WHY LOVE LEADS TO JUSTICE

This book tells the stories of notable historical figures who, by resisting patriarchal laws condemning adultery, gay and lesbian sex, and sex across the boundaries of religion and race, brought about lasting social and political change. Constitutional scholar David A. J. Richards investigates the lives of leading transgressive artists, social critics, and activists including George Eliot, Benjamin Britten, Christopher Isherwood, Bayard Rustin, James Baldwin, Eleanor Roosevelt, and Margaret Mead. Richards shows how ethical empowerment, motivated by love, allowed these figures to resist the injustices of anti-Semitism, racism, sexism, and homophobia, leading to the constitutional condemnation of these political evils in the United States, Britain, and beyond. Love and law thus grow together, and this book shows how and why.

Drawing from developmental psychology (including studies of trauma), political theory, the history of social movements, literature, biography, and law, this book will be a thought-provoking tool for anyone interested in civil rights.

David A. J. Richards is Edwin D. Webb Professor of Law at New York University School of Law, where he teaches constitutional law and criminal law. He is the author of nineteen books, including recently *The Deepening Darkness: Patriarchy, Resistance, and Democracy's Future* (with Carol Gilligan, 2009); *Fundamentalism in American Religion and Law* (2010); and *The Rise of Gay Rights and the Fall of the British Empire* (2013). He lives with his partner, Donald Levy, in New York City.

Why Love Leads to Justice

LOVE ACROSS THE BOUNDARIES

DAVID A. J. RICHARDS

New York University

CAMBRIDGE
UNIVERSITY PRESS

CAMBRIDGE
UNIVERSITY PRESS

32 Avenue of the Americas, New York NY 10013-2473, USA

Cambridge University Press is part of the University of Cambridge.

It furthers the University's mission by disseminating knowledge in the pursuit of education, learning and research at the highest international levels of excellence.

www.cambridge.org
Information on this title: www.cambridge.org/9781107569829

© David A. J. Richards 2016

First published 2016

A catalogue record for this publication is available from the British Library

Library of Congress Cataloguing in Publication data
Richards, David A. J.
Why love leads to justice : love across the boundaries / David A. J. Richards.
    pages   cm
Includes bibliographical references and index.
ISBN 978-1-107-12910-8 (hardback) – ISBN 978-1-107-56982-9 (paperback)
1. Homosexuality.   2. Interracial dating.   3. Adultery.   4. Love.   5. Social justice.
6. Patriarchy.   I. Title.
HQ76.25.R49   2015
303.3'72–dc23   2015024645

ISBN 978-1-107-12910-8 Hardback
ISBN 978-1-107-56982-9 Paperback

For Donald Levy

All I have is a voice
To undo the folded lie . . .
We must love one another or die.

W. H. Auden
"September 1, 1939"

Contents

Acknowledgments

All my work on this book profited from ongoing conversations with Carol Gilligan, with whom I have co-taught a seminar, now called Resisting Injustice, at the New York University School of Law for well over ten years. Our conversations led not only to a co-authored book (*The Deepening Darkness: Patriarchy, Resistance, and Democracy's Future*, Cambridge, 2009), but to my own continuing research and writing on the themes of our book, including one of its central themes, resisting the Love Laws (*Fundamentalism in American Religion and Law: Obama's Challenge to Patriarchy's Threat to Democracy*, Cambridge, 2010; *Resisting Injustice and the Feminist Ethics of Care in the Age of Obama: "Suddenly, ... All the Truth Was Coming Out,"* Routledge, 2013). This book arose very much in conversation with Carol about these themes, and she read it closely and gave me detailed comments that saved me from many mistakes. She is the most generous and inspiring of friends, as anyone graced by her astonishing intelligence and loving care and concern knows.

Conversations with two other friends were enormously helpful to me as well. Nicholas Bamforth of Queens College, Oxford, took two year-long leaves at the New York University School of Law, the first of which led to our co-authored book, *Patriarchal Religion, Sexuality, and Gender: A Critique of New Natural Law* (Cambridge, 2008), and the second of which critically illuminated and advised my work on my book *The Rise of Gay Rights and the Fall of the British Empire: Liberal Resistance and the Bloomsbury Group* (Cambridge, 2013), which in turn suggested to me that I work on this book. For several years I have co-taught a seminar with Dr. James Gilligan on retributivism at the New York University School of Law. No one understands the psychology of patriarchal manhood, including its propensities to violence, better than Jim, and conversations with him helped me understand the role resistance to violence played in the men and women I study in this book.

John Berger, my editor at Cambridge University Press, enthusiastically supported my work on this book from the time I first mentioned it to him, and secured the excellent readers who helped me improve it; his assistant, Stephen Acerra, was also most helpful. It was through John that I secured the invaluable editorial services of David Lobenstine. David worked closely with me on both the form and content of the book, helping me see where I must improve my writing and sharpen and deepen my analysis. He is an extraordinary editor, indeed, a dream of what good editing is and can be.

I must also acknowledge my gratitude for discussions with Phillip Blumberg about the psychological arguments I make in this book, which included how and why these arguments arise and clarify my own personal life; he also referred me to many works that enormously advanced my understanding of the life histories of the men and women I study in this book. Phillip is a person of remarkable humane intelligence and empathic feeling, both of which sustained and enriched my work on this book.

My friends, LaShonda Katrice Barnett (whose first novel, *Jam on the Vine*, has just been published) and her partner Ruth Heit, enthusiastically supported my work on this book when I needed such support and showed me the path forward on issues I did not fully understand until I conversed with them. I grieve at Ruth's recent death and cherish the memory of her warm enthusiasm in support of my writing this book.

I am grateful as well for the comments on the book of my friend Thomas P. Dickson.

I received invaluable criticism of earlier drafts of the book from students in the two seminars at the New York University School of Law who read it. With respect to the seminar Resisting Injustice (fall 2014), I thank Kylie Barbosa, Lauren Brachman, Sarah Brafman, Stephen Brown, Monica Bruzzio Galvez, Ngoc Quang Bui, Aimee Carlisle, Ian Dummett, Ijeoma Eke, Duncan Fraser, Vaneesha Jain, Margaret Marron, Lisette Martinez, Juan Camillo Mendez Guzman, Alexa Rozell, Amanda Russo, Derry Sandy, Brittany Simington, Naomi Snider, Deborah Taeid, Rafael Taraszkiewicz Sowk, Cort Welch, Harrison White, Paul White, Rachel Wisotsky, and Evan Zatorre. And, with respect to the seminar Free Speech, Ethical Transformation, and Social Change: Race, Gender, and Sexual Orientation (Spring 2015), I must thank David Billingsley, Vincent Cesare, Donald Cooley, Candis Davis, Ryan Davis, Ian Dummett, Luke Fredericks, Tsion Gurmu, Emily Juneau, So Yung Kang, Caillie Lefevre, Joao Oliveira, Chelsea Plyer, Landon Reid, Naomi Snider, Michael Stachiw, and Dian Yu.

The book was researched and written during sabbatical leaves and summers, supported in part by generous research grants from the New York University School of Law Filomen S'Agostino and Max E. Greenberg Faculty Research Fund. I am grateful as well to the support of our former dean, Richard Revesz, and our current dean, Trevor Morrison, and for the assistance of Lavinia Barbu in preparing the book for publication.

My debt to Donald Levy, Professor of Philosophy, emeritus, Brooklyn College, is profound. He opened my heart and mind to what love is, love that nourishes our lives together, including work on this book.

Introduction

Love Resists Injustice

This is a book of love stories. It is a book that I never, ever expected to write. I have been writing about the workings of the law for well over forty years. Love is not something that I write about, certainly not in the way I do here. And yet this is a book about love, because there was no other way to tell this story.

Much to my surprise, the more I write about the law, the more I realize how incomplete the methods of the law are in and of themselves. Instead, this book argues for a deep connection between two subjects usually disconnected: our ability to love and our ability to resist injustice. I use methods of argument, and thus whole disciplines, that are usually sealed off from one another: normative political theory, psychology, history, and biography. But why love, and why love stories, in an argument by a law professor of all people? One of the abiding interests of my life is about the boundaries of our world – the restrictions that both shape our lives and constrict our lives – and the ways that we overcome those boundaries. It is now clear to me that nothing enables us to get across those boundaries like love. And an argument about love across the boundaries has required me to break interdisciplinary boundaries, not least the boundary between law and love, the topic of a wonderful poem, "Law Like Love," by one of the artists at the center of this book, Wystan Auden.[1] Auden's poem was written in the year he met – disastrously, as it turned out – the love of his life, Chester Kallman. Written to his lover, it is an urgent description of the law. He argues that law – both scientific and normative – is:

> Like love I say.
>
> Like love we don't know where or why,
> Like love we can't compel or fly,
> Like love we often weep,
> Like love we seldom keep.[2]

[1] W. H. Auden, "Law Like Love," in W. H. Auden, *Collected Poems*, edited by Edward Mendelson (New York: Vintage International, 1991), pp. 262–64.

[2] See *id.*, p. 264.

Auden's visceral experience of love led him to make connections not usually made, precisely because love – as he and the other lovers I study in this book came to experience it – enabled him to resist societal restrictions and embrace new creative possibilities.

What marks the love at the heart of this book is precisely that it crosses boundaries, and thus is condemned by the social norms that are so effective at setting up boundaries in the first place. Here we find love involving adultery; love between people of different castes or religions or ethnicities or races; love between men and love between women. Such love has not only been traditionally condemned, but has often been incendiary, giving rise to sometimes extraordinary forms of violence against the partners to such relationships. The question, which has absorbed me for some time, is why – in light of all this condemnation and violence – people continue to engage in and often flourish in such relationships. And what are the consequences of these relationships, not only for those involved but for the wider cultural world that we share.

It is these questions that led me to see that this kind of boundary-crossing love has often been central to human resistance – central to humanity's ongoing fight against the structural injustices that have afflicted and continue to afflict humankind – extreme religious intolerance (for example, anti-Semitism), racism, sexism, and homophobia, all of whom condemn, unjustly, loves across the boundaries – whether adultery or loves of different castes or religions or ethnicities or races, or of the same genders. Love's daring, its insistence on resistance to injustice, has been followed – very slowly – by cultural and legal shifts. The injustices that love has for so long resisted are now condemned by basic principles of constitutional law in a growing number of constitutional democracies. So, love and law are, as it were, bedfellows; any concern with law and the justice of law, then, must take seriously an approach that combines political theory, psychology, history, and, as I have come to see, love.

My approach to these matters in several recent books has integrated a political theory of liberalism (including a theory of basic human rights and of forms of structural injustice that arise from abridgment of those rights) with a political psychology that explains how irrational prejudices arise from and support such structural injustices. At the center of my interests is the question of how, historically, such deeply rooted injustices have been resisted by social movements, such as the civil rights, antiwar, feminist, and gay rights movements, a resistance that led, in turn, to greater justice in our political and constitutional arrangements both in the United States and abroad. As I explain more fully in Chapter 1 of this book, my understanding of both structural injustice and the psychology of prejudice has been deepened by connecting both to a patriarchal understanding of authority in both public and private life that has flourished for a very long time. Starting in the Neolithic period, it dominated the high cultures of Babylonia, Egypt, India, and China.

It flourished in the Roman Empire and the forms of later political and religious authority influenced, often uncritically, by its example. Resistance to such structural injustice arises from a democratic and egalitarian resistance to patriarchy, as Carol Gilligan and I have argued at length elsewhere.[3] Whereas patriarchy rests on enforcement of the gender binary and a hierarchy that places one gender over another, democratic equality challenges both the gender binary and its hierarchy, calling for a free and equal voice and relationships that resist both. One important form of such resistance is to what we call the Love Laws, which condemn precisely the loving relationships across the barriers patriarchy imposes and violently enforces.

What was needed to do justice to this topic was an investigation of such loves in all their complexity. I knew, from an earlier study of the liberal resistance of the Bloomsbury Group, that resistance to the Love Laws led both to new forms of friendship and love-empowered political resistance to British imperialism.[4] What I found there inspired me to look more closely at both the struggles and consequences of such loves, in particular, when they led and when they did not lead to resistance.

What I found quite surprised me, and hopefully it will surprise you – namely, that at the very center of their love stories, the ones that resisted the Love Laws, was the way in which, against such odds, they sexually loved another person as a person against the grain of patriarchal stereotypes. For many of them for the first time in their lives, they loved and were loved as the persons they were precisely because such loves, on terms of freedom and equality, released them from the stereotypes that patriarchy enforces. Patriarchy rests on hierarchy, not equality, and violently represses free voice that would challenge the stereotypes. What I found in the love stories at the heart of this book's argument is that love, when it led to resistance, arose from a voice in the lovers that love freed from patriarchal controls. Sexual love, when rooted in the body and mind of two persons in love as equals, breaks patriarchy's hierarchies (including the hierarchy of mind over body) and exposes its lies and violence against voice. Freed through love from the patriarchal controls that suppress voice, the lovers find their free and equal voices, as democratic equals, through a resistance rooted in the intimate truths of love. It is this voice that expressed itself in sometimes quite remarkable resistance to structural injustices in the transformative civil rights, antiwar, feminist, and gay rights movements that have reshaped both our understanding of justice and of constitutional law. Hence, we cannot appreciate the vast changes over the last two hundred years and

---

[3] See Carol Gilligan and David A. J. Richards, *The Deepening Darkness: Patriarchy, Resistance, and Democracy's Future* (Cambridge: Cambridge University Press, 2009).

[4] David A. J. Richards, *The Rise of Gay Rights and the Fall of the British Empire: Liberal Resistance and the Bloomsbury Group* (Cambridge: Cambridge University Press, 2013).

earlier,[5] about the purpose of the law and the aims of justice, without reckoning with the power of love.

What guided my investigation was the relational structure of resistance to patriarchal controls. Such controls are often quite rigidly enforced by caretakers, yet sometimes the caretakers themselves resist patriarchy and impart their skepticism to their sons and daughters. We shall discover different patterns of such resistance in all of the loves this book studies in some depth – George Eliot (Marian Evans) and Henry Lewes, Harriet Taylor and John Stuart Mill, Benjamin Britten and Peter Pears, Christopher Isherwood, Wystan Auden, Bayard Rustin, James Baldwin, and Margaret Mead and Ruth Benedict (as well as Eleanor Roosevelt and Lorena Hickok). Many of them come to regard the patriarchal demands of their caretakers and the cultures they reflect as unjust, often seeking support and care in more egalitarian relationships, some of which take the form of passionate sexual relationships that break the Love Laws and flourish sometimes brilliantly for precisely that reason.

Some of these stories deeply move me, Benjamin Britten and Peter Pears, for example, perhaps because they are closest to my own continuing experience of loving relationship to the man I have loved and with whom shared my life for some forty years. Others astonished me with their restless search for a loving relationship and its empowering connection to finding an artistic voice; Christopher Isherwood, for example, truthfully spoke both of gay love in Berlin after World War I and the reactionary horrors of German fascism, which would, like a deadly snake, paralyze and destroy German political decency. Still others fascinated me as love stories that went so wrong. Wystan Auden, for example, came disastrously to accept a homophobia he once had resisted, and yet still wrote so sensitively later in life of the anxieties of patriarchal manhood in the wake of World War II, as we shall see. The interracial gay sexual relationships of Bayard Rustin and James Baldwin cast an unexpected light not only on the psychological roots and political creativity of nonviolence (which Rustin pioneered long before other more conventional black leaders), but also on Baldwin's remarkable insights into how American racism destroyed love for blacks and whites, men and women, gay and straight. And, the passionate lesbian love of Margaret Mead and Ruth Benedict revealed to me something I had not suspected, namely, that it was through such love, based on freedom and equality, that each of them found their voice to resist the gender stereotypes that unjustly afflict both women and men, straight and gay. And, through her love for Lorena Hickok, Eleanor Roosevelt found and spoke in the remarkably progressive ethical voice (speaking of and addressing poverty; resisting American anti-Semitism, racism, and sexism; and, later in her life, playing a crucial role in shaping the

---

[5] For a recent compelling historical argument that these developments, including respect for moral individuality and human rights, were prepared by certain radical developments within Christianity, see Larry Siedentop, *Inventing the Individual: The Origins of Western Liberalism* (London: Allen Unwin, 2014).

Universal Declaration of Human Rights as the ideal of the post–World War II order) that has no parallel among other American first ladies. In the case of Ruth Benedict, love also yielded astonishing insights into the injustice of homophobia, racism, and the roots of the fascist violence of Japanese imperialism. My experience of writing this book was one of continuing surprise, which suggests how much its investigations compelled me to go into places I had not previously explored.

Why these lovers, when I could have studied many others, some much more contemporary? The gay love stories I tell and investigate are of three artists (Benjamin Britten, Christopher Isherwood, and Wystan Auden), a black civil rights activist and pioneer of nonviolence (Bayard Rustin), a black gay artist and civil rights activist (James Baldwin), America's most ethically progressive first lady (Eleanor Roosevelt), and two cultural anthropologists, Margaret Mead and Ruth Benedict, whose lesbian love illuminated their lives and astonishing achievements. All of them are closer to my generation than they are to the millennial generation (whom I now teach), some of whom may read this book. Of course, remarkable achievements in the political and constitutional recognition of basic human rights have occurred since the time the gay and lesbian people I study in this book lived and wrote, not least, a black president, the constitutional decriminalization of gay sex, the removal of homophobic restrictions on military service, and an emerging right to same-sex marriage. However, there is a story still to be told about the struggles that made these developments possible. What has not been seen is the role love played across the patriarchal boundaries in the resisting voices to injustice exemplified by the lives and works of the persons I study in this book.

Patriarchy rests on a psychology of trauma, showing itself in loss of voice and memory. No one today, including millennials, would or should want to act out the psychological logic of patriarchal disassociation by not taking seriously what this study shows, namely, that a struggle for love between equals released the patriarchal controls on voice that had made deep injustice seem to be in the nature of things. Otherwise, they may misunderstand and misuse the equality and freedom they enjoy, and should struggle to deepen and extend. All of the people I study in this book not only loved across the boundaries, but, through the experience of love, found a resisting voice to tell the truth about the lies and violence that had condemned and repressed such love. Many of them are artists, whose struggles for creative voice often explore and illuminate, as artists often do, the psychology – personal and political – of resistance to injustice in ways more academic disciplines do not, or not yet. I chose to study these persons because all of them illuminate the struggles, pitfalls, and brilliant voices that their loves made possible, and their achievements touch not only on homophobia and gay rights but on the evils of racism and sexism and imperialism.

These are love stories we need to remember and value not only for their impact on the greater justice of our own law and politics, but because they tell us something about what love has been and can be, for each and every one of us, when love flourishes on terms of equality and free voice in relationship. What such love tells us is that love is at the center of our ethical natures and democratic values, and that patriarchy, being toxic to love, is not.[6]

Many of the love stories I tell are British, or, at least I begin there because they continue and build on the love stories implicit in my study of the Bloomsbury Group. However, at least two of the Britons I study (Isherwood and Auden) settle in America, and fall in love with Americans, and both of their love stories, including their love for one another (such as it was), took them to Berlin, where Isherwood falls in love with a German. This explains his pacifism (Isherwood could not imagine killing his former lover, who, against his will, served in Hitler's army). All the rest of the love stories I study (Rustin, Baldwin, Eleanor Roosevelt, Mead, and Benedict) are of Americans, but again one of them, James Baldwin, finds his resisting voice only in Europe as an exile from an American racism that repressed his voice and finds the love of his life in Europe with a white European. Rustin, though deeply American, learned from and traveled to Gandhi's India to study the aims and strategies of Gandhi's nonviolent satyagrahas. Love across the boundaries transcends national as well as cultural boundaries, because the hunger for love and voice is universal and love sometimes finds its heart's desire only in self-conscious exile from its repressive homeland (Isherwood and Baldwin). What this shows, I believe, is that the right to love, while the most intimate of our basic human rights, is also the most universal.

The love stories I investigate are far from the love stories of your average romantic comedy. The complexity of these relationships include not only the lovers, but their early caretakers, their friends, and their creative vocations as artists and pathbreaking, ethically creative thinkers who have advanced our understanding not only of love but of justice and of ethics itself. Still, they are all very much love stories, which must be told and understood in all their struggles, often against heavy odds, to appreciate the ethical power of love, its roots in our human nature. So, love is, I have come to believe, the heart of the matter, and resistance to patriarchy is the key issue in understanding and appreciating the ethical power of sustaining love in a life well and justly lived. If we cannot see this, it is because patriarchy darkens our ethical intelligence.[7] We need to look, and look truthfully, at love as the key not only to our happiness, but also to our sense of justice. It is for this reason that this book is about both love and justice. Resistance to injustice is, very much to my surprise, at the very heart of the love stories I have tried to tell truthfully in all their astonishing human complexity, including their disappointments and their successes. The stories we will explore are like no love story I have read or seen in film or theatre, yet it is closer,

---

[6] On the tragic love stories that patriarchy tells, and the psychological possibility of resistance to such tragic love stories, see Carol Gilligan, *The Birth of Pleasure: A New Map of Love* (New York: Vintage, 2003).

[7] See, on this point, Carol Gilligan and David A. J. Richards, *The Deepening Darkness: Patriarchy, Resistance, and Democracy's Future* (Cambridge: Cambridge University Press, 2009).

I believe, to the role love plays in our lives and has certainly played in my own life. Why do we have such difficulty in seeing our lives as they are? Perhaps, this book's originality is that it helps us take this question seriously, and even perhaps helps us to answer it with an honesty and authenticity based in a democratic experience very much before our eyes.

I begin my argument in Chapter 1 by reviewing the concepts and work on which it builds, and then explore its explanatory fertility in exploring adultery both in Hawthorne's great novel, *The Scarlet Letter*, and in the relationships of George Henry Lewes and Marian Evans (George Eliot) and Harriet Taylor and John Stuart Mill. Following this initial exploration of love across the boundaries in heterosexual relationships, my argument focuses on gay/lesbian relationships.

I focus on the close study of gay/lesbian loving relationships precisely because the forces that condemn them have been culturally entrenched and uncontested for so long and have taken the remarkable form, not found in the same way with other prejudices such as anti-Semitism and racism, of regarding the sex acts expressive of gay love as, literally, not to be spoken or given any voice whatsoever, "a crime not fit to be named, '*peccatum illud horrible, inter christianos non nominandum*,'" as Blackstone put it.[8] The history of Christian and later forms of secular anti-Semitism, as well as forms of racism, have been ethically monstrous and ultimately genocidal (gassing Jews, lynching blacks), but there has long been cultural space for resisting voices to contest such injustices, for example, the abolitionist movement in Britain and the United States. Homosexuals have, however, long lived under a more total form of unspeakability. Homophobia not only led to and rationalized extraordinary forms of repressive violence (burning at the stake) directed against gay men and lesbians, but mandated codes of manhood and womanhood that entered and shaped the psyches of homosexuals, unleashing intrapsychic violence against a loving gay voice. It is such extraordinary cultural repression that makes so interesting and compelling – in the general study of how love matters to justice – the closer study of the circumstances in which gay men and lesbians through loving relationships find their ethical voice to resist injustice – as Britten and Pears do through music dramas, which give expression to and resist destructive homophobic forces; as Isherwood does in his novels and his late defense of gay rights; as Auden does in his poetry about the anxieties of manhood; as Rustin does in his pathbreaking development of nonviolence – long before other black leaders – as the resistance strategy for the civil rights movement; as Baldwin does in his remarkable novels and essays about how patriarchy destroys love and enforces racism; as Eleanor Roosevelt does in speaking and writing in an ethical voice that challenged deep injustices at home and abroad; as Margaret Mead does in her debunking of gender stereotypes and critique of American sexism as on a par with American racism; and as Ruth

---

[8] Quoted in David A. J. Richards, *Women, Gays, and the Constitution: The Grounds for Feminism and Gay Rights in Culture and Law* (Chicago: University of Chicago Press, 1998), at p. 292.

Benedict does in her brilliant indictments of European and American racism and homophobia and her pathbreaking study of the patriarchal violence underlying Japanese fascist imperialism in World War II. In coming into loving relationships against such extraordinarily powerful external and internal forces, they all tell us something true and deep about the force of loving relationships in human life and how such relationships do matter and matter profoundly to our psychological competence, as persons, to resist justice.

There is another reason for a work of this sort to be of interest to everyone – male and female, straight or gay. All of us increasingly understand that patriarchy is and remains toxic to love, and we aspire to loving relationships of free and equal persons, unencumbered by patriarchal demands. This obviously remains a central problem in heterosexual relationships in which patriarchal conceptions of gender have long defined both men and woman. Heterosexual couples now struggle for loving relationships in which patriarchal conceptions of gender no longer play the destructive role they have in the past.[9] What should count as a just understanding of free and equal voice in love is, however, as urgent a question for homosexuals as it is for heterosexuals, perhaps more urgent. It is precisely because the idea of a human right to loving relationship is completely new for homosexuals that the relationships they form in light of this new normative understanding must be of as much interest to heterosexuals as it is to homosexuals. The fact that both parties to the relationship are men or women may be taken to render such relationships by definition equal, but this is, of course, false. Gay men of my generation, for example, were brought up under a regime of aggressive homophobia, rooted in patriarchal conceptions of what counts as a man that condemned sexual love between people of the same gender as unspeakable, incendiary because it both challenged the gender binary and its hierarchy. However, we carry these self-conceptions into our personal relationships, and patriarchy is as toxic to loving relationships here as elsewhere. Patriarchy bears particularly heavily and rigidly on men and at an early stage of boyhood when, through traumatic breaks in relationship, they have little capacity to resist its demands. Women stay in relationship much longer, and patriarchal demands impinge on their lives at a later stage when they are more able to resist them, as Carol Gilligan's developmental work clearly shows.[10] For this reason, gay

[9] See Carol Gilligan, *The Birth of Pleasure: A New Map of Love* (New York: Vintage, 2003).

[10] See Lyn Mikel Brown and Carol Gilligan, *Meeting at the Crossroads: Women's Psychology and Girls' Development* (Cambridge, MA: Harvard University Press, 1992); Carol Gilligan, "The Centrality of Relationship in Human Development: A Puzzle, Some Evidence, and a Theory," in *Development and Vulnerability in Close Relationships*, edited by K. Fisher and G. Noam (New York: Erlbaum, 1996); Carol Gilligan, "Joining the Resistance: Psychology, Politics, Girls and Women," *Michigan Quarterly Review* 24, no. 4 (1990): 501–36; Carol Gilligan, Annie G. Rogers, and Deborah Tolman, eds., *Women, Girls, and Psychotherapy: Reframing Resistance* (New York: Hayworth Press, 1991); Carol Gilligan, Nona P. Lyons, and Trudy Hanmer, eds., *Making Connections: The Relational Worlds of Adolescent Girls at Emma Willard School* (Cambridge, MA: Harvard University Press, 1990); Jill McLean Taylor, Carol Gilligan, and Amy Sullivan, *Between Voice and Silence: Women and Girls, Race and Relationship* (Cambridge, MA: Harvard University Press, 1995).

relationships may be, if anything, more burdened by patriarchy than are heterosexual relationships (in which one party is a woman) and perhaps than lesbian
relationships. For this reason, the closer study of the circumstances when these
relationships do resist patriarchy is of enormous general interest to our understanding of why love matters to justice. If love gives rise to resistance to injustice here
against such extraordinary repressive odds, the transformative power of love should
never be underestimated by those subject to less punishing odds.

Why these love stories? My choices here arose, of course, from my own life as a gay
man who found love only through resistance to the homophobia so central to the
American manhood and womanhood that was, during my early life, assumed to be
axiomatic, including by the parents I loved and who loved me. These struggles were
much part of my own experience, as a gay man and constitutional lawyer who was
one of the first legal scholars of my generation to write about and defend gay rights.
My interest in the love stories in this book arose from reflection on the trajectory
of my life (I am now 71), finding love with the man I loved and who loved me
and, because of this enduring and deepening love, a resisting voice as a moral
philosopher and constitutional law professor. These convergent choices of love
and vocation married at the same time (1973). I knew my story was more fortunate
than many other gay men of my generation, but what drew me to the persons studied
in this book was the deeper study of this broadly shared struggle, which was my
struggle and the struggle of so many others of my generation I knew (some of whom
died of AIDS[11]), showing the remarkable power of love in resisting patriarchy during
a period when American homophobia was hegemonic, and resisting it publicly was
subject to criminal sanctions and social contempt. So, I write from within my own
public and private experience – an experience that I learned, through writing this
book, was shared by so many others. What I also learned was how different such
experience was, but yet how common was the role of resisting patriarchy in releasing
an ethical voice long quashed by a homophobia largely unquestioned for millennia.
It is, if I am right, an important discovery, because it shows close connections
between love in certain contexts and the growth of an ethical voice that resists
deep injustices.

Breaking the Love Laws has historically been visited with catastrophic punishments and losses. Many during the period I study – whether adulterers or others
loving across forbidden patriarchal boundaries – led lives shrunken into quiet misery
by homophobia; but others led rich and creatively inventive lives, and some openly
resisted. It is for this reason all the more important to understand and take seriously
the lives and works of the persons here studied – what it was about these people and
the circumstances in which they lived that made psychologically possible for them
forms of love and resistance that, against such odds of irrational hatred supported by

---

[11] For a remarkable recent documentary on the AIDS activists, who resisted the homophobia during the
AIDS crisis, see David France, *How to Survive a Plague* (DVD, MPI Media Group, 2012).

law and culture, have been ethically transformative both for them and the wider cultures in which they lived. Why, for them, did love across the boundaries lead to ethical dignity not only for them but for others?

Only taking seriously their struggles for love – both their successes and failures – can reveal the ethical power of love in resisting the evils dividing us from our common humanity (the root of ethics) that patriarchy enforces – religious intolerance, racism, sexism, and homophobia. What drew me to the lovers I study is the role resistance to patriarchal stereotypes played in their loves, and the form the resistance took, namely, their creative *voices* as artists, or as activists, or as some of the most profound students of culture of their time, all of them challenging then-dominant stereotypes of religion or race or gender or sexual orientation. Their voices broke the silences that had supported homophobia for millennia. In breaking this silence, they broke as well the silences that had supported and sustained the evils of anti-Semitism, racism, and sexism, and its attendant evil, imperialism. Their breaking of the silence inspired me when, still a young man, I heard in the musical voices of Benjamin Britten and Peter Pears the love that made their voices possible, and I knew – from the depths of my repressed body and overdeveloped mind – that there was an alternative life for me, a love rooted in the body and the mind and the resisting voice such love made possible. Or, I heard in the indignant voice of James Baldwin and the nonviolent voice of Bayard Rustin – gay black leaders in the civil rights movements that transformed the lives of all Americans – that the resisting voices against American racism and homophobia was a voice available to me and every other person striving for ethical dignity as the person they were. No one makes such a discovery on one's own, but only in relationship to other persons. We build on the struggles of others, as I did, nourished by other resisters and the web of relationships that sustain and support us. Creativity is often much more relational and social, arising from sustaining networks of love and friendship, than our models of the lonely artist would suggest.[12] Such networks, including creative pairs, are often not rooted in sexual love, but sometimes they are.

In this book, I focus on homosexual love relationships, ones in which the sexual love itself not only broke the Love Laws, but resisted them, leading to extraordinarily creative expressions of ethical voice that exposed and resisted injustice, including a homophobia based in enforced unspeakability, and called us to resistance. I want to show here these struggles in all their relational complexity (including their risks and disappointments), so that the generation today will know what has made possible my own life and their own freer and more democratic lives, something I see all about me in the gay men, lesbians, and transgendered people who live and work in the city I love, and thrive personally and politically because they defy the gender binary and

[12]   See, on this point, Joshua Wolf Shenk, "The End of 'Genius,'" *The New York Times, Sunday Review,* Sunday, July 20, 2014, pp. 6–7; Joshua Wolf Shenk, *Powers of Two: Finding the Essence of Innovation in Creative Pairs* (New York: An Eamon Dolan Book/Houghton Mifflin Harcourt, 2014).

hierarchy that held hostage so many in my generation.[13] With knowledge based on experience breaking through disassociation, we better understand our own ethical responsibilities as free people. Breaking the silence is the key, and its heart is a love that resists patriarchy, whose continuing psychological power over our lives and politics, whatever our sexual orientation, rests on loss of voice and memory. This book is an effort to make clear to millennials, among others, how important it remains that they break the silence if patriarchal psychology is not, unconsciously, to dominate and devastate their lives and choices in love and in work.

---

[13] See, for a recent example in New York City public life of such a gay man, Anemona Hartocollis, "Credibility Among Gay Men Gives Leverage to City's New Chief of H.I.V. Prevention," *The New York Times*, Tuesday, July 22, 2014, p. A22.

1

Breaking the Love Laws as Resistance

How and why does love matter to justice, or, more precisely, the struggle for justice?

To answer this question, we need to understand patriarchy, both its psychology, and its tension with, indeed contradiction to, democratic values in both our public and private lives. Patriarchy – both its structure and psychology – supports and indeed enforces the antidemocratic structural injustices of extreme religious intolerance, racism, sexism, and homophobia. One of the ways it has done so is through its enforcement of the patriarchal Love Laws, an idea central to Arundhati Roy's brilliant novel, *The God of Small Things*.[1] Roy's novel is one of many examples in my collaborative work with Carol Gilligan (Hawthorne's *The Scarlet Letter* is another) in which we have found that great artists illuminate the psychology of patriarchy, its roots in trauma, loss of voice, and disassociation,[2] and the tension between love and patriarchy.[3] It is only when we take seriously both patriarchy and its psychology, as well as the role of the Love Laws in their unjust demands, that we can begin to understand how and why sometimes love across boundaries enforced by the Love Laws plays the role it does in resisting injustice. Therefore, I first explore patriarchy and the Love Laws, and then investigate the creative role breaking the Love Laws can and has played in resisting injustice. My examples in this chapter are all heterosexual, showing, from the very beginning of my argument, that my analysis addresses a real issue for all sexual orientations. I begin with Hawthorne's astonishing novel, and then turn to the remarkably creative voices resisting patriarchy that arose from the relationships of several Victorian adulterous couples – Henry Lewes and George Eliot (Marian Evans), and Harriet Taylor and John Stuart Mill.

[1] Arundhati Roy, *The God of Small Things* (New York: Harper Perennial, 1997).
[2] The marks of trauma are loss of voice and memory. See, on this point, Bessel A. van der Kolk, Alex C. McFarlane, and Lars Weisaeth, eds., *Traumatic Stress: The Effects of Overwhelming Experience on Mind, Body, and Society* (New York: The Guilford Press, 1966); Judith Herman, *Trauma and Recovery* (New York: Basic Books, 1997).
[3] Carol Gilligan and David A. J. Richards, *The Deepening Darkness: Patriarchy, Resistance, and Democracy's Future* (2009); Carol Gilligan, *The Birth of Pleasure*, whose epigraph makes this point: "The power of love upsets the order of things," Genesis Rabbah LV8.

Patriarchy "is an anthropological term denoting families or societies ruled by fathers. It sets up a hierarchy – a rule of priests – in which the priest, the *hieros*, is a father, *pater*. As an order of living, it elevates some men over other men and all men over women; within the family, it separates fathers from sons (the men from the boys) and places both women and children under a father's authority."[4] So, in patriarchy, the father – *pater* – fulfills the function of the priest, occupying the top of authority in its various dimensions (family, religion, politics, and the like). It is this structure of authority that we see in the priest-rulers, sometimes viewed as gods, of the autocratic high civilizations of ancient Babylonia, Egypt, China, and the Roman Empire (after Augustus abolished the republic),[5] in which absolute monarchy and imperialistic wars were the rule. Even the Greek democracies, notably Athens, were patriarchal in their treatment of women and slaves, a tension that one of its greatest artists, Aeschylus in *The Oresteia*, exposed and explored as a tragedy, personal and political,[6] and which may explain Athens' ultimately self-destructive imperialism.

Patriarchy, as the dominant structure of authority in personal and political life, was probably a relatively late development in the history of the human species, arising in the Neolithic period when we settled into an agrarian life,[7] a period "Jared Diamond has called ... the greatest catastrophe in the history of humanity."[8] Patriarchy may not have been dominant during the long period of human history when we were hunter-gatherers (99.5 percent of our history as a species). During this period when human populations were quite small and highly vulnerable to extinction, the politics that existed was much more democratic than it was later to be. Relations between men and women were egalitarian and flexible. Such flexible arrangements may have included what we find today in some contemporary hunter-gatherers, men acting as caretakers, as women play economic roles in gathering nuts and fruits. Against this background, it is not an empirically reasonable understanding of the evolutionary record that our species was hardwired for patriarchy. What marks our species is its intelligent flexibility in changing survival strategies as circumstances changed. What may once have made sense in the circumstances of the Neolithic period no longer makes sense today, and it is for this reason that patriarchy is increasingly understood as a cultural form subject to criticism and change.[9]

---

4   See Carol Gilligan and David A. J. Richards, *The Deepening Darkness*, p. 22.
5   For a fuller, in-depth discussion of Roman patriarchy, both under the republic and empire, see Gilligan and Richards, *The Deepening Darkness*.
6   See, for fuller exploration and discussion of this point, Gilligan and Richards, *The Deepening Darkness*, pp. 12–15.
7   See Gerda Lerner, *The Creation of Patriarchy* (New York: Oxford University Press, 1986).
8   Quoted at p. 21, David A. J. Richards, *Resisting Injustice and the Feminist Ethics of Care in the Age of Obama* (New York: Routledge, 2013).
9   See, for supporting argument and citations for this analysis, David A. J. Richards, *Resisting Injustice and the Ethics of Care in the Age of Obama*, pp. 19–23. For development of a similar argument, see Ian Morris, *Foragers, Farmers, and Fossil Fuels: How Human Values Evolve* (Princeton, NJ: Princeton University Press, 2015).

The most important reason for this criticism is that patriarchy is inconsistent with democracy because it accords hierarchical authority to priest-fathers over women and other men and boys, rationalizing its authority on the basis of the repression of the moral voices and experience of well over half the human species. In contrast, democracy calls for equal care and respect for all persons, including their equal human rights to free conscience and voice. The history of modern democracy, based on respect for universal human rights, may plausibly be understood in terms of the struggle for democratic values against patriarchy.[10] The United States and other constitutional democracies have, no doubt, made enormous progress in deepening democracy, in particular, after the defeat of fascism in World War II. However, our advances in the United States – energized by the movements for civil rights, antiwar, feminism, and gay rights – have led to reactionary political forces both at home and abroad that can best be understood as attempts to reinstate patriarchy.[11] It is for this reason all the more important to take seriously the role patriarchy still plays in our lives and to study how to resist it, which is why the argument of this book is so contemporary and alive.

What has made this struggle so long and difficult is that patriarchy gave rise to a personal and political psychology that supports patriarchy and the injustices that patriarchy enforces – to wit, dividing us from one another on unjust grounds of religion, race, ethnicity, gender, and sexual orientation. Its psychology thus legitimated irrational prejudices now increasingly constitutionally condemned in constitutional democracies as a basis for law and policy (the antidiscrimination principle that condemns religious hatred, sexism, racism, and homophobia as the basis for laws and policies[12]). To understand what makes these divisions acceptable or believed to be acceptable, we must turn to "the contemporary literature on trauma and its effects of human neurophysiology and psychology," a developmental psychology that traumatically breaks real relationships between children and caretakers (boys much earlier than girls[13]).

The now well-documented consequence of trauma is loss of voice and of memory, in particular, loss of the voice of intimate relationship. The loss or suppression of voice, however, is often covered by an identification with the voice of the person who imposed the trauma and internalization of the demands that this more powerful person imposes on one's life. The crucial mechanism here is dissociation: the psychological process through which the surviving self separates itself from the self that was overwhelmed. A voice that speaks from experience is silenced in favor of a voice that carries more authority, leading to a replacement of one's personal sense of

---

[10] See, for extensive argument for this historical thesis, Carol Gilligan and David A. J. Richards, *The Deepening Darkness.*
[11] See David A. J. Richards, *Resisting Injustice and the Feminist Ethics of Care in the Age of Obama.*
[12] See, for an illuminating general study, Nicholas Bamforth, Maleiha Malik, and Colm O'Cinneide, *Discrimination Law: Theory and Context* (London: Sweet & Maxwell, 2008).
[13] See, on this point of developmental psychology, Carol Gilligan, *The Birth of Pleasure.*

emotional presence and truth with what Sandor Ferenczi, the Hungarian psycho-analyst, describes as an "identification with the aggressor," the taking on as one's own voice the voice and demands of the oppressor. The process, leading to what Ferenczi observed as false compliance, is in itself largely unconscious, due in part to the loss of memory that follows the traumatic rupture of relationships.[14]

Identification with stereotypes replaces real relationship, the stereotypes defining a sense of reality based on disassociation, not experience, as if women did not often have masculine qualities (courage and reason), and men feminine qualities (care and emotion). The loss of voice, at a young age for boys, disables them from contesting such stereotypes, in particular, the patriarchal gender binary of masculine versus feminine, and the masculine as hierarchically superior to the feminine, a structure on which other unjust stereotypes are modeled[15] (I shall call this pattern hereafter, the gender binary and hierarchy, or patriarchal gender stereotypes). Lacking the psychology to contest such patriarchal gender stereotypes on grounds of justice, the child often acts out the repressive logic of patriarchy, bullying other boys and girls who violate the gender binary (as some boys and many girls do). The psychological marks of such disassociation, based on identification with gender stereotypes, are the idealization of those men and women who comply with the stereotypes, and the denigration of those who do not, none of which is based on experience, indeed willfully denies and falsifies experience. It is because of this psychology that patriarchy so often distorts and sometimes destroys the search for real relationships with other persons, as the individuals they are. It is a threat to love itself.

Another mark of the psychology of such disassociation is violence against any challenge to the gender stereotypes. Propensities to fascist violence thus arise from any challenge to the gender binary, experienced by patriarchal psychology as a shaming of manhood. Indeed, political fascism is most plausibly defined not by its political theory (it has none), but by its legitimation of impulses of mindless violence directed at any supposed challenge (often scapegoats like the Jews, or other margin-alized groups, homosexuals) to the leader's patriarchal authority.[16] It is no accident that the struggle between democracy and patriarchy should in the twentieth century have taken the form of the catastrophic aggressive violence of Mussolini's and Hitler's and Tojo's fascism, based on restoring patriarchal values, self-consciously at war with liberal democracy precisely because they saw it as such a threat to a patriarchal autocracy modeled on the Roman Empire.[17]

---

[14] Carol Gilligan and David A. J. Richards, *The Deepening Darkness*, p. 25.

[15] See, for a historically based exploration of the links between the subjection of women under patriarchy and slavery and other evils, Gerda Lerner, *The Creation of Patriarchy* (New York: Oxford University Press, 1986).

[16] See, for an excellent exposition of this view, with which I agree, Robert O. Paxton, *The Anatomy of Fascism* (New York: Vintage Books, 2004).

[17] For fuller discussion and defense of this position, see Carol Gilligan and David A. J. Richards, *The Deepening Darkness*.

What is distinctive about this patriarchal psychology is its violent repression of any resisting voice, in particular, of those groups subject to its dehumanizing stereotypes who would otherwise reasonably challenge its injustice. For example, the shaming of manhood, whenever it deviates from patriarchal demands, reflects the intrapsychic dimension of the way patriarchy used gender stereotypes to repress voice.[18] Patriarchal demands on men can be severe and quite onerous. They are enforced much earlier on boys than girls, making boys more vulnerable, because they are more immature, to their demands. Such demands, internalized in their psyches, require them to stay strictly within the confines of the patriarch-ally enforced gender binary and hierarchy. Since the demands are often enforced in the young childhood of boys through traumatic breaks in relationship and the violent bullying of boys by boys that arise from such trauma, such boys uncritically internalize such demands and thus strictly monitor not only other boys, but themselves.

Although we have made great progress as an increasingly democratic culture in resisting patriarchy, including in child-rearing, patriarchal psychology remains alive in our experience, as we can see in the stark divisions among contemporary Americans on a range of matters, including punitive and more nurturant patterns of bringing up children.[19] The issue is evident in the psychological development of boys, as several important recent empirical studies show us. Judy Chu's important study of these processes in young boys (organizing themselves into mean teams – often invisible to parents – that enforce the gender binary and hierarchy both against girls and other boys) reveals how early in the development of boys patriarchy continues to be enforced;[20] and Niobe Way's study of what happens to these boys in adolescence shows how they both cover their own powerful loving relationships to other boys (as inconsistent with the gender binary) and come to self-destructively repudiate these relationships, often to dispel any suggestion of homosexuality ("no homo," as they put it).[21]

This violence against resisting voice shows itself in the Love Laws. Arundhati Roy defines the Love Laws as "the laws that lay down who should be loved and how. And how much."[22] Since the norm under patriarchy was arranged marriage by the patriarch, the Love Laws forbade any loving sexual relationship across the barriers of religion, ethnicity, race, and, of course, gender that patriarchy enforced (adultery was forbidden, as was love with a person of another religion or ethnicity or race or a

---

[18]   See, for a brilliant analysis of shaming manhood as the root of violence in men, James Gilligan, *Violence: Reflections on a National Epidemic* (New York: Vintage Books, 1996).

[19]   See, for a brilliant investigation of these divisions, George Lakoff, *Moral Politics: How Liberals and Conservatives Think* (Chicago: University of Chicago Press, 1996, 2002).

[20]   See Judy Y. Chu, *When Boys Become " Boys": Development, Relationships, and Masculinity* (New York: New York University Press, 2014).

[21]   Niobe Way, *Deep Secrets: Boys' Friendships and the Crisis of Connection* (Cambridge, MA: Harvard University Press, 2011); for "no homo," see pp. 220, 235–36.

[22]   Arundhati Roy, *The God of Small Things*, p. 31.

person of the same gender). The patriarchal control of women's sexuality was crucial to patriarchal authority, whatever the desires and passions of women themselves. Roy's novel investigates the role that the Love Laws play in enforcing the Indian caste system in which fathers and mothers exercise their patriarchal authority over their daughters, in order to advance their ends, by arranging the daughter's often loveless marriages only within one's caste. The consequence of violating the Love Laws is homicidal violence: Velutha, the untouchable with whom Ammu has a loving sexual relationship in violation of the Love Laws, is murdered. Such violence, keyed to maintaining caste distinctions, remains vividly alive in India today[23] and elsewhere (honor killings). We should not think of ourselves as remote from this world, as the violence against religious and ethnic minorities as well as women and gays clearly shows. The depth of Roy's psychological analysis is that it shows us not just Indians, but ourselves.

The violence elicited by breaking the Love Laws plays a pivotal role in enforcing patriarchy. Its exemplary violence constrains and inhibits impulses of humane ethical connection that would otherwise lead to reasonable doubt and debate about the injustice of patriarchal demands in general. It is what George Eliot, who, as we shall see, broke the Love Laws and resisted patriarchy, came to see in her great novel, *Middlemarch*, about the corruption of morality and religion: "There is no general doctrine which is not capable of eating out our morality if unchecked by the deep-seated habit of direct fellow-feeling with individual fellow-men."[24] The very fact that the force of love reaches so naturally across the boundaries patriarchy enforces suggests that its dehumanizing stereotypes are based on lies and coercion, nothing else. It is for this reason that breaking the Love Laws is so incendiary within patriarchy.

The question – the question that this book attempts to answer – is how and why against such odds people not only break the Love Laws but come through love to find and creatively speak in an ethical voice that resists the injustices patriarchy enforces. I begin my argument by turning to a novel, published in the United States in 1850, during a period of remarkable cultural ferment over issues of both race and gender, including the abolitionist feminists who questioned the justice not only of American slavery, but of American racism and sexism, which they regarded as interlinked evils.[25] Nathaniel Hawthorne, the author of this great American novel, *The Scarlet Letter*, was on intimate terms with the abolitionist feminists; his sister-in-law, Elizabeth Peabody, was one of them. "Hawthorne, a boy raised by his mother, who was scorned by the more aristocratic family of his father (a sea captain, who died

---

[23] See Amana Fontanella-Khan, "India's Feudal Rapists," *The New York Times*, Thursday, June 5, 2014, at p. A27.

[24] See George Eliot, *Middlemarch* (Oxford: Oxford University Press, 2008), at p. 582.

[25] See, for a historical analysis of the abolitionist feminists and their importance in American constitutional development, David A. J. Richards, *Women, Gays, and the Constitution: The Ground for Feminism and Gay Rights in American Culture and Law* (Chicago: University of Chicago Press, 1998).

when Nathaniel was four),"[26] was acutely sensitive to his mother's unjust suffering and the voice of resistance he sensed in her and the abolitionist feminists. He "wrote *The Scarlet Letter* in a rush of intensity and passion in the year following his mother's death. 'I think I have never overcome my own adamant in any instance,' he subsequently reflected in his journal."[27] It offers a remarkable psychological analysis of the connection of resistance to patriarchy to breaking the Love Laws, one based on Hawthorne's close study of the resistance of the women he loved and what he had come to believe was the problem they had not yet addressed (namely, unjust patriarchal controls on women's freedom to love sexually).

The novel is set in Puritan New England in the year 1649, the year that the Puritans in Great Britain executed Charles I. "It was an age," Hawthorne observes, "in which the human intellect, newly emancipated, had taken a more active and wider range than for many centuries before. Men of the sword had overthrown nobles and kings."[28] Hawthorne counterpoints such Puritan liberal resistance to absolute monarchy to this Puritan New England community's moral and legal horror of Hester Prynne's adultery, shown by her pregnancy and birth of a child, Pearl, during a period of her husband's continuing absence and indeed putative death. Hester refuses to disclose the name of her lover, Dimmesdale, her minister. Hester's punishment is the shame of wearing an "A" sewn onto her garments. The good women of the town, however, regard death as more appropriate. But why death for adultery?

Within patriarchy, or the attempt to better enforce patriarchy, adultery is elevated to a high crime, because adultery flouts patriarchal controls on women's sexuality. For example, when Augustus, establishing absolute monarchy after the fall of the Roman Republic, seeks to enforce the demands of imperial, antirepublican rule, his *Lex Julia* imposed unprecedented criminal penalties for adultery, making it a crime against the state. Augustus had required his own intelligent and witty daughter, Julia, to enter into several loveless marriages; when Julia defied him, having many sexual affairs outside marriage with men she desired, her furious father, pursuant to his own law, exiled her to an island.[29] Early Christian emperors, eager to enforce their aggressively autocratic rule, extended to adultery the dreaded punishment of the sack (the victim was enclosed in a sealed sack with a dog, a cock, a viper, and a monkey, and then thrown into a river). That punishment had been previously reserved for parricide, thus equating adultery with the killing of a father, the ultimate crime within patriarchy.[30] Death for adultery thus makes sense against the background of aggressively patriarchal religious and political constraints on women's sexual freedom.

---

[26]   See Carol Gilligan, *The Birth of Pleasure*, p. 136.
[27]   *Id.*
[28]   Nathaniel Hawthorne, *The Scarlet Letter* (New York: Penguin, 1983), p. 143.
[29]   See, on this point, Carol Gilligan and David A. J. Richards, *The Deepening Darkness*, pp. 41–49.
[30]   See *id.*, p. 2.

Hester Prynne, however, was in love with Dimmesdale, and refuses to identify him as her lover in part as an expression of her love. In contrast, Hester never loved her much older husband, Chillingworth, whom she (not unreasonably) thought dead at the time of her affair with Dimmesdale. Hester never accepts her community's condemnation of her love, and indeed secures Dimmesdale's help when the Puritan elders question her custody of her daughter. After Dimmesdale's death, Hester leaves New England with her daughter, but later returns on her own, "people brought all their sorrows and perplexities, and besought her counsel, as one who had herself gone through a mighty trouble."[31] In effect, Hester becomes what Dimmesdale was not, a humane minister to human suffering, Hester had come, through love, to "cast away the fragments of a broken chain. The world's law was no law for her mind." Having suffered from the patriarchal Love Laws that condemned adultery (including both her loving relationship to Dimmesdale and to their daughter, Pearl), Hester comes ethically to question such Laws:

> Men of the sword had overthrown nobles and kings. Men bolder than these had overthrown and rearranged – not actually, but within the sphere of theory, which was their most real abode – the whole system of ancient prejudices, wherewith was linked much of ancient principle. Hester Prynne imbibed this spirit.[32]

By the end of the novel, Hester imagines that at some future time, "when the world should have grown ripe for it, . . . a new truth would be revealed, in order to establish the whole relation between man and woman on a surer ground of mutual happiness."[33]

As Hawthorne shows us, what makes Hester's ethical resistance possible is her "lawless passion,"[34] starting from and assuming the political liberalism of Puritan ethical ideals of the priesthood of all believers (the direct relationship of each believer to God without the intermediary of a patriarchal priesthood), a liberalism that justifies the Lockean democratic right to revolution against authorities that abridge basic human rights (the "men of the sword" overthrowing "nobles and kings").[35] Hester can, however, as others had "within the sphere of theory," expand and deepen the underlying liberal ideal of free and equal ethical voice to question the role patriarchy played not only in politics and religion but intimate life. It is from this perspective that we can understand how Hester's breaking the Love Laws empowers the ethically resisting voice of Hester that is at the heart of the novel. It is because Hester loves Dimmesdale and the child of their union, Pearl, that she

---

[31] Nathaniel Hawthorne, *The Scarlet Letter*, at p. 227.

[32] *Id.*, p. 143.

[33] *Id.*, p. 227.

[34] *Id.*, p. 144.

[35] On Locke's political theory and its importance to American revolutionary constitutionalism, see David A. J. Richards, *Toleration and the Constitution* (New York: Oxford University Press, 1985).

comes to see how the patriarchal Love Laws condemn relationships between men and women to unhappiness.

Both men in Hester's life – her lover, Dimmesdale, and her husband, Chillingworth – are treated in the novel as remarkable, humane, and generous men (Chillingworth, for example, wills his estate to Pearl, even though she is not his natural daughter). However, their ethical intelligence has been darkened by the ways in which patriarchy frames their self-conceptions of manhood: A gifted and loving ethical leader, Dimmesdale, has become dim (unable to acknowledge his love for Hester and Pearl), and the heart of a generous and humane physician, Chillingworth, one who had learned to heal from Native Americans, has been chilled when he is shamed by his wife's breaking of the patriarchal Love Laws and, for this reason, does not, as a physician, minister to Dimmesdale when he falls ill, but, like some psychotic psychoanalyst, exacerbates his guilt-ridden misery until he dies.[36] The dimness of ethical intelligence and the coldness of the heart are consequences of the gender binary and hierarchy central to patriarchy, an intelligence (masculine) divided from feeling (feminine) that cripples ethical thought and feeling (for example, legitimating the hierarchies among ethnic groups central to cultural racism[37]), which requires both. Such intrapsychic divisions and hierarchies are what patriarchal moral development imposes even on good men, dividing not only, as Hawthorne shows, men from women, but men from men, and expresses itself in violence elicited by the shaming of manhood and womanhood (homophobia, lashing out at relationships between men that both defy the gender binary and the hierarchies that divide men, illustrates this dynamic). The division between Dimmesdale and Chillingwood is enforced by such political violence, keyed to insults to manhood.

The isolation of Dimmesdale and Chillingworth from one another bespeaks the shadow patriarchy casts over the hearts and minds of men in general, even men who are not violent criminals[38] or victims of war trauma.[39] What Hawthorne shows us in Dimmesdale and Chillingworth is how patriarchy, here enforced by religious authority, inflicts on mature, good men a moral injury that cuts them off from humane relationships, not only to women, but to one another – Chillingworth's sadistic deepening of Dimmesdale guilt, and Dimmesdale's incapacity to embrace the love Hester offers him, leading to illness and death.[40] Such men are also

---

[36] I am indebted for this point to Carol Gilligan.

[37] See, on this point, Francisco Bethencourt, *Racisms: From the Crusades to the Twentieth Century* (Princeton, NJ: Princeton University Press, 2013).

[38] See James Gilligan, *Violence: Reflections on a National Epidemic* (New York: Vintage Books, 1996).

[39] See Jonathan Shay, *Achilles in Vietnam: Combat Trauma and the Undoing of Character* (New York: Scribner, 1994).

[40] On moral injury, see *id.* Shay's study of Vietnam War veterans identifies, describes, and explores what he calls the moral injury to the character of these men arising from structures of authority that require these men in high-stakes war situations of life and death to do things they know to be wrong, traumatically injuring their moral character in ways that lead some men to go berserk, wantonly injuring and killing innocent persons without any sense of limit or accountability to personal

vulnerable to the shaming of manhood, which often leads to violence against women, one another, and, intrapsychically, themselves.

Hester Prynne, however, exists in a very different place: She lives in but also outside patriarchy. It is not merely that she has broken the Love Laws, but that she has held onto the loving relationships to her lover and daughter that the Love Laws would condemn and break. The good women of New England, who would condemn her to death, are shamed by her adultery, as Hester would be, were she still within patriarchy. However, Hester no longer accepts such patriarchal demands: "The world's law was no law for her mind."[41] Because Hester no longer accepts the patriarchal stigmatization of adultery, she does not experience the shame for her sexual love of which the good women of New England are so acutely aware. The point is made by the way Hester insists on continuing to wear "A," the patriarchal symbol of her infamy, but also by the way in which she ornaments it, as something to be celebrated, and in the way others come to regard the "A" to mean not "Adultery," but as "Able." Hester has come to a position of pride in her love and loving relationships.

Although Hester first thinks she herself might be the "prophetess"[42] of a new anti-patriarchal ethical order, she comes to see that what is required for such an ethically prophetic role is a woman, unlike her, not "stained with sin, vowed down with shame, or even burdened with a life-long sorrow."[43] Throughout the novel, Hester is quite alone except for her loving relationship to her daughter whom she takes away from New England. However, Hester returns alone, and was never joined in her resistance by the man she loved. It is this "life-long sorrow" that may explain the realism of her coming to see that she, who could not bring her patriarchally crippled lover to resist, was not the ethical voice who would find resonance at this time in this still very patriarchal culture. Her return to New England alone suggests that if she could not herself be a leader of social change, she could at least show others that a person, who stayed in loving relationship as she did (indeed, still loving her now dead lover), could express her love by humanely ministering to human suffering, finding the strength to be the kind of prophetic minister her lover was not able to be. "A" indeed means "Able."

The question left open by Hawthorne's exquisitely observed artistic exploration of resistance to patriarchy is what further steps would be required for someone in Hester's position not only to resist, but to do what Hester comes to believe she cannot

conscience. Here, I suggest, due to my discussions with Carol Gilligan, that patriarchy itself inflicts moral injury on those who accept its demands, as Hawthorne shows us in Dimmesdale and Chillingworth. I return to this question in the Conclusion. See, on this point, Carol Gilligan, "Moral Injury and the Ethic of Care: Reframing the Conversation about Differences," *Journal of Social Philosophy*, 45, no. 1 (2014): 89–106; Carol Gilligan, "Strong Democracy: A Different Voice, What Stands in the Way," unpublished essay, 2014.

[41]   Nathaniel Hawthorne, *The Scarlet Letter*, p. 143.

[42]   *Id.*, p. 227.

[43]   *Id.*, p. 228.

do alone, namely, find in herself and speak publicly in her ethically resisting voice with a resonance that would lead to a social movement of resistance to patriarchy in both public and private life. There are studies of two remarkable Victorian couples, both studied by Phyllis Rose in her *Parallel Lives*,[44] that suggest what might in addition be required.

The two couples – Harriet Taylor and John Stuart Mill,[45] and George Eliot (Marian Evans) and George Henry Lewes[46] – were, first and foremost, adulterers. When each couple met one another, Harriet Taylor and George Henry Lewes were already married. Soon after, Taylor started an intimate relationship with John Stuart Mill, and Lewes did the same with George Eliot. These new relationships were, needless to say, condemned by Victorian social morality. Victorian Britain was not, however, seventeenth-century New England, and adultery, while condemned by Victorian social morality, would not be visited by state-imposed sanctions.[47] Patriarchal controls on adultery were much weaker in nineteenth-century Britain than in seventeenth-century New England (in part because the liberal democratic strands in British life had led to resistance to its patriarchal, imperial strands[48]). In both cases, the spouse knew about and accepted the adultery. Furthermore, Harriet's children were now adults, and her daughter became a close friend of Mill; Lewes's wife had herself had sex with other men, and her children by other men were supported by Lewes. Nonetheless, both relationships scandalized Victorian social morality: Both clearly broke the Victorian Love Laws.

What is remarkable in both cases is, in contrast to Hester Prynne and Dimmesdale, that both couples stayed in a loving, reciprocal relationship until one of them died. In both cases, like Hester, the women – Harriet Taylor and George Eliot (Marian Evans) – not only broke the Love Laws, but were able to extract the stigma from such relationships, avoiding that irrational shame over their sexual love that more patriarchal women did experience. Unlike Hester, however, both women stayed in relationship to the men they loved, and the men stayed in relationship to them. What such reciprocal, loving relationships made possible was, in both cases, an astonishing freeing of ethical voice from the Love Laws, making psychologically possible new forms of ethical, political, and artistic creativity in works that exposed the injustices of patriarchal demands on both men and women and called for more democratic, egalitarian forms of public and private life. In short,

---

[44] Phyllis Rose, *Parallel Lives: Five Victorian Marriages* (New York: Vintage, 1983). For a similar study, see Katie Roiphe, *Uncommon Arrangements: Seven Marriages* (New York: Dial, 2007).

[45] See Phyllis Rose, *Parallel Lives*, pp. 95–140.

[46] *Id.*, pp. 193–238.

[47] At British common law, adultery, known as criminal conversation, was a civil tort, calling for damages. Criminal conversation was abolished by statute in 1857. See Wikipedia.org/wiki/Adultery.

[48] On these two strands in British cultural life and their larger political importance in explaining both British imperialism and the resisting voices to imperialism of the Bloomsbury Group, among others, see David A. J. Richards, *The Rise of Gay Rights and the Fall of the British Empire: Liberal Resistance and the Bloomsbury Group* (Cambridge: Cambridge University Press, 2013).

through loving relationships that self-consciously broke the Love Laws, both couples found and spoke or supported speaking in an ethically prophetic voice in a way Hester came to believe she alone could not. George Eliot and Harriet Taylor found a resonance for their voices in the men they loved, empowering new social movements that would transform ethics, politics, and art.

Prior to falling in love with Lewes, Marian Evans was a notable Victorian bluestocking, who translated leading German works on Bible criticism and aspired to become yet another high Victorian intellectual. What she had not imagined was she had literary gifts, let alone gifts that would make her one of the leading novelists of her era or of any later era. With an ambition to be taken as seriously as the male Victorian intellectuals she admired and even loved (particularly Herbert Spencer[49]), Evans understandably defined her talents within the metric of the era's gender hierarchy. Status and recognition were associated primarily with nonfiction written on high intellectual topics; "women's literature," on the other hand, occupied some nether region far below. One of the features of love can be coming to see the beloved as the individual she or he is, sometimes in ways the beloved cannot see. It was Lewes who recognized and pointed out to Marian Evans her remarkable insights into the human psyche and human relationships, a recognition that led Marian Evans – George Eliot – to write a series of novels that culminate in two masterpieces, *Middlemarch* and *Daniel Deronda*. Lewes's love enabled her to break free from the Victorian gender binary and hierarchy that confined her ambition, empowering her to find and speak in an artistic voice comparable to the very greatest male novelists – Tolstoy, for example. Breaking the Love Laws was an important ingredient in thus releasing and empowering creative voice, exposing the ravages patriarchy sometimes imposed on both men and women in Victorian marriages. For Eliot, these ravages were not only to personal life but to ethics itself, as we saw in the earlier cited quote: "There is no general doctrine which is not capable of eating out our morality if unchecked by the deep-seated habit of direct fellow-feeling with individual fellow-men."[50]

Middlemarch, written by a woman not married to the man she loved, is a piercing, revelatory study of two disastrous Victorian marriages – one by a remarkable woman, Dorothea, and one by a remarkable man, Lydgate, both of whom address the two questions posed for a well-lived life – how to live and what to do in love and vocation so as to invest and fulfill one's moral nature as a responsible ethical person. And both make disastrous choices. Dorothea marries an older man whom she thinks will elevate and challenge her, but comes to see as an intellectually empty, controlling patriarchal man incapable of the kind of loving relationship or vocational

---

[49] On Eliot's unrequited passion for Spencer and his impact on her thinking, see Nancy L. Paxton, *George Eliot and Herbert Spencer: Feminism, Evolutionism, and the Reconstruction of Gender* (Princeton, NJ: Princeton University Press, 1991).

[50] See George Eliot, *Middlemarch* (Oxford: Oxford University Press, 2008), at p. 582.

accomplishment for which Dorothea had hoped. Lydgate, a highly ambitious physician with strong interests in the sciences, marries a frivolous woman incapable of understanding his gifts and ambitions, and comes to see that she never loved him, nor understood his aspirations, leading to a life without love and without the accomplishment of which he knew he was capable. What Eliot is able to show us is how patriarchal conventionality can be equally destructive, both of love and of vocation, both of women and of men. Only after her husband's death does Dorothea come into loving relationship with a man, Will Ladislaw, who loves her. The man, not coincidentally, is an ethnic and religious outsider (a Pole and a Jew[51]), so, in loving him, Dorothea breaks the Love Laws. Eliot's point is clear: So long as marriage remains patriarchal, it is dangerous to the hearts and minds of both men and women.

One of the remarkable features of *Middlemarch* is its poignant exploration of the loneliness of a woman, Dorothea, in a loveless, patriarchal marriage.[52] Eliot describes both a loss of voice and a submerged rage, a kind of spiritual death of the soul: "we should die of that roar which lies on the other side of silence."[53] In her last novel, *Daniel Deronda*,[54] she continues to explore the psyche of a woman, Gwendolen Harleth, much more conventional in her ambitions than Dorothea and less ethically inhibited (thus, her rage is, in contrast to Dorothea's, not submerged), but one who, precisely because of her conventional ambitions for wealth and status, enters into a loveless marriage with an aristocratic, empty, patriarchal man she comes to hate and, in not saving him when he falls into the ocean from their boat, may have acted on her hate, and is arguably ethically responsible for his death. Eliot counterposes to the shrunken world of an exemplary, high-status British patriarchal marriage the ultimate outsider to British patriarchy, a Jew, Daniel Deronda, whose still intact humane ethical feeling for others alone can touch and redeem Gwendolen from the hell in which she finds herself. However, Deronda loves another and seeks an alternative for his people, the most patriarchally despised of religious groups, the Jews, in Palestine. Long before the Dreyfus Affair was to lead Herzl to call for a Jewish state to protect European Jews from the ravages of European anti-Semitism, Eliot sees the problem and moreover sees, in an outsider to European patriarchy, an ethical alternative.[55]

The loving relationship of Harriet Taylor and John Stuart Mill, while Taylor was married to another man, scandalized Victorian society, exposing them to social opprobrium, including by Mill's own family (after her husband's death, the couple do marry). Their relationship led to work on two books that Mill always

[51] See, on this point, George Eliot, *Middlemarch* (Oxford; Oxford University Press, 2008), at pp. 676, 727.
[52] See, for example, *id.*, pp. 399–400.
[53] *Id.*, p. 182.
[54] George Eliot, *Daniel Deronda* (Oxford: Oxford University Press, 2009).
[55] See, for illuminating discussion, Gertrude Himmelfarb, *The Jewish Odyssey of George Eliot* (New York: Encounter Books 2009).

acknowledged to be conceived and written in genuine collaborative with Harriet Taylor, namely, *On Liberty* and *The Subjection of Women*.[56] Both works are now reasonably regarded as establishing the two principles of political liberalism: The basic human rights that government must protect (*On Liberty*), and the principle of antidiscrimination (*The Subjection of Women*) (today condemning the expression through public law of the irrational prejudices of religious intolerance, racism, sexism, and homophobia). While Mill tried to justify these principles in terms of his interpretation of the utilitarian principle, later liberals, like John Rawls and myself, have defended the two principles but on anti-utilitarian, deontological grounds of equal respect for human dignity.[57] The principle of basic equal liberties rests not on utility, but on dignity, the protection of the higher-order interests we have in deciding on and pursuing our ends as persons, exercising our powers of rationality and reasonableness.[58] The principle of antidiscrimination condemns the expression through law or policies of deeply entrenched, irrationalist cultural prejudices. I have elsewhere explored in depth the cultural background of such prejudices in terms of what I called "moral slavery."[59] By moral slavery, I understand a long-standing cultural prejudice – whether an extreme religious intolerance like anti-Semitism, or racism, or sexism, or homophobia – all of which may reasonably be understood and explicated in terms of an entrenched patriarchal culture that uses the gender binary and hierarchy to target with hostility, as feminine and thus subject to men or the manly, whole groups of persons in terms of insults to the dignity of their moral powers: First, the group in question is deprived of all the basic human rights accorded other persons (not only the rights of conscience and speech but of intimate life and work); and second, such abridgment of basic human rights is rationalized in terms of dehumanizing stereotypes (whether anti-Semitic, or racist, or sexist, or homophobic) whose force depends, in a vicious circularity, on the abridgment of the basic human rights of the group.

My interest here is how and why the relationship of Taylor and Mill, breaking the Love Laws, empowered them to make their arguments, a profoundly anti-patriarchal

---

[56] See John Stuart Mill, *On Liberty and The Subjection of Women*, edited by Alan Ryan (London: Penguin 2006) (*On Liberty*, first published, 1859; *The Subjection of Women*, first published, 1869).

[57] See David A. J. Richards, *Sex, Drugs, Death and the Law: An Essay on Human Rights and Overcriminalization* (Totowa, NJ: Rowman & Littlefield, 1982); see Rawls's treatment of this matter, John Rawls, *Lectures on the History of Political Philosophy* (Cambridge, MA: The Belknap Press of Harvard University Press, 2007), at pp. 251–316.

[58] For Kant's formulations of the Categorical Imperative, based on the value of dignity, see Immanuel Kant, *Foundations of the Metaphysics of Morals*, translated by Lewis W. Beck (New York: Liberal Arts Press, 1959) (first published, 1784); for Rawls's contractualist statement of Kant's position, see John Rawls, *A Theory of Justice* (Cambridge, MA: Harvard University Press, 1971). For fuller defense and explication of rationality and reasonableness as moral powers, see David A. J. Richards, *A Theory of Reasons for Action* (Oxford: Oxford at the Clarendon Press, 1971).

[59] For further discussion, see David A. J. Richards, *Women, Gays, and the Constitution: The Grounds for Feminism and Gay Rights in Culture and Law* (Chicago: University of Chicago Press, 1998).

argument because it questions both the repression of voice central to patriarchy as well as the justice of the dehumanizing stereotypes patriarchy has enforced. What made psychologically possible their making such arguments, which remain relevant to the fabric of our lives today?

On Liberty and *The Subjection of Women* are pathbreaking articulations of the two main principles of political liberalism, that of basic human rights and antidiscrimination, arguments that can be better defended in terms of equal respect for dignity, a value that is, I believe, clearly implicit in the argument of both books. The argument of *On Liberty* not only defends a robust right of conscience and speech, but also a right of autonomy when neither the state nor dominant social morality can justify its sanctions in terms of harms to other persons, a right that can also be grounded in dignity.[60] And, the argument of *The Subjection of Women* clearly develops an argument akin to "moral slavery" in the domains of race and gender that applies as well to religion and sexual orientation. What is of interest to me here is not ongoing contemporary debates of how both principles should be understood, principles now central to constitutional law in many democracies, including the United States and the nations of the European Union, including Great Britain. Rather, my question – the subject matter of this book – is why a loving relationship that broke the Victorian Love Laws should have empowered this kind of ethical creativity in the articulation and defense of basic principles of political liberalism, some of which clearly challenged then-dominant moral, religious, and political views in Britain and elsewhere.

What is at the heart of the matter is what Harriet Taylor and John Stuart Mill confronted when they fell in love, namely, that their relationship was condemned. *On Liberty* is thus written out of a sense of liberal indignation not only at the state of British criminal law, but, equally central to its argument, at conventional social morality, which was outraged by such adultery. Such outrage at adultery is, as we have seen, the mark that patriarchy still very much governs ethical, religious, and political life, holding both women and men in conformity to the patriarchal Love Laws, seeking to break and disrupt all such relationships. However, the loving relationship of two free and equal persons, coming to love and know one another as the individuals and persons they are, leads not only to breaking the Love Laws, but empowers the ethically resisting voice of both Harriet Taylor and John Stuart Mill to expose the injustice of patriarchal arrangements that are inconsistent with democratic values of equal voice and dignity. It is for this reason that *On Liberty* offers that most muscular defense of freedom of conscience and speech ever made, for it was precisely the violent repression of voice that had made patriarchy seem for so long simply the natural order of things. The long argument in *On Liberty* about the history of the repression of thought and speech must be understood against this

---

[60] See David A. J. Richards, *Sex, Drugs, Death and the Law: An Essay on Human Rights and Overcriminalization* (Totowa, NJ: Rowman & Littlefield, 1982).

background, exposing the lies and violence that were required to enforce patriarchy. Only a regime of free thought and speech can empower the kind of resisting voice that can expose such injustices, and empower reform and reconstruction in terms of justice. A social morality resting on the violent repression of free and equal voice is a morality not worthy of the rational and reasonable persons we are, and the societies we have a right to demand and expect.[61]

The same liberal indignation – breaking the gender binary of thought versus emotion – explains the defense in *On Liberty* of the right of personal autonomy that can only be coercively abridged, either by law or by social morality, on grounds of fair distribution of goods and opportunities (the argument is not economically libertarian) or when the acts of one person inflict real harms (taking of life or property or security) on other persons; the argument rules out as well most forms of paternalism, aimed to protect the agent from herself or himself (Mill is, I believe, particularly concerned with the sexist abuse of arguments of self-destruction when women and men challenge conventional gender roles). The argument is clearly aiming to condemn appeals to conventional majoritarian views as such, ungrounded in any reasonable argument of fairness or harm. Since conventional morality often rests on the repression of free and equal resisting voice, such appeals violate the values of equal dignity central to constitutional democracy.

While the argument of *On Liberty* does not narrowly define the right to autonomy that he defends, it is reasonably clear that the central example for Mill of this right is the right to intimate life, the right to intimate loving relationships. It was, after all, the social opprobrium from family and friends, as well as the wider British society, that Harriet Taylor and he experienced for their loving relationship that crystallized for Mill the callous cruelty, indeed the inhumanity, of the patriarchal demands imposed on intimate life. Mill had experienced, for the first time in his life, a reciprocally loving relationship, a human connection of shared intimate voice to another person, a connection that released him from the sense of empty, mechanical disassociation, the depression, left by the patriarchal control of his demanding father for impersonal ends of utilitarian aggregation (based on the hierarchy of thought over emotion), described in his autobiography.[62] What, for Mill, is at the heart of human dignity and individuality is our choices about our intimate love lives, and what appalled him in the coercive demands of the patriarchal Love Laws is their violent repressive attack on what makes us human and bearers of basic human rights. Protecting love is the liberal heart of the matter.

---

[61] For a sensitive recent exploration of how their love may have led to their ethical insights, see Cass R. Sunstein, "John & Harriet: Still Mysterious," *The New York Review of Books*, April 2, 2015, Vol. LXII, no. 6, pp. 67–70.

[62] For Mill's own statement of this history, see John Stuart Mill, *Autobiography*, edited by John M. Robson (London: Penguin, 1989) (first published, 1873).

The Subjection of Women is, as I have suggested, an argument about what I have called the structural injustice of moral slavery, and patriarchy – the gender binary and hierarchy – is the viciously circular irrationality that Mill and Harriet Taylor expose. What they came to see is that the patriarchal heart of darkness lies in the ways patriarchy has entered into our psyches, defining love itself in the terms of the gender binary and hierarchy. It is surely because their own loving relationship, based on free and equal voice, exposed patriarchal gender stereotypes as based on lies and violence that their mode of breaking the Love Laws empowered ethical voice in resisting patriarchy, which is the subject of both *The Subjection of Women* and *On Liberty*.

In my judgment, certain works in political and ethical theory mark ethical progress, a deeper understanding of what ethics is and how far we fall short of its demands. The Buddha's critique of the caste system is one of these works,[63] and both *On Liberty* and *The Subjection of Women* are yet others. What compels me in the study of breaking the Love Laws is when this leads, as it did in the case of these collaborative works by Harriet Taylor and John Stuart Mill, to such astonishing forms of ethical emancipation and progress, in effect, loving relationship making possible a deeper understanding of injustice and thus of justice.

What our closer study of *The Scarlet Letter* and these two remarkable Victorian couples shows is that breaking the Love Laws can have an emancipatory ethical significance, empowering ethical voices of resistance to the structural injustice I have called moral slavery. What distinguishes the resistance of Hester Prynne from that of Lewes and Eliot and Taylor and Mill is that Hester is alone in a way neither Eliot and Taylor are, joined by their lovers in resistance to the patriarchal forces around them that would condemn their relationship and separate them. When Hester at the end of the novel comes to believe she cannot be the prophetess of the new ethical order that justice requires, her judgment reflects not only a sense of realism about when an ethically resisting voice can give rise to a social movement of ethical transformation, but also her own isolation. What empowers resistance to patriarchy to go public is relationship, often against extraordinary forces of ignorance, stupidity, and fascist violence.

These observations are consistent with the role of relationship and resisting voice that I investigated in *The Rise of Gay Rights and the Fall of the British Empire: Liberal Resistance and the Bloomsbury Group*.[64] What I show there is how central breaking the Love Laws was to the forms of ethical resistance to patriarchal

---

[63] See, for example, The Buddha, *The Dhammapada: The Sayings of the Buddha*, translated by John Ross Carter and Mahinda Palihawadana (Oxford: Oxford University Press, 2008). For illuminating commentary on this point, see Richard Gombrich, *What the Buddha Taught* (London: Equinox, 2009), pp. 186–89, 195.

[64] See David A. J. Richards, *The Rise of Gay Rights and the Fall of the British Empire: Liberal Resistance and the Bloomsbury Group* (Cambridge: Cambridge University Press, 2013).

demands, including British patriarchal imperialism, of the writers and artists of the Bloomsbury Group. I focus on the emergence in their relationships and discourse of gay rights, although the argument explains as well their feminism and their anti-imperialism. Homosexuality has existed both in animals and in human cultures for a very long time. In the ancient world of Greece and Rome, homosexuality was accepted in a way it was not under Christianity, which severely condemned it (by burning at the stake[65]). In Greece and Rome, homosexuality, under a rigidly defined system of gender segregation, was common and accepted, but largely thought of in highly patriarchal forms: defined by its sexist contempt for the passive role in gay sex, and associated, as in Rome, with slave boys and, in Greece, with boys and often slaves.[66] In contrast, the claim that gay/lesbian sexual relationships are forms of enduring loving relationship between adults to which gays have a basic human right is modern and, as I show, made possible by the new view of their homosexual relationships that Lytton Strachey and John Maynard Keynes came to take under the moral influence and philosophy of their teacher and friend, G. E. Moore, at Cambridge University. Moore had argued that friendship and love are human goods, and Strachey and Keynes made ethical sense of their homosexual relationships, as loving relationships, along these lines. Gay love does, of course, break the patriarchal Love Laws, which define sexual love as exclusively between a man and a woman. Both Strachey and Keynes knew this to be false, but only came to see their loves as a ground for ethical resistance when Moore's ethical philosophy, which they regarded as a major breakthrough in moral philosophy, enabled them to see loving relationships, of all kinds, as a basic ethical good, an experience that was deepened and expanded by meeting Vanessa and Virginia Stephen in London, the remarkable sisters of their good Cambridge friend Thoby Stephen. Lytton Strachey and Virginia became close friends and literary competitors, and Strachey, who had first asked Virginia to marry him, thought better of it, and was the matchmaker in her eventual marriage to Leonard Woolf, a Jew. Virginia Woolf herself broke the Love Laws by falling in love with and marrying a Jew. In her own later passionate lesbian affair with Vita Sackville-West, she again breaks the Love Laws that forbid both same-sex love and adultery (Vita was married to Harold Nicolson, himself a gay man, and both were well aware of the other's extramarital affairs[67]). It is Strachey and Virginia Woolf, who not only break the Love Laws but come – via loving relationship to others as well as their own loving friendship to one another – to speak and write in a creative ethical voice that indicts the patriarchal demands that would condemn them and to connect this ethically

---

[65] See, on this point, William Blackstone, *Commentaries on the Laws of England* (1765–69) (Chicago: University of Chicago Press, 1979), 4:215–16. For commentary, see David A. J. Richards, *Women, Gays, and the Constitution: The Grounds for Feminism and Gay Rights in Culture and Law* (Chicago: University of Chicago Press, 1998), p. 292.

[66] See Kenneth J. Dover, *Greek Homosexuality* (London: Duckworth, 1978); Craig A. Williams, *Roman Homosexuality*, 2nd ed. (New York: Oxford University Press, 2010).

[67] See Nigel Nicolson, *Portrait of a Marriage* (New York: Athenaeum, 1973).

resisting voice to a larger criticism of British patriarchy both in private and public life, including British imperialism.[68] Not all members of the Bloomsbury Group linked their understanding and experience of gay rights to a feminist critique of gender stereotypes (E. M. Forster, for example, did not, though he certainly shared their critique of British imperialism), but Strachey and Woolf did so, exemplifying those circumstances when breaking the Love Laws leads to ethical advances in the understanding of injustice through loves that lead to resistance.

The resistance of the Bloomsbury Group, linked to their loves that broke the Love Laws, raises the question of how the next generation both loved and resisted and with what consequences for new forms of voice that exposed the injustices of patriarchy. I begin with Benjamin Britten and Peter Pears.

---

[68] See, for elaboration of all these points, David A. J. Richards, *The Rise of Gay Rights and the Fall of the British Empire*, pp. 97–139.

2

Benjamin Britten and Peter Pears: Love and Resistance

The Bloomsbury Group's acceptance of gay/lesbian love and their anti-imperialism informed the gradual liberalization of British and American public opinion and law after World War II. We explore here how breaking the Love Laws related to the comparable resistance of four gay British men – Benjamin Britten, Peter Pears, Christopher Isherwood, and Wystan Auden – who come to young manhood after the Bloomsbury Group. They were, however, certainly influenced by them – Virginia Woolf, as we shall see, and, notably, the novelist E. M. Forster. Forster was a friend of and major influence on Isherwood (indeed, shared with Isherwood and sought his comments on his only explicitly gay novel, *Maurice*, published after Forster's death). He collaborated with Benjamin Britten on the libretto for Britten's exploration of repressed gay love in his opera, *Billy Budd*, Britten's most explicitly gay work until his final opera, *Death in Venice*.

What makes these four particular gay men – a composer, a singer, a novelist, and a poet – of interest is that their resistance leads to forms of art that in various ways contest homophobia, breaking the silencing of voice on which homophobia rests. During the 1930s, they are good friends and supporters of one another, indeed embedded in a web of relationships so close – as gay men and artists – that any fair study of any of them must include the others. The love story of Benjamin Britten and Peter Pears, the subject of this chapter, arises within this web of such friendship, a relational web that frames the later divergences among these friends, including, in the case of Britten and Auden, the breaking of their friendship, very much linked to their quite different erotic choices and love stories. Creativity, friendship, and love are often intimately connected, and, when they are, we cannot fairly discuss one without the other. Consider, in the United States, the comparable friendships among the gay poet, Allen Ginsberg, and the gay novelist, William Burroughs, and the bisexual novelist, Jack Kerouac, whose creative support for one another was indispensable in their artistic development and love stories.[1] My argument here begins by setting the stage for

---

[1] See, for illuminating commentary, Barry Miles, *Allen Ginsberg: Beat Poet* (Croydon, UK: Virgin Books, 2014); Jane Kramer, *Allen Ginsberg in America* (New York: Random House, 1969); Barry Miles, *Call Me Burroughs* (New York: Hachette Book Group, 2013).

exploring the later love stories of two of the artists I study (Isherwood and Auden) in the next two chapters, and the love story of Britten and Pears here.

During this period, Isherwood and Auden were particularly close friends, indeed were sex partners over the period between 1926 and 1938,[2] although Isherwood emphasized the sexual dimension of their relationship, implicitly denying anything deeper between them.[3] It is doubtful that Auden, who may have been in love with Isherwood, shared this view. Isherwood and Auden, who had first met as boys at school and then meet again seven years later (Auden was now at student at Oxford),[4] collaborate on at least three plays and a travel book on China at war (more on all this later).

Auden is nearly seven years older than Britten when they meet in 1935; Isherwood is even older (by two and one-half years). Britten is impressed by their Oxbridge educations (Isherwood at Cambridge, Auden at Oxford), which he lacked (he attended the Royal College of Music in London), and also by their artistic flair and sexual experience. Both urge Britten, who is shy and much less sexually experienced than they, to be more sexually active, and he has at least one serious sexual affair with a German youth.[5] Over the next several years, Britten collaborates with Auden, writing music (for example, on the coal industry, or running the railroads, or the history of British imperialist racism),[6] all under the heavy influence of socialist realism. He writes music as well to several Auden poems,[7] including the song cycle, *Our Hunting Fathers* (attacking, *inter alia*, "the rituals and values of the hunting set,"[8] and quoting Lenin's wife on her husband's revolutionary aims[9]), and later collaborates with Auden in the United States on their American opera, *Paul Bunyan*. Auden, who may have been erotically drawn to Britten, writes at least two poems to and for his friend, one of which, "Underneath the abject willow," urges him to be more sexually adventurous:

> Underneath the abject willow,
> Lover, sulk no more,
> Act from thought should quickly follow:
> What is thinking for? . . .
> Walk then, come,
> Into your satisfaction.[10]

[2] See Peter Parker, *Isherwood: A Life Revealed* (New York: Random House, 2004), p. 115.
[3] See, on this point, Christopher Isherwood, *Christopher and His Kind* (Minneapolis: University of Minnesota Press, 2001) (first published, 1976), p. 264.
[4] Peter Parker, *Isherwood*, pp. 104–5.
[5] See, on this point, John Bridcut, *Britten's Children* (London: Faber and Faber, 2006), pp. 89–110.
[6] For a recent recording, see Martin Brabins, conductor, Birmingham Contemporary Music Group, *Benjamin Britten on Film* (London: NMC Recordings, 2007).
[7] See the CD recording of these poems, Benjamin Britten, *Settings of Poems by W.H. Auden* (London: Collins Classics, 1998).
[8] See Paul Kildea, *Benjamin Britten: A Life in the Twentieth Century* (London: Allen Lane, 2013), p. 120.
[9] See *id.*
[10] See libretto to CD, Benjamin Britten, *Settings of Poems by W.H. Auden* (London: Collins Classics, 1998), at p. 23.

Britten sets both poems to music.[11] Isherwood and Auden come to America in 1939, Auden settling in New York City, Isherwood in Los Angeles, California. Britten follows later that same year with his good friend, the singer, Peter Pears.

Britten and Pears met in Britain in 1937, but the relationship between them only gradually develops into a deeply loving, sexual relationship when they are traveling in 1939 in Grand Rapids, Michigan, which is marked in their correspondence as the sexual culmination and expression of their love (their marriage, as it were),[12] which was to last until Britten's death in 1976. Britten and Pears, in contrast to Isherwood and Auden, return to Britain during World War II. In 1942, while traveling in California, they read an article by E. M. Forster, analyzing a poem by the Suffolk poet George Crabbe on Peter Grimes, a Suffolk fisherman who killed an apprentice.[13] The article inspires them both, and Pears begins sketching a libretto. Britten's first operatic masterpiece, *Peter Grimes*, would premiere in London in 1945, with Pears singing the leading role.

Although these four artists shared so much in the 1930s, their later artistic development diverges: Isherwood in California converts to Vedanta Hinduism, and writes screenplays and a series of novels dealing with increasingly explicit homosexual themes, and, under the influence of his lover Don Bachardy, would end his life with an explicit defense of gay rights, *Christopher and His Kind*.[14] Auden in New York City converts to a liberal but still homophobic version of Anglican Christianity, which, as we shall see, importantly rationalizes the misery of his enduring love for Chester Kallman, and collaborates with Kallman in writing opera librettos, at least one of which – for Stravinsky's *The Rake's Progress* – is a masterpiece. And Britten, upon his return to Britain with Peter Pears, emerges as Britain's most important opera composer since Henry Purcell and creates, with Pears as his muse and indeed his musical voice, a number of works, including operas, that explore the intrapsychic ravages of British patriarchal homophobia during a period when homosexuality remained criminal in Great Britain. What Britten and Pears do is, remarkably, to give powerful ethically resisting voice through music to what Britain's political and legal culture had long regarded, and continued to regard, as the unspeakable.[15]

In the 1930s, however, what these artists shared was a common perspective on and critical exploration of the cultural ideals and educational system that had sustained British imperial manhood, and in particular its conception of the war hero. All four young men, like others of their generation, had come to doubt the conception of imperial manhood that had led Britons enthusiastically to embrace fighting in

[11] See *id.*, which includes both settings.
[12] See Neil Powell, *Benjamin Britten: A Life for Music* (New York: Henry Holt and Company, 2013), at p. 169.
[13] See Paul Kildea, *Benjamin Britten*, p. 184.
[14] See Christopher Isherwood, *Christopher and His Kind* (Minneapolis: University of Minnesota Press, 2001) (first published, 1976).
[15] See, for an excellent discussion along these lines, Paul Kildea, *Benjamin Britten*.

World War I, a war many found unjust both in its ends and means, and which in turn, through the unjust and humiliating terms of the Treaty of Versailles, set the stage for the emergence of the violently patriarchal, antidemocratic politics of fascism in Italy and later Germany and finally Spain and Japan.[16] Isherwood's father had been killed in World War I and had been memorialized by his wife and Isherwood's mother as a war hero in a way that Isherwood came to see as empty, false to his own memories of his gentle and liberal father, and tragically complacent about the links between patriarchal manhood and violence.[17] Isherwood's resistance to his mother's image of his father was lifelong and, as we shall see, one of the sources of his remarkable creative voice as an artist. Auden's poem, *The Orators*, published in 1932, challenged the polemical conceptions of heroic manhood that he believed disastrously pervaded British social and political life, including education.[18] Britten was shocked by the use of corporal punishment in the education of young British boys,[19] and while at Gresham's (attended earlier by Auden), he refused to participate in the officer training corps[20] and so objected to the bullying of boys by other boys that he thought of organizing among the boys "an effort against bullying."[21] What was the educational and family structure to which all these artists came to take such exception?

Kwasi Kwarteng, in his book *The Ghosts of Empire*,[22] shows us the remarkably similar education of the small elite who administered the British Empire: as young boys; destined to serve the Empire at home and abroad, they were separated from their parents at young ages, entering into the rigors of highly hierarchical public school education in which flogging and sexual abuse were rampant.[23] The trauma of such separations led to identification with the patriarchal definition of manhood imposed by such schools, including the hierarchical authority that older boys visited, sometimes sadistically, on younger boys. Athletic teamwork was much emphasized, preparing the small elite of British rulers for the kinds of collaborative work at home and abroad that imperial service would call for. University education at Oxford and Cambridge centered on classical languages, namely Greek and Latin, idealizing

---

[16] See, two illuminating studies, Paul Fussell, *The Great War and Modern Memory* (New York: Oxford University Press, 2013) (first published, 1975); Peter Parker, *The Old Lie: The Great War and the Public School Ethos* (London: Humbledon Continuum, 2007) (first published, 1987).

[17] See, on all these points, Peter Parker, *Isherwood*, pp. 32–41.

[18] See W. H. Auden, *The Orators: An English Study* (London: Faber and Faber, 1966) (first published, 1932, revised edition, 1934). For illuminating discussion of this and others works by Auden and Isherwood during the 1930s, see Samuel Hynes, *The Auden Generation: Literature and Politics in England in the 1930's* (New York: The Viking Press, 1976).

[19] See, on this point, Humphrey Carpenter, *Benjamin Britten: A Biography* (New York: Charles Scribner's Sons, 1992), pp. 10–11, 12–13.

[20] See *id.*, p. 27.

[21] *Id.*, p. 30.

[22] Kwasi Kwarteng, *Ghosts of Empire: Britain's Legacies in the Modern World* (New York: Public Affairs, 2011).

[23] *Id.*, pp. 237–39.

ancient patriarchal manhood as a model for life today.[24] Athletics remained important, as did social life generally: many did not complete university education.[25]
Homosexuality, under such a rigid system of gender hierarchy and segregation, was
common. However, having sex with another man was primarily a physical act, not
an enduring emotional and sexual relationship, sometimes lifelong, between two
adult men as equals. Rather, what predominated was a highly patriarchal vision of
homosexuality, just as in the ancient Greek and Roman worlds: defined by its
sexist contempt for the passive role in gay sex, and associated, as in Rome, with
slave boys and, in Greece, with boys and often slaves.[26] Homosexuality was also
condemned as unspeakable by the Augustinian sexual morality that was enforced
at large. Such patriarchally enforced silencing about the facts of human sexuality
in all its variants locked both men and women into a rigidly defined patriarchal
understanding of permissible sexuality immune from reasonable argument and
experience.

As under Roman patriarchy, relationships between spouses and between parents and their children were often quite shallow. Robert Graves observes how, at
his public school, a boy showed no grief at the death of his father (whom he hadn't
seen for two years), commenting that such a boy "lives in a world completely
dissociated from home life" with "a different moral system, even different voices,"
the consequence of parents who "lose all intimate touch with their children."[27]
Such training prepared men and women, as in Rome, for the long absences of
husbands from wives, and of parents from children that imperial service abroad
required. Indeed, as in the Roman armies, marriage in the British military was
discouraged, and "married men were not selected for the SPS [civil service]."[28]
George Orwell, who would serve in the British imperial police force in Burma for
five years, wrote late in his life *Such, Such Were the Joys*, a nightmarish account of
the preparatory school experience that had prepared him for his imperial role.[29]
Orwell's remarkable defense of liberal voice in his novels and essays arose,
I believe, from questioning both his school experience and the imperial service
to which it led on the basis of a value he increasingly placed on a network of
personal relationships among the lower classes in Britain and elsewhere and on

---

[24] See, for an illuminating recent treatment, Simon Goldhill, *Victorian Culture and Classical Antiquity: Art, Opera, Fiction, and the Proclamation of Modernity* (Princeton, NJ: Princeton University Press, 2011).

[25] See, in general, David Gilmour, *The Ruling Caste: Imperial Lives in the Victorian Raj* (New York: Farrar, Straus & Giroux, 2005). See also Michael Rosenthal, *The Character Factory: Baden-Powell's Boy Scouts and the Imperatives of Empire* (New York: Pantheon, 1986).

[26] See Kenneth J. Dover, *Greek Homosexuality* (London: Duckworth, 1978); Craig A. Williams, *Roman Homosexuality*, 2nd ed. (New York: Oxford University Press, 2010).

[27] Robert Graves, *Good-Bye to All That* (New York: Anchor, 1998) (first published, 1929), p. 20.

[28] Kwarteng, *Ghosts of Empire*, p. 242.

[29] See George Orwell, *Such, Such Were the Joys*, in George Orwell, *Essays* (New York: Everyman's Library, 1969), pp. 1291–332.

his two marriages and adopted child.[30] In contrast, several of the leading imperialists –
Lord Herbert Kitchener in the military[31] and Cecil Rhodes in South Africa[32] – clearly
flourished outside marriage and better met the demands of British imperialism
because they preferred men to women in hierarchical relationships more consistent
with the extraordinary demands they imposed on themselves as agents of British
imperialism. The resulting emotional vacuum at the heart of personal life fueled a
psychology of male honor embedded with surprising levels of aggressive violence, as
in Kitchener and Rhodes, in response to any challenge to the patriarchal demands
made by British imperialism.[33]

What Isherwood, Auden, Britten, and Pears broadly shared and was the basis for
their sometimes collaborative friendships in the 1930s was an acute sensitivity to the
roots of the problem in British family and educational life. There was, in particular,
the hierarchical bullying of British public school experience, which they had known
at first hand, including its secretive, hierarchical, and exploitative homosexual
culture, including the sexual abuse of boys by boys and sometimes by teachers.[34] It
is, I believe, no accident that these sensitive and intelligent artists had sex with but
rarely found reciprocal love with men who shared their background of hierarchical,
exploitative same-sex experience. Isherwood would find love only with German
working-class boys and later with an American, Don Bachardy; Auden would fall
passionately in love with a New York Jew, Chester Kallman. Only Benjamin
Britten falls in love with a fellow Briton, Peter Pears, but Pears, who came from a
family of military officers, had revolted against his background and had become a
singer and a pacifist, highly critical of the imperial traditions of his own family. He
was willing and able to join Britten in their remarkable musical art voicing ethical
resistance to British imperial patriarchy and its patriarchal homophobia.[35] Between
them, there was a sense of equal, complementary authority in working together,[36] as
well as of free and honest voice and criticism, not always welcomed by the sensitive
Britten.[37] It was much the most free and equal sexual relationship of any of the

---

[30] For an important biography of Orwell's development, see Bernard Crick, *George Orwell: A Life*
(London: Penguin 1992). For a recent power defense of Orwell against his critics, but criticizing his
homophobia, see Christopher Hitchens, *Why Orwell Matters* (New York: Basic Books, 2002);
for criticism of his homophobia, and comments on its possible sources, see *id.*, pp. 19–20, 80, 99,
101, 145–46, 164.

[31] See, on this point, Philip Magnus, *Kitchener: Portrait of an Imperialist* (New York: E.P. Dutton, 1968),
pp. 10, 127, 152, 235, 238, 245.

[32] See, on this point, Robert I. Rotberg, *The Founder: Cecil Rhodes and the Pursuit of Power* (New York:
Oxford University Press, 1988), at pp. 92, 403–4, 404–8, 680.

[33] On Kitchener's growing taste for violence, see Magnus, *Kitchener*, p. 227; and, on Rhodes's lack of guilt
and shame, see Rotberg, *The Founder*, p. 685.

[34] See, for an illuminating study, Peter Parker, *The Old Lie*.

[35] See, on these points, Christopher Headington, *Peter Pears: A Biography* (London: Faber and Faber,
1992), especially, pp. 6–13.

[36] See, on this point, Paul Kildea, *Benjamin Britten*, p. 238, 299.

[37] See *id.*, p. 324.

Britons here studied, and perhaps for this reason the most creative for both of them over their lifetimes together.

It is difficult today to understand the pacifism that was embraced by Britten and Pears and by Isherwood as well that which persisted during and after World War II (Auden was sympathetic, but ultimately came to accept a Christian just war theory that condemned most wars, but certainly not World War II). However, their pacifism was so linked to their resisting voices as gay men and their love stories that it must be taken seriously. At bottom, their pacifism arose, like that of many others at this time, from the political experience of World War I and later, before the world had absorbed the moral atrocities of the Holocaust and Stalinist and Maoist totalitarianism, which were almost unimaginable during the 1930s and were difficult for many to face honestly even when they knew these atrocities had occurred (consider contemporary forms of Holocaust denial). The British Empire remained intact although many in Britain had come to see it as not in Britain's interests and rooted in a racism that was as problematic as the monstrous anti-Semitism of Hitler's imperialistic fascism.

No one had more profoundly explored these issues than Virginia Woolf, whose work, connecting fascism to injustices in both public and private life, clarifies how Britons like Britten and Isherwood thought in the 1930s. Virginia Woolf's *Mrs. Dalloway*[38] and *To the Lighthouse*[39] are among the most astonishing and revelatory artistic explorations of the power of patriarchy in the lives of women and men. Like *A Farewell to Arms* and *Lady Chatterley's Lover*,[40] they explicitly evoke the violence and trauma of World War I. Woolf's great plea for resistance to patriarchal violence, *Three Guineas*, written in the 1930s, directly explores what her novels exposed: the patriarchal roots of the fascist violence that would shortly erupt in the cataclysm of World War II. In this work, artistic resistance becomes political resistance.

What Woolf shows us so astutely in *Mrs. Dalloway* is the trauma of patriarchy, the losses inflicted on women and men. The novel pivots around a woman and a man who never meet – Mrs. Dalloway and Septimus Warren Smith – yet whose lives have been truncated by the patriarchal roles they have played. Mrs. Dalloway, the name capturing her evisceration as patriarchal wife and mother, has in effect lost her voice and her self. It is only in the very last word of the novel that we hear her own name, as she finally appears as herself: "There she was: Clarissa." By this point, she has learned of the suicide of Septimus, the World War I soldier traumatized by the loss of Evans, the comrade he loved.

The loss of love, or rather the relinquishment of love, has similarly traumatized Clarissa. As a young woman, she had been in love with her friend Sally Seton and also with Peter Walsh, a lively threesome joined in resistance to convention.

[38] Virginia Woolf, *Mrs. Dalloway* (San Diego, CA: Harvest, 1997) (first published, 1925).

[39] Virginia Woolf, *To the Lighthouse* (San Diego, CA: A Harvest Book, 1981) (first published, 1927).

[40] See, for discussion of these novels, Gilligan and Richards, *The Deepening Darkness*, pp. 201–3, 217–24.

In choosing to forgo these loves to marry the emotionally constricted "Dalloway" (as Sally insists on calling him), she opts to play her required role as the wife of a successful politician, spending her day preparing to give the dinner party that ends the novel. But Mrs. Dalloway is no Leopold Bloom. She is deeply lonely and unhappy, cut off emotionally from her daughter as well as from her husband and from herself. Woolf shows us the underlying psychology of loss that had turned the vibrant Clarissa into Mrs. Dalloway. Both Peter and Sally show up at the party, but in their own ways they too have succumbed. There is seemingly no way of avoiding the power of patriarchy. But Woolf also alludes to the loss of a story about love that had shown a way out.

In the middle of the day that ends with Septimus's suicide and Clarissa's recognition of her own despair, Woolf suddenly introduces an Apuleian reference. Crossing a busy street in London, Peter Walsh and also Septimus and his wife, Rezia, hear an old woman singing in a public garden, "the voice of no age or sex, the voice of an ancient spring spouting from the earth ... singing of love – love which has lasted a million years ... love which prevails and millions of years ago, her lover" (p. 47). The reference suggests the old woman in Apuleius's *Metamorphoses* who tells the despairing Charite the story of Cupid and Psyche. However, although the subject – love – is unmistakable, the story itself has become incomprehensible, the path of resistance reduced to fragmented syllables.[41]

Long before Judith Herman and other students of trauma had seen the analogies and drawn the connections between the lives of shell-shocked soldiers and women in abusive relationships,[42] Woolf forged the link in *Mrs. Dalloway*. When the news of Septimus's suicide slices into Mrs. Dalloway's party, she feels for the first time the depth and force of her own despair. She thinks of committing suicide herself, but in the end she resists, emerging finally from the shell of her marriage to appear, at least to herself, as Clarissa. In showing us the different but analogous role that traumatic loss plays in the psychology of the women and men who take up their patriarchal destiny as wives and soldiers, Woolf also hints at the different capacities of men and women to resist and survive such trauma.

To the Lighthouse, Woolf's most autobiographical novel, portrays the patriarchal marriage of her remarkable parents, but also, in the character of Lily Briscoe, the role of the artist as resistor – the one who paints the portrait. At the center of Woolf's canvas we see Mrs. Ramsey, a woman so completely identified with her patriarchal role that she too has no name of her own, so selfless that she has no self, yet so compulsive in her enactment of the patriarchal narrative that "she was driven on, too quickly she knew, almost as if it were an escape for her too, to say that people must

---

[41] See, on the Cupid and Psyche story in Apuleius, Carol Gilligan, *The Birth of Pleasure: A New Map of Love* (New York: Vintage, 2003).

[42] See Judith Herman, *Trauma and Recovery* (New York: Basic Books, 1997).

marry; people must have children" (p. 60). The portrait of Mr. Ramsey, off to one side, shows a man physically present but emotionally distracted in the midst of a family life centered on facilitating and supporting his compulsive work on his encyclopedia:

> It was a splendid mind. For if thought is like the keyboard of a piano, divided into so many notes, or like the alphabet is ranged in twenty-six letters all in order, then his splendid mind had no sort of difficulty in running over those letters one by one, firmly and accurately, until it had reached, say, the letter Q. He reached Q. Very few people in the whole of England ever reach Q. (p. 33)

Yet Mr. Ramsey is obsessed with getting to the letter R. The patriarchal burdens weighing on him are such that despite his accomplishment, he is left with a gnawing sense that "he had not done the thing he might have done" (p. 45).

If *Mrs. Dalloway* reveals the shattering effects of trauma on the psyches of women and men under patriarchy, *To the Lighthouse* captures its blighting effects on creativity (Mr. Ramsey). Patriarchal violence, the implicit subject of both novels, moves to center stage in Woolf's late essay, *Three Guineas*. Her beloved nephew, Julian Bell, had been killed in the Spanish Civil War in 1937, the year Neville Chamberlain became prime minister of Great Britain. What Woolf came to see, in the rise of an aggressively violent fascism in Spain, Germany, and Italy – a fascism that had killed her nephew – was something Winston Churchill had also seen, leading him to call for resistance before it was too late: namely, that the aggressive violence of fascism was rooted in humiliated manhood.[43] Woolf brilliantly carries Churchill's insight one step analytically further to expose the patriarchal roots of fascist violence and to explore the possibilities for resistance on the part of the daughters of educated men.

What makes the analysis of *Three Guineas* so astonishing is not only Woolf's pathbreaking analysis of the patriarchal origins of fascist violence, but also her larger call for a resistance in which women join with men, as she had been joined by Lytton Strachey and her husband, Leonard Woolf.[44] At issue, she argued, was what Josephine Butler called "the great principles of Justice and Equality and Liberty." Addressing men, Woolf comments:

> The words are the same as yours; the claim is the same as yours. The daughters of educated men who were called, to their resentment, "feminists" were in fact the advance guard of your own movement. They were fighting the same enemy that you are fighting and for the same reason. They were fighting the tyranny of the patriarchal state as you are fighting the tyranny of the Fascist state. (p. 121)

---

[43] See, on this point, David A. J. Richards, *Disarming Manhood*, pp. 198–218.

[44] Woolf's description of the great procession of patriarchal men in British culture certainly echoes Strachey's critique of "eminent Victorians." See, Virginia Woolf, *Three Guineas*, Jane Marcus edition (Orlando, FL: A Harvest Book, 2006) (first published, 1938), pp. 18–39.

The same moral and political values justify resistance to both patriarchy and fascism: namely, the values of democracy, "the democratic ideals of equal opportunity for all" (p. 119). Woolf clearly sees in the antidemocratic injustice and violence of what we have called moral slavery, the common patriarchal roots of anti-Semitism, racism, and sexism.[45]

Woolf frames her argument, however, by focusing on "the daughters of educated men" (p. 16), whom she sees as having an independence men do not have, caught up as they are in the great patriarchal processions of British professional and public life.[46] This independence reflects the four teachers of women who have historically resisted the patriarchal demands imposed on them: poverty, chastity, derision, and freedom from unreal loyalties. Women's resistance to patriarchy has, Woolf suggests, certain advantages in part because the disadvantages heaped on their resistance – their four teachers – render them more impervious to its seductions and threats. Even the injustice done to women in the area of sexuality ("how great a part chastity, bodily chastity, has played in the unpaid education of our sex") can be reinterpreted to the advantage of women's resistance: "It should not be difficult to transmute the old ideal of bodily chastity into the new ideal of mental chastity – to hold that if it was wrong to sell the body for money it is much more wrong to sell the mind for money, since the mind, people say, is nobler than the body" (p. 99). For this reason, she calls upon women to pledge "not to commit adultery of the brain because it is much more serious than the other" (p. 112).

Woolf anchors her call for women's resistance in a recognition of difference: It is because women are "[d]ifferent ... as facts have proved, both in sex and in education," that "our help can come, if help we can, to protect liberty, to prevent war" (p. 123). Their distinctive strengths can flourish as grounds for resistance, if the women who gain access to education and the professions form an "Outsiders' Society," finding their own voices as moral agents and speaking in a different voice, a voice nourished by their own "unpaid-for education" – the relational experience and emotional intelligence that would lead women to question and to resist patriarchal demands on men as well as on themselves:

> The Society of Outsiders has the same ends as your society – freedom, equality, peace, but it seeks to achieve them by the means that a different sex, a different tradition, a different education, and the different values which result from those differences have placed within our reach. (p. 134)

Woolf thus concludes by suggesting that women can best help men prevent war "not by repeating your words and following your methods but by finding new words and creating new methods" (p. 159). In doing so, women will refuse the function Woolf had earlier observed them playing in patriarchy, a function to which men had become addicted:

---

[45] See, on this point, Woolf, *Three Guineas*, p. 122.
[46] See *ibid.*, pp. 23–28.

Women have served all these centuries as looking-glasses possessing the magic and delicious power of reflecting the figure of men at twice its natural size. Without that power probably the earth would still be swamp and jungle. The glories of all our wars would be unknown.[47]

In *Three Guineas*, Woolf seeks to break the hypnotic spell of a patriarchally rooted male narcissism – the wounded honor or shame that fueled the mass appeal of Hitler and Mussolini.[48] What makes her argument pathbreaking is the way she connects the forms of public and private violence she had examined so sensitively in *Mrs. Dalloway* and *To the Lighthouse* to the aggressive fascism Britain faced in the 1930s, and the importance she accords to this linking of private worlds and public tyrannies. To examine these connections critically, she urges that "it is time for us to raise the veil of St. Paul and to attempt, face to face, a rough and clumsy analysis" of how the Christian tradition has treated women.[49] Finally, in recognizing how far women have come in resistance to patriarchy, she observes how aggressive the response has been to such resistance.

Many of my central points in this book were first stated or at least suggested by Woolf. Once again, we are aware how deeply artists, like Hawthorne and Woolf, can see into the problems of patriarchy, even when the religion, politics, and psychology around them are in thrall to its conceptions and institutions. In Woolf's terms, women are, or can be, "a Society of Outsiders," with perhaps unique insights (like Hester Prynne) as to how to stand at once within and apart. The four gay artists – Britten, Pears, Isherwood, and Auden – are, I believe, in an analogous position, a Society of Outsiders, sharing her sense of the difficulties of love, whether straight or gay, under British patriarchy, and concerned as well with the violence of patriarchal manhood that supported the injustice of the British Empire as well as the injustice of Hitler's aggressive imperialism. Of the four teachers that had for Woolf placed women in a position to resist patriarchy (poverty, bodily chastity, derision, freedom from unreal loyalties), the four gay artists clearly experienced derision and freedom from unreal loyalties (the basis of much of their art). The sexual lives certainly did not rest on chastity, but Woolf herself regarded the role of chastity in women's lives as, to say the least, damaging to creativity, and had called for economic freedom and privacy for women.[50] What, for Woolf, taught women how and why to resist patriarchy applied clearly to these four gay men and artists. What joined them to Woolf was their sense that the repressive violence of patriarchy extended to both private and public life, in particular, to the repressive violence of homophobia against gay voice (unspeakability) and, as Britten, Pears, and Isherwood came to see, gay love. Love for these men – breaking the Love Laws – required resistance.

---

[47] Virginia Woolf, *A Room of One's Own* (San Diego, CA: A Harvest Book, 1981) (first published, 1929), p. 35.
[48] See, on this point, Woolf, *Three Guineas*, pp. 132, 135.
[49] *Ibid.*, p. 153.
[50] See Virginia Woolf, *A Room of One's Own* (San Diego, CA: A Harvest Book, 1981) (first published, 1929).

It is this perception that enables us to understand the attractions of pacifism for Britten, Pears, and Isherwood. If the propensities for unjust violence of patriarchal manhood had led Britain and Germany and others into the injustice of World War I largely over competing imperialisms, the same violence now threatened to lead to an even more catastrophic conflict. I should make clear that I do not agree with their pacifist views; in my judgment, George Orwell in his two great essays of 1940 and 1941, *My Country Right or Left*[51] and *The Lion and the Unicorn: Socialism and the English Genius*,[52] makes a compelling case for why Britain must be defended against the fascist onslaught and what it was in British culture, including its liberalism, that must be defended. Pacifism was, for Orwell, a deplorable political and ethical position, wholly failing to take seriously liberalism and the threat of fascism to its values and institutions.[53] However, before the aggressive violence of Hitler's fascism, including its genocidal racism, became apparent, pacifism may have seemed a more reasonable position than it does today. Both Richard Gregg's *The Power of Non-Violence*[54] and Aldous Huxley's *Ends and Means*[55] pointed in the 1930s to the effectiveness of Gandhi's use of nonviolence in both South Africa and India, and Huxley appealed to the history of warfare (for example, the Napoleonic wars) to show that such violence invariably had led to more injustice (for example, post-Napoleonic hostility of many European powers to liberal democracy, although Napoleon's rule and imperialism were neither liberal nor democratic, whatever his meritocratic policies and his lip service to the ideals of the French Revolution).

The attraction of pacifism for Isherwood and Britten was not only based on the reasonable arguments of Gregg and Huxley, but on something very alive in their experience as gay men coming to love other men; Orwell was at least onto something when he linked their pacifism to their homosexuality, the "pansy-left,"[56] putting the point, I fear, homophobically (many gay men were not pacifists, including Auden and Forster, and some straight men were pacifists, like Huxley). What Britten and Isherwood saw in their own experience was that patriarchy warred on loving relationships between equals in general (as Virginia Woolf saw), and, because of the patriarchal Love Laws, on loving gay relationships in particular. It was a theme Isherwood and Britten recognized in the works and words of E. M. Forster, a member of the Bloomsbury Group both men knew and admired. No one was more peculiarly local and British than Forster, and yet – in the midst of the rise of fascism and its aggressively violent challenge to British values – Forster articulated a

[51] See George Orwell, *Essays* (New York: Everyman's Library, 2002) (first published, 1961), pp. 281–90.

[52] See *id.*, pp. 291–348.

[53] See, on this point, George Orwell, *Essays*, pp. 326–27, 343, 398–99, 389–90.

[54] See Richard B. Gregg, *The Power of Non-Violence* (Ahmedabad, India: Navajivan Publishing House, 1938).

[55] See Aldous Huxley, *Ends and Means: An Inquiry into the Nature of Ideals* (New Brunswick, NJ: Transaction, 2012) (first published, 1937).

[56] See George Orwell, *Essays* (New York: Everyman's Library, 1978), p. 397.

universalistic liberalism centered on friendship and love: "I hate the idea of causes, and if I had to choose between betraying my country and betraying my friend, I hope I should have the guts to betray my country."[57] Forster defends democracy because of the value it places on liberty in general and on free speech in particular. However, he points, citing Shelley, to the deeper values of "Democracy, 'even Love, the Beloved Republic, which feeds upon Freedom and lives.'"[58] Forster wrote these words long before gay rights had become a live issue in British politics, which would, in time, protect gay love as a human right. For this reason, he resists the association of Democracy in the Britain of his time with "the Beloved Republic." In his greatest novels, Forster had written both of how deep relational love was in our natures and yet how difficult it was under patriarchy to take it seriously:

> It did not seem so difficult. She need trouble him with no gift of her own. She would only point out that salvation that was latent in his own soul, and in the soul of every man. Only connect! That was the whole of her sermon. Only connect the prose and the passion, and both will be exalted, and human love will be seen at its height. Life in fragments no longer. Only connect, and the beast and the monk, robbed of the isolation that is life to either, will die.[59]

But, in light of what has happened since Forster wrote, we may see Forster's liberalism as expressing his own resisting voice according gay love the dignity it had achieved for him in living his own life and the gay relationships he chose. Isherwood and Britten resonated to Forster's views because they spoke intimately to their own struggles for loving gay relationships, "the Beloved Republic."

Neither Forster nor Virginia Woolf defended pacifism, and both, unlike Britten, Pears, Isherwood, and Auden, remained in Britain as war approached (a threat so apparently credible that it informed Virginia Woolf's suicide). However, Forster's and Woolf's views on how patriarchy wars on love illuminates how Isherwood and Britten came to such a position, associating, as they did, gay love with pacifism.[60] We know that Isherwood was drawn to coming to Los Angeles and to pacifism through his friendship with Huxley and Gerald Heard, both of whom moved to California in 1939 in part because of Heard's fears about the oncoming cataclysm from a German invasion.[61] Heard, a gay man, was now celibate,[62] but Huxley, a straight man, certainly was not.

---

[57] E. M. Forster, *Two Cheers for Democracy* (New York: A Harvest Book, 1938), at p. 68.

[58] E. M. Forster, *Two Cheers for Democracy*, at p. 69.

[59] E. M. Forster, *Howards End* (New York: Vintage International Edition, 1989), at p. 195.

[60] On the contemporary difficulties in understanding Britten's pacifism, see Adam Roberts, "No jingo! Benjamin Britten and Pacifism," *Times Literary Supplement*, November 22, 2013, no. 5773, at pp. 13–15.

[61] See, on this point, Sybille Bedford, *Aldous Huxley: A Biography* (Chicago: Ivan R. Dee, 1974), pp. 327, 339.

[62] Gerald Heard, a learned polymath who spoke frequently on the BBC on science and religion, had been the gay lover of Christopher Wood, the charming heir to a grocery fortune, and they came together to Los Angeles. Heard embraced celibacy in 1935, but continued to live with Wood. See Alison Falby, *Between the Pigeonholes: Gerald Heard 1889–1971* (Angerton Gardens: Cambridge Scholars Publishing, 2008), at pp. 12–14, 84, 103, 108–9, 112.

Huxley deals suggestively with the personal motives that brought sensitive artists, like Isherwood and Britten, to pacifism, which at least clarifies the psychology that led them to pacifism. In Huxley's novel, *Eyeless in Gaza*,[63] the central figure, Anthony Beavis, is converted to pacifism not through reflections on its consequences, but through remorse about how he had come to betray a male friend by sleeping with the woman the friend loved, leading to the friend's suicide. Huxley had been a close friend of the novelist D. H. Lawrence,[64] one of whose most profound and revelatory points about how industrial modernity had crippled our capacity for love was to argue that the problem was not just seen in the difficulties of men loving women, but in men loving men, whether the men were straight or gay.[65]

Huxley investigates this difficulty in *Eyeless in Gaza*: what he shows us in the development of Anthony Beavis is precisely what Virginia Woolf shows us in *Mrs. Dalloway*, how patriarchy destroys the capacity for love in both women and men, only here focused on a man as psychologically crippled as Mrs. Dalloway and Septimus. Huxley exposes how this happens, a narrative of traumatic breaks in relationship, identification with patriarchal stereotypes of manhood, and a propensity to violence against other men when such manhood is challenged. Beavis, a tender and loving boy, had, through the traumatic loss of his mother and his public school and later education, become a patriarchal man, sexually active with women but incapable of love, and manipulatively shamed and prodded by one of his female lovers to betray a childhood friend who had fallen deeply in love with a woman, a betrayal that leads to the friend's suicide. The portrait of Beavis is very like the unloving coldness of Gerald in Lawrence's *Women in Love*, only Beavis does not end in suicide in the frozen wastes of the Swiss mountains (an image of Gerald's heartlessness), but turns remorsefully from the violence and lovelessness of patriarchal manhood to a manhood that can love other men, a humane pacifism, which Huxley bases on "[l]ove, compassion and understanding or intelligence," "the primary virtues" of ethics.[66] Love for men as well as for women is here psychologically linked to a humane ethics that refuses complicity with what is believed to be unjust patriarchal violence, interpreted by Huxley as requiring pacifism.

Analogously, when Isherwood later explained his pacifism, he did not appeal to the Vedanta Hinduism he learned from Huxley and Heard, but to his loving relationship with a German youth who had been conscripted into and fought in Hitler's armies, even though he had no sympathy with fascism.[67] Staying in

---

[63] Aldous Huxley, *Eyeless in Gaza* (New York: Harper Perennial, 1995) (first published, 1936).

[64] See Sybille Bedford, *Aldous Huxley*, at pp. 178–79, 191–92, 223–28.

[65] The issue is at the heart of the relationship between Birkin and Gerald in Lawrence's *Women in Love*. See D. H. Lawrence, *Women in Love* (London: Vintage, 2008) (first published, 1921), pp. 27–28, 195, 200, 269, 347–48, 358, 434, 471, 474–75.

[66] Aldous Huxley, *Ends and Means*, at p. 348.

[67] See Christopher Isherwood, *Christopher and His Kind* (Minneapolis: University of Minnesota Press, 2001) (first published, 1976), pp. 334–37.

relationship to an enemy that one loved or had loved explained, for Isherwood, his pacifism, and the moral heart of Britten's powerful *War Requiem*, as we shall see, is the common calamity of a British and German soldier killed in World War II, which expresses the same view.

Britten's consistent pacifism throughout his life has another psychological basis in his early experience, which contrasts to that of both Isherwood and Auden, who, more conventionally, were sent away from home to public schools and either Cambridge (Isherwood) or Oxford (Auden). Britten had also been sent to public school, but resisted its bullying, and stayed in much closer relationship to his parents, in particular, his mother, who took a nurturing interest in developing his obvious musical abilities (Britten starts composing at an early age), including study in London with Frank Bridge, an important British composer of the period and also a pacifist.[68] No one has explored more sensitively such mother–infant relationships than the British pediatrician and psychoanalyst, D. W. Winnicott, who traces creativity to the imaginative play of mothers and infants in and about transitional objects, which bridge the gap between the infant's subjective experience of the mother and a more objective work of common play.[69] Britten's mother was musical and sang, and her son experienced in this relationship the play of music as a transitional object he shared with her and would eventually share with Peter Pears and the wider world. However, the close and continuing relationship to his supportive and nurturing mother may also explain why, strikingly, he objects early on to both British corporal punishment and bullying. As I earlier observed, on the basis of Judy Chu's study of little boys and Niobe Way's study of adolescent boys, boys are often required to identify with the codes and scripts of masculinity. This forces rather traumatic separations from their mothers and from aspects of themselves coded "feminine"; they cannot be like her or close to her and live as a real boy or a real man.[70] Nonetheless, boys' desire for relationships with other boys persists into adolescence, although often covered and even denied; and, under the impact of homophobia, such relationships are often broken. Britten's continuing relationship to his parents and their support for his artistic interests suggest a rather unusual psychological development for a boy of his period, one less burdened by the effects of traumatic separation than other British boys (including both Isherwood and Auden) and thus less burdened by patriarchal gender stereotypes and the hierarchies they enforce. Because he stayed in real relationship to his mother, Britten did not experience the world through the prism of identification with patriarchal gender stereotypes, and thus had still intact the psychological strength to resist, as he did, the violence (including bullying) that enforced such stereotypes. It is also likely that, because gender stereotypes had less of a hold on him, he may not have been less

[68] See Humphrey Carpenter, *Benjamin Britten*, p. 14.

[69] See D. W. Winnicott, *Playing and Reality* (London and New York: Routledge, 1971)–(first published, 1971), pp. 1–34.

[70] I am indebted to this way of putting this point from comments by Carol Gilligan.

subject to the idealization and denigration of his mother and women and men generally, an idealization and denigration that can make later real, honest personal relationships so fraught and difficult, whatever one's sexual orientation.[71] Although Britten later in his life admitted that he was sexually abused by one of his teachers, and acknowledged his father's sexual interest in boys, those challenges were not compounded by the usual enforced aggression and separation of British boys.[72] What this unusual development suggests is something Britten acknowledged to friends, his sense of retaining the sensitivity and vulnerabilities and openness of a boy, on which he drew as the basis for his art throughout his life. In explaining why he wrote so well for boys' voices, he stated: "It's because I'm still thirteen."[73] This may explain Britten's rather high-strung sensitivities in his adult life, sometimes abruptly ending friendships with collaborators, and the fact that his lifelong loving relationship with Peter Pears should, like Britten's mother, have elicited an enduring trust throughout their relationship of remarkable mutual understanding and caring support, finding and giving expression to their creative ethical voices as artists and resisting gay men. Friends who knew both Britten's mother and Pears were struck by the similarities in their singing voices.[74] What their relationship shows is how ethically and personally liberating breaking the Love Laws is when in service of a relationship between men that resists the gender binary and hierarchy that locks men into a patriarchal understanding of what a man must and can be, as if men are not human, not sharing in the full range of human sensibilities and experiences including the need for intimate relationships with both men and women based on free and equal voice. Britten, who first experienced this complexity in his real relationship to his mother, experienced it as well in his relationship to men. Gay love, for this reason, came easier to him than it did for Isherwood and Auden.

The most telling example of Britten's breaking of relationship with a friend and collaborator is his break with Wystan Auden, which reveals as much about Auden as it does about Britten and their very different gay love stories. As we have seen, Auden and Britten had been close friends and collaborators, including, when they were both in New York, collaboration on their American opera, *Paul Bunyan*. Auden had produced a problematic libretto for a form, opera, of which he then knew little and about a country he and Britten knew even less; it is a flawed work, and was badly received by American critics, who "resented what they considered a patronizing lecture, an imperial report card."[75] "For Britten, the production of *Paul Bunyan* and

[71] See, on this point, Jacqueline Rose, "Mothers," *London Review of Books*, 36, no. 12 (June 19, 2014), pp. 17–22; D. W. Winnicott, "Hate in the Countertransference," in D. W. Winnicott, *Through Paediatrics to Psycho-Analysis: Collected Papers* (New York and London: Brunner-Routledge, 1992), at pp. 194–203.

[72] See, on these points, Humphrey Carpenter, *Benjamin Britten*, pp. 19–25.

[73] John Bridcut, *Britten's Children*, p. 8.

[74] See *id.*, p. 11.

[75] Paul Kildea, *Benjamin Britten*, at p. 179.

his departure from Middagh Street [in Brooklyn, where Pears and Britten had lived with Auden and other artists[76]] signaled the beginning of a gradual estrangement from Auden in both life and work."[77] Auden thought of himself as very well informed about psychoanalysis and human psychology generally, but Isherwood's portrait of Auden, his close friend, as Hugh Weston, in his autobiographical *Lions and Shadows* bespeaks not Auden's deep or sensitive study of psychology, but "his magpie brain … a hoard of curious and suggestive phrases from Jung, Rivers, Kretscher and Freud."[78] Auden's close friend, Stephen Spender, trenchantly observed that Auden's exaggerated "self-awareness and self-confidence" and claims to know others rested on willfulness and insensitivity, and yet

> we are intimidated by our awareness of his perception and therefore he does not know us as we are among other people, or alone. Auden, despite his perceptiveness, lacked something in human relationships. He forced issues too much, made everyone too conscious of himself and therefore was in the position of an observer who is a disturbing force in the behavior he observes. Sometimes he gave the impression of playing an intellectual game with himself and with others, and this meant that in the long run he was rather isolated.[79]

When a sexually inexperienced and rather shy gay man, Britten had valued Auden's brilliance and bravado, and had been drawn to and learned from him. However, he was now passionately in love with Peter Pears and Pears with him, while Auden had fallen in love disastrously with Chester Kallman (more on this later). "Auden was neither an equable companion, nor a sympathetic, imaginative, soothing lover. His admiration of others was often possessive. … He misjudged people's reactions to his advice,"[80] including letters to one friend, Harold Norse, which had a "shattering effect" on Norse, who "later described Auden as 'a dogmatic tyrant' who was 'rude and unfair.'"[81]

In early 1942, when Britten and Pears were about to leave the United States to return to Britain and Britten wrote Auden about their imminent departure, Auden responded with a long letter that began with an expression of affection and sense of loss, "I need scarcely say, my dear, how much I shall miss you and Peter, or how much I love you both," but then turned into the kind of insensitive, hurtful advice Auden had given to others as well. Writing of "the dangers that beset you [Britten] as a man and artist," he explained that all great art required

---

[76] See, on Middagh Street, Sherill Tippins, *February House* (Boston: Mariner, 2005).

[77] Neil Powell, *Benjamin Britten: A Life for Music* (New York: Henry Holt and Company, 2013), p. 193.

[78] Christopher Isherwood, *Lions and Shadows* (London: Vintage Books, 2013) (first published, 1938), p. 143.

[79] Stephen Spender, *World Within World* (New York: The Modern Library, 2001) (first published, 1951), at p. 60.

[80] Richard Davenport-Hines, *Auden* (New York: Pantheon, 1995), at p. 208.

[81] *Id.*

a perfect balance between Order and Chaos, Bohemianism and Bourgeois Convention. Bohemian chaos alone ends in a mad jumble of beautiful scraps. Every artist except the supreme masters has a bias one way or the other.... Technical skill always comes from the bourgeois side of one's nature.[82]

Britten's bent was to Bourgeois Conventions:

> Your attraction to thin-as-board juveniles, i.e., to the sexless and innocent, is a symptom of this. And I am certain, too that it is your denial and evasion of the demands of disorder that is responsible for your attacks of ill-health, i.e. sickness is your substitute for the Bohemian. Whenever you go you are and probably always will be surrounded by people who adore you, nurse you, and praise everything you do, e.g. Elizabeth, Peter (Please show this to P to whom all this is addressed). Up to a certain point this is fine for you, but beware. You see, Benjy, dear, you are always tempted to make things too easy for yourself in this way, i.e. to build yourself a warm nest of love (of course, when you get it, you find it a little stifling) by playing the lovable talented boy.[83]

Carpenter, one of Britten's biographers, observes that the gay composer Michael Tippett wondered whether these observations were motivated by jealousy of the Britten–Pears relationship, as Auden by this time had been sexually abandoned by his own lover.[84] Auden continues:

> If you are really to develop to your full stature, you will have, I think, to suffer, and make others suffer, in ways that are totally strange to you at present, and against every conscious value that you have, i.e. you will have to be able to say what you never yet have had the right to say – God, I'm a shit ...
>   All my love to you both, and God bless you,
>   Wystan[85]

Britten evidently objected, in a lost letter, to the way Auden characterized his relationship to Pears. Auden, in turn, replied:

> Dearest Ben,
>   Of course, I don't mean to suggest that your relationship with Peter was on the school boy level. Its danger is quite the reverse, of you both letting the marriage be too caring. (The escape for the paederast is that a marriage is impossible.) You understand each other so well, that you will always be both tempted to identify yourselves with each other.[86]

Britten was evidently most deeply mortified by the arrogant terms in which Auden questioned his relationship to Pears, and was later exasperated by the long, unwieldy

---

[82] Humphrey Carpenter, *Benjamin Britten: A Biography* (New York: Charles Scribner's Sons, 1992), cited at p. 163.

[83] *Id.*, at p. 164

[84] See *id.*

[85] Cited at *id.*

[86] Cited at *id.*, pp. 164–65.

libretto of Auden's poem "For the Time Being" (which he hoped Britten would set to music) sent by Auden to Britten after his return to Britain with Pears. After 1947, the estrangement of Britten from Auden was irreparable, which Britten refused to revive.[87] In contrast, although Auden and Isherwood would live on opposite coasts of the United States, their friendship continued. Auden's attempts to revive the friendship with Britten were rebuffed, and he acknowledged their estrangement as "a constant grief to me."[88] When Britten, himself then quite ill, heard of Auden's death in 1973, Donald Mitchell, who was with Britten when he heard the news, "says it is the only time he ever saw the composer cry."[89]

There are many remarkable, revelatory features in Auden's 1942 letters to Britten. Britten's return to Britain as well as the remarkable acceptance he and his work were eventually to receive there certainly confirm the perceptiveness of Auden's description of his friend's bent to Bourgeois Conventions: Britten and Pears would become pillars of the British establishment, including founding the Aldeburgh Music Festival as a British rival to Bayreuth ("Bayreuth without the poison," as the conductor Simon Rattle put it[90]), in a way Auden and Isherwood do not. What Auden, however, quite misses is the courage of the return to Britain in 1942 of two committed pacifists (they would both be exempted in virtue of their services to art as performers during the war[91]) and the courage with which two gay men, clearly and conspicuously lovers, would in homophobic Britain of the war years and long thereafter publicly perform, often together, works dealing with gay love, sometimes quite explicitly. Anyone, like myself, who attended one of these performances (Britten at the piano, Pears singing) in Boston, where I was then a student at Harvard in the mid-1960s, was struck by their wild joy and pleasure in performing together, an image of playful pleasure in relationship, a memory that is still alive in my mind after some fifty years: how, I then wondered as a young gay man yet distant from any experience of either sex or love, dare they show such pleasure in gay love – in public, and in Boston of all places? I was awed. These performances – read by many in the way I read them – were themselves public acts of resistance for both them and others, and remained a prominent feature of their lives together, from the very beginning. For gay men and lovers who came through love to resist and challenge the patriarchal norms that had held gay men for generations in a supine and shrunken private world, going public in this way marks the links between their love and their resistance in both their private and their public lives. The public/private division – so axiomatic for earlier generations of gay men – made as little sense to them as it did for feminists like

---

[87] See, on these points, Richard Davenport-Hines, *Auden*, pp. 219–20.

[88] Humphrey Carpenter, *W.H. Auden: A Biography* (Boston: Houghton Mifflin Company, 1981), p. 375.

[89] Neil Powell, *Benjamin Britten: A Life in Music*, p. 448.

[90] Quoted at Neil Powell, *Benjamin Britten: A Life in Music*, p. 411.

[91] See, on this point, Humphrey Carpenter, *Benjamin Britten*, at pp. 174, 176–77. The pacifist gay composer, Michael Tippett, was not exempted and went to jail. See *id.*, pp. 194–95.

Woolf, for whom the distinction masked the profound and linked injustices to women in both public and private life. Shortly after their return to Britain, Britten and Pears thus publicly performed at London's Wigmore Hall, in September 1942, Britten at the piano, Pears singing, a work explicitly about gay love and thus about their love, namely, Britten's "Seven Sonnets of Michelangelo,"

> written [by Michelangelo] for the handsome young Italian Tommaso dei Cavalieri, Ganymede to Michelangelo's Zeus. "My will is in your will alone, my thoughts are born in your heart, my words are on your breath. Alone, I am like the moon in the sky which our eyes cannot see save that part which the sun illumines." That was their relationship, Pears later said.[92]

Britten's bel canto setting of the Michelangelo poems, the first in the style of Puccini, beautifully displayed Pears's voice, and the connection, explicit in the poem just cited, "my thoughts are born in your heart, my words are on your breath" acknowledges how Britten and Pears, inspired by their relationship, had found a voice to give public expression of their love in ways that Auden could not even imagine and indeed misunderstands, distorts, and falsifies. Auden, rigidly locked (as we shall later see) into a homophobic understanding of gay love, including his own, can make no sense, indeed willfully distorts, a gay relationship, like that of Britten and Pears, that self-consciously forges an ethically resisting voice to patriarchy in general and patriarchal homophobia in particular. Indeed, as I shall now try to show, it is the subject matter of their art in a way Auden's certainly was not and Isherwood's would become only after much struggle to speak and write in a voice honest to his gay experience and loving relationships.

I shall later investigate what it says about Auden that he should insist in his 1942 letter to Britten on his need, as an artist and man, "to suffer, and make others suffer." However, it is astonishing that Auden, a sensitive artist and putative friend to and collaborator with Britten, should not have seen what Leonard Bernstein saw in Britten's music, commenting after his death, "When you hear Britten's music, if you really hear it, not just listen to it superficially you become aware of something very dark. There are gears that are grinding and not quite meshing, and they make a great pain."[93] In 1942, Auden would not have heard *Peter Grimes*, which Bernstein later conducted at Tanglewood,[94] but Britten had already composed *Sinfonia da Requiem*, a Mahlerian, deeply moving exploration of Britten's terrors and grief and rage at the death of his parents, ending with a redemptive march of hope into the future. What Auden failed to appreciate was the extent to which the musical exploration of suffering, often the unjust suffering of gay men, would be the subject matter of Britten's art, exposing a suffering Auden always stoically covered, to a grievous cost in his personal happiness.

---

[92] Paul Kildea, *Benjamin Britten*, p. 174.
[93] *Id.*, p. 14.
[94] See Humphrey Carpenter, *Benjamin Britten*, p. 240.

There is now substantial, sophisticated musicological literature on this point, most notably, the works of Philip Brett,[95] which persuasively show how much the patriarchal silencing of voice, including gay voice, is what Britten's art, in particular, the operas, is about. My own analysis that follows draws upon this literature. What is, I believe, at the heart of the matter is the wedding of Britten's remarkable experience and sensibility, holding onto his relationship to his mother's voice, to the sensibility and voice of Peter Pears (similar in quality to his mother's voice). This loving relationship opened their hearts and minds to a voice that resisted the homophobia that has traditionally silenced their loving voice, as unspeakable. When Britten first met Pears, long before they became a couple, Britten with friends heard Pears sing his own setting of Auden's "On This Island," and expressed qualified enthusiasm, writing in his diary: "to hear Peter sing my new songs & are considerably pleased – as I admit I am. Peter sings them well – if he studies he will be a very good singer. He's certainly one of the nicest people I know, but frightfully reticent."[96] Pears's biographer explains that "his reticence and even occasional shyness must also have had something to do with frustration over his voice,"[97] and that what inspired Pears to work harder on his voice was several recitals with Britten.[98] Pears was still largely an ensemble and choral singer, and traveled to America in 1937 to perform with the New English Singers. It was when Pears traveled with Britten to America in the Spring of 1939, still only friends, following the lead of Isherwood and Auden, that Pears came to the "possibly painful awareness that while his friend was already established in his career, he himself still had far to go."[99] It was in New York in 1940 that Pears, now Britten's lover since 1939,[100] worked closely with music teachers to improve his voice, and Britten, noting in a letter that Pears was "singing 100% better,"[101] started work on his first song cycle with Pears, *The Seven Sonnets of Michelangelo*. When Britten and Pears return to Britain, "[t]hose who had heard Pears sing before the war were amazed at the transformation."[102]

What a loving relationship between these two gay men, breaking the patriarchal Love Laws, made possible is something we saw in Chapter 1 in the relationships of Lewes and Eliot and Taylor and Mill, namely, finding through relationship an ethical voice to challenge a patriarchy that rests on the violent suppression of such voice. What shows the ethical strength of such relationships or rather, the strength

[95] See Philip Brett, *Music and Sexuality in Britten: Selected Essays*, edited by George E. Haggerty (Berkeley: University of California Press, 2003).

[96] Quoted in Christopher Headington, *Peter Pears: A Biography* (London: Faber and Faber, 1992), at p. 74.

[97] *Id.*, pp. 74–75.

[98] See *id.*, p. 75.

[99] See *id.*, p. 84.

[100] See *id.*, pp. 87–88.

[101] Cited at *id.*, p. 98.

[102] Humphrey Carpenter, *Benjamin Britten*, p. 177.

to resist that the relationship makes possible, is that these two gay men, both pacifists, would decide that returning to wartime, homophobic Britain was the place and time where they might find or forge a resonance for their resisting voices, while Isherwood and Auden remain, much more comfortably, in the United States. What motivates them is something they came to see during a stay in California, an article by E. M. Forster on Peter Grimes, a Suffolk fisherman who killed an apprentice. The Suffolk poet George Crabbe had recently published a poem on Grimes, which Forster reviewed. Britten was from and loved Suffolk and the people of Suffolk, but, as a gay man, he felt the damage and violence such communities inflict on outsiders, through both punishment and social condemnation and, intrapsychically, by shaping the psyche of the outsider, making love and relationship impossible and inflicting violence on the self. In Crabbe's poem, Grimes is a ruffian and murderer. By contrast, in their opera, Grimes is not a murderer (the deaths of apprentices are accidental), but rather an innocent man harried to death by the irrational violence of a community that suspects him of murders of which he is innocent. Britten told *Time* magazine in February 1948, just before the first New York performance of the opera, "The more vicious the society, the more vicious the individual," saying that the Grimes affair was "a struggle very close to my heart – the struggle of the individual against the masses."[103]

In an early sketch for the libretto for the opera, written when Pears and Britten were still in California, Pears touched on the issue of Grimes's repressed homosexuality:

[Peter] admits [the apprentice's] youth hurts him, his innocence galls him, his uselessness maddens him. He had no father to love him, why should he? His father only beat him, why should not he? "Prove yourself some use, not only pretty – work – not only be innocent – work do not stare; would you rather I loved you? You are sweet, young etc. – but you must love me, why do you not love me? Love me darn you."[104]

However, on the boat back to Britain, after hearing some of the score and perhaps after discussions with his partner, Pears revises the scene to emphasize Grimes's violence:

The more I hear of it, the more I feel that the queerness is unimportant & doesn't really exist in the music (or at any rate obtrude) so it mustn't do so in words. P.G. is an introspective, an artist, a neurotic, his real problem is expression, self-expression.[105]

However, the problem of expression is the problem of voice, which gave Britten and Pears a way of revealing through the powers of musical art the terrifying

[103] Cited in Philip Brett, *Music and Sexuality in Britten*, p. 38.
[104] Cited in *id.*, p. 39
[105] Cited at *id.*, p. 40.

forces – external and internal – that homophobia brings to bear, intrapsychically, on resisting voice and thus on the possibility of loving relationships. As Peter Pears observed, writing about Britten's terrifying music for the storm in an interlude in *Peter Grimes*,

> the Storm takes hold of him. Grimes is very near to Nature, with all its up and downs; and the storm belongs to him ... Pride, irritation, oversensitiveness, and of course a guilty conscience – not for anything he has *done*, but something (conforming) which he has *not* done: all these drive him to violence, the violent slap at Ellen, and the violent shaking of the boy in the Hut.[106]

In the previous chapter, I sketched a developmental psychology of boys under patriarchy, traumatic breaks in relationship that lead to identification with unjust sexist gender stereotypes, and the loss of a voice and memory that might reasonably challenge such injustice. Such a psychology shows itself in a disassociation of thought from feeling dictated by the gender binary and hierarchy that establishes patriarchy. Great artists, many of whom work through a kind of free association, sometimes – like Hawthorne or George Eliot or Virginia Woolf – break through this disassociation, and thus free in themselves a resisting voice that is otherwise buried in the psyche. I use the word "buried" precisely to make the point that the human psyche is rarely entirely colonized, as we can see in the young boys studied at different developmental stages by Judy Chu and Niobe Way, who hide, but don't lose, their desire for real relationships. What artists can do is, by breaking the patriarchal disassociation that afflicts others, give voice to resisting thoughts and feelings that sometimes deeply resonate, even during periods when patriarchy is otherwise unquestioned and unquestionable.

We have already seen in the loving relationships of Lewes and Eliot and Taylor and Mill how breaking the Love Laws may empower transformative ethically resisting voices, and we now can explore how two gay men, breaking the Love Laws precisely because as men and as free and equal persons they fall in love and, remarkably, stay in love and do so in a way that demands that they break the taboo on speakability that has afflicted homosexuals for so long. One of the features of patriarchal disassociation, as Carol Gilligan and I have shown in depth elsewhere,[107] is the darkening of our ethical intelligence, dividing us from parts of ourselves and fueling irrationalist prejudices such as anti-Semitism, racism, sexism, and homophobia. What the loving relationship of Britten and Pears shows us is how, precisely by breaking the Love Laws in the way they did, they came to experience, probably for the first time in their lives, a relationship in which they were known, understood, tenderly nurtured and supported, and in which they explored delightful erotic play by and with another person, each as the individual they were, their complementary talents harnessed to a love and vocation that deepened throughout

---

[106] Quoted in Christopher Headington, *Peter Pears*, at p. 308.
[107] See Carol Gilligan and David A. J. Richards, *The Deepening Darkness*.

their lives together. A loving relationship of this sort released both Britten and Pears from the patriarchal disassociation so common in the men, straight and gay, colonized by the ideals of British imperial manhood. Since they associated such imperial manhood with the hierarchies and exploitation of British public schools, their shared pacifism may be understood as resisting these often violently enforced hierarchies, as they moved into a new kind of free and equal loving relationship between men, and British men at that. It was as if finally, for these two men in and through their loving free and equal relationship, the light of their ethical intelligence was switched on and they came to see not only the truth and value of loving relationships of equals, but also the lies and violence that homophobia inflicted on even the thought of such relationships. Their collaborative art would expose and examine these lies and violence.

Auden and Isherwood certainly had once shared much with their younger friend, Benjamin Britten. However, Auden, as we shall see, was locked into a patriarchal masculinity that darkened both his private and public life, and Isherwood had certainly been in love, but he was puzzled by why he was yet unable to love his equals.[108] When Britten asks Isherwood to write the libretto for *Peter Grimes*, Isherwood declines, perhaps frightened by its pederastic content and not understanding, I believe, the emotional depths that the work would explore.[109] Neither Auden nor Isherwood were yet in a place to understand what Britten and Pears had discovered in and through loving relationship, and why what they discovered moved them to do something Auden and Isherwood found at that time unthinkable; namely, that it would make sense to a gay, pacifist British couple to seek and find a home for their relationship and anti-homophobic art in homophobic Britain. In contrast, both Isherwood and Auden spent much of their lives as young gay men, searching for sexual experience abroad unburdened by British homophobia, endlessly traveling both in Europe and China, and, finally, coming to rest in America where, as outsiders but respected for their achievements, they may have felt freer than American gay men of that period would and did (more on this later). Consider Oscar Wilde's exhilarating sense of freedom during his American journey.[110]

In contrast, the decision of Britten and Pears to return, as lovers and collaborators, to war-time Britain is rooted in the strength of their love for one another, as the British men they were, and perhaps as well, their love for Britain in all its complexities – its liberal democracy and its imperialism. In this, Britten and Pears, although pacifists of the sort Orwell condemned usually homophobically, apparently shared Orwell's British patriotism, which objected to its imperialism

---

[108] On this point, see Christopher Isherwood, *Christopher and His Kind* (Minneapolis: University of Minnesota Press, 1976) (first published, 1959), at pp. 3, 114–15, 122, 272.

[109] See, on this point, Peter Parker, *Isherwood*, pp. 411–12.

[110] See Roy Morris, Jr., *Declaring His Genius: Oscar Wilde in North America* (Cambridge, MA: Belknap Press of Harvard University Press, 2013).

but regarded it as a bastion of liberalism and, as Orwell argued, socialism (the war, Orwell prophetically argued, would lead to British socialism).[111] Another non-violent pacifist, Gandhi, had shown how powerfully appealing a nonviolent voice, rooted in liberal democratic values that many Britons shared, could be to the British conscience in questioning its own imperialism. Orwell both respected and criticized Gandhi,[112] and acknowledged, in a late essay, nonviolent protest had a place within a democracy like Britain that respected freedom of speech, indeed only made sense in such a democracy: "we must begin struggle against it [oppression] by non-violent means. The first step towards sanity is to break the cycle of violence."[113] Britten and Pears, who certainly admired how far so English a novelist and gay man like E. M. Forster had gone in questioning British imperialism in India, not unreasonably may have thought there might be an opening, even a resonance, for their resisting voice as well. It supports this claim that Britten and Pears saw themselves in this way, as part of an already existing tradition of gay resistance, that they would engage E. M. Forster to assist them in writing the libretto for *Billy Budd*.

There is, of course, this great difference between them and E. M. Forster: Forster never dared in his novels published before World War II to challenge British homophobia directly (his gay-themed novel, *Maurice*, is published posthumously and well after the war). Neither Britten nor Pears were, like Isherwood and Auden, writers, and it may be precisely that they were, in the case of Britten, a creative musical composer, and, in the case of Pears, a vocal performing artist, that made it possible for them collaboratively to think that they might give voice to issues that could not otherwise be discussed under British homophobia and in a way that might find resonance. Music is expressive of our emotional lives, including emotions we might otherwise find difficult to express or acknowledge. As I earlier suggested, the human psyche remains alive even under patriarchal disassociation, and music may, precisely because of its emotional appeal, find a way around and under patriarchal constraints, touching the psyche, including the silenced voices and emotions in the underworld that patriarchy cannot entirely colonize. When music takes the form of song, as it largely did in the collaborative work of Britten and Pears, it may touch and enliven a sense of broadly shared experiences, including experiences of injustice, as in the role song played in the civil rights and antiwar movements in the United States,[114] or the role rock music played in awakening the Czechoslovak resistance to communism.[115]

---

[111] See George Orwell, *The Lion and the Unicorn, op. cit.*
[112] See George Orwell, *Reflections on Gandhi*, in George Orwell, *Essays*, pp.1349–57.
[113] See George Orwell, *Essays*, p. 1013.
[114] See, for example, Ruth Feldstein, *How It Feels to Be Free: Black Women Entertainers and the Civil Rights Movement* (New York: Oxford University Press, 2014).
[115] See Tom Stoppard's play on this theme, *Rock 'n' Roll* (New York: Grove Press, 2006).

In an earlier book, *Tragic Manhood and Democracy: Verdi's Voice and the Powers of Musical Art*,[116] I show, through the close study of Giuseppe Verdi's post-Risorgimento operas, that opera in appropriate circumstances may join music and voice in ways that powerfully reveal the ravages patriarchy unjustly inflicts on the psyches of men and women, calling for resistance. Verdi's Risorgimento operas played the role they evidently did in empowering the Italian people to embrace an Italian nationalism ostensibly in the liberal spirit of Mazzini. However, nationalism can become highly patriarchal, unifying a people on unjust, racist grounds (Mussolini). All Verdi's mature post-Risorgimento operas struggle with and against his worries about patriarchy, and he develops a musical art along these lines, quite like Britten and Pears. In Verdi's case, the pivotal loving relationship was also of a composer to a singer, Giuseppina Strepponi, with whom he defiantly lived outside marriage for some time (eventually, they marry). Living in a loving sexual relationship outside marriage in this way challenged Italian patriarchy because Strepponi had conspicuously not conformed to Italian patriarchal standards of a good woman: she had worked independently as a distinguished singer of opera (including brilliantly singing in Verdi's early opera, *Nabucco*) and had had several lovers and illegitimate children. Her indefatigable work as a singer in numerous bel canto operas, earning money with which she supported her family of origin, had destroyed her voice. In light of this background, her relationship to Verdi defied Italian patriarchal social morality, which rigidly controlled women's sexuality. Giuseppina had defied such patriarchal controls, and Verdi's love for her brought on the couple the condemnation of and contempt for her of Verdi's own parents and close friends and neighbors. Deep love can upset and shift the framework of a lover's world, and even change the world, exposing injustices that call for resistance. Verdi, deeply in love with Strepponi, came to see Italian patriarchy through her eyes and experience it for the injustice it was, and was indignant, as a lover and artist, at such violence against a loving relationship of free and equal persons. Verdi came to see and resist the same patriarchal Love Laws that Britten and Pears came to see, and, like them, he joins forces with Giuseppina to wed music and voice in a new, highly original way, exposing through the voices of his often tormented heroines and heroes how patriarchy destroys and wars on love and pits men against one another, innovating what I call Verdi's voice, like that of no other composer before or since. For example, the opera, *La Traviata*, was written in close collaboration between Verdi and Strepponi. Its subject matter echoes the Verdi–Strepponi relationship: a Parisian courtesan falls deeply in love with a young man with whom she decides to spend the rest of their lives in a loving relationship, a relationship broken by the demands of her lover's patriarchal father, who had his own views about whom his children should marry. The opera gives expression to the harrowing voice of Violetta's

---

[116] See David A. J. Richards, *Tragic Manhood and Democracy: Verdi's Voice and the Powers of Musical Art* (Brighton: Sussex Academic Press, 2004).

patriarchally imposed, unjust separation from her lover culminating in her death, speaking of the unspeakable (the unjust suffering of resisting women under patriarchy) in a deeply moving, riveting, and shattering way. The unjust cruelty of patriarchy is unforgettably exposed, as we are pierced by the loving voice of its victims, women and men who aspire to freedom and equality in sexual love and are crushed under the grinding wheels of patriarchy for this reason. Music drama of this sort makes its critical points against patriarchy under the radar of patriarchy when a more explicit critique would not be tolerated. Transgressive art, precisely because it resonates in the human psyche, shows that the psyche is never wholly colonized by patriarchy, but may and can resist, preparing the way for more explicit critique.

The loving relationship of Britten and Pears was of the same kind, as they came to acknowledge in a remarkable exchange of letters near the end of Britten's life when Britten was too ill to travel and Pears was performing their last opera, *Death in Venice*, at the Metropolitan Opera in New York City. Britten writes:

> My darling heart (perhaps an unfortunate phrase – but I can't use any other),
>
> I feel I must write a squiggle which I couldn't say on the telephone without bursting into those silly tears – I do love you so terribly, & not only glorious *you*, but your singing. I've just listened to a re-broadcast of Winter Words (something like Sept. '72) and honestly you are the greatest artist that ever was – every nuance, subtle & never overdone – those great words, so sad & wise, painted for one, that heavenly sound you make, full but always coloured for words & music. What *have* I done to deserve such an artist and *man* to write for? I had to switch off before the folk songs because I couldn't [take] anything after – "how long, how long." How long? Only till Dec. 20th – I think I can *just* bear it.
>
> But, I love you,
>   I love you,
>   I love you[117]

Pears responded:

> My dearest darling,
>
> No one has ever had a lovelier letter than the one which came from you today. You say things which turn my heart over with love and pride, and I love you for every single word you write. But you know, Love is blind – and what your dear eyes do not see is that it is you who have given me everything, right from the beginning, from yourself in Grand Rapids! Through Grimes & Serenade & Michelangelo and Canticles – one thing after another – right up to this great Aschenbach. I am here as your mouthpiece and I live in your music – And I can never be thankful enough to you and to Fate for all the heavenly joy we have had together for 35 years.
>
>   My darling, I love you.
>   P.[118]

---

[117] Philip Reed and Mervyn Cooke, eds., *Letters from a Life, The Selected Letters of Benjamin Britten, Volume Six: 1966–1976* (Woodbridge, Suffolk: The Boydell Press, 2012), at p. 645.

[118] See *id.*, p. 646.

The sense in these letters is that the art of one, Britten, lived in the voice of the other, and that the voice of Pears lived in the music of Britten, or, more precisely, what the Michelangelo poem, earlier cited, expresses: "My will is in your will alone, my thoughts are born in your heart, my words are on your breath. Alone, I am like the moon in the sky which our eyes cannot see save that part which the sun illumines." It is only through the experience of their love as intimately relational – the thought of one becoming real in the voice of the other – that they can see one another. What gives such poignant sense and motivating force both to their interlinked love and their vocations is that, having seen one another as the individuals and persons they are, they forge an art that exposes the irrational forces that demand such love not be seen, let alone acknowledged.

This approach to their lives and art – rooted in a love that resisted its invisibility and denigration – helps make interpretive sense of the broad sweep of the major music dramas on which Britten and Pears worked: *Peter Grimes* (1945), *The Rape of Lucretia* (1946), *Albert Herring* (1947), *Billy Budd* (1951), *Gloriana* (1953), *The Turn of the Screw* (1954), *A Midsummer Night's Dream* (1960), *War Requiem* (1961), *Curlew River* (1964), *The Burning Fiery Furnace* (1966), *The Prodigal Son* (1968), *Owen Wingrave* (1970), and *Death in Venice* (1973).[119]

Of these works, only three of them are performed after the decriminalization of gay sex in Britain in 1967, yet the most powerful and piercing exploration of the destructive force of homophobia comes with the first of them, *Peter Grimes* (1945), in one of the most homophobic periods of modern British history (under the influence of aggressive American homophobia after World War II[120]). In their ongoing discussions of the narrative, as earlier noted, Pears says "that the queerness is unimportant," "P.G. is an introspective, an artist, a neurotic, his real problem is expression, self-expression." It is certainly understandable, in the circumstances of Britain during the war years, why Britten and Pears may have wanted not to deal in any explicit way with the issue of Grimes's possible, but repressed, homosexuality. However, the issue is suggested, as a possible unconscious motive (counterphobically turning repressed desire into violence), in the way he treats the young apprentice in the opera, who, strikingly, never speaks. The boy is certainly not treated in the way Ellen Orford, a widow and school teacher whom Grimes says he wants to marry, urges Grimes to treat him (giving the boy a day off). The boy is overworked and terrified, and there are marks on his body that suggest to Ellen he has been beaten; and Grimes is himself obsessed by work and success, and he will not marry Ellen

---

[119] See, for an illuminating study of all these works along the lines I suggest, Paul Kildea, *Benjamin Britten*. See also Philip Brett, *Music and Sexuality in Britten*; Humphrey Carpenter, *Benjamin Britten*; and Neil Powell, *Benjamin Britten*. See also Heather Wiebe, *Britten's Unquiet Pasts: Sound and Memory in Postwar Reconstruction* (Cambridge: Cambridge University Press, 2012); Mervyn Cooke, ed., *The Cambridge Companion to Benjamin Britten* (Cambridge: Cambridge University Press, 1999).

[120] See, on this point, David A. J. Richards, *The Rise of Gay Rights and the Fall of the British Empire*, pp. 140–65.

until he is successful. Finally, when Ellen challenges him, he hits her. None of this is conclusive on the issue of actual repressed homosexuality, but there is little doubt that the community's almost paranoid suspicion of Grimes and its collective violence against him reflect homophobia. Even his wife-to-be Ellen and his putative friend, Bulstrode, yield to such collective violence, acquiescing in Grimes's suicide as a punishment for something of which he is in fact innocent (the boy died accidentally). What this work reveals is the destructive power of homophobia even over good people, over putative friends and lovers, who should, of course, know better. What is, however, most musically piercing is how its violence has entered into the psyche of Grimes himself, cutting him off from the friendship and love of both women and men, making of an innocent man a scapegoat for the community's violence against a man who is seen as different in any way, alone with visions he cannot share, so, as Pears put it, "his real problem is expression, self-expression." Violence, in this case, violence against the self (suicide), replaces voice.[121]

If the underlying theme of *Peter Grimes* is to disclose and explore the repressive violence of patriarchal control on male sexual voice, their next work, *The Rape of Lucretia* (1946), discloses the same repressive violence of patriarchal control over female sexual voice. With their interest in an art that exposes the violence that enforces patriarchy, Britten and Pears here explore the founding myth of Roman patriarchy: the rape of a good Roman woman by Tarquinius, the son of the ruling tyrant, Tarquin, which leads to a suicide that shames Roman men into finally resisting the tyranny. In the opera, Lucretia is the wife of the Roman general Collatinus, and is loving and faithful, in contrast to the sexual freedoms taken by many other Roman wives at this time, including the wives of other generals, Junius and the Etruscan prince, Tarquinius. The opera begins with a competitive drinking bout between Collatinus, Junius, and Tarquinius; evidently, Junius and Tarquinius and others had tested the fidelity of their wives by returning unexpectedly to Rome from the front and finding all their wives to be sexually unfaithful with other men; only Collatinus did not go, and in fact his wife, Lucretia, had been and was faithful. Tarquinius, shamed by Lucretia's fidelity, goes to Rome to seduce her, but in fact rapes her. The rape takes place at night when Tarquinius enters her home; at first, imagining him to be Collatinus, she feels sexual desire, but then resists when she realizes who he is. Although Collatinus clearly regards her as morally innocent, as she clearly is, Lucretia is evidently so shamed by feeling any sexual desire at all that she commits suicide, and her sacrifice motivates Roman resistance to the tyranny of Tarquin and his son.

Briitten and Pears, who were pacifists, explore in this work the roots of violence under Roman imperial patriarchy, which was very much the model for British

---

[121] On the inverse relationship of violence and voice, see James Gilligan, *Violence: Reflections on a National Epidemic* (New York: Vintage Books, 1997).

imperial patriarchy, as I argue at length elsewhere.[122] Here, the music drama rivets attention not only on the predatory violence against women of a man like Tarquinius, but in the way such violence shows itself in repressive controls on women's sexuality, so that even Lucretia's quite understandable experience of sexual desire should elicit self-inflicted violence, as if women have or should have no sexual desire or voice whatsoever. It is such violence, whether imposed by others (as in Augustus's *Lex Julia*, see Chapter 1) or by the violent sacrifice of the self, that enforces the patriarchal Love Laws. What *Peter Grimes* reveals of the intrapsychic ravages patriarchy works on the psyches of men, *The Rape of Lucretia* reveals in the psyches of women. Both works end in suicide.

It is a feature of the way the gender binary and hierarchy work under patriarchy that the gender stereotypes of male and female who are repressively enforced against any reasonable voice that might challenge them takes the form of the idealization of the men and women who conform (as heroes or good women) and the denigration of those who do not (thus the unspeakability of gay sex, let alone love, and the some-times homicidal violence directed at women who pursue sex and love in violation of patriarchal controls, i.e., the Love Laws). If *Grimes* shows us both the external and internal forms of homophobic violence directed against a denigrated, supposedly deviant man, *Lucretia* shows us the idealization of a good women and the sexist violence elicited by any deviation from this ideal.

The suicide of Lucretia, idealized under Roman patriarchy as what a good Roman woman would do to preserve from any doubt the image of her purity, shows how far Britten and Pears could go in the exploration of patriarchal violence as early as 1946. Here they follow in the feminist footsteps of Virginia Woolf. Virginia Woolf, who came from a patriarchal British family,[123] wrote perceptively of its deadening intrapsychic effects on women's imagination and intelligence, imposing on "good" women a self-sacrificing and self-abnegating idea, the angel in the house, of service to the patriarchy that kills a real human voice, the basis for creativity. In "Professions of Women," Virginia Woolf, considering the psychological blocks she had encoun-tered as a creative woman, wrote of

> the Angel in the House, I will describe her as shortly as I can. She was intensely sympathetic. She was immensely charming. She was utterly unselfish. She excelled in the difficult arts of family life. She sacrificed herself daily ... in short she was so constituted that she never had a mind or a wish of her own, but preferred to sympathize always with the minds and wishes of others. Above all – I need not say it – she was pure. Her purity was supposed to be her chief beauty – her blushes, her great grace. . . . And when I came to write I encountered her with the very first words. The shadow of her wings fell on my page; I heard the rustling of her skirts in the room. Directly, that is to say, I took my pen in hand to review that novel by a famous

---

[122] See David A. J. Richards, *The Rise of Gay Rights and the Fall of the British Empire.*

[123] See, on her controlling father, Noel Annan, *Leslie Stephen: The Godless Victorian* (Chicago: University of Chicago Press, 1984).

man, she slipped behind me and whispered: "My dear, you are a young women. You are writing about a book that has been written by a man. Be sympathetic; be tender; flatter; deceive; use all the arts and wiles of our sex. Never let anybody guess that you have a mind of your own. Above all, be pure." And she made as if to guide my pen. I now record the one act for which I take some credit to myself, though the credit rightly belongs to some excellent ancestors of mine who left me a certain sum of money ... so that it was not necessary for me to depend solely on charm for my living. I turned upon her and caught her by the throat. I did my best to kill her. My excuse, if I were to be had up on a court of law, would be that I acted in self-defense. Had I not killed her she would have killed me.[124]

The self-sacrifice of Lucretia, idealized under Roman patriarchy, is a Roman version of "the Angel in the House," so anxious to preserve the image of her purity that she will kill herself. The same unjust patriarchal violence that leads to the suicide of Grimes leads as well to the suicide of Lucretia. It is her very suicide that Romans idealized as patriarchally heroic, leading to their resistance against tyranny. However, the idealization of the sexual purity of its women in this way was, in turn, to rationalize Rome's own limitless appetite for imperialistic violence, triggered by any insult, real or imagined, to Roman manhood and womanhood.

Britten and Pears begin in these operas the investigation of how patriarchy, including its ideals of manhood and womanhood, often rests on and indeed requires the violent sacrifice not only of women, but of children, a central preoccupation of Britten and Pears, connected to their experiences of British public schools. Clearly, their pacifism was in part rooted in the questions of many in Britain after World War I about how and why both the government and the people of Britain had so mind-lessly fought, at enormous loss of lives, a war unjust both in its ends and its means, including why there had been so little resistance.[125] And, many of these questions were directed at the role the British public school ethos had played in a conception of heroism in war that rested murderously on lies.[126]

Such questions are beautifully illustrated in *Regeneration*, Pat Barker's novel based on true events.[127] The novel explores the conflicted role of the distinguished anthropologist and psychiatrist, Dr. William Rivers, in treating the few war resisters there were to World War I. At Craiglockhart War Hospital, these men are seen as a medical problem. The heart of the novel is Rivers's treatment of an acclaimed World War I war hero and gay man, the poet Siegfried Sassoon, who in 1917 refused to

---

[124] Virginia Woolf, "Professions of Women," in Virginia Woolf, *Women and Writing*, edited by Michele Barrett (Orlando, FL: A Harvest Book, 1980), pp. 57–63, at p. 59.

[125] See Paul Fussell, *The Great War and Modern Memory* (Oxford: Oxford University Press, 2013) (first published, 1977).

[126] See, for a brilliant study, Peter Parker, *The Old Lie: The Great War and the Public School Ethos* (London: Hambledon Continuum, 2007) (first published, 1987).

[127] See Pat Barker, *Regeneration* (New York: Plume, 1993).

participate any longer in the war and went public with his resistance.[128] Rivers, in questioning during a church service what he has done (therapy that leads Sassoon to return to the front, a decision that troubles Rivers), looks at the representation on a church window,

> looking at Abraham and Isaac. The one on which all patriarchal societies are founded. If you, who are young and strong will obey me, who am old and weak, even to the extent of being prepared to sacrifice your life, then in the course of time you will peacefully inherit, and be able to exact the same obedience from your sons. Only we're breaking the bargain, Rivers thought. All over northern France, at this very moment, in trenches and dugouts and flooded shell-holes, the inheritors were dying, not one by one, while old men and women of all ages, gathered together and sang hymns.[129]

In thinking about his relationship as a therapist to Sassoon, Rivers reflects on his relationship to his father, a speech therapist, and how difficult it had been for his father to hear what his son said as opposed to the way he said it.[130] Had he failed Sassoon in the same way?

The issue of the patriarchal sacrifice of boys or young men is the subject of several works. In *Billy Budd* (1951), Budd is unjustly hanged, although Captain Vere could have saved him. *The Turn of the Screw* (1954) is a remarkable, poignant work with an innovating voice and music (including pentatonic scales and celesta)[131] expressing the psychic confusion, disassociation, and loss of a sense of the real and imagined of an abused boy, exacerbated by a homophobic culture that refuses to acknowledge, let alone take seriously, such abuse or how to deal with the damage it inflicts. It is a work that, unsurprisingly, Britten (preoccupied from boyhood with the patriarchal violence inflicted on boys) called "nearest to me."[132] In this work, Miles dies, torn between the imagined presence and homoerotic desire of the boy and the now-dead Peter Quint, his former tutor, who probably sexually abused the boy, and the homophobic denial of the governess. And in *Owen Wingrave* (1970), Owen, who wants to break the long-standing patriarchal family tradition of serving in the military, is opposed by his family and fiancée; the oldest male member of the family, General Sir Philip Wingrave, is played by Peter Pears (also the opera's narrator), who, in fact, had, like Owen, broken with his family tradition of imperialistic military service, but, unlike Owen, had the support of the person he loved. Owen locks himself in an allegedly haunted room where an ancestor killed a boy and, like

---

[128] For an illuminating biography of Sassoon, see Max Egremont, *Siegfried Sassoon: A Life* (New York: Farrar, Straus and Giroux, 2005).

[129] *Id.*, at p. 149.

[130] See *id.*, pp. 153–56.

[131] See, for illuminating discussion, Humphrey Carpenter, *Benjamin Britten: A Biography* (New York: Charles Scribner's Sons, 1992), pp. 337–40.

[132] Quoted in Neil Powell, *Benjamin Britten: A Life for Music* (New York: Henry Holt and Company, 2013), at p. 327.

the boy, is found dead in the morning. In each case, innocent boys or young men are destroyed by a patriarchal culture that will not see or acknowledge the culture's unjust demands on the vulnerable and the innocent.

The patriarchal sacrifice of young men is also the subject of *War Requiem* (1961), the most musically well-articulated, powerful, and ambitious expression of the pacifism of Britten and Pears. *The War Requiem* prominently uses the antiwar poetry of Wilfred Owen, who was killed fighting in World War I, and its conception called for soloists from three of the leading nations of World War II: Great Britain (Peter Pears), Germany (Dietrich Fischer-Dieskau), and the Soviet Union (Galina Vishnevskaya).[133] Fischer-Dieskau had, in fact, fought on the German side in that war. The emotional cornerstone of the work are the settings of two Owen poems, sung by the tenor, Peter Pears, and the baritone, Fischer-Dieskau. The first is the Owen poem, "The Parable of the Old Man and the Young," which the work sets in the original Owen version:

> So Abram rose, and clave the wood, and went,
> And took the fire with him, and a knife,
> And as they sojourned both of the them together,
> Isaac the first-born spake and said, My Father,
> Behold the preparations, fire and iron,
> But where the lamb for this burnt-offering? ...
> When lo! An angel called him out of heaven,
> Saying, Lay not thy hand upon the lad, ...
> But the old man would not so, but slew his son,
> And half the seed of Europe, one by one.[134]

The other is a redacted version of Owen's poem, "Strange Meeting"[135]:

> It seemed that out of battle I escaped
> Down some profound dull tunnel, ...
> Yet also there encumbered sleepers groaned,
> Too fast in thought or death to be bestirred.
> Then, as I probed them, one sprang up, and stared
> With piteous recognition in fixed eyes,
> Lifting distressful hands as if to bless ...
> "Strange friend," I said, "here is no cause to mourn.
> "None," said the other, "save the undone years,
> The hopelessness ....

[133] Because of opposition from the Soviet bureaucracy, Vishnevskaya was unable to sing at the premiere of the work at Coventry Cathedral, which had been bombed by the Germans during the war; but, the three voices for whom the work was written are heard on the recording of the *War Requiem*, Benjamin Britten conducting, on the London label, and available on CD, recorded in Kingsway Hall, London, January 1963.

[134] See Wilfred Owen, *The Collected Poems of Wilfred Owen*, edited by C. D. Lewis (New York: New Directions Book, 1963) (first published, 1920), p. 42.

[135] For Owen's full version, see *id.*, pp. 35–36.

> ... I mean the truth untold,
> The pity of war, ...
> I am the enemy you killed, my friend.
> I knew you in this dark; for so you frowned
> Yesterday through me as you jabbed and killed.
> I parried, but my hands were loath and cold.
> Let us sleep now.[136]

Britten and Pears make their artistic case for pacifism in a work of both thunderous indignation and piercing pity, which gives some sense of what lay behind their lifelong pacifism. There was the searing sense of many Britons after World War I that Britain had sacrificed young men in a war unjust in its ends and means and catastrophic in its consequences (World War II). The Owen poem about Abraham and Isaac is the vehicle to express their indignation for the same reason Pat Barker uses it to frame Rivers's remorse in *Regeneration*: Abraham's willingness to kill his own son shows the root of unjust violence in patriarchal manhood, a violence that severs intimate connections. And the musical setting of Owen's "Strange Meeting," which ends the work, embraces in an inclusive pity both the British (Pears) and the German (Fischer-Dieskau) soldiers, whom patriarchy has divided from their common plight and common humanity.

The alternatives to such patriarchal sacrifice of the young are posed by the three parables for church performance: *Curlew River* (1964), based on a Japanese Noh drama, tenderly explores the relationship between a mother and son (the boy, who is missing, has been murdered, and his mother, driven mad by his loss, is comforted when his spirit appears to her and tells her what happened); in *The Prodigal Son* (1968), a father lovingly and nonjudgmentally accepts the return of a wayward son he thought he had lost forever; and *The Burning Fiery Furnace* (1966) celebrates Jewish resistance to their unjust persecution for failure to worship Babylonian gods.

Alternatives of both resistance and unconventional love are also explored in the only two comedies of Britten and Pears, *Albert Herring* (1947) and *A Midsummer Night's Dream* (1960).

Albert Herring returns to the same kind of Suffolk community that hounded Peter Grimes to death. But here, those Puritanical community leaders are satirized. They meet to discuss candidates for the community's yearly May Queen, but when they realize there are no female candidates who meet their standards of sexual propriety, then decide to give the award to a mother-dominated good boy. Albert, however, uses the award to go on a bend (its nature is unspecified) and is missing and believed dead, leading to a quite moving musical threnody mourning him. He disappoints the mourners when he reappears and tells them he has been drunk. The shocked

---

[136] The redacted version omits some lines from the original, and adds two lines near the end. For the full redacted version, see libretto to Benjamin Britten, *War Requiem*, conducted by Benjamin Britten, London, at pp. 50 and 52.

community leaders leave, and Albert finally asserts his independence from his mother.

A *Midsummer Night's Dream*, redacted by Britten and Pears from the Shakespeare play, gives the most ravishing, musically expressive voice to Titania in her sexual affair with Bottom, transformed into a donkey. Britten and Pears make of a putatively unnatural act an ecstatic romantic love not matched by any other in the work. Their serious point, made through obscene humor, could not be more obvious: what is condemned as an unnatural act may be as deep a love as any, indeed deeper.

The problem of love under patriarchy is the subject of two operas about homosexual love, *Billy Budd* (1951) and their last work, *Death in Venice* (1973), and of one opera about heterosexual love, *Gloriana* (1953). *Gloriana*, a work commissioned for the coronation of Elizabeth II, is based on Lytton Strachey's remarkable *Elizabeth and Essex: A Tragic History*.[137] Strachey's study, much admired by Sigmund Freud, frames patriarchy as what makes Elizabeth's love for Essex disastrous and tragic for both. Because Essex is rigidly locked into a gender binary and hierarchy that disables him from seeing that Elizabeth is a much better ruler than he could ever be, he demands what Elizabeth cannot surrender, her moral sovereignty. And, Elizabeth, traumatized by her father's murder of her innocent mother, Anne Boleyn, sees in Essex a violent patriarch who would murder her, and responds, self-defensively, by killing him.[138] Strachey's narrative of how patriarchy destroys love understandably appealed to Britten and Pears as a problem they knew intimately.

Britten's interest in Herman Melville's novella, *Billy Budd*, arose from E. M. Forster's desire to collaborate with Britten on a new opera. "The men were not close, though Britten felt a sense of gratitude toward Forster for introducing him to Crabbe's poetry, repaying him by dedicating *Albert Herring* 'to E. M. Forster, in admiration'."[139] Britten was much more courageous in dealing with explicit gay themes than Forster, whose gay novel, *Maurice*, written in 1913, was published only after Forster's death. However, the men, both gay and in loving relationships (Forster with a policeman), shared a common sensibility about the value of gay love and friendship. Unsurprisingly, it was Britten who proposed *Billy Budd* to Forster.

Billy Budd appealed to Britten as a parable about how patriarchy both destroys love and legitimates imperial violence. Its hero is an honest and handsome sailor who had been impressed into the British navy at the time of the French Revolution. Budd is beloved by everyone who knows him except for John Claggart, the captain-at-arms. Claggart, a man twisted by homophobia, is sexually attracted to Budd, but

---

[137] See Lytton Strachey, *Elizabeth and Essex: A Tragic History* (San Diego, CA: A Harvest Book, 1956) (first published, 1928).

[138] See, for a fuller discussion, David A. J. Richards, *The Rise of Gay Rights and the Fall of the British Empire*, pp. 118–20.

[139] Paul Kildea, *Benjamin Britten*, p. 324.

maliciously decides to destroy him, a counterphobic response to the very idea of gay love, destroying, as homophobia requires, the thing one loves. The very idea of loving the boy leads Claggart to destroy the boy and himself. Claggart falsely accuses Budd of mutiny. Budd, who has a stammer, cannot express his indignation in words, and instinctively strikes out at Claggart, killing him. Captain Vere, the scholarly captain of the ship, understands perfectly well Claggart's malice, and "fully comprehends that Claggart's vindictive attraction to Billy is the real crime."[140] When Claggart dies, however, Vere follows his role as patriarchal captain of the military hierarchy of a ship at war, and convenes the required court to follow to the letter the Mutiny Act, which would condemn Budd to death. Budd is found guilty and hanged. Claggart is buried at sea with full military honors.

Forster began work on a libretto (Eric Crozier, who assisted, was initially skeptical: "Who had ever heard of an opera with an all-male cast?"[141]). Although he preserved much of Melville's dialogue, Forster's most important change of keeping Vere alive after the events in the novella, making of the opera a memory drama in which Vere, now an old man, reflects on his remorse that he performed the role imperial patriarchy required of him and killed a boy he, like others, loved.

The collaboration between Forster and Britten was tempestuous. Some of it was age: "Forster was seventy-one and slowing down,"[142] Britten was in his mid-thirties; Forster "could not comprehend Britten's fast pace and full diary."[143] Forster, not a musician, could not appreciate the orchestral colors of the orchestration intended for Forster's setting of Claggart's aria voicing his motives to destroy Billy (Britten played for him only the piano version). Forster, in a letter to Britten, objected:

> I want *passion* – love constricted, perverted, poisoned, but nevertheless *flowing* down its agonizing channel; a sexual discharge gone evil. Not soggy depression or growling remorse. I seemed [to be] turning from one musical discomfort to another, and was dissatisfied.[144]

Britten was deeply hurt and crippled in his work, and sought solace from Pears and others. Except for Auden, Britten had never worked with a librettist as much his artistic equal as Forster, and, as for Forster, "[n]othing in his previous friendship with Britten prepared him for the composer's single-mindedness."[145] Nonetheless, they continued to collaborate at the highest level of creative accomplishment, as composer and writer, leading to a work that "has legitimate claim to being Britten's greatest opera."[146]

---

[140] See *id.*, p. 326.
[141] *Id.*, p. 327.
[142] *Id.*, p. 343.
[143] *Id.*, p. 343.
[144] Quote at *id.*, p. 346.
[145] *Id.*, p. 146.
[146] *Id.*, p. 347.

What Britten and Forster show us in *Billy Budd*, in which Pears (a resister to his own family's military background) plays the role of Captain Vere is nothing less than the structure and psychology of patriarchy through the microcosm of an imperial ship at war with the rights of man. The authority structure of the ship is rigidly organized in terms of the gender binary and hierarchy, and this extends not only to their hierarchically ordered roles on the warship, but to the psyches of the officers and men and boys and their lack of real relationship to one another, including the counterphobic violence of both Claggart and Vere who, locked in the patriarchal commands of hierarchy, kill the boy they love. When Billy is publicly executed, after exclaiming "Starry Vere, God bless you," the music explodes, a delayed expression of the crew's inarticulate raging indignation, which is then silenced by the officers who feel their authority at threat. The opera ends with Forster's setting of Vere as an old man, realizing that he is as guilty as Claggart for endorsing the death of a boy he loved and who clearly loved him:

> I could have saved him. . . . But he has saved me, and blessed me, and the love that passeth understanding has come to me. I was lost on the infinite sea, but I've sighted a sail in the storm. . . . There's a land where she'll anchor for ever.[147]

The music swells into an anthem of a world in which loving relationships are free and equal, a world that Britten and Forster see as coming and celebrate, joined as the great artists they were, in this remarkable work that premiered in homophobic Britain in 1951, in prophetic ethical resistance to patriarchy.

Britten's last collaboration with Pears is *Death in Venice* (1973), based on Thomas Mann's novella.[148] Whereas *Billy Budd* – both the novella and opera – combine public and private worlds, Mann's *Death in Venice* is almost entirely intrapsychic, exploring the internal life of an accomplished and celebrated German novelist, Gustav von Aschenbach. He has led a highly conventional life as a husband (his wife now deceased) and father (of a daughter now married) but now, on a trip to Venice, enters into crisis as he falls in love with a young Polish boy, Tadzio. Mann sets the stage for the crisis by his opening exploration of what Aschenbach had forged in his art, namely, "the new type of hero he preferred, a type recurring in numerous incarnations in his work, that it was the concept of an intellectual and youthful masculinity that grits its teeth in proud modesty and stands by calmly while its body is pierced by swords and spears."[149] His ideal of beauty in art is thus the violent death of St. Sebastian, a sacrifice of the self, imagining "that the only kind of heroism that existed at all was the heroism of weakness," from which "derives the strength to humble an entire haughty nation at the foot of the Cross."[150] Aschenbach, "an addict of the intellect, had

---

[147] See libretto, *Billy Budd*, conducted by Benjamin Britten, London CD, at pp. 69–70.
[148] See Thomas Mann, *Death in Venice*, translated by Stanley Appelbaum (New York: Dover, 1995).
[149] See *id.*, p. 8.
[150] *Id.*, p. 8.

overexploited knowledge,"[151] suggesting "the questionable nature of art and even the role of the artist," and then, having experienced "the acrid and bitter appeal of knowledge," becomes a master of art that expresses disgust with human weakness and its "indecent psychological learnings," indeed with any human behavior that "tends in the slightest to paralyze, discourage or debase willpower, action, the emotions, and even the passions," disowning "all sympathy with the abyss."[152] It is an art that resonates with German conservative culture and values, leading the German ruler to bestow "a personal title of nobility on the author of *Frederick the Great*,"[153] a patriarchal icon of German imperialism, adored by Adolf Hitler.

What is remarkable about Mann's characterization of Aschenbach as an acclaimed German artist is that his work as an artist fits so rigidly into the same gender binary and hierarchy as an imperialist like Frederick the Great. Intellect and will mark the masculine hero – whether artist or warrior – and place him hierarchically over the disgusting man of (feminine) sympathy and feeling. However, at the same time this hero and his masculinity volunteers for violent sacrifice and abject submission "at the foot of the Cross" and to the conservative German imperial state.

Aschenbach, in other words, has devoted his rigid life and art to the Love Laws. Falling in love with Tadzio, not surprisingly, is devastating. Aschenbach never even speaks to the boy, although he follows him and his family around Venice for some time. Aschenbach's love is a fantasy, based only on the erotic appeal of the boy's body; he knows little about him, and is never in any kind of relationship with him. Indeed, he even fails to warn Tadzio and his family that the plague has come to Venice, a failure of elementary moral obligation to them, leading Aschenbach self-destructively, indeed suicidally, to risk death by staying in Venice when he knows of the danger (later he dies of the plague). This is not love as relationship, let alone ethical relationship, for Aschenbach the artist has no voice by which he might express such love to another person; indeed, as patriarchy requires, Aschenbach has no moral self. Gripped by irrational obsession, Aschenbach contemplates Plato's great dialogues on love, *Phaedrus*, and its vision of homoerotic desire that is more about an ideal than an actual person.[154] It is this Apollonian conception of homo-erotic love that Aschenbach first entertains, the one more consistent with his rational will, as the sexual component is not acknowledged. Eventually, however, Aschenbach has a dream, which Mann describes as coming from the depths far beneath Aschenbach's rational will:

[151] See *id.*, p. 9.

[152] *Id.*, p. 9.

[153] *Id.*, p. 10.

[154] On this point, see Gregory Vlastos, "The Individual as an Object of Love in Plato," in Gregory Vlastos, *Platonic Studies*, 2nd ed. (Princeton, NJ: Princeton University Press, 1981), pp. 3–42. But, see Donald Levy, "The Definition of Love In Plato's *Symposium*," in Alan Soble, *Sex, Love, and Friendship: Studies of the Society for the Philosophy of Sex and Love, 1977–1992* (Amsterdam: Rodopi, 1997), pp. 15–21.

Although it came to him when he was fast asleep in complete independence of his will and his senses were fully alert, nevertheless he did not see himself as a separate participant moving in a space external to the events, rather, their theater was his soul and they broke in from outside, violently overcoming his resistance – a profound, intellectual resistance – forced their way through, and, when they had passed, left his existence, and his lifetime's accumulation of culture, totally destroyed and annihilated.[155]

The content of the dream is Dionysian, with appetite both sexual and violent, what Aschenbach's repressed self imagines homosexual sex with Tadzio to be. It is after this dream that Aschenbach, now terminally ill, imagines that "flight and death might remove all surrounding interference by living people, and he might be left alone on this island with the beautiful boy. . . . his monstrous wish seemed like a real hope to him and morality seemed to be null and void."[156] While sitting on the beach watching Tadzio in the water, Aschenbach dies. The last, suicidal expression of how the gender binary and hierarchy has colonized Ashenbach's psyche is his dichotomous division of good and bad homoerotic love into the Apollonian and Dionysian, and, consistent with the Love Laws, moving from the one to the other requires punishment, in this case, a kind of suicide.

Britten's *Death in Venice* (1973) is his work that most frankly deals with homosexual erotic desire and, more indirectly, gay love. Gay sex had been decriminalized in Great Britain in 1967, but for reasons that had little or nothing to do with appreciating gay love as a human right (that would come much later).[157] Britten and Pears, as usual, bravely push the envelope of their resisting artistic voice by collaborating on an opera, in which Aschenbach would be sung by Pears himself, based on a novella that studies an artist who, unlike Britten and Pears, was so rigidly locked into the patriarchal gender binary that his experience of what he comes to see as not only homosexual desire, but gay love, cannot be expressed, and indeed kills him, yet another of the stories endlessly told under patriarchy of how breaking the Love Laws must result in tragedy and death.[158]

The libretto by Myfanwy Piper imaginatively frames the narrative in terms of Aschenbach and a figure of Death, suggesting the two sides of Aschenbach's psychic division, framed by the gender binary, but otherwise follows the novella closely. Piper is clearly trying to introduce some dramatic conflict into a novella that lacks it, as whatever drama there is in the work is intrapsychic. Clearly, what Britten and Pears wanted from Piper was what they got, a libretto much closer to the literary work that inspired it than any of their earlier operas, namely, not a music drama, but a musical and vocal expression of the psyche of an artist like Aschenbach who, locked

---

[155] Thomas Mann, *Death in Venice*, p. 55.
[156] *Id.*, p. 17.
[157] See, on these points, David A. J. Richards, *The Rise of Gay Rights and the Fall of the British Empire*, pp. 144–207.
[158] See, on this point, Carol Gilligan, *The Birth of Pleasure*.

in a rigidly intellectual understanding of art, has no voice to express his love (more a song cycle than an opera). Britten's setting of it, in a period when he knew he was dying, is, at its best, frankly homoerotic (the dance sequences on the beach of the boy Tadzio and his friends) and beautifully autumnal, subjects not usually linked in drama or opera. What remains memorable about the opera is its subject matter, as if the divided, self-destructive psyche of Aschenbach touched something deep in Britten and Pears, namely, what they had overcome and had to overcome to form the loving relationship that gave rise to their resisting artistic voice. Aschenbach is, for them, a cautionary warning, a memento mori, of what the stakes are of the refusal of relationship. It is because of the strength of their own loving relationship that they demand that we see the narcissistic hall of mirrors, the echo chamber, of the suppressed voice that patriarchy exacts of its victims, which is, potentially, all and every one of us. Britain may at this time have removed criminal sanctions from adult gay sexual acts, but the problem of love – for everyone, straight and gay – remains so long as patriarchy retains its hold on our psyches, as it clearly does in Aschenbach's. As the great artists they are, Britten and Pears show us how deeply patriarchy damages our capacity for love and thus for ethical relationship, and thus how far we have yet to go to grapple with such moral injury and find our way to the reparative love, which was the basis of their lives together, a love through which they found together the ethical voice to forge an art that resisted such injustice.

We should no more idealize than denigrate such a loving relationship of free and equal persons, which had all the complexity of any real relationship between persons as individuals who love and respect another, a hallmark of which is finding in one another an honest voice and resonance, a kind of moral compass. Although lovers, Britten and Pears were different people. Britten may have been more ambivalent about his sexuality than Pears,[159] or, perhaps more accurately, ambivalent about any form of sexuality not based on a loving, long-term monogamous relationship. Indeed, we have seen how Britten's relationships with boys were caring and absorbing, not sexual,[160] built on an openness to and feeling for the voices of boys, including writing for their voices, "because I'm still thirteen."[161] Britten's distaste for any loving sexual relationship that was not long-term and monogamous is shown by his disapproval of what he probably took to be the sexually promiscuous gay world, including even for the word "gay"[162] (a word originally applied to prostitutes and then transposed to homosexual[163] was not something Britten could happily embrace) and his furious rejection of his erstwhile good friend and supporter Lord

---

[159] See, for example, Humphrey Carpenter, *Benjamin Britten*, pp. 178–79.

[160] See John Bridcut, *Britten's Children* (London: Faber and Faber, 2006).

[161] *Id.*, p. 8.

[162] Paul Kildea, *Benjamin Britten*, p. 516.

[163] See, on this point, David A. J. Richards, *Women, Gays, and the Constitution: The Grounds for Feminism and Gay Rights in Culture and Law* (Chicago: University of Chicago Press, 1998), p. 295.

Harewood when Harewood committed adultery.[164] During their long life together, Britten was not sexually active outside the relationship as Pears may have been.[165] Britten, as he aged, became more absorbed in his art, more temperamentally difficult, and more in need of care than Pears was always willing to supply; in part for this reason, Pears was sometimes away pursuing his career as a performer, always missed by Britten.[166] However, the relationship, sometimes fraught, always was vital, honest, alive, responsive, caring, and collaborative, and always drew them back to one another, and remained at the center of both of their lives. Britten dies in the arms of Pears in 1976.[167] And, Britten and Pears, against all the homophobic odds, bravely gave expression in their collaborative art to a voice that, in all the works discussed here, resisted the homophobic unspeakability of gay love.

Against this background, whatever its flaws as music drama, *Death in Venice* may be their most musically profound, sensitive, and sometimes harrowing exploration of the intrapsychic dimension of how homophobia kills the voice of gay love and thus of the larger point that patriarchy in all its forms kills love in all its forms.[168] What must have made Aschenbach so poignant for Britten and Pears, I believe, is that Aschenbach is an artist with no voice to express his love even to his beloved, let alone in his art. There is, for this reason, an emptiness at the heart of this work, for Aschenbach has no self. However, the work is one of great pity and compassion for such unjust suffering. Their own lives and relationship showed there was an alternative resisting path for both gay love and art. There was no better way to make this point than for Britten and Pears, as Britten faced death in the arms of his lover, to show through their collaborative art how love made such an alternative possible and feasible not only for gay men, but for each and every one of us.

In our own era of much greater toleration and, via gay marriage, even legitimation of gay love, it is easy to lose sight of just how remarkable were the lives and art of Benjamin Britten and Peter Pears, who lived openly as a gay couple and produced two of their most remarkable works, *Peter Grimes* (1945) and *Billy Budd* (1951), during one of the most homophobic periods of modern British history. We should not make their achievement more comfortable to our sensibilities by suggesting it was easier for them than it was. If they had wanted an easier life, they would have followed the American path of Isherwood and Auden. In Britain, quite shabby expressions of homophobia afflicted them both,[169] but would have been and were

---

[164] See, on this point, Paul Kildea, *Benjamin Britten*, p. 536; Neil Powell, *Benjamin Britten*, pp. 356–57, 391–92.

[165] On how and when Pears may have contracted syphilis, which was asymptomatic and not reasonably detectable, and may have transmitted it to Britten, a fact discovered only during the operation on his heart, see Paul Kildea, *Benjamin Britten*, pp. 534–36.

[166] See, on this point, Paul Kildea, *Benjamin Britten*, pp. 459, 562.

[167] See Paul Kildea, *Benjamin Britten*, pp. 559–60.

[168] For an illuminating discussion of the work, see *id.*, pp. 522–31.

[169] See, for illuminating discussion of this point, Paul Kildea, *Benjamin Britten*, pp. 234, 338, 375–77, 380, 381, 434, 435–36.

particularly wounding to Britten's highly strung sensitivities, which may explain why he broke with so many friends. Such indignities included, in the homophobic panic after the Burgess–MacLean scandal in the early 1950s,[170] the questioning of Britten by Scotland Yard.[171] It is shocking today to realize how common such homophobia once was in Britain, darkening the intelligence of even so sophisticated operagoer and liberal stalwart like Isaiah Berlin, who objected in 1958 to Britten's appointment as music director of Covent Garden because he was a homosexual. In terms of breathtaking stupidity both about opera and about Britten, Berlin said "Not to put too fine a point upon it, opera is an art essentially heterosexual, and those who do not feel affinity with this tend to employ feeble voices, effeminate producers etc."[172] It is against this background that we should appreciate what is most remarkable about the art and life of Benjamin Britten and Peter Pears, namely, their courage. Their courage was made possible by their love, just as their love was made possible by their courage. So, in studying them as a resistance pair who both broke the Love Laws and challenged the gender binary and hierarchy, we discover what would not surprise us if we could and would free our intelligence from the distorting lens of patriarchy, namely, that courage, conventionally gendered male, and love, conventionally gendered female, do not, in fact, correspond to the terms of the gender binary and hierarchy, but work together collaboratively in the creative relationships of equals that make and keep us human.

---

[170] For a recent study on the role of British patriarchy in protecting Kim Philby, one of these spies, from accountability, see Ben Macintyre, *A Spy Among Friends: Kim Philby and the Great Betrayal* (New York: Crown Publishers, 2014).

[171] See Paul Kildea, *Benjamin Britten*, pp. 376–79.

[172] Quoted in John Banville, "Learning a Lot About Isaiah Berlin," *The New York Review of Books*, December 19, 2013, Vol. LX, no. 20, pp. 44–47, at p. 47.

3

Christopher Isherwood's Struggle for a Resistant Voice

Christopher Isherwood came from a wealthier and more privileged background than Britten and Auden, his ancestors including the judge who ordered the execution of Charles I. The great struggle of both his life and work was defined both by his homosexuality and by his deep skepticism about the ideal of the war hero that had led Britain, disastrously, into World War I. What made this struggle so personal for him was that his father, a professional officer in the military, was killed in World War I when Christopher was eleven, and then was passionately idealized by his mother and set up as a model for her two sons. But Christopher, the older son, had known his father, and thus knew a truth about the man behind his mother's myth making.

His father was not a conventional military professional. Before attending military college at Sandhurst, he had had a broad liberal arts education; "he had been to school at Cheltenham College and university at Clare College, Cambridge.... He was widely read, played the piano well, composed songs, and was keenly interested in art and architecture."[1] Even more fascinating, "Frank often played female roles in amateur theatricals, his luxuriant moustache presumably adding to the comedy of the proceedings."[2] The relationship between father and son was affectionate, and the father, in a letter to his wife from the front of World War I, expressed an interest in the liberal education of his son that would nurture his individuality:

> The whole point of sending him to school was to flatten him out, so to speak, and make him like the other boys, and when all is said and done I don't know that this is at all desirable or necessary, and I for one would much rather have him as he is.[3]

This was not, however, to be the attitude of Isherwood's mother, Kathleen, after her husband's death. Kathleen was the independent-minded child of difficult parents, and she had an interest in excursions that prefigured her son's travels, co-authoring a book, *Our Rambles in Old London*, that had been published to polite

---

[1] Peter Parker, *Isherwood*, p. 11.

[2] *Id.*, p. 12.

[3] Quoted at *id.*, p. 38.

reviews in 1895.[4] When her husband died, Kathleen was forty-seven, and "her principal identity was war widow":

> By dying in the war, Frank ... underwent an instant metamorphosis from fond parent to distant icon. Well-meaning adults began to hold him up as a hero worthy of emulation: the man whom Isherwood was able to amuse with his conjuring tricks and his jokes suddenly became a god who had to be placated by decorous behavior.[5]

Kathleen, traumatized by the death of her husband, idealized him on the patriarchal terms that Isherwood was to resist for the rest of his life.

Isherwood was at school when his father died:

> Although the bereaved were accorded respect by their fellow-pupils, teachers often berated the newly orphaned for not living up to the standards set by their hero-fathers. For boys the loss of a father was a case of "bad luck", Christopher Isherwood recalled, and the crepe-marked child would be excused the rough-and-tumble of the playground.... For teachers, however, a dead father was a useful stick with which to beat a troublesome pupil. The effect of this was often scarring. Isherwood began to reject the image of his father as a Dead Hero and with it he rejected all sense of duty this figure was supposed to instill.[6]

As Isherwood began to reject the Myth of the Dead War Hero, which British culture aggressively memorialized in the wake of World War I, his resistance would become increasingly personal, indeed intra-familial, soon resisting his mother and the demands she placed on him. His first two novels, *All the Conspirators* (1926)[7] and *The Memorial* (1932),[8] are thinly disguised explorations of his own conflict with his mother, the first about a mother's refusal to take seriously her son's artistic ambitions, the second about a son's dilemma about whether to emulate his mother's idealized portrait of his dead father or his father's roguish friend who survives the war and throws himself into gay life. Isherwood's mother wanted him to be an academic, a don, she hoped, at Cambridge or Oxford, and she refused to take seriously his artistic ambitions; Isherwood had been a good student of history, but at Cambridge he self-consciously flunked his exams so that he could not pursue the path his mother wanted for him. His intentional derailing is the proud subject of Isherwood's revelatory first autobiography, *Lions and Shadows*.[9] Resistance to his patriarchal mother was an ambition that followed him to the end of his life.[10]

---

[4] *Id.*, p. 10.

[5] *Id.*, p. 41.

[6] See Peter Parker, *The Old Lie*, pp. 259–60.

[7] Christopher Isherwood, *All the Conspirators* (New York: A New Directions Book, 1979) (first published, 1926).

[8] Christopher Isherwood, *The Memorial: Portrait of a Family* (New York: Farrar, Straus and Giroux, 2013) (first published, 1932).

[9] Christopher Isherwood, *Lions and Shadows* (London: Vintage Books, 2013) (first published, 1938).

[10] See, for fuller biographical details, Peter Parker, *Isherwood*.

In the opening passage of *Swann's Way*, Marcel Proust's narrator remembers his desperate need as a young child to be kissed by his mother before he went to bed.[11] His father, however, urged the mother not to comply so readily to her son's emotional demands, as it made him less emotionally self-sufficient, less manly. One evening, the mother refuses to kiss him, complying with her husband's expectation. The father, however, is the patriarchal authority, and thus can change the law as he wills, and he tells the mother to go kiss her son. The boy thus glimpses the structure of patriarchal authority: His mother will break her relationship as her husband demands, but lacks the freedom, which her husband the patriarch has, to make such decisions on her own. In *The Birth of Pleasure*, Carol Gilligan uses this moment to delineate the role of mothers under patriarchy:

> His mother and her mother become agents of his initiation into patriarchy. Breaking relationship at the command of the father, they encourage the boy to become like the father, withholding themselves for his own good. So that in time, he will become more sporadically in touch with people's feelings, more quixotic in relationships, able to make and to break the law, to act on his will.[12]

Isherwood came to observe in his mother what Proust, also an artist and gay man, had observed in his mother: she saw herself as executing the demands of the patriarch and altered her relationship to her son as her understanding of the patriarch required. Gilligan's phrase for this, "breaking relationship," captures the traumatic emotional weight and significance for a young child of such loss of connection, a breach of the care and trust the child had come to expect from his mother above all with sometimes enduring psychological consequences. Isherwood came to distrust his mother in the same way Proust's narrator does in *Swann's Way*. But his distrust cut more deeply into his psyche because, since he had known his father, he realized that his mother was worshiping an idealized myth of his father, the Myth of the War Hero, which did not correspond to – indeed falsified – the man he had known as an affectionate and liberal parent interested in his son's individuality. Kathleen's idealization led her to a rigid identification with what she believed to be the duties of patriarchal imperial manhood, which she assumed her son would take as his guides in life. Proust's sense of closeness to his own mother remained at the center of his creativity (*In Search of Lost Time* was first conceived as a letter to his mother).[13] However, once Isherwood came to see what Peter Parker has called "the old lie"[14] of the Myth of the War Hero, his distrust of his mother led to a resistance to her views that was to continue to the end of her life. Resistance took the form of a psychological imperative in her son that, to become the artist and man he wanted to be, he had to separate himself not only from her but from Britain itself, an

[11]   See Carol Gilligan, *The Birth of Pleasure*, pp. 81–84.
[12]   *Id.*, p. 84.
[13]   See, on this point, Carol Gilligan, *The Birth of Pleasure*, p. 81.
[14]   See Peter Parker, *The Old Lie*.

imperative that explains his successive travels through Europe and Asia and later to America. This separation remained at the center of his creative life and work, as much as Proust's closer connection to his mother remained at the core of his. At the end of his life, having achieved a kind of balance and serenity, Isherwood acknowledged as much. Perhaps through his loving relationship to Don Bachardy, he was able to write a long study of his father and mother, *Kathleen and Frank*,[15] in which he pays, finally, loving tribute to his mother's voice that had been so often in disagreement with his own, and acknowledges hers as the basis of and stimulus for his own voice, without which he would never have become the artist he became.[16] In his remarkable essay "The Capacity to Be Alone," the psychoanalyst D. W. Winnicott suggests that a secure and caring early relationship between mother and child allows the child, playing in the presence of his mother, to experience creative play when alone: It is "only when alone (that is to say, in the presence of someone) that the infant can discover his own personal life."[7] At the end of his life, Isherwood sees his creative resisting voice as arising from his mother's care in precisely this way: The angry resistance to his mother rested, he came to see, on her love, neither idealized nor denigrated, but a love with voice in real relationship to her son.

However, that understanding was many years in the making. As a young man, distrust of his mother and the absence of any real relationship to his deceased father left a vacuum, a sense of loss of reliable loving relationship. The question of his very identity or authenticity would be in doubt for much of the rest of his life. As he explained in his diary in 1938, reflecting on the choices before him,

> I once read the title of a German novel (I forget the author's name [it was Robert Musil], *Der Mann ohne Eigenshaft* [sic][usually translated *The Man Without Qualities*]. That, I've come to feel more and more, just described me ... I really don't exist ... I cannot believe in my own soul. No, I am a chemical compound, conditioned by environment and education. My "character" is simply a repertoire of acquired tricks, my conversation a repertoire of adaptations and echoes, my "feelings" are dictated by purely physical, external stimuli. And yes, of course, like everybody else, I make a certain average impression upon the outside world.
>
> What impression? Most of my friends think of me, apparently, as a diplomatist, rather amusingly sly. Wystan [Auden] finds me completely unscrupulous – capable of anything to further my own designs. There is a lot of talk about my "will". Very few people trust me, I think – and how right they are. *Der Mann ohne Eigens[c]haft* is never to be trusted.[18]

[15] Christopher Isherwood, *Kathleen and Frank* (London: Vintage Books, 2013) (first published, 1971).
[16] See *Id.*, pp. 507–9.
[17] D. W. Winnicott (1958). "The Capacity to Be Alone," *Int. J. Psycho-Anal.* 39:416–20, quoted at p. 418.
[18] Quoted in Peter Parker, *Isherwood*, p. 340.

The sense of himself as a man never to be trusted reflects his loss of trust early in his life. Without any reliable guides, and with reasons to distrust the distorting influence of patriarchal ideals, Isherwood felt himself as an outsider from the time he was a teenager. The patriarchal standards into which he was born, and which most boys of his class had no reason to question, felt more and more like a lie to him. It was this self-conscious sense of himself as an outsider, very much one of Virginia Woolf's Society of Outsiders (see Chapter 2), that was a basis for the development of the resisting voice that found expression in his artistic voice.

What made that voice so artistically creative was that, precisely because it was formed in self-conscious resistance to patriarchal lies, it was less disassociated from experience, indeed it hungered for and was open to experience (including the experience of friendship and love) as a more reliable basis for sustaining a sense of trust. Isherwood is perhaps best known for his statement, "I am a camera with its shutter open, quite passive, recording, not thinking."[19] The statement makes little sense when we consider the active critical intelligence and empathy that motivated Isherwood's best work. However, it does make sense in light of his lifelong search for a reliable basis in experience, unburdened by the imperialist patriarchal lens of his mother and British culture, and the ways that lens distorted and falsified what was before their eyes. When he marks his art as "recording, not thinking," he is distinguishing his art from that of his close friend, Wystan Auden, whose love of grand theories filled his "magpie brain,"[20] theories not based on and sometimes ignoring and even distorting experience. Isherwood's close observation of his good friend, appearing in *Lions and Shadows* as Hugh Weston, as domineering and willful, suggests in Isherwood the same resistance to patriarchal manhood that had led Britten to break with Auden (see Chapter 2). Isherwood gave voice to his resistance, however, not by breaking with Auden, as Britten felt impelled to do, but by observing and writing precisely about what such residues of patriarchy cost Auden in personal relationships, as in his poignant portrayal of Auden in his diary during their trip to China together: "Wystan in tears, telling me that no one would ever love him, that he would never have my sexual success."[21] Isherwood distrusted patriarchy and what patriarchy did to people, and all his work expresses his relationality, his love of people, shown by his close, nonjudgmental observation of people, including his friend Auden. In showing us what patriarchy had done to a friend like Auden, a sensitive and gifted artist, Isherwood resists patriarchy by showing us what it would cover, and conceal and suppress: a free voice based on experience. Isherwood's remarkable psychological intelligence, expressed throughout his art, here traces Auden's problem both in love and in his art,

---

[19] See Christopher Isherwood, *The Berlin Stories* (New York: A New Directions Book, 2008) (*Mr. Norris Changes Trains*, first published, 1936; *Goodbye to Berlin*, first published, 1939), p. 207.

[20] Christopher Isherwood, *Lions and Shadows*, p. 143.

[21] Quoted in Christopher Isherwood, *Christopher and His Kind*, p. 304.

including his later turn to a still homophobic Anglican Christianity and to his idealized mother and his failure to resist her patriarchal demands.[22]

Isherwood's growing sense of himself as an artist was closely connected psychologically to his sense of himself as a gay man, and took the form of a larger resistance to both British patriarchal manhood and its homophobia. Isherwood's education as a boy and young man, however, followed the standard of patriarchal British culture: As we've seen, not only early separation from parents, but immersion into the all-male preparatory and public schools (Isherwood's prep school was St. Edmund's, and his public school was Repton), and their inculcation into hierarchy enforced via corporal punishment, bullying of boys by boys, and sexual exploitation of boys by boys and sometimes of boys by teachers. Isherwood took to this education at Repton with enthusiasm, showing no signs of Britten's early resistance to officer training, corporal punishment, or bullying. Young Isherwood accepted them all as perquisites of young men of his class. This included at least two relationships to younger boys, who he would later refer to fondly as "My fags, Darling and Betty."[23] These relationships, in the words of his best biographer, Peter Parker, were "strictly hierarchical, that of master and servant," which included Isherwood's caning of Darling for losing a pair of football shoes.[24]

His public school education included one quite good teacher, Graham Burrell Smith, who taught his students to think critically about history,[25] and perhaps more importantly, had "a profound and even more subversive influence upon Isherwood,"[26] namely, his friendship, which was to be lifelong, with Edward Upward. Isherwood wrote of him: "Everything about him appealed to me. He was a natural anarchist, a born romantic revolutionary."[27] Isherwood had been quite conventional at St. Edmund's (where he first met Auden), but meeting Upward at Repton changed all that. It was through his relationship to Upward that he came, like Upward, to question that role of the Officers' Training Corps in his public school, which, in conformity to the mythos of the postwar years, was "still pursued with appropriately martial solemnity by the authorities."[28] As he later recalled, writing about himself in the third-person voice that would be the hallmark of some of his most important later work:

> It was easy for these impressive adults to make a suggestible little boy feel guilty. Yet he soon started to react against his guilt. Timidly and secret at first, but with passion, with a rage against The Others which possessed him to the marrow of his bones.

[22] See, on this point, James J. Berg and Chris Freeman, *Conversations with Christopher Isherwood* (Jackson: University Press of Mississippi, 2001), p. 186; Christopher Isherwood, *Christopher and His Kind*, pp. 241–42, 306.

[23] Peter Parker, *Isherwood*, p. 63.

[24] *Id.*, p 64.

[25] See *id.*, pp. 63–64.

[26] *Id.*, p. 53.

[27] Quoted at *id.*, p. 53.

[28] *Id.*, p. 55.

He rejected their Hero-Father. Such a rejection leads to a much larger one. By denying your duty toward the Hero-Father, you deny the authority of the Flag, the Old School Tie, the Union Solder, The Land That Bore You, and the God of Battles.[29]

Upward and Isherwood created between them "an entire category of people who represented 'the other side' and who earned their sneers and condemnation."[30] This sense of a shared imaginative world, which would define their resistance to the Myth of the Dead War Hero, would flower when they were both at Cambridge into the Montmere stories. They wrote collaboratively with one another for their own amusement about a village, called Montmere, in which obscene and bizarre events took place,[31] subjecting to ridicule the "antics of the Poshocracy."[32] Isherwood's sense of his vocation as an artist crystallized at the same time that he "really began to turn against his mother and everything she stood for,"[33] which led him to flunk his exams at Cambridge and free himself from his mother's ambition that he should be a don. Upward was not gay, although he was more sexually advanced than Isherwood. Isherwood had two gay sexual encounters at Cambridge, but largely channeled his sexuality "into the imaginary world he and Upward had begun to create."[34]

It was after he left Cambridge, when Isherwood was working for a gifted violinist, that Isherwood met again Wystan Auden, then an undergraduate at Oxford, whom he had known seven years previously at their prep school. Auden was now a poet, and Isherwood, two and half years older, offered criticisms of his work that Auden took seriously. There was a great deal of laughter in their relationship, and they became lovers from 1926 to 1938.[35] Isherwood published his first novel in 1926, and thus his relationship with Auden would be defined by their common sense of artistic vocation as well. During the 1930s, they would collaborate on the writing of three highly political plays that deal with the problems of both manhood and love under patriarchy (more on these plays in Chapter 4).

Isherwood was later to understate the depth of the sexual relationship:

The friendship was rooted in schoolboy memories and the mood of its sexuality as adolescent. They had been going to bed together, unromantically but with much pleasure, for the past ten years, whenever an opportunity offered itself, as it did now. They couldn't think of themselves as lovers, yet sex had given friendship an extra dimension. They were conscious of this and it embarrassed

---

[29] Quoted at *id.*, p. 55.
[30] *Id.*, p. 55.
[31] See, on this point, *id.*, pp. 79–82.
[32] *Id.*, p. 84.
[33] *Id.*, p. 84.
[34] *Id.*, p. 79.
[35] See *id.*, p. 115.

them slightly – that is to say, the sophisticated adult friends were embarrassed by the schoolboy sex partners.[36]

Isherwood admitted that he "couldn't relax sexually with a member of his own class and nation,"[37] and observed in a letter to Stephen Spender, "I can't imagine that I ever could or should be able to live intimately with an equal for long."[38] Was that the problem between him and Auden? Auden's desperate outburst to Isherwood about his lovelessness during their trip to China suggests something deeper and more poignant, namely, that Auden's greater investment in patriarchal manhood (his domineering willfulness) made it difficult to stay friends with (Britten) or to remain in loving relationship to him (Isherwood). The problem was not, as Isherwood supposed, that it was a relationship between equals, but precisely that it could not be psychologically understood or valued by them as such a relationship. Isherwood's conception of homosexual sex had been framed by the patriarchal hierarchies of the British public school, enforced by corporal punishment and bullying, and the world of exploitative sex by boys of boys and masters of boys. It is not psychologically surprising that gay men from this world, as both Isherwood and Auden were, should come to see a sexually loving relationship between "sophisticated adult friends" as undermined or "embarrassed" by the sense of themselves as still "schoolboy sex partners," the traumatized boy – without voice to resist patriarchy – still very much alive in the man he has become. Breaking the Love Laws is very different from resisting them as well. It is easy enough, since gay sex of any kind violates their broad prohibitions, to break the Love Laws. However, that does not necessarily mean that you are resisting the Love Laws, as long as patriarchy dictates the terms of the relationship. The relationship of Britten and Pears shows how much resisting the Love Laws extends beyond merely breaking them, as the love between free and equal persons joined them and released in them an astonishing creative voice that exposed the patriarchal violence that warred, both socially and intrapsychically, on such love. For them, the close marriage of their voices as composer and singer arose from their love, and their resistance, as artists, sustained and deepened their love over a shared lifetime together against the homophobic forces that ignored and denigrated the very possibility of such love.

It was Auden, who had already lived in Berlin, who suggested to Isherwood that the comparative sexual freedom of Berlin would make it a congenial place for him to explore his craving for experiences, including sexual experiences, unburdened by British homophobia. Isherwood made his first trip there in 1929, and, having received regular money allowances from a sympathetic gay uncle, went back there in 1930 and, with some interruptions, lived there until 1933. He would describe his

---

[36] Christopher Isherwood, *Christopher and His Kind*, p. 264.
[37] Quoted at Peter Parker, *Isherwood*, p. 200.
[38] Christopher Isherwood, *Christopher and His Kind*, p. 115.

first trip as "one of the most decisive events in my life."[39] Nothing defied Isherwood's mother more than looking for enlightenment in Germany, the nation that had killed her husband in World War I. However, Isherwood encountered there a public culture that not only acknowledged but scientifically studied homosexuality, something unthinkable on this scale in a homophobically repressive Britain that had become notorious for the criminal prosecution of Oscar Wilde in 1895[40] (with the notable exception, in the late nineteenth and early twentieth centuries, of the resisting life and works of Edward Carpenter, a decisive influence on E. M. Forster[41]), in the form of the Institute for Sexual Science of Dr. Magnus Hirschfeld and his longtime lover, Karl Giese. Hirschfeld's work included political activism for the repeal of Paragraph 175 that criminalized gay sex,[42] activism not to be seen in Britain until the Wolfenden Commission of 1957.[43] Isherwood also fell deeply in love for the first time in his life. The effect on his life and work was transformative.

However, first, he had to move beyond his own British inhibitions. Isherwood observed of himself, referring to himself as "Christopher":

> Christopher was suffering from an inhibition, then not unusual among upper-class homosexuals; he couldn't relax sexually with a member of his own class or nation. He needed a working-class foreigner.[44]

He was released from those inhibitions in Berlin by the availability of working-class German boys, most of them heterosexual, who were available for sex for money; Isherwood, like Auden, availed himself of such services. Breaking the Love Laws in Berlin came to mean something deeper, for Isherwood, evidently because it involved not only sex with men, but with men not of one's nationality and not of one's class.

The most important of these, for Isherwood, was his relationship with Heinz Neddermeyer, a sixteen-year-old Berliner, not conventionally attractive, but, in contrast to his smarter and more exploitative other lovers, "emotionally innocent, entirely vulnerable, and uncritical, whom he could protect and cherish as his own."[45] Heinz was probably bisexual (he later married and had a child), and the relationship may have begun as sex for money. With Heinz, however, Isherwood would form "a relationship which would be much more serious than any he had had in his life."[46] When Isherwood leaves Berlin in 1933, after Hitler takes power, he

---

[39] *Id.*, p. 3.
[40] See, on this point, David A. J. Richards, *Women, Gays, and the Constitution*, pp. 315–16.
[41] On the importance of Carpenter, among others, as an early gay activist and feminist, see David A. J. Richards, *Women, Gays, and the Constitution*, pp. 310–27. See also Sheila Rowbotham, *Edward Carpenter: A Life of Liberty and Love* (London: Verso. 2008).
[42] See Christopher Isherwood, *Christopher and His Kind*, pp. 15–19.
[43] See David A. J. Richards, *The Rise of Gay Rights and the Fall of the British Empire*, pp. 144–65.
[44] Christopher Isherwood, *Christopher and His Kind*, p. 3.
[45] Quoted in Peter Parker, *Isherwood*, p. 205.
[46] Quoted in *id.*, p. 205.

takes Heinz with him and desperately tries to preserve the relationship, first by bringing him to Britain, and then, when a bureaucrat refuses Heinz's entry, tries to secure a visa to a foreign nation (Mexico, for example) where Heinz would not be subject to German conscription, and where the two might live together. Despite Isherwood's strenuous efforts, in 1937, the plan falls through, and Heinz is arrested and compelled to serve in the German army;[47] Isherwood is bereft, writing of what Heinz had aroused in him, "That aching, melting tenderness."[48] He would not see Heinz again in Berlin until 1952, now married and the father of a son.[49] Their relationship is the main subject of *Christopher and His Kind*, probably Isherwood's most honest and personally revelatory book.

It was during and because of their loving relationship that Isherwood writes his two remarkable novels about Berlin, *Mr. Norris Changes Trains* (1935) and *Goodbye to Berlin* (1939), now available as *The Berlin Stories*.[50] Because of his background of distrust of his mother's Myth of the Dead War Hero, Isherwood lived increasingly outside British patriarchy and found his resisting voice in an art based on his search for experience that contested the idealizing and denigrating stereotypes that patriarchy enforced. Isherwood was led to Berlin, following Auden's lead, because he could explore there a sexual freedom as a gay man impossible for him in Britain and experience as well, in the life and work of the Jewish Magnus Hirschfeld, a public and politically active gay culture that challenged the homophobic unspeakability of gay sex. What this context made possible for Isherwood was falling in love with a man in a way he never had before, and a man who was both of a different and, in Britain, despised nationality and of a lower class. Breaking the Love Laws – in an enemy country, with a person of a lower class – freed in Isherwood a voice based on an experience of "That aching, melting tenderness" of a man in love with another man. The experience enabled him as an artist truthfully and humanely to enter into the world of the men and boys he came to love and to sympathetically show as well the inner world of Berlin's monsters and their victims.

The novels are, of course, autobiographical (in *Mr. Norris Changes Trains*, William Bradshaw is Isherwood; in *Goodbye to Berlin*, Isherwood writes as himself, using "I"), with a variety of characters based on real people Isherwood came to know and love in Berlin, including his lovers. Some of these real characters (notably, Gerald Hamilton, on whom Arthur Norris is based) led a long life even more disgraceful than Isherwood portrays.[51] However, he always shows them in all their attractive and repelling complexities, including Arthur Norris's vitality and cowardice, and Sally Bowles's exuberant sexual freedoms with which Isherwood, as a sexually active gay man, strongly identified. The exploration of the world of fascism's

[47] See Christopher Isherwood, *Christopher and His Kind*, pp. 159–290.
[48] Quoted in Peter Parker, *Isherwood*, p. 205.
[49] See Peter Parker, *Isherwood*, p. 535.
[50] See Christopher Isherwood, *The Berlin Stories*.
[51] See, on this point, Peter Parker, *Isherwood*, pp. 181–86.

victims is particular notable, breaking the silence of a European anti-Semitism that failed to take seriously until too late its worst monsters. Isherwood, finding his way to a resisting voice about the violence of patriarchy to its victims, insists the we see clearly, based on experience, the violence not only against gays and sexually free women, but German Jews.

The portrait of the members of a wealthy Jewish family, the Landauers, very much at threat from the growing political violence of fascist anti-Semitism, is among the most poignant in these books. Isherwood's portrait of Natalia Landauer is of a highly intelligent and responsible young woman, very much in contrast to the flamboyant and witless Sally Bowles. Her father, Herr Landauer, is the most ethically civilized and reasonable German in the book, pressing Isherwood with ethical doubts about British homophobia: "Your dramatist, Oscar Wilde ... this is another case. I put this case to you Mr. Isherwood. I would like very much to hear your opinion. Was your English Law justified in punishing Oscar Wilde, or was it not justified? Please tell me what you think?"[52] Isherwood does not respond. However, the most penetrating of these portraits is of Natalia's cousin, the probably gay business-man, Bernhard, who confesses an internalization of Prussian patriarchal discipline (in contrast to what he regards as British freedom[53]) and tries to speak intimately with Isherwood about his Jewish background and personal life, and observes Isherwood's disgust at such an attempt at intimacy: "You are a little shocked. One does not speak of such things. It disgusts your English public-school training, a little – this Jewish emotionalism."[54] Isherwood, now in love with German lower-class youths, could not find an intimate voice to speak with a gay German man much more his equal and clearly seeking such intimacy. His honesty is such that he insists we see his own emotional lapses and frailties in interpersonal relationships. And later Bernhard observes, when Isherwood questions him about German politics, that he feels quite disassociated by the events around him and was "troubled by this hallucination of the non-existence of Landauers'"[55] (imagining, prophetically, genocide). Isherwood later writes of German politics, "these people could be made to believe in anybody or anything,"[56] and observes that Nazi bullies, "looking hungrily for more German womanhood to rescue,"[57] touching on the incendiary violence patriarchy visits on breaking the Love Laws, which forbid sexual relationships between non-Jews and Jews. We later learn that Bernhard Landauer has been killed.

---

[52] See Christopher Isherwood, *The Berlin Stories*, p. 354.
[53] See *id.*, p. 363.
[54] See *id.*, p. 374.
[55] *Id.*, p. 383.
[56] *Id.*, p. 394.
[57] *Id.*, p. 394.

Isherwood had long been self-consciously at war with the constraints British imperial patriarchy placed on him as a man and as a gay man, as his two earlier novels, *All the Conspirators* (1926)[58] and *The Memorial* (1932)[59] show about personal life, and as his collaborative plays with Auden later show about public life (more on this in Chapter 4). The artistic expression of his resistance to British patriarchal manhood deepened, however, through the experiences of Berlin, including loving relationships with Germans who were Briton's enemies in both World War I and were to be their enemies in World War II. Love across the boundaries released Isherwood from the shackles British patriarchy had fixed on his imagination, and his artistic voice, freed from the idealizing and denigrating stereotypes that patriarchy enforces, recorded the complex and varied life of people in Berlin among whom Isherwood came to feel more at home than he ever did in Britain. While Isherwood liked to portray himself as a player of roles without any core of moral personality, the experience of loving relationship gave rise to a resisting ethical voice in Isherwood that he was to be the basis both for his art and life for the rest of his life, including his lifelong pacifism. It is this voice that enables him to give such a complex and loving portrait of both the unforgettable monsters and victims that he shows us nonjudgmentally in *The Berlin Stories*. What is so moving is that Isherwood himself, the narrator, has the strength in the second novel (which he writes from his experience as Isherwood himself), to expose and explore his own frailties, as in the revelatory conversation with Bernhard Landauer who comments on Isherwood's difficulties with honest emotional intimacy, the lingering residue of his British disassociation, "your English public-school training," as Bernhard perceptively puts the point. What Isherwood reveals, in both his characters and in himself, is how difficult under patriarchy is both friendship and love, and how the most honest ethical voices, the Jewish Landauers and Hirschfeld's public gay resisting voice, are the objects of murderous fascist rage (Bernhard is murdered, Hirschfeld's Institute is destroyed by Nazi mobs). What Isherwood shows us, several years before Hitler's genocidal rage was to murder 6 million innocent European Jews, is what was coming. Few artists of this period had such a truthful ethical voice both about the incubation of monsters in Germany and one more prophetic, because more based on experience, of the havoc these monsters would wreck on European and indeed world civilization.

It was during this period, when Isherwood was in Britain desperately trying to arrange visas for himself and Heinz to go to Mexico, that Isherwood was to work with the Austrian director, Berthold Viertel, in writing a script for a movie Viertel was directing in Britain.[60] Isherwood loved movies, and this was to be his first experience

[58] Christopher Isherwood, *All the Conspirators* (New York: A New Directions Book, 1979) (first published, 1926).

[59] Christopher Isherwood, *The Memorial: Portrait of a Family* (New York: Farrar, Straus and Giroux, 2013) (first published, 1932).

[60] See Peter Parker, *Isherwood*, pp. 236–37.

of creative work in making films that prefigures his later work in Hollywood as a screenwriter (the love of movies was one of the bases for the mutual attraction of Isherwood and his American life partner, Don Bachardy). Viertel was Jewish, and much concerned, during the making of the movie, about what was happening in Austria, where his wife lived. Isherwood becomes a close confidante of Viertel at this time, and their feeling for one another would be the basis of a brilliant novel Isherwood would write in America, *Prater Violet.*[61] The portrait of Viertel in the novel is as complexly alive as any of the characters in *The Berlin Stories,* and Isherwood's voice (writing as himself, Isherwood) is as honest as he comes into a loving, albeit brief friendship with this passionate and brilliantly observant Austrian director, realizing at the end that he finds in Viertel the kind of real relationship to a father he never had.[62] The relationship to Viertel leads Isherwood to raise the most basic questions: "What makes you go on living? Why don't you kill yourself? Why is all this bearable? What makes you bear it?"[63] The answer Isherwood gives is loving relationship, in this case, gay love.[64] The lover in the novel is identified as "J." At the time, Heinz was Isherwood's lover, his J.

Although Isherwood writes this book in Los Angeles after his forced separation from Heinz, it was conceived and written from the same experience of loving relationship, and further illustrates how important that relationship was to empowering Isherwood's resisting voice as an artist, as the author of *Prater Violet* clearly writes as a gay man and Viertel, albeit straight, is a kind of emotional surrogate for what Heinz had meant to Isherwood. Isherwood is feeling his way into honest loving relationships to other men, nonsexual and sexual, and through such relationships he finds a voice to speak honesty from experience about how such love for other men, of a German or Austrian or, in Viertel's case, Jewish background, frees ethical imagination from its patriarchal blinkers on the range of humane concern.

The loss of Heinz was devastating for Isherwood, and may further have inflamed his indignation at the patriarchal forces that had separated them. One of the most telling scenes in *Christopher and His Kind* targets Britain for such indignation. Isherwood, Auden with him, is at Harwich to meet Heinz's boat from Europe. Isherwood had arranged for his mother, Kathleen, to write a letter of invitation for Heinz, which would be the basis for his admission to Britain. However, the British official raises questions because Heinz's passport indicates he is a worker, and why would Mrs. Isherwood want a working-class German in her home? Heinz is not admitted, and Auden observes to Isherwood

[61] Christopher Isherwood, *Prater Violet* (Minneapolis: University of Minnesota Press, 1973) (first published, 1945).
[62] See *id.,* p. 127.
[63] See *id.,* p. 123.
[64] See *id.,* pp. 124–25.

that he, the official, is "one of us,"[65] a homosexual, who, homophobically and pursuant to the Love Laws, wars on gay love between a Briton and a German. It may seem like a small point, but for Isherwood it would have crystallized his sense of estrangement from imperial Britain and being more at home abroad where British patriarchy would not reach; Isherwood would thus later observe: "Not until after the Second War, when England had ceased to be imperial and had become a minor power with cosmopolitan population, did Christopher begin to love it, for the first time in his life. It had turned into the kind of country he had always wanted it to be."[66] The civil war in Spain, in which Britain remained neutral against fascism, deepened Isherwood's sense of estrangement, and he leaves Britain with Auden for a trip to China to report on the war there, which would lead to their book, *Journey to a War*.[67] Auden had gone to Spain during the civil war and had some sense of the carnage of war. For Isherwood, the war in China was his first such experience, and it crystallized his commitment to pacifism, and thus his disgust with the war clearly coming in Europe, a war he may have supposed to be, such as World War I, essentially a war between British and German imperialism. Auden and Isherwood decide to move to the United States in 1939. Auden settling in New York City, Isherwood in Los Angeles.

They found an apartment together in New York City, but just a month later, Auden fell in love with Chester Kallman, a Jewish Brooklyn College undergraduate. Isherwood no longer found Auden a sufficient attraction to remain in a city that he quickly came to loathe. What drew him to Los Angeles was twofold. First, there was work in the movie industry (a taste stimulated by his earlier work with Viertel in Britain); Isherwood would write a number of screenplays, for which he was well paid, although few of them were made into movies.[68] Second, a man so absorbed by friendship was drawn to Los Angeles by his two close British friends there, Aldous Huxley and Gerald Heard, who were both pacifists (see Chapter 2). Heard had come to Los Angeles from Britain with Christopher Wood, his wealthy and close friend and erstwhile lover. When they visited Isherwood and Auden in Berlin, they were lovers; Isherwood observed: "Chris Wood was about ten years younger than Gerald, handsome, shy, but friendly, rich."[69] Whereas Auden and Heard "would withdraw to Gerald's room for abstruse scientific conversation," Isherwood and Wood "quickly became intimate"[70] as friends. Heard was a scientific polymath who had been a BBC commentator on science and religion, and wrote a number of books, including one that developed a progressive understanding of gay sex as an aspect of the plasticity

---

[65] Christopher Isherwood, *Christopher and His Kind*, p. 162.

[66] Christopher Isherwood, *Christopher and His Kind*, p. 316.

[67] See W. H. Auden and Christopher Isherwood, *Journey to a War* (London: Faber and Faber, 1986) (first published, 1939).

[68] For a notable exception, see *The Loved One* (1965), screenplay by Terry Southern and Christopher Isherwood, directed by Tony Richardson, available in CD.

[69] Christopher Isherwood, *Christopher and His Kind*, p. 102.

[70] *Id.*, p. 103.

and depth of human sexuality[71] and a complex theory of the five stages of the evolution of human psychology.[72]

It was through Huxley and Heard that Isherwood was introduced in Los Angeles to Vedanta Hinduism and developed a close personal relationship to a man he came to call his guru, Swami Prabhavananda. Isherwood was not drawn to pacifism or to Vedanta by abstract theories such as those of Huxley and Heard, although he valued the scientific rationality that led Huxley and Heard to take Vedanta seriously. His pacifism, as he acknowledged, was rooted in his loving relationship to Heinz, who was now fighting on the German side in World War II, and whom Isherwood could not imagine himself killing under any circumstances.[73] His attraction to Vedanta arose from his personal relationship to the Swami, a man he came to love and admire, like Viertel, as a good and tolerant and caring father. His love for the Swami gave rise to several books that both explained their relationship and made a case for both Vedanta and pacifism.[74] When Isherwood was asked how much his defense of Vedanta reflected his own views, he denied he was "in any sense a guru," his books reflecting the views of a man he admired "put into a rather more readable language," denying they reflected "independent thinking in the sense of making something up or even thinking something out."[75]

Early on in their relationship, Isherwood raised with the Swami the question of his homosexuality and sexual relations with his current lover, Vernon, to which Isherwood tells us the Swami replied, "You must try to see him as the young Lord Krishna."[76] Peter Parker, Isherwood's best biographer, questions whether the Swami and Vedanta were in fact this tolerant, suggesting the Swami made an exception to Vedanta's sexual asceticism to secure so useful a convert.[77] Heard, who had once been the gay lover of Chris Wood, had become celibate in 1935,[78] and Huxley had come to question the morality of sexual freedom[79] and embraced, rather paradoxically, "pre-nuptial chastity and absolute monogamy,"[80] along with the equality of women. However, although Isherwood took the Swami's advice seriously and even lived in his monastery for several years,[81] there are matters on which he did not yield.

[71] See Gerald Heard, *Pain, Sex, and Time: A New Outlook on Evolution and the Future of Man* (Rhineback, NY: Monkfish Book Publishing Company, 1967) (first published, 1939), p. 41.

[72] See Gerald Heard, *The Five Ages of Man: The Psychology of Human History* (New York: The Julian Press, 1963).

[73] See, on this point, Christopher Isherwood, *Isherwood and His King*, pp. 335–36.

[74] See, for example, Christopher Isherwood, *My Guru and His Disciple* (Minneapolis: University of Minnesota Press, 2001) (first published, 1980); *Ramakrishna and His Disciples* (Hollywood, CA: The Vedanta Press, 1965); *An Approach to Vedanta* (Hollywood, CA: The Vedanta Press, 1963).

[75] James J. Berg and Chris Freeman, eds., *Conversations with Christopher Isherwood*, p. 132.

[76] Quoted in Peter Parker, *Isherwood*, p. 422.

[77] See, on this point, Peter Parker, *Isherwood*, pp. 422–23, 712–14.

[78] See Alison Falby, *Between the Pigeonholes*, p. 84.

[79] See Aldous Huxley, *Ends and Means*, pp. 316–18.

[80] Id., p. 368.

[81] See Peter Parker, *Isherwood*, pp. 440–41, 472.

For example, although the Swami discouraged him in 1944 from working on novels, Isherwood started *Prater Violet* soon thereafter.[82] And, Isherwood continued to have sexual relations with men, and indeed was attracted to the Swami's version of Vedanta because one of its central figures, Ramakrishna, may have drawn on homosexual desires he never fully understood but expressed in his sometimes gender-bending life and work.[83]

While Isherwood wrote and published one of his best novels, *Prater Violet*, after coming to America, it was a novel very much rooted in his past – in Berlin and his loving relationship to Heinz and, in Britain, his friendship with Viertel. Some of his closest friends in California, notably, Dodie Smith, were shocked when Isherwood showed them drafts of his latest novel, which was published in 1952 as *The World in the Evening*.[84] In contrast to all of Isherwood's other novels, it is not written with the authority of autobiographical voice, which suggests a lingering disassociation that his love for Heinz and Viertel had overcome when he wrote *Prater Violet*. Isherwood draws upon his experience with the Quakers he met in Pennsylvania while a conscientious objector during World War II, whose pacifism and integrity he grew to admire. Its central character, Stephen Monk, is not a novelist, but had been married to a distinguished female novelist, now dead, to whom he been unfaithful with an actress, Jane. After his wife's death he marries Jane, only to suspect her of infidelity; furious, he goes to Pennsylvania to stay with his Aunt Sarah, a Quaker. There he meets a gay male couple. Eventually, he learns that Jane was not unfaithful (the man was gay), and he returns to her. Aside from the sympathy of the relatively brief treatment of the gay couple, the novel lacks focus and point. Dodie Smith "blamed its failure on the company Isherwood kept in California. 'It is destroying his sense of values and even his taste,' she complained. 'He needs the company of his peers – as almost every writer does. I believe America has almost ruined his talent.'"[85] It is quite an indictment of the price Isherwood, the artist, paid for settling in America in general and Los Angeles in particular. The problem, however, may not have been what Dodie Smith thought it was, as Isherwood certainly had "the company of his peers" in California (Huxley, Heard, Wood), and, at a distance in New York, Auden, and many others in Britain and elsewhere. The Swami, who never understood Isherwood's artistic voice or sympathized with his sex life, may have been a problematic influence, but the key may have been a sex life in California that continued to break the Love Laws, but lacked the emotional depth that had nurtured the resisting voice of his best work. Some evidence for this is the

---

[82] See Peter Parker, *Isherwood*, pp. 455–56.

[83] See, for argument along these lines, Jeffrey J. Kripal, *Kali's Child: The Mystical and the Erotic in the Life and Teachings of Ramakrishna* (Chicago: University of Chicago Press, 1995). For Isherwood's own study of Ramakrishna, see Christopher Isherwood, *Ramakrishna and His Disciples*.

[84] Christopher Isherwood, *The World in the Evening* (Minneapolis: University of Minnesota Press, 1980) (first published, 1952).

[85] Peter Parker, *Isherwood*, p. 544.

quality of his artistic work after he met and fell in love with his lifelong partner, Don Bachardy.

In 1953, Isherwood meets Don Bachardy, who is eighteen although he looks younger; Isherwood is forty-eight. They would shortly move in together, and would live together as a couple for the next thirty-two years, until Isherwood's death in 1985. Bachardy looked so young that even Isherwood's closest friend, Evelyn Hooker, was shocked. Hooker had produced one of the first and pathbreaking empirical studies of how little gay men differed from other men (challenging then dominant views, based on biased samples of prisoners and neurotics, that all gay men were sick and worse);[86] at the time Isherwood began his affair with Bachardy, he was living in a house on her property, Hooker asked the couple to vacate the house on her property where they were staying; the relationship looked too scandalously pederastic even for the tolerant Hooker and her academic husband.[87] Bachardy, then going to UCLA, had a brother who was mentally disturbed, and he was impressed by Isherwood's understanding and loving support (Isherwood had a younger brother who was also quite troubled). Over the years of their relationship, Isherwood nurtured and encouraged Bachardy's artistic interests. Parker perceptively observes:

> Past experience had shown Isherwood the consequences of having a partner with no proper occupation, and whenever Bachardy felt insecure about his talent and his vocation or felt that his longed-for career was never going to materialize, Isherwood was there to encourage him. There was always the risk, as Isherwood well knew, that once he was independent of Isherwood, Bachardy might develop a taste for freedom, but it was a risk Isherwood knew he had to make.[88]

The risk was increased when Isherwood helped Bachardy secure a place at the Slade School of Fine Arts in London, "where generations of leading British painters had trained."[89] Bachardy would be in London for six months. Isherwood visited him there, and Bachardy was now an accomplished portraitist and was to have a distinguished artistic career, making prized portraits of many of Isherwood's friends as well as of Isherwood himself. There was to be a show in London of his work, and Isherwood "was aware that in some ways Bachardy was keen for him to return to America. 'It's the old story,' Isherwood noted, 'he can't have any friends of his own as long as I'm around, because, even if he finds them, they take more interest in me as soon as we meet.'"[90] It was an often fraught relationship, and both men had affairs with other men. In a joint interview of Isherwood and Bachardy about this aspect of their relationship, Bachardy observed to Isherwood: "You didn't encourage me to see people on the side, but you behaved fairly well about it. But if he thought there was

[86] See *id.*, p. 513.
[87] *Id.*, pp. 541–42.
[88] Peter Parker, *Isherwood*, p. 601.
[89] *Id.*, p. 601.
[90] *Id.*, p. 609.

any danger of my getting involved with anybody, he made it clear that he didn't like the idea, which is really what I wanted. It was a way of testing love."[91] For both men, the relationship remained the central one in their lives, and Isherwood's concern for Bachardy's own development, independence, and voice as an artist made it a much more equal loving relationship certainly than Heinz had been, and one in which both men had a voice. It would have been unthinkable for Heinz to have read Isherwood's works in draft, let alone give valued critical comments on them, as Bachardy did. Isherwood and Bachardy also shared a common passion for movies, and they collaborated on the writing of the screenplay for the movie, *Frankenstein*, and collaborated as well on a stage version of *Down by the River* that was staged unsuccessfully in New York City.[92] Isherwood's collaborative work with Bachardy was never at the level of that of Britten and Pears, who were, after all, much closer in age and sensibility, more happily monogamous, and whose complementary gifts (composer and singer) enriched the art and life of both of them. However, even such a very different relationship (Isherwood and Bachardy) strikingly led not only to support of one another as artists, but to collaborative work together. Reflecting on his life with Bachardy, Isherwood struck a rather different note on love than the extraordinary love letters of Britten and Pears (see Chapter 2): "With love there *ought* to be a need to worry, every moment. Love isn't an insurance policy. Love is tension. What I value in a relationship is constant tension, in the sense of never being under the illusion that one understands the other person. . . . He's eternally unpredictable – and so you are to him, if he loves you. And that's the tension. That's what you hope will never end."[93]

Isherwood was to publish three novels during his relationship to Bachardy. *Down There on a Visit* (1959),[94] *A Single Man* (1964),[95] and *A Meeting by the River* (1967),[96] as well as the most important of his autobiographies, *Christopher and His Kind* (1976).[97] *Down There on a Visit* was inspired by the play, *I Am a Camera*,[98] and the musical, *Cabaret*,[99] both based on *The Berlin Stories*, and, on the model of *The Berlin Stories*, centers around four more persons who came from that period in his life and later, all before he met Bachardy. *A Meeting by the River* is based on Isherwood's relationship to the Swami, dividing his psyche here into two brothers, one of whom becomes a Hindu monk in India, the other much more

[91] James J. Berg and Chris Freeman, eds., *Conversations with Christopher Isherwood*, p. 194.

[92] See Peter Parker, *Isherwood*, pp. 674–75, 704–6.

[93] Id., pp. 105–6.

[94] Christopher Isherwood, *Down There on a Visit* (Minneapolis: University of Minnesota Press, 1999) (first published, 1959).

[95] Christopher Isherwood, *A Single Man* (Minneapolis: University of Minnesota Press, 2001) (first published, 1964).

[96] Christopher Isherwood, *A Meeting by the River* (Minneapolis: University of Minnesota Press, 1999) (first published, 1967).

[97] See Christopher Isherwood, *Christopher and His Kind*.

[98] See Peter Parker, *Isherwood*, pp. 523–24, 528–29, 538, 581, 647, 695.

[99] On both the musical and film see Peter Parker, *Isherwood*, pp. 647, 655, 670–72.

secular. Their conflict reflects Isherwood's own tensions between the Swami and his life with Bachardy. The other two works, *A Single Man* and *Christopher and His Kind*, are among Isherwood's best works and grow directly out of his relationship to Bachardy.

A Single Man was written during an especially fraught period in his relationship to Bachardy when, as Bachardy frankly admitted, "I always suspected he was imagining what it would be like if we split up because I remember that period was a very rough time for us, and I was making a lot of waves. I was being very difficult and very tiresome."[100] The voice of the novel is an academic, George, who teaches literature at a local college and is a gay man whose lover died in a motor accident while visiting his family. Isherwood had taught courses of this sort at many universities over the years, and George is very much Isherwood as an aging and literate gay man reflecting on the loss of the most fulfilling relationship in his life. Isherwood gives voice to anger in part at Bachardy (whom he might at this point have wished dead), but also anger and indignation at the unspeakability of homophobia, which George explicitly analogizes in a lecture to his students to other forms of irrational prejudice, such as anti-Semitism and racism. The novel is a day in George's life – from waking in the morning, to teaching, to an alcoholic dinner with his unhappy British friend and fellow émigré Charlotte, to further drinks with an attractive male student whom George takes home but then passes out before they have sex. In the closing pages of the book, George dies. It is revelatory of the anger that gay men feel at a culture that will not see them or their loving relationships and the corrosive effects that this has on the psyche and its hunger for love and relationship. Isherwood had already experienced in his love for Heinz how patriarchy breaks such relationships, and now again experienced the difficulties of love in his relationship to Bachardy, which American homophobic culture did everything to pull apart. It says something about Isherwood's confidence as an artist and as a gay man at this point in his life that he can give voice to an anger that his pacifism, perhaps not unlike that of Britten and Pears, did not allow him to express. And, it may be a mark of the degree to which homophobic unspeakability had released its strangle hold on the honest voice of gay artists like him that he could now break this silence, and make such anger and indignation at injustice the subject of one of his best novels and, shortly, his most important autobiography. If so, it suggests how important his love for Bachardy and Bachardy for him had become in the development of Isherwood's artistic voice, now exploring new emotional depths of personal anger and indignation. Britten and Pears, because their loving relationship had reached this point of mutual support and trust so much earlier in their relationship and had gone so much deeper, find the strength through their relationship to give shattering artistic expression to this indignation in their earliest collaborative work together and probably their greatest, *Peter Grimes*, an indignation that they explore in all their later works together.

[100] James J. Berg and Chris Freeman, eds., *Conversations with Isherwood*, p. 193.

For Isherwood, the relationship came later and the role of anger and indignation both in *A Single Man* and *Christopher and His Kind* come late in Isherwood's art as well. However, the dynamic of love and resistance in Britten and Pears and in Isherwood and Bachardy are, I believe, similar.

What places *A Single Man* among Isherwood's best work (with *The Berlin Stories* and *Prater Violet*) is that his love for Bachardy, like his love for Heinz and Viertel, did not lead to idealization or denigration (the mark of patriarchal stereotypes) but was based on experience of another complex human being, made possible by a mutual love between two equal persons in relationship, but a love sometimes mixed with disappointment and anger, as love sometimes is. It is sometimes revelatory of the depth of a loving relationship that the partners discover that the honest expression of anger does not destroy, but deepens the relationship, precisely because such expression shows it is based on a free and equal voice, a kind of moral compass to emotional truth in relationship. It is the truth to gay experience, both of gay relationships and of a surrounding homophobic culture, that makes *A Single Man*, like *The Berlin Stories*, so remarkable in its artistic and ethically resisting voice, a voice that arises from Isherwood's experience of his love for Bachardy, which survived and flourished despite disappointment. In *The Berlin Stories*, Isherwood drew upon his love to show both his lovers and Berlin's monsters and victims in all their humane complexity. *A Single Man* draws in the same way on love and the honest voice, based on experience, it makes possible.

Christopher and His Kind, dedicated to Bachardy, speaks in a voice we have not heard from Isherwood before, namely, the voice of the American resisting movement of gay rights, of which it is an important, indeed pathbreaking statement. Strikingly, It is a work of historical memory in which Isherwood traces his own current sense of gay rights, as a social, political, and ethical movement, to what liberated him in Berlin – both the voice of gay rights advocated by Magnus Hirschfeld and of his loving relationship to Heinz. The book ends as Auden and Isherwood come to America: It does not deal with his life and work in the United States, nor with his relationship to Bachardy. Yet, it is probably Isherwood's most American book, conceived and written in the voice made possible by his relationship to his American lover, a relationship based on a free and equal voice unlike any of Isherwood's earlier relationships. Why, then, is it a work of memory and memory largely of Berlin and of Heinz? It was the experience and relationships of Berlin that finally released Isherwood's voice from the disassociation of British patriarchy, and, although Berlin becomes the capital of aggressively homophobic and anti-Semitic German fascism and although he was separated from the man he loved, what remained most real for Isherwood was what he had found there, a life and voice rooted in relationships. And, in telling an American story of gay rights, Isherwood, the truth teller about human relationships and the patriarchal forces that destroy them, insists that it be seen not as an American story but as a story that transcends parochial nationalisms, putting the narrative in a larger historical perspective of a period of great promise for a humane politics of human and gay rights and of the European tragedy, warring on such rights, that abruptly ended it.

Isherwood was never tempted by celibacy (unlike Heard) or by strict monogamy (unlike Huxley and Britten), and, at the end of his life in a joint interview with Bachardy, he dismissed the notion – fretted over by Auden and many others – that God's will forbade gay sex: "You know, fuck God's will. God's will must be circumvented, if that's what it is."[101] Isherwood was in many gay sexual relationships throughout his life, all of which broke the Love Laws. Only a few of them, however, gave rise to resisting voice. What makes his life and art so interesting, from the perspective of this work's study of love and resistance, is that his life's struggle was not over having gay sex, but finding gay sexual relationships so free from the patriarchal hierarchies of his past that he could experience what such love could bring to a more just and humane private and public life, what Forster, citing Shelley, called "Love, the Beloved Republic, which feeds upon Freedom and lives."[102] What made this a struggle for him was that the idealized and denigrated forms of love (including gay sex) under British patriarchy came to seem to him to be based on lies and indeed promoted or legitimated unjust violence (as in World War I). Isherwood's struggle for voice as an artist was for this reason closely connected to his search for gay sexual experience outside the framework of British patriarchy, which meant for him a gay sexual experience not burdened by the hierarchies of British homophobia, supported by the lies and disassociation on which British imperialist patriarchy rested.

Why, for Isherwood, was gay sexual experience the heart of the matter and, in particular, his experience in Berlin so important to the trajectory of his struggle for resisting voice? It was not gay sex in itself that was pivotal, for Isherwood had had such sex long before Berlin, including his long sexual affair in Britain with Wystan Auden. The issue of trust was central to Isherwood's struggle. Once he had decisively broken with his mother over the falsifying Myth of the War Hero, what relationships or persons could be trusted? Gay sex could not itself be trusted, for British hierarchy extended here as it did to straight sex, framing such relationships in terms of a gender binary and hierarchy, which idealized and denigrated the marks not of a real relationship but of the traumatic break of such relationships. It suggests why British patriarchy was, for men like Isherwood, so psychologically powerful and so crippling that it could extend to something to intimately personal as sexual experience. If intimate personal life could be so drained of personal connection, then no experience could be trusted. If patriarchy could colonize the intimately personal, it could destroy all humane feeling, as the twentieth-century totalitarianisms, which war on private life, clearly show. What is remarkable about Isherwood is that, unlike other British men (gay and straight) of his period, he came to see this

[101] James J. Berg and Chris Freeman, *Conversations with Christopher Isherwood*, p. 191.
[102] E. M. Forster, *Two Cheers for Democracy*, quoted at p. 69.

problem, and was moved to search for an alternative. Berlin was so important to Isherwood's life and work because he found there a form of gay sexual experience, his love for a youth of a different ethnicity and class – breaking the patriarchal boundaries not only of gender but of ethnicity and class – that opened his heart and mind to persons outside the limited boundaries of patriarchal concern. Such love expressed itself in an art based on resisting voice, seeing the Germans he loved not as stereotypes but as the complex people, including monsters and victims, they were.

We can see what a struggle this was for Isherwood in his sense of himself as playacting, as lacking any core of moral personality, as he experimented with new forms of gay experience in Berlin and later as he experimented in his art with different ways of writing about gay life and relationships in the voices of various characters and sometimes in his own voice and, eventually, in the third-person voice of "Christopher," the voice he uses in *Christopher and His Kind*. Only in his worst novel, *The World in the Evening*, does he abandon any attempt to speak in this own voice, and the result is disastrous.

It is, for this reason, quite moving that all pretension and evasion are put aside when he writes *Christopher and His Kind*, and he writes in an ethically resisting voice, which was to be resonant with and empowering of the resistance movement we now call gay rights. Isherwood was the least political of artists, centering himself, like E. M. Forster, in liberal individuality, which was never tempted by the antiliberal strain in communism to which his friends Edward Upward and Stephen Spender gravitated. Whatever authority the Swami had over Isherwood arose from his relationship to a man he found to be a caring and loving father; from the beginning of the relationship, it was clear, at least from Isherwood's perspective, that nothing in Vedanta stood in the way of his continued gay sexual relationships. Isherwood, unlike his gay friend Gerald Heard, never interpreted Vedanta to require celibacy, nor did he, like Heard, hermetically seal himself off in a monastery, and in disassociated abstractions that led Heard's critics to see Heard's stance as a Vedanta yogi to be as patriarchally totalitarian as a Stalinist commissar.[103]

In contrast, Isherwood always stayed close to democratic experience and to relationships; experience of a democratic love is what gave authority to his art. In an interview with Bachardy, Isherwood, now near death, says about religious homophobia in all its forms: "You know, fuck God's will. God's will must be circumvented, if that's what it is." At the end, Isherwood, the least political of artists, found his political and ethical voice, having centered himself in a loving relationship of equals with a moral authority free of all patriarchal controls, which is love itself.

---

[103] See, for this criticism, Arthur Koestler, *The Yogi and the Commissar and Other Essays* (New York: The Macmillan Company, 1945), pp. 3–14, 218–47.

4

Wystan Auden on the Anxiety of Manhood

Wystan Hugh Auden (more commonly known as W. H. Auden) played an important role, as we have seen, in the lives of both Benjamin Britten (Chapter 2) and Christopher Isherwood (Chapter 3). Like them, he was a gay man and an artist, and he collaborated artistically with both of them – as a friend of the younger Britten, and close friend and lover of the older Isherwood. Although Isherwood always emphasized the boyish, sexual dimension of his relationship with Auden, it was, I believe, a more deeply loving relationship, on Auden's part, than he ever acknowledged, perhaps even to himself. We can see this both in their quite psychologically radical collaborative plays during the 1930s in which they explore the lovelessness and violence of British patriarchal manhood, and in Auden's poetry during this period, among his best work. Auden's later work continued to be absorbed by the problem of manhood, in particular, by associated anxieties, and he wrote some distinguished poetry and many penetrating essays. However, the psychological and artistic depths Auden's work plumbed when he was in a still lively sexual and personal relationship to Isherwood, very much his equal as a man and artist, came to an end, as Isherwood moves to Los Angeles and Auden falls disastrously in love with Chester Kallman. Isherwood and Auden remained friends, albeit at a distance, but the relationship was no longer intimate and ongoing in the way it had once been. Auden's relationship to Britten, however, ended, broken, as we have seen (Chapter 2), by Britten's indignation at Auden's imperious questioning of both his love for Pears and his vocation as an artist.

What divided Auden from his formerly intimate friends and collaborators was not their sexual lives: All loved other men, and thus all broke the Love Laws that forbad such love across the boundaries. It was something else, namely, their understanding of the relationship of their loves to patriarchy. The foundation of the loves of Britten and Pears – expressed in their collaborative art from *Peter Grimes* onward – was an art that exposed the violence and injustice of patriarchy; and, Isherwood's own struggles as an artist – informed by his loves for Heinz and Don Bachardy – gave expression to a voice that resisted British imperial manhood and, finally, homophobia itself as Isherwood found his voice as an ethical advocate of gay rights as a universal human right. The relationship between Auden and Isherwood, while it lasted as a lively, sexual relationship between two artists very much equals, also expressed itself in their remarkable collaborative plays. The great difference between Britten, Pears, and Isherwood, as gay men, and Auden came later. The lives and works of Britten, Pears, and Isherwood not only continued to break the Love Laws but took the form of increasingly self-conscious ethical resistance to both patriarchy and homophobia, whereas, as we shall see, Auden did not. All were or fell deeply in love with other men, but Auden's love not only did not resist patriarchy, but took a patriarchally homophobic form. So, the closer study of Auden's rather different gay love story clarifies and deepens my exploration of when and how breaking the Love Laws sometimes calls for resistance, and sometimes does not. And, resistance or lack of resistance to patriarchy is, as we shall see, the heart of the matter.

Auden was the youngest of three sons of George Augustus Auden and Constance Rosalie Bicknell.[1] His father was a physician educated at Repton School and Christ's College, Cambridge, and his mother, at a time when few women went to university, studied French at Royal Holloway College, graduating with a gold medal in 1891. "She was a devout Christian, with High Church tastes, and qualified as nurse with the intention of becoming a medical missionary."[2] Auden wrote of his father: "He was the gentlest and most unselfish man I have ever met – too gentle, I used sometimes to think, for as a husband he was often henpecked."[3] Dr. Auden pursued broad cultural and scientific interests, and a common interest shared by father and son was in psychology, the father publishing a number of articles on the more practical aspects of child psychology.[4] His mother, in contrast, "was excitable and domineering," and Auden's "identification with maternal discipline became increasingly eccentric after his mother's death in 1941. He turned the admonishing internal voice of guilt into a maternal voice. He would say, almost as her deputy, of some act, 'Mother would never have allowed that.'"[5]

Auden's interests were in science when he met Isherwood, a three and half-years older boy, at their prep school, St. Edmund's,[6] and Isherwood was surprised that he had become a poet when the two met again some seven years later. Auden's turn to poetry, which he associated with his being introverted, had begun at his public school, Gresham's, later attended by Britten. Gresham's "had virtually no fagging or beating, no privileges for older boys,"[7,8] but its honor system imposed what Auden

[1]   Humphrey Carpenter, *W.H. Auden: A Biography* (Boston: Houghton Mifflin Company, 1981), p. 3.
[2]   Richard Davenport-Hines, *Auden* (New York: Pantheon Books, 1995), p. 7.
[3]   Quoted at *id.*, p. 10.
[4]   *Id.*, pp. 22–23.
[5]   Richard Davenport-Hines, *Auden*, p. 11.
[6]   See *id.*, pp. 35–37.
[7]   *Id.*, p. 37.
[8]   *Id.*, p. 37.

later condemned as "the conditions of 'a fascist state' "[9] (Britten objected to both the bullying he encountered and the officer corps at Gresham's, a sensitivity Auden apparently did not share). Auden's college at Oxford was Christ Church, and he initially enrolled in PPE (Philosophy, Politics, and Economics), but transferred to the English School, influenced by having met Isherwood again, who, having deliberately spoiled his exam results at Cambridge, was now living in London as social secretary to a violinist. "One common point between Auden and Isherwood was their rebellion against the small, smothered morality of their mothers"[10] (both had now abandoned their mothers' Christianity and shared, of course, their homosexuality). "Isherwood was a youth of limited sexual experience when he re-met Auden in 1925. Auden set out to broaden his outlook with shameless and inflammatory anecdotes of his own escapades: both young men recognized that transgressive sexuality would service their literary needs,"[11] Auden as poet, Isherwood as novelist. Soon, they were having sex together. Both shared a passion for travel outside Britain, including, of course, Berlin and, for Auden, Iceland, as well as many other destinations. Their travels end with their long journey as journalists to China during World War II,[12] and then to America, where they decide to emigrate to after their return to Britain.

The poetry for which Auden is now universally known was largely written in the 1930s before or shortly after he and Isherwood came to America, and is poignantly sensitive to the loss of faith in British imperialism after the debacle of World War I, the appeal of socialism and even communism (inspired by the Soviet Union), the troubling rise of fascism in Italy and then Germany and Japan, all of which soon became preludes to what looked like yet another catastrophic war, only now enveloping not only Europe but Asia. Auden rapidly became the leading poet for this generation, which by the 1970s would become known as the Auden generation: socialist in politics, anti-fascist, and anti-imperialist, with an acute sensitivity to developments in both British and European politics.[13]

Auden's interests in the psychopathology of British imperial manhood make this the subject of his early, influential poem, *The Orators: An English Study* (1932, 1934).[14] The poem combines prose and poetry to indict the political rhetoric of aggressive imperialist manhood that suicidally inspired the young men of Britain to take pleasure in going to war in World War I[15] and inspired, at the time Auden wrote,

[9] *Id.*, p. 38.

[10] *Id.*, p. 54.

[11] *Id.*, p. 54.

[12] The journey leads to their collaborative book, W. H. Auden and Christopher Isherwood, *Journey to a War* (London: Faber and Faber, 1986) (first published, 1939).

[13] See, for a brilliant study, Samuel Hynes, *The Auden Generation: Literature and Politics in England in the 1930's* (New York: The Viking Press, 1976).

[14] See W. H. Auden, *The Orators: An English Study* (London: Faber and Faber, 1966) (first published, 1932, revised edition, 1934). For illuminating analysis of the poem, see Samuel Hynes, *The Auden Generation*, pp. 87–95.

[15] See, for example, W. H. Auden, *The Orators*, p. 66.

the aggressively violent politics of Mussolini and Hitler.[16] In a remarkable section, "Letter to a Wound," Auden, as a kind of literary psychiatrist, speaks to the wound in the psyche that gives rise to such propensities to violence,[17] locking aggressors and victims into a vicious cycle of self-destruction.[18] The leaders we take as our imperialist heroes, like Lawrence of Arabia (who was, of course, gay), express not strength, but a wounded manhood.[19] The poem traces the rhetoric that shames men into such unjust violence to speeches at British public schools, and prominently includes in such shaming rhetoric homophobic epithets: "poofs and ponces,"[20] "cissy,"[21] "queer,"[22] and a father to his son, acting "just like a girl."[23] As a study of the gendered rhetoric of violent manhood, the poem, although hermetic, is remarkably contemporary and psychologically acute.

We earlier saw that Isherwood's resisting voice, as an artist, was first inspired by resistance to his mother's idealization of his father as a war hero. Auden – much closer to both his mother and father – did not share this background, but both his break with the Christianity of his parents and his associated homosexual love life led him, as a secular humanist, to explore what he came to see as the twisted psychology underlying British imperial manhood, including its homophobia. Auden's poem, *The Orators*, is very much along these lines (including its indictment of homophobic bullying), and the three plays on which they collaborated during the 1930s – *The Dog Beneath the Skin*[24] (1935), *The Ascent of F6*[25] (1936), and *On the Frontier*[26] (1937–38) – take as their central theme what they had collaboratively (like Virginia Woolf in *Three Guineas*) come to see as the dangers of imperialist patriarchal manhood to both public and private life. The plays are framed as political theatre in the style of Brecht, whose plays and cabaret theatre they knew from Berlin,[27] just as Auden's movie scripts around this time for film documentaries, for which Benjamin Britten wrote the music, are British versions of Soviet socialist realism.[28]

[16] See *id.*, p. 88.
[17] See *id.*, pp. 35–38.
[18] See *id.*, p. 73.
[19] See *id.*, p. 77.
[20] *Id.*, p. 86.
[21] *Id.*, p. 90.
[22] *Id.*, p. 92.
[23] *Id.*, pp. 95–96.
[24] W. H. Auden and Christopher Isherwood, *Plays*, edited by Edward Mendelson (Princeton, NJ: Princeton University Press, 1988), pp. 189–292.
[25] *Id.*, pp. 293–356.
[26] *Id.*, pp. 357–420.
[27] For an example of one's of Brecht's early expressly anti-imperialist plays, located in British India in 1925, showing how an ordinary man may be bullied into losing his identity and abandoning his wife and becoming a savage killing machine, see Bertolt Brecht, *A Man's A Man*, in Bertolt Brecht, *Three Plays*, edited by Eric Bentley (New York: Grove Press, 1964), pp. 103–98.
[28] See, for these scripts, W. H. Auden and Christopher Isherwood, *Plays*, pp. 421–36.

The most bizarre of these quite bizarre plays is *The Dog Beneath the Skin*. Alan Norman has been asked by a British community to find the long lost heir to its lands, Sir Francis Crewe. Norman searches with a dog, who, we eventually figure out, is Francis disguised as a dog. When the dog is revealed as Francis, Francis gives a long speech about what it is like "to start seeing people from underneath,"[29] and condemns the people of his community for the need for a "dictator"[30] and the failure to "speak with the only authority there is, the authority of experience,"[31] demonizing people they should love, like the Germans. He is condemned by the community, and dies.

The Ascent of F6 debunks the psychology of heroic manhood of British patriarchal imperialism. The mountain F6 stands between a British colony and another of its enemy, and the natives have come to believe that whichever of the two nations, Britain or its enemy, first climbs F6 will be their leader. Sir James Ransom in the Foreign Service believes it is imperative, to secure Britain's imperial supremacy, that a Briton climb the mountain and asks his brother, Michael Ransom, the best British climber, to climb the mountain. Michael first rejects the proposal, knowing it to be wrong, but then agrees to do so when prodded and shamed by both his competitive brother and his domineering mother. One of his friends dies while they are climbing, and Michael realizes that he has become a hero like Caesar, willing to sacrifice those they love for ideals in which they do not believe.[32] Michael dies in the attempt although acclaimed by his brother and mother as a national hero. The heart of the play is the patriarchal mother who sacrifices her son for the patriarchy. He in turn can be bullied by her to do anything, like Coriolanus in Shakespeare's great study of Roman patriarchal manhood.

On the Frontier, dedicated to Benjamin Britten, examines two nations that regard one another as enemies on the verge of armed conflict; one of them ruled by a dictator, clearly modeled on a fascist leader, who is supported by an amoral businessman. The leader is killed by a soldier who comes to see the lies underling his rule, and the business leader is killed when he fails to take seriously the injustices he did the soldier and his family and even humiliates him further. Eric, the son of one family, is a pacifist, and refuses to take up arms, and falls in love with Anna, the daughter of a family in the other nation; both regard their love as transcending all barriers between them. Their love would, of course, break the patriarchal Love Laws. War separates the couple, Eric in jail for his pacifism, Anna a nurse for the wounded, as the Love Laws require.

What is of interest in these collaborative works is how both gay artists and at this time, lovers, examine what they take to be the central problem of contemporary European politics through a conception of the violent, lying, and self-deluded

---

[29] See *id.*, p. 285.
[30] *Id.*, p. 286.
[31] *Id.*, p. 286.
[32] See *id.*, p. 336.

patriarchal hero. The role of patriarchy in supporting ethnic nationalism, which divides peoples into enemies, is clearly the heart of the matter. What seems quite contemporary in these works is the psychological frailty of patriarchal manhood, a "dictator," as Francis the ex-dog puts it, who creates scapegoats, but one, as Michael Ransom realizes, whose independent ethical voice has been crushed by a patriarchal mother and brother. And finally, they connect the psychology that supports patriarchal violence to one that enforces the Love Laws and thus makes impossible the loving relationships that might break the disassociation that sustains the need for false authority.

We know, of course, that the problem of gay love in a homophobic culture, not surprisingly, was an urgent concern of both Isherwood and Auden as gay men at this time in their lives. What made the experience and relationships of Berlin so liberating for Isherwood was that, now outside the framework of British homophobia, he could experience relationships he could not otherwise have imagined.

Auden's poetry in this period (January 1937) shows he is in a very different place. Sometimes, the problem is his own faithlessness:

> Lay your sleeping head, my love,
> Human on my faithless arm;
> Time and fevers burn away
> Individual beauty from
> Thoughtful children, and the grave
> Proves the child ephemeral:
> But in my arms till break of day
> Let the living creature lie
> Mortal, guilty, but to me
> The entirely beautiful.[33]

And, sometimes as in a poem of March 1936, the problem is the faithlessness of the other:

> Dear, though the night is gone,
> Its dream still haunts to-day, . . .
> What hidden worm of guilt
> Or what malignant doubt
> Am I the victim of,
> That you then, unabashed,
> Did what I never wished,
> Confessed another love,
> And I, submissive, felt
> Unwanted and went out.[34]

---

[33] See W. H. Auden, *Selected Poems*, selected and edited by Edward Mendelson (New York: Vintage International, 1989), p. 50.

[34] W. H. Auden, *Collected Poems*, edited by Edward Mendelson (New York: Vintage International, 1991), pp. 137–38.

What makes these poems so moving is their exposure of such intimate personal need, in contrast to what Auden in "Law Like Love" (September 1939) calls "Law":

> And always the loud angry crowd
> Very angry and very loud,
> Law is We,
> And always the soft idiot softly Me . . .
>
> Like love we don't know where or why,
> Like love we can't compel or fly,
> Like love we often weep,
> Like love we seldom keep.[35]

The Orators shows that Auden was well aware how patriarchal manhood was polemically enforced, and his collaborative plays with Isherwood show a penetrating psychological insight into the intrapsychic landscape of such manhood, its need for scapegoats, its frailty, its lovelessness. However, Auden shows in these love poems that underneath the armor of his own rather stoic British manhood, there remained a need for intimate voice and relationship that could not be entirely stilled, as he gives expression to that voice and exposes his own remarkable sensitivity. The man who emigrated to America with Isherwood in 1939 was a man desperate for love; as Isherwood, his closest friend, put it, "there were these extraordinary scenes – Wystan in tears, telling me that no one would ever love him, that he would never have any sexual success."[36]

Auden, as a poet, was unusual for his strong scientific interests (including in critical history and psychology) that he shared with his beloved father. Some of his best poetry during this period was about the history of the unfolding European tragedy of the 1930s. It linked past to present and insisted on our choices, taking moral responsibility, as a matter of ethical conviction, for our futures, which included our capacity to act responsibly on such conviction. Edward Mendelson describes one of these, *In Time of War*, as "Auden's most profound and audacious poem of the 1930's, perhaps the greatest English poem of the decade."[37] The poem[38] starts with Creation, or rather, the contrasting place of man and the flora and fauna in the earth's evolution:

> So from the years the gifts were showered; each
> Ran off with his at once into his life:
> Bee took the politics that make a hive,
> Fish swam as fish, peach settled into peach . . .

---

[35] *Id.*, pp. 263–64.

[36] Christopher Isherwood, *Christopher and His Kind*, p. 304.

[37] Edward Mendelson, *Early Auden* (Cambridge, MA: Harvard University Press, 1981), p. 348; for his illuminating commentary on this poem, see *id.*, pp. 348–57. See also Edward Mendelson, *Later Auden* (New York: Farrar, Straus and Giroux, 1999).

[38] See *In Time of War*, in W. H. Auden, *Selected Poems*, pp. 64–78.

> Till finally there came a childish creature
> On whom the years could model any feature,
> And fake with ease a leopard or a dove;
>
> Who by the lightest wind was changed and shaken,
> And looked for truth and was continually mistaken,
> And envied his few friends and chose his love.[39]

His evocation of man, that "childish creature," continues and soon he delineates the problematic psychological consequences. Out of our frailty and the self-consciousness of our ethical freedom comes our anxiety:

> The life of man is never quite completed;
> The daring and the chatter will go on:
> But, as an artist feels his power gone,
> These walk the earth and know themselves defeated.
>
> Some could not bear nor break the young and mourn for
> The wounded myths that once made nations good,
> Some lost a world they never understood,
> Some saw too clearly all that man was born for.
>
> Loss is their shadow-wife, Anxiety
> Receives them like a grand hotel; but where
> They may regret they must; their life, to hear
>
> The call of the forbidden cites, see
> The stranger watch them with a happy stare,
> And Freedom hostile in each home and tree.[40]

In his great poem, "Spain," based on his going to Spain to support the republican cause in the civil war (as an ambulance driver), Auden poignantly combines a sense of the country's history with its present plight as the victim of fascist violence, ending with a call to resistance:

> Yesterday all the past. The language of size
> Spreading to China along the trade-routes; the diffusion
>   Of the counting-frame and the cromlech [prehistoric monument];
> Yesterday the shadow-reckoning in the sunny climates . . .
>
> To-day the makeshift regulations; the shared cigarette,
> The cards in the candlelit barn, and the scraping concert,
>   The masculine jokes, to-day the
> Fumbled and unsatisfactory embrace before hurting.

---

[39] See *id.*, pp. 64–65.
[40] See *id.*, p. 75.

The stars are dead. The animals will not look.
We are left alone with our day, and the time is short, and
     History to the defeated
May say Alas but cannot help nor pardon.[41]

With these poems, Auden gives voice to a haunting anxiety about the use and abuse of our ethical freedom to resist or not resist injustice, often centering on inhibitions arising from manhood. This had been the subject of *The Orators* as well as his plays with Isherwood, and one he would explore to the end of his life. The problem was not only propensities to fascist violence. During the 1930s Auden, like Isherwood, was anti-fascist and sympathetic to the socialist left, but when he went to Spain during the civil war to lend aid to the republican cause (as an ambulance driver), he was shocked that republicans were mindlessly murdering priests.[42] And, when he settled in New York City and went in 1939 to a movie in Yorkville where many German-Americans lived, he was shocked yet again that, when the Germans were shown invading Poland, the audience exploded in vicious hatred of the Poles, shouting "Kill them."[43] Propensities to unjust violence lurked in our human natures, Auden saw again and again, and could not be simply mapped onto ideological divides. So too there was our indifference to suffering and tragedy (as America and Britain ignored the civil war in Spain), the subject of Auden's remarkable poem, *Musée des Beaux Arts*[44]: "how everything turns away/Quite leisurely from the disaster."[45] At this time still a secular humanist, Auden's deeply moving *In Memory of Sigmund Freud*[46] saw Freud's contribution along these lines:

Of course, they called on God: but he went his way,
Down among the Lost People like Dante, down
     To the stinking fosse where the injured
     Lead the ugly life of the rejected.

And showed us what evil is: not as we thought
Deeds that must be punished, but our lack of faith,
     Our dishonest mood of denial,
     The concupiscence of the oppressor.[47]

It was Freud's understanding of the feelings – violent and erotic – we would deny that, Auden argued, made possible a more human voice. Such a voice:

---

[41] See "Spain," W. H. Auden, *Selected Poems*, pp. 51–55, at pp. 51, 55.
[42] See Humphrey Carpenter, *W.H. Auden: A Biography*, pp. 11–12.
[43] See Carpenter, *W.H. Auden*, pp. 282–83.
[44] See W. H. Auden, *Selected Poems*, pp. 79–80.
[45] *Id.*, p. 80.
[46] See *id.*, pp. 91–95.
[47] *Id.*, p. 93

Would restore to the larger the wit and will
The smaller possesses but can only use
    For arid disputes, would give back to
    The son the mother's richness of feeling . . .[48]

One rational voice is dumb: over a grave
The household of Impulse mourns one dearly loved,
    Sad is Eros, builder of cities,
    And weeping anarchic Aphrodite.[49]

The summit of Auden's psychological, historical, and political art – reflecting on
the events leading to World War II – is *September 1, 1939*. The poem is long, and
I suggest here its continuing power and appeal by quoting and reflecting on brief
excerpts. The poem opens with Auden, now in New York City in America, reflecting
on the demonic 1930s ending in catastrophic war:

    I sit in one of the dives
    On Fifty-Second Street
    Uncertain and afraid
    As the clever hopes expire
    Of a low dishonest decade:
    Waves of anger and fear
    Circulate over the bright
    And darkened lands of the earth,
    Obsessing our private lives;
    The unmentionable odour of death
    Offends the September night.

It then turns to an analysis of the roots of the catastrophe deep in European culture
and its unending imperialist cycle of violence:

    Accurate scholarship can
    Unearth the whole offence
    From Luther until now
    That has driven a culture mad,
    Find what occurred at Linz,
    What huge imago made
    A psychopathic god:
    I and the public know
    What all schoolchildren learn,
    Those to whom evil is done
    Do evil in return . . .

    But who can live for long
    In an euphoric dream;

[48] *Id.*, p. 24.
[49] *Id.*, p. 95.

> Out of the mirror they stare,
> Imperialism's face
> And the international wrong . . .

The poem then reflects on our own frailties and failures, and appeals to a voice released by personal love to resist false authority:

> Lost in a haunted wood,
> Children afraid of the night
> Who have never been happy or good . . .

> For the error bred in the bone
> Of each woman and each man
> Craves what it cannot have,
> Not universal love
> But to be loved alone . . .

> All I have is a voice
> To undo the folded lie,
> The romantic lie in the brain
> Of the sensual man-in-the-street
> And the lie of Authority
> Whose buildings grope the sky;
> There is no such thing as the State
> And no one exists alone;
> Hunger allows no choice
> To the citizen or the police;
> We must love one another or die . . . [50]

Paradoxically, Auden's moving encomium to love comes when he falls in love with a man who was to frustrate Auden's hopes for love.

Within a month after moving to New York, Auden met eighteen-year-old Chester Kallman, a Jewish undergraduate at Brooklyn College. Auden was fourteen years older. Kallman's friend Harold Norse described him at this time:

Both sexes merged with androgynous appeal: willowy grace combined with a deep, manly voice. Not at all effeminate, just young and blond, he was tall, unathletic, with slightly stooped shoulders, a spinal curvature, and a heart murmur from rheumatic fever in childhood. He disliked all physical exercise except cruising, which developed his calf muscles. He picked his nose with long spatulate fingers, dirt-rimmed, and thoughtfully examined the product, a sure sign of a Brooklyn intellectual. [51]

Kallman and Norse sat in the front row of a poetry reading by Auden and Isherwood; Auden was "typically disheveled, and Kallman hissed, 'Miss Mess.'"[52] Isherwood had

---

[50] See *id.*, pp. 86–89 (excerpted).
[51] Quoted in Richard Davenport-Hines, *Auden*, at p. 187.
[52] *Id.*, p. 187.

given Norse a card with their address and phone number, and when Kallman visited Isherwood, "Auden opened the door, hoping to find an athletic student who had been at the meeting, he whispered to Isherwood, 'It's the wrong blonde.' Yet their first conversation was a success, and when Kallman returned to the apartment a second time, they became lovers."[53] Auden was ecstatic, writing his brother John, "Mr. Right has come into my life.... Not only can I talk to him as an equal but he understands sex like no one I've ever met."[54] "There seems to have been a proposal, or the exchange of marriage vows, which for Auden had sacramental meaning. He began wearing a ring, though this apparently was soon discarded."[55] The physical dimension did not last long, as the men were not sexually compatible (Auden objected to anal intercourse, which Kallman preferred[56]), and Kallman soon had an affair with another young man, who was not aware of the connection to Auden, and was to have many others until the end of his life. Auden's heart was broken, and he was so enraged that one night he put his fingers around Kallman's neck and pressed hard before Kallman pushed him away, and admitted to several friends he "contemplated murdering his rival."[57]

Nonetheless, Auden chose Kallman as the love of his life, lived with him in New York and in Southern Italy (where they vacationed) and in Austria (where Auden bought a home, near Vienna), and supported Kallman both financially and as a poet (Kallman published several books of poems[58]), although, in their later years, Kallman lived most of the year apart from Auden in Athens. Perhaps the most charitable interpretation of Kallman was given by Lincoln Kirstein, the founder of New York City Ballet and a sexually active gay man, who, like many such men in his position at that time,[59] had married (Leonard Bernstein was yet another[60]), and became a friend of both Auden and Kallman. Kirstein observed:

> Chester was cast, or cast himself, in an "impossible" role. He was competitive, although he knew perfectly well that he hadn't much right to be, but he insisted on the pose out of pure orneriness. On one level Wystan took him as a sort of hair-shirt and put up with him as an article of undoubting faith. But there a lot of romance, and perhaps romanticism, involved.... Chester was always – as far as I can recall – extremely witty. The horrors of life struck him with an ancestral expectation of the

[53] *Id.*, p. 188.

[54] Quoted at *id.*, p. 188.

[55] Richard Davenport-Hines, *Auden*, pp. 194–95.

[56] See, on this point, Richard Davenport-Hines, *Auden*, p. 212. See also Humphrey Carpenter, *W.H. Auden: A Biography*, p. 261.

[57] See Richard Davenport-Hines, *Auden*, p. 214.

[58] See, for example, Chester Kallman, *The Sense of Occasion* (New York: George Braziller, 1971).

[59] See, for an excellent biographical treatment, Martin Duberman, *The Worlds of Lincoln Kirstein* (Evanston, IL: Northwestern University Press, 2007).

[60] See Humphrey Burton, *Leonard Bernstein* (New York: Doubleday, 1959).

worst, and he could turn the worst off by camping. He reigned over this province of formalized sensibility by appropriating the emotional world of 19th century Italian grand opera. But he was not a screaming queen; his tone was moderate and, for this, much funnier.

He also, of course, had a real musical knowledge, sense, and understanding. He broadened Wystan's taste and information. He had a very good ear, and his own light verse, often dirty but often brilliant, was original and skillful. He was a real pain in the ass on many occasions and caused Miss-Master [Auden] plenty of trouble. . . . He could be very nasty, even about Wystan, which did not make one love him. . . . He was extremely intelligent analytically, and this, in addition to everything else, Wystan found useful.[61]

Auden remained so loyal to Kallman that few friends realized the extent of Kallman's infidelities and cruelties to Auden and Auden's miseries. Only occasionally did Auden give expression to his deeper feelings. Stephen Spender, once sitting in a café with them, saw Auden's response to Kallman's sexual approach to a young man: "though Auden went on talking, there were tears running down his cheeks."[62] Kallman's callous carelessness about Auden, who still financially supported him, became painfully evident later in their lives when Kallman lived largely apart in Athens and Auden's loneliness and deplorable lack of care and support shocked his friends. Hannah Arendt, who became a close friend to Auden, remarked on the change in demeanor, "those deep wrinkles as though life itself had delineated a kind of face-scape to make manifest the 'heart's invisible furies' . . . I finally saw the misery, somehow realized vaguely his compelling need to hide it behind the 'count-your-blessings' litany, and still found it difficult to understand fully what made him so miserable, so unable to do anything about the absurd circumstances that made everyday life so unbearable to him."[63] Finally, loneliness and misery in New York led him to choose even greater misery abroad: "in the last year of life, he found himself in an Antarctic camp of his own devising called the Christ Church Common Room."[64]

Kirstein's trenchant remark about Auden's love for Kallman "as a sort of hair-shirt and put up with him as an article of undoubting faith," plausibly connects Auden's love for Kallman with his conversion to the homophobic Anglican Christianity of his mother (Auden resumes going to church in early 1940,[65] after he meets Kallman): The conversion is connected to two traumas of loss: the loss of Kallman's love and, shortly thereafter, the death of his mother. Auden's response to such traumatic loss is identification with patriarchal stereotypes (Auden, as it were, becomes his mother, often referring to himself as "Mother"). Isherwood, one of Auden's closest friends

---

[61] Quoted in Richard Davenport-Hines, *Auden*, pp. 189–90.

[62] Humphrey Carpenter, *W.H. Auden*, p. 316.

[63] See Hannah Arendt, "Remembering Wystan H. Auden," pp. 181–87, at pp. 182–83, in Stephen Spender, ed., *W.H. Auden: A Tribute* (New York: Macmillan Publishing Co., 1975).

[64] Richard Davenport-Hines, *Auden*, p. 339.

[65] See Humphrey Carpenter, *W.H. Auden*, p. 286; Richard Davenport-Hines, *Auden*, pp. 200–1.

who knew Auden's mother well, said of her: "his mother, in other circumstances, might have become a nun, even a saint, she was an extraordinary woman and he was deeply influenced by her."[66] When discussing Isherwood's relationships to his mother (Chapter 3), I made reference to Carol Gilligan's discussion of how Proust shows how a young boy comes to see the different relationships of his father and mother to patriarchy, the father having discretion to suspend its demands, the mother more tightly bound by patriarchy not to kiss her son at bedtime in order to make him more manly. Isherwood's whole direction as an artist was formed in finding a voice to resist his mother's patriarchal devotion to the Myth of the Dead War Hero. If Isherwood grew as an artist by rejecting his mother's myth making, then Auden did nearly the opposite. Auden was evidently much closer to both parents, and Isherwood, although he acknowledged Auden's conversion, said "Auden was always deeply religious,"[67] referring, I believe, to the importance always to Auden of ethical conviction as, even in his liberal humanist period, the test for our choices. That ethical seriousness was imparted by both his parents but, in particular, by his demanding mother. The one matter on which Auden was in conflict with his parents was their condemnation of and anxiety about his homosexuality,[68] and both his loss of his faith and his gay life reflect resistance to such condemnation. The focus of his art during the 1930s on anxieties about the demands of patriarchal manhood suggests that his artistic voice was also empowered by such resistance, nourished by his sexual relationship to Isherwood.

Benjamin Britten had been at least as close to his mother, perhaps more so, as Auden, but the closeness took a rather different form, namely, her own musical voice, as a singer, nourishing her son's creative voice as an artist, a subject of mutual delight between them that was to continue and flourish later in Britten's loving sexual relationship, as a composer of operas, to the singing voice of Peter Pears. It is Britten's continuing relationship to his mother that illuminates not only both his later love life and creativity, but his early ethical voice as a boy that resisted the violence and exploitation of boys by boys and by masters in British education. Auden's relationship to his mother was quite different, and the difference illuminates his remarkable letter to Britten, cited in Chapter 2, in which he questions both Britten's love life and art because you, Britten, "build yourself a warm nest of love." In contrast, "If you are really to develop to your full stature, you will have, I think, to suffer, and make others suffer."[69] The letter is written after Kallman sexually abandons Auden, and bespeaks how and why Auden came to see gay sexual love and resistance in such a different way than Britten. What Britten came, through his love for his mother and Pears, to question in British patriarchy, Auden came, through the dual losses of his mother and Kallman, to

[66] James J. Berg and Chris Freeman, *Conversations with Christopher Isherwood*, p. 186.

[67] *Id.*, p. 186.

[68] See, on this point, Richard Davenport-Hines, *Auden*, pp. 48–49, 66.

[69] Cited in Humphrey Carpenter, *Benjamin Britten*, at p. 164.

accept as the unquestionable patriarchal framework both for his sexual love and his work as an artist, relentless industry and a despair and suffering stoically unacknowledged. How should we understand this, when Britten, Pears, and Isherwood made such different choices as gay men and as artists?

Although Auden had sexual relationships with women,[70] his sexual relationships were dominantly with men throughout his life, long after his conversion and up to his death, sometimes for money.[71] However, after his conversion, Auden never wavered in his expressed conviction that gay sex was a sin and wrong.[72] In a conversation with a friend, Auden put the point thus:

> I've come to the conclusion that it's wrong to be queer, but that's a long story. Oh, the reasons why are comparatively simple. In the first place, all homosexual acts are acts of envy. On the second, the more you're involved with someone, the more trouble arises, and affection shouldn't result in that. It shows something's wrong somewhere.[73]

Auden is thinking, of course, of Kallman, the love of his life, but a love life he came to accept on terms, as he saw it, of the necessary role of masochistic, and implicitly sadistic, suffering in love between men. However, there is a framework for thinking of love in this way, namely the patriarchal Christianity of Augustine of Hippo that Auden had come to accept, only in Augustine the doubts about love extended to all forms of human sexual love. We more clearly see the connection between Auden's choice of Kallman as the love of his life and his conversion to Christianity if we place both in the framework of Augustine's arguments on sexual love, the love of his patriarchal mother, and the love of God, all of which were, for both Augustine and for Auden, closely related. How?

In his remarkable psychoanalytically informed biography, *Augustine of Hippo*, Peter Brown frames the trajectory of Augustine's development in terms of his relationship to his mother – fleeing from her,[74] but drawn deeply back to her highly personal religion of Christian piety. Her piety centered on the sense of her "heroes, as a man 'predestined,' the course of his life already ineluctably marked out by God." Her religious psychology was at the root of one of her son's most remarkable and influential beliefs, "Augustine's grandiose theory of predestination: and, as with so many very clever people, such simple roots were all the stronger for being largely unconscious."[75] God's love for Augustine is modeled on

---

[70] See Humphrey Carpenter, *W.H. Auden*, pp. 342–49.

[71] See, for example, Richard Davenport-Hines, *Auden*, pp. 300–1.

[72] See *id.*, pp. 215, 245.

[73] Alan Ansen, *The Table Talk of W.H. Auden* (Princeton, NJ: Ontario Review Press, 1990), p. 80.

[74] See, on this point, Augustine, *The Confessions*, pp. 81–82.

[75] Peter Brown, *Augustine of Hippo* (London: Faber & Faber, 1967), at p. 175. See also, in general, Peter Brown, *The Body and Society: Men, Women, and Sexual Renunciation in Early Christianity* (New York: Columbia University Press, 1988).

that of his mother: "[S]he loved to have me with her, but much more than most mothers."[76]

Augustine, a philosophical rationalist, had turned to Christianity only when he had found a way, through neo-Platonism,[77] to make personal sense of the Christian immaterial conception of God as an inner voice, the voice of a perfectly sensitive and responsive lover to whom *Confessions* is passionately addressed, but a lover decidedly without a body. (Porphyry wrote of the leading neo-Platonist Plotinus that he "seemed ashamed of being in the body.")[78] Augustine could believe in his mother's God only when, philosophically, he could make sense of the Christian God in such terms and when, theologically, Ambrose of Milan had given him a living example of a Christian clerical life that exercised responsible political authority and made metaphorical interpretive sense of both the Old and New Testament in integrated Christian terms.[79] Through these, Augustine came to the conviction, underlying his conversion, that Bible interpretation was the reasonable basis for ultimate authority in religious and ethical matters (based on the evidence of miracles, and the like). What compelled him, at the moment of conversion, were the epistles of Paul, in particular *Romans*, texts that he construed as requiring celibacy as the only way of hearing God's voice within, and later as requiring original sin through his interpretation of the Adam and Eve narrative.[80]

The method of biblical interpretation in question had been reasonably contested by Christians before Augustine, and would be contested by even more Christians after Augustine.[81] My interest here is in the powerful personal and political psychology that led Augustine to take the interpretive views he did, and why those views were so hegemonically dominant for so long. Why, once he arrives at a conception of an immaterial lover/God, does that psychologically lead him associatively (certainly not logically or philosophically) to celibacy? I believe that a psychology of idealization and loss, based on regarding patriarchy as in the nature of things, explains not only Augustine's conversion but also its enormous continuing power during periods when patriarchy and its supporting psychology remained largely uncontested.

[76] Augustine, *Confessions*, p. 82.
[77] See, on this point, *ibid.*, pp. 111–32. The central text would have been Plotinus, *The Enneads*, translated by Stephen MacKenna (London: Penguin, 1991), parts of which Augustine read in Latin translation (Plotinus wrote in Greek). On the parts of Plotinus he read, see Eugene TeSelle, *Augustine the Theologian* (Eugene, OR: Wipf and Stock, 2002), at pp. 43–45, 53, 68; John M. Rist, *Augustine: Ancient Thought Baptized* (Cambridge: Cambridge University Press, 1997), p. 188.
[78] Porphyry, *The Life of Plotinus*, translated by Stephen McKenna (Edmonds, WA: Holmes Publishing Group, 2001), at p. 5.
[79] See Neil B. McLynn, *Ambrose of Milan: Church and Court in a Christian Capital* (Berkeley: University of California Press, 1994).
[80] See Augustine, *Confessions*, pp. 131, 134, 141, 153. See also, for illuminating commentary, Stephen Menn, *Descartes and Augustine* (Cambridge: Cambridge University Press, 2002), at pp. 192–206.
[81] See, on these points, Elaine Pagels, *Adam, Eve, and the Serpent* (New York: Random House, 1988).

Augustine's denigration of sexuality rests on his acceptance, as axiomatic, of the highly patriarchal Roman conception of women. Honor codes exemplify the unjust demands of patriarchy on the psychology of men, a manhood that places sons and daughters under the hierarchical authority of fathers, for example, dictating the arranged marriages of daughters for dynastic ends.[82] A father's or brother's or lover's or husband's sense of honor, as a man, is defined in terms of his control over the chastity or fidelity of women, irrespective of personal feeling or desire. Any challenge to such control was an insult that triggered violence as a condition of manhood under patriarchy.

Where women do not exist as persons with moral individuality, let alone sexual agency and subjectivity, it becomes impossible to imagine with women the kind of intense friendship Augustine found in his relationships with men, a companionship based on equal voice. Rather, he came to regard sexual experience as inimical to any such relationships, which explains why in *The Confessions* he tells a story in which he identifies his sexual experience as what kept him from the love of God, a love conceived on terms that dignified the lover and beloved as full persons.[83] God, who is the addressee of *Confessions*, is the most satisfying and absorbing of lovers, with whom Augustine lives in the most confidential, trusting, and loving of relationships ("physician of my most intimate self").[84] His love song to this lover is highly erotic:

> Yet there is a light I love, and a food, and a kind of embrace when I love my God – a light, voice, odour, food, embrace of my inner man, where my soul is floodlit by light which space cannot contain, where there is sound that time cannot seize, where there is a perfume which no breeze disperses, where there is a taste for food no amount of eating can lessen, and where there is a bond of union that no satiety can part. That is what I love when I loved my God.[85]

The developmental narrative Augustine tells so truthfully is a love story of a certain remarkable sort, suggesting traumatic breaks in real relationships and a covering over of the trauma with a mythologizing conception of gender that divides women into asexual good women (his mother) and sexual bad women (his lover). While he insists at the end of his narrative that women have "an equal capacity of rational intelligence," he regards such capacity as undermined "by the sex of her body," which "is submissive to the masculine sex."[86] Women are equal but, as sexual, unequal, a contradiction that Augustine's divided psychology accepts as in the nature of things, as his patriarchal mother had taught him.

---

[82] See, on this point, Gilligan, *The Birth of Pleasure*, pp. 4–5.
[83] See, on this point, Augustine, *The Confessions*, Henry Chadwick translation (Oxford: Oxford University Press, 1991), at pp. 127, 134, 141, 145.
[84] *Ibid.*, p. 180; see also p. 202.
[85] *Ibid.*, p. 183.
[86] See *ibid.*, p. 302.

What makes Augustine's conversion so psychologically riveting is that he comes to it in a way that is strikingly anti-patriarchal, that is, through his relationship to his mother's experience and voice, which he came to regard as ethically and religiously authoritative. Monica's personal form of Christianity led her to a remarkable understanding of and ability to deal with the Roman patriarchal violence of her husband, something her son clearly admired and valued in her. It is quite consistent with this interpretation that Augustine in *The City of God* should offer one of the first serious and profound criticisms of Roman imperialistic violence as, more often than not, unjust both in its ends and means (giving rise to the just war traditions of Western thought).[87] However, Monica's insights never fundamentally questioned the Roman patriarchy she assumed to be in the nature of things, a fact clearly shown by her own role in arranging her son's marriage to an appropriate girl to assure his upward mobility, even at the expense of requiring him to give up his relationship to the woman he tells us he sexually loved. Augustine shows himself very much to be a good son when he accepts his mother's patriarchal demands, though in the honesty of his confessions, he tells us that it broke his heart.

Augustine reveals at the beginning of *Confessions* that he adored, before his conversion, the Dido-Aeneas episode in Virgil's *Aeneid*.[88] In fact, Augustine's conversion reenacted this tragic story of love under Roman patriarchy as he also repudiates the woman he loved because of the patriarchal demands of his mother (Monica as Venus). Yet Augustine insists on making himself suffer even more than his mother ever demanded of him, and certainly more than Venus ever demanded of Aeneas: He will give up sex entirely, something his mother never did, although men she much admired, like Ambrose, had.[89] Not only does Augustine dutifully obey his mother's commands, like pious Aeneas, but he also sets himself the competitive goal of exceeding her in piety, inflicting on himself, because of her, both the loss of the woman he sexually loved and the abandonment of sexuality itself.

Augustine plays the patriarchal Roman hero of his confessional narrative as much as Aeneas does in Virgil's narrative of Roman manhood. Aeneas is a heroic man because he leaves the woman he loved when patriarchy demands such abandonment. At a time when the western Roman Empire is near its end, Augustine tells a story of his own heroism, shown by his abandonment of the woman he loved and of his sexuality, all, as he came to believe, demanded by patriarchy. Since Augustus, the Roman Empire had lived under an autocratic political system in which both political and religious authority was hierarchically centered in the emperor. Since Constantine, the emperors had been largely Christian, and centered in themselves

---

[87] See, on this point, Augustine, *The City of God*, Henry Bettenson translation (Harmondsworth, Middlesex, England: Penguin, 1972), at pp. 97–99, 104, 139, 142, 154–55, 205–7, 207–12, 401.

[88] See Augustine, *Confessions*, pp. 15–16.

[89] See, on this point, *ibid.*, pp. 91–92.

the same authority over Christianity as the emperors had enjoyed over Roman pagan religion. Augustine works within the framework of this autocratic conception, calling for a heroic form of religious and political leadership, namely, a celibate male priesthood, which will support such a patriarchal conception of authority even when the empire collapses, as it does during Augustine's lifetime. A member of this celibate male priesthood is "the soldier of the heavenly host,"[90] underscoring the militaristic model for patriarchal authority that he absorbed from Roman politics into his conception of the priesthood appropriate to the Christian religion. What makes such a soldier possible, whether Aeneas or Augustine, is the renunciation of sexual love.

Augustine is not the first or last sexually conflicted, highly sensitive man of genius who turned to celibacy as the only way to free himself from patriarchally framed sexual relationships to women that disabled him from hearing or listening to their real voices as equals. Both Tolstoy and Gandhi turned to celibacy for such reasons.[91] What is striking in thinkers of ethical genius, like Augustine, Tolstoy, and Gandhi, is that they can extend critical ethical thought to many areas, although not to the patriarchal assumptions governing their most intimate sexual lives, feelings, and relationships. These they accept as in the nature of things, or in the nature of sexuality. It is important to take seriously the suffering that patriarchy inflicts on men as well as women, in particular, highly sensitive, ethically demanding men who experience sex under these terms as lacking the relational personal significance and value they associate with the passionate friendship and affection of equals.

Like Augustine, Auden comes to God through his mother, and, again like Augustine, he does so after his heart was broken by the breaking of sexual relationship to the person he loved. Both Augustine's and Auden's mothers enforce the patriarchal Love Laws on their sons – Augustine must leave the woman he loved for a marriage to a suitable woman arranged by his mother, Auden must not love men and, if he does so, he must be punished or punish himself. Augustine comes to regard all forms of sexual love as inadequate and turns to the only reliable and satisfying lover, God, and becomes celibate, a turn his mother did not want or expect. After his traumatic break with Kallman, Auden does not become celibate and does not give up having sex with men, but he tenaciously and willfully holds on to a relationship he regards as the love of his life on terms of suffering to both that are both idealizing and denigrating, masochistic and sadistic, a turn that might well have shocked his mother. Since he never challenges his mother's patriarchal understanding that gay sex is wrong, he regards sexual love between men as defective and wrong and calling for punishment, and thus accepts that his sexual love for Kallman is wrong and, if it continues as love, its wrongness will call for suffering as

---

[90] *Ibid.*, p. 206.
[91] See, for study of this point, David A. J. Richards, *Disarming Manhood: Roots of Ethical Resistance in Jesus, Garrison, Tolstoy, Gandhi, King, and Churchill* (Athens, OH: Ohio University Press, 2005).

condign punishment, a suffering Auden embraced, as a mark of manhood, until the bitter end of an increasingly miserable life. Everything that was wrong in his relationship to Kallman is ascribed to its homosexuality, never to the patriarchal terms of the relationship, one more of master and slave than mutually responsive lovers. Auden came to believe that Kallman's defects as a lover meant no man could be loved and love, in the same way Augustine found all women incapable of the love of equals. Misogyny and homophobia are, in this respect, the same: both deeply sexist, as if no woman and no gay man (more woman than man) could possibly love deeply, responsively, and mutually, as a free and equal person in loving relationship. Like Augustine, Auden finds that the only responsive and sensitive lover he allowed himself to have is God. Thus, in a remarkable and long letter (excerpted here) to Kallman after his betrayal, Auden framed the misery of their relationship in redemptive theological terms:

Christmas Day, 1941.

Dearest Chester

Because it is in you, a Jew, that I, a Gentile inheriting an O-so-genteel anti-Semitism have found my happiness:

As this morning I think of Bethlehem, I think of you.

Because, suffering on your account the torments of sexual jealousy, I have had a glimpse of the infinite vileness of masculine conceit;

As this morning I think of Joseph I think of you . . .

Because the necessarily serious relation of a child to its parents is the symbol, pattern, and warning of any serious love that may later depend upon its choice, because you are to me emotionally a mother, physically a father, and intellectually a son;

As this morning I think of the Holy Family, I think of you.

Because on account of you, I have been, in intention, and almost in act, a murderer;

As this morning I think of Herod, I think of you . . . .

Because in the eyes of our bohemian friends our relationship is absurd;

As this morning I think of the Paradox of the Incarnation I think of you . . .

As this morning I think of the Good Friday and Easter Sunday already implicit in Christmas day, I think of you.[92]

The letter shows the depth of Auden's love for Kallman, as, in characterizing what Kallman means to him, he does so in terms that break the terms of the patriarchal gender binary, "to me emotionally a mother, physically a father, and intellectually a son."[93] However, the letter shows as well how much, for Auden, his suffering was defined in the terms of orthodox Christian homophobia.

[92] Quoted in Dorothy J. Farnan, *Auden in Love: The Intimate Story of a Lifelong Love Affair* (New York: New American Library, 1984), pp. 65–66.
[93] I am grateful for this point to Vincent Cesare.

It is, of course, an orthodox interpretation of Christianity that God's sacrifice of his son was vicarious atonement for Adam's fall and, consistent with this view, Auden reads his own suffering in terms of what God the Father required of His Son, namely, sacrifice of self. There are within the Christian tradition alternative interpretations, like that of Anselm of Canterbury, that reject as irrational that the patriarchal sacrifice of an innocent child could ever be a reasonable understanding of a just God (Anselm argues that Jesus chooses to die as the most reasonable way to impart his ethical teaching).[94] Why, then, must a reasonable Christian like Auden, quite theologically well informed, opt for a less reasonable reading of his own tradition? It is confirmation of Anselm's worries about irrationalism rather than justice as the heart of Christian ethics that Auden could so interpret Christianity to regard his disastrous choice of lover as sacramental, indeed a crucifixion modeled on Jesus's suffering. As Lincoln Kirstein perceptively observed, Auden chose Kallman "as a sort of hair-shirt and put up with him as an article of undoubting faith," because that idea made sense of their fraught relationship in terms of his Augustinian religious faith.

Auden's Christianity was never one of fundamentalist certitude. He came to it through experience of the evil of human nature (suggesting Original Sin) he observed in Spain (the killings of priests) and in Yorktown, and the anxiety and doubt and the need for grace (part of his experience of love) he found in Kierkegaard.[95] He was influenced by the Anglican theologian Charles Williams[96] and Reinhold Niebuhr's Protestant political liberalism, that reinterpreted Original Sin in terms of irrational prejudices like anti-Semitism and racism that must be resisted.[97] Having fallen in love with a Jew, another way of breaking the Love Laws, Auden was repelled[98] by T. S. Eliot's Christian anti-Semitism.[99] Just as Augustine's conversion to his mother's Christianity supported his own ethical judgments that were critical of Roman patriarchal violence in its imperialistic wars, Auden's conversion to his mother's Christianity gave support for his judgments of our ethical freedom, including our liberal responsibility to take seriously and resist, following Niebuhr's interpretation of Original Sin, evils like religious intolerance and racism. However, like other men, like Augustine, whose sense of Christianity was imparted through mothers who retained patriarchal conceptions of gender and sexuality, the superbly intelligent Auden could not bring his critical intelligence to bear on something as intimately personal as homophobia. Patriarchy, rooted in intimate

---

[94] See Anselm of Canterbury, *Why God Became Man*, pp. 260–356, in Anselm of Canterbury, *The Major Works* (Oxford: Oxford University Press, 2008).

[95] See, for example, W. H. Auden, *The Living Thoughts of Kierkegaard* (New York: New York Review Book, 1999) (first published, 1952), pp. xii–xiii.

[96] See, on this point, Humphrey Carpenter, *W.H. Auden: A Biography*, at pp. 283–86.

[97] See, for a good general treatment of Auden's Christianity, Arthur Kirsch, *Auden and Christianity* (New Haven, CT: Yale University Press, 2005).

[98] See Arthur Kirsch, *Auden and Christianity*, p. 87.

[99] See Christopher Ricks, *T.S. Eliot and Prejudice* (London: Faber and Faber, 1994), at pp. 40–41.

life, thus intractably darkens our intelligence about our intimate lives and relationships.

The contrast to Isherwood is illuminating here (Chapter 3). Both Isherwood and Auden broke their mother's religious understanding of the patriarchal Love Laws. Such resistance made possible their gay sexual lives (including sex with one another) and their collaborative works exposing both the violence and lovelessness of patriarchal manhood. However, their paths diverged when it came to resisting homophobia itself. Both continued to break the Love Laws, but Isherwood's takes the form of an ethically grounded resisting voice that, like that of Britten and Pears, exposes the lies and violence underlying patriarchy in general and homophobia in particular. Isherwood, as seen in Chapter 3, came to distrust how patriarchal mythology disassociated people from experience, indeed rested on the refusal to take experience seriously. He stayed close to the experience of human relationships in order to free himself from the patriarchal blinkers that dominated British manhood. The experience of loving gay relationships to Heinz and later to Bachardy made this voice psychologically possible for Isherwood, and his best art gives voice to what loving experience across the boundaries had shown him both about himself and others; as for religion, "You know, fuck God's will. God's will must be circumvented, if that's what it is." There is also another important contrast between Isherwood's relationship to his mother and Auden's. Isherwood, later in his life, came to regard his disagreements with his mother as a root of his creative voice, suggesting that his sense of being able to disagree with her was a way of staying in relationship to her and having a voice in relationship, a source both of his capacity for love and of his ethical independence. Isherwood's relationship to his mother is quite different from Auden's, which suggests not relationship, but identification. Isherwood also observed of Auden, a friend he loved and studied, "his magpie brain [was] ... a hoard of curious and suggestive phrases from Jung, Rivers, Kretscher and Freud."[100] Theories, for Auden, sometimes took the place of experience, perhaps never more disastrously than the disassociation from experience after his loss of Kallman, which he framed in terms of a homophobic interpretation of Christianity, yet another grand theory, itself not based on experience. For these reasons, Auden's experience with Kallman could not be more different than Isherwood's of Heinz and Bachardy, which arose from an experience skeptical of patriarchal distortion. Kallman brought to his relationship with Auden an affection distorted by masochism and sadism, which, for Auden, mirrored his own willful needs for such masochism and sadism, rooted probably in what the psychoanalyst, Sheldon Bach, calls a childhood "fantasy about being mistreated by someone as a sign that he loves you."[101] As one of Auden's psychologically

---

[100] Christopher Isherwood, *Lions and Shadows* (London: Vintage, 2013) (first published, 1938), p. 143.

[101] Sheldon Bach, *The Language of Perversion and the Language of Love* (Northvale, NJ: Jason Aronson, 1994), p. 54.

astute biographers comments, "Auden ... came to recognize that their similar need of pain was a stronger tie to Kallman than homosexuality."[102] Auden for this reason mistook his own need for suffering with his homosexuality because he read his experience through the prism of a Christian homophobia he never seriously questioned. Auden saw himself and Kallman through the broken mirror of patriarchy. From this perspective, any anti-patriarchal love must be one of suffering as punishment.

The contrast to Britten is, as I earlier suggested, also instructive. Both Britten and Auden were quite close to their mothers, but in quite different ways: Britten by early coming to his creative voice through his mother's singing voice, Auden by first disavowing his mother's patriarchal controls (part of the psychopathology of manhood in his plays with Isherwood), then identifying with these controls. Britten's creativity centered in the continuing sense of himself as a boy resisting patriarchal violence, very much part of his continuing relationship to his mother's responsive care and singing voice, the basis of his creative relationship to Peter Pears. Auden first found his creative voice, supported by his relationship to Isherwood, through resistance to the patriarchal controls he had known as a boy and young man. However, the loss of both his mother and the man he loved reinstated the boy in the man, only not the boy, like Britten, who resisted patriarchal demands, but the boy whose demanding mother had imparted to her beloved son patriarchy as a badge of honorable British manhood. The artist who had once indicted controlling patriarchal mothers as quashing conscience now himself became "Mother."

No relationship even of this sort could or would have lasted so long between men as gifted and intelligent as Auden and Kallman, if, despite all its negative features, it had not also brought them something deeply satisfying and fulfilling. As Lincoln Kirstein observed, Auden came to value Kallman's wit and critical mind and the way Kallman opened his mind and heart to the profundities of opera, including not only Wagner but Italian opera, culminating in Verdi's musical art. Auden, the much greater poet, always supported Kallman's work as a poet. Friends, who observed them closely together, observe the wit and the laughter, the honesty and aliveness of their voices even when arguing, the pleasures of relationship and of the food and life they shared (Kallman was a chaotic but good cook).[103] Their happiest experiences as a couple were to "work together as equals on libretti and translation – a productive and entirely happy partnership."[104] Two of these libretti, *The Rake's Progress*[105] and

---

[102] Richard Davenport-Hines, *Auden*, p. 190.

[103] See, for example, Thekla Clark, *Wystan and Chester: A Personal Memoir of W.H. Auden and Chester Kallman* (New York: Columbia University Press, 1995); Dorothy J. Farnan, *Auden in Love: The Intimate Story of a Lifelong Love Affair* (New York: New American Library, 1894).

[104] Humphrey Carpenter, *W.H. Auden*, p. 395.

[105] See W. H. Auden and Chester Kallman, *Libretti and Other Dramatic Writings* 1939–1973 (Princeton, NJ: Princeton University Press, 1993), pp. 47–93.

The Bassarids,[106] are masterpieces of the form, and one of them, *The Rake's Progress*, inspired Stravinsky's marvelous neoclassical musical setting, one of the summits of twentieth-century operatic art.[107] It is surely notable that these two libretti express deeply personal features of the Auden–Kallman relationship (the first, the steadfast lover and the faithless beloved; the second, violence unleashed by the denial of erotic love). It is psychologically revealing that, in working on their collaborative masterpiece, *The Rake's Progress*, Auden wrote the part of the faithless beloved, Tom Rakewell, Kallman that of the steadfast lover, Anne Truelove, reversing their quite different roles in their fraught relationship; Kallman later said he found writing Anne's words "a task approaching penance."[108] Why penance? What this suggests, I believe, is that collaboration strengthened and empowered both their artistic voices to go further than they could otherwise have gone separately, perhaps because they could express so truthfully what they had come to know, as a couple, so intimately and could, at least in art, acknowledge to themselves and others as the pathos of their own relationship – for Kallman, in particular, "penance," for Auden a suppressed rage, expressed by Shadow (the devil) striking Rakewell insane. The last scene of the opera is one of exquisite pathos, as Anne sees that her lover lives in another world and no relationship with him will ever be possible. The libretto is a remarkable personal and artistic achievement, which Stravinsky sets in his most beautiful neoclassical style.

The same cannot be said of the quality of Auden's work as a poet after the interconnected events of his love for Kallman and his religious conversion.[109] Auden's great poem of transition, *New Year Letter* (January 1, 1940),[110] puts in broad historical perspective his sense of what coming to America would mean to the art and lives of him and his fellow emigres to America from Europe:

> However we decide to act,
> Decision must accept the fact
> That the machine has now destroyed
> The local customs we enjoyed,
> Replaced the bonds of bloom and nation
> By personal confederation.
> No longer can we learn our good
> From chances of a neighbourhood
> Or class or party, or refuse

---

[106] See *id.*, pp. 249–313.

[107] On this collaboration, see Humphrey Carpenter, *W.H. Auden*, pp. 352–53.

[108] See, on this point, *id.*, p. 354.

[109] For a range of views on this point, see Alan Jacobs, *What Became of Wystan: Change and Continuity in Auden's Poetry* (Fayetteville: The University of Arkansas Press, 1990); Alexander McCall Smith, *What W.H. Auden Can Do for You* (Princeton, NJ: Princeton University Press, 2013); Edward Mendelson, *Later Auden*.

[110] W. H. Auden, *Collected Poems*, pp. 199–243.

As individuals to choose
Our loves, authorities, and friends, . . . [111]

Being cut off from traditional ties, including their families, would make possible, indeed require a new kind of ethical choice, "[c]ompelling," as he put it, "all to the admission/Aloneness is man's real condition."[112] In fact, however, both falling in love and his conversion were to bring Auden into much closer dependence on the values of his patriarchal mother than had been the case when he still lived and worked in Britain, leading to an artistic voice that many have found less compelling than the voice of his previous poems. It is a mark of this shift in voice that one of his most justly admired earlier poems, the already quoted *September* 1, 1939, now was a poem Auden repudiated, excluding it (as well as "Spain") from the collected edition of his work;[113] because, after he fell in love with Kallman and his religious conversion, the first poem's conclusion, "We must love one another or die," expressed a conviction about the redemptive value of personal love that no longer made sense to the now religious Auden, who looked for such love to God, who Auden believed or needed to believe might give it, not to Kallman, who Auden now knew certainly could and would not. In fact, Auden was more alone than he had ever been (Isherwood, his closest good friend, was now in California). Breaking the kind of ongoing, intimate relationship he once had had to Isherwood may have been experienced by Auden as yet another trauma, in addition to his loss of his mother and his loss of Kallman. If so, we can see the consequences of such loss in the shift in Auden's artistic voice away from the piercing ethical honesty and psychological penetration of his earlier poetry, some of which he now repudiated (in contrast, Auden continued to produce intelligent and incisive critical essays, including a study of Shakespeare, until the end of his life[114]). George Orwell in Britain had admired Auden's earlier poetry, including "Spain," "this poem is one of the few decent things that have been written about the Spanish war."[115] What he objected to in the poem was Auden's choice of the words, "necessary murder," which showed he had not confronted what Orwell clearly had in the civil war, "the terror, the hatred, the howling relatives, the post-mortems, the smells."[116] Auden, unlike Orwell, had not actually fought in

---

[111] *Id.*, p. 238.

[112] *Id.*, p. 238.

[113] See Edward Mendelson, *Early Auden*, pp. 324–30; W. H. Auden, *Selected Poems*, p. 305.

[114] See W. H. Auden, *The Complete Works of W.H. Auden: Prose*, Volume 1, 1926–1938, edited by Edward Mendelson (Princeton, NJ: Princeton University Press, 1996); W. H. Auden, *The Complete Works of W.H. Auden: Prose*, Volume II, 1939–1948, edited by Edward Mendelson (Princeton, NJ: Princeton University Press, 2002); W. H. Auden, *The Complete Works of W.H. Auden: Prose*, Volume III, 1949–1955, edited by Edward Mendelson (Princeton, NJ: Princeton University Press, 2008); W. H. Auden, *The Complete Works of W.H. Auden: Prose*, Volume IV, 1956–1962, edited by Edward Mendelson (Princeton, NJ: Princeton University Press, 2010); W. H. Auden, *Lectures on Shakespeare*, edited by Arthur Kirsch (Princeton, NJ: Princeton University Press, 2000).

[115] See George Orwell, *Essays* (New York: Everyman's Library, 2002) (first published, 1961), p. 236.

[116] See *id.*, p. 237.

the war, let alone been seriously injured, and Orwell objected accordingly to the use of words, "necessary murder," that suggested to him a disassociation from moral reality not unlikely the way in which Hitler and Stalin rationalized their murderous atrocities. For Orwell, Auden's later shift in poetic voice was even more disassociated from experience because even less based in ethical judgment of our inadequate responses to political injustice. Orwell, like many others in Britain (including members of Parliament), regarded Auden's and Isherwood's staying in America when Britain was at war as moral cowardice, reflecting yet another lapse in responsible ethical judgment.[117] Orwell, who in 1941 wrote eloquently in *The Lion and the Unicorn: Socialism and the English Genius*[118] about the anti-fascist, liberal decency of the British people and why taking up arms against the fascist attack on Britain was called for (including, prophetically, that it would lead to socialism),[119] regarded Isherwood and Auden leaving for America as confirmation of his long-held view that "the English intelligentsia" suffered from "severance from the common culture of the country."[120] Of Auden's shift in voice in his poetry, such poetry was beyond the pale of responsible art; Orwell commented acidly: "Auden is watching his navel in America."[121]

Three long poems express this shift: *For the Time Being* (1941–42),[122] *The Sea and the Mirror* (1942–44),[123] and *The Age of Anxiety* (1944–46).[124] Auden subtitled *For the Time Being* as "A Christmas Oratorio," and had hoped Britten would set it to music (Britten wrote a few parts, and then, finding the work unwieldy, gave up). The poem is dedicated to Auden's mother who had died in 1941, and acknowledges his religious conversion to God in striking terms, combining a need for some personal truth with anxiety:

> He is the truth.
> Seek Him in the Kingdom of Anxiety;
> You will come to a great city that has expected your return for years.[125]

The Sea and the Mirror, subtitled "A Commentary on Shakespeare's *The Tempest*," is Auden's statement of his artistic credo, in which Caliban, the monster who is also a poet, speaks in Auden's voice, but notably largely in rather flat prose, "about accident and tragedy: the circumstances in the life of an individual which unavoidably

---

[117] See Humphrey Carpenter, *W.H. Auden: A Biography*, pp. 288–93.

[118] See George Orwell, *The Lion and the Unicorn: Socialism and the English Genius*, in George Orwell, *Essays* (New York: Everyman's Library, 1968), pp. 291–348.

[119] See also his 1940 essay, *My Country Right or Left*, in George Orwell, *Essays*, pp. 281–90.

[120] George Orwell, *Essays*, p. 311.

[121] See George Orwell, *Essays* (New York: Everyman's Library, 2002), p. 474.

[122] See W. H. Auden, *Collected Poems*, pp. 347–400.

[123] See *id.*, pp. 401–46.

[124] See *id.*, pp. 447–538.

[125] *Id.*, p. 400.

cause some natural aim or desire to end in catastrophe when carried out."[126] It is a self-absorbed work on art and artists, not on the political world Auden had once so powerfully and acutely studied.

The most revealing of these works is *The Age of Anxiety*, a poem for four characters – two older men, a younger Jewish woman, and a younger man, a soldier in uniform. The poem opens in a bar, where we hear each of the character's inner thoughts in isolation from one another. Eventually, the four talk to one another and go to the young woman's apartment, where she dances with the young man. The two older men leave, thinking the younger couple wants to be alone. In fact, the young man, quite drunk, falls into a deep sleep. The young woman is left with her own thoughts, which include acknowledging her Jewish background. The poem ends with the thoughts of one of the older men on the need for God:

> His Truth makes our theories historical sins,
> It is where we are wounded that is when He speaks
> Our creaturely cry, concluding His children
> In their made unbelief to have mercy on them all
> As they wait unawares for His World to come.[127]

The Age of Anxiety had resonance for postwar Americans: It won the Pulitzer Prize, and was set by Leonard Bernstein, another conflicted gay man, as the narrative basis for his Symphony No. 2, "The Age of Anxiety," a kind of tone poem for orchestra and piano (Jerome Robbins, another gay man, would make a ballet to the Bernstein score).[128]

Why should anxiety be so central both to Auden's religion and, increasingly, his poetry? And, why so resonant in postwar America? Auden from his earliest poems had found his distinctive poetic voice in writing his doubts about patriarchal British imperial manhood and expressing an altogether more complex sense of what men were, challenging the gender binary and hierarchy. Think, for example, of the lines, earlier cited:

> And always the loud angry crowd
> Very angry and very loud
> Law is We,
> And always the soft idiot softly Me.[129]

Anxiety over one's manhood would always be something gay men, like Auden, would feel in a culture as homophobic as Britain was, a homophobia Auden clearly internalized. However, a poetry giving voice to such anxiety would have a wider and deeper resonance in American culture after World War II, which unsettled gender

---

[126] See Richard Davenport-Hines, *Auden*, p. 224.
[127] W. H. Auden, *Collected Poems*, p. 335.
[128] See, on these points, Humphrey Burton, *Leonard Bernstein*, pp. 188–91, 197.
[129] W. H. Auden, *Selected Poems*, p. 90.

roles as women worked in American factories during the war and then were abruptly returned to their conventional roles after the war, and men returned to peacetime life after a war that traumatized many of them against an enemy motored by aggressive patriarchal fury at its humiliation by defeat in World War I. Old patriarchal values had proved more dangerous than anyone had anticipated, and new values of universal human rights now had an appeal they had never had before. However, it was yet unclear what this new order would mean for conceptions of manhood and womanhood long framed by patriarchy. How to live in this tension?

What Auden shows us in *The Age of Anxiety* are men and a woman whose manhood and womanhood is more in doubt than ever before and who experience themselves as cut off from one another and yet, hungry for love, anxiously turn to God who is, as Auden put it, "the Truth . . . in the Kingdom of Anxiety." Anxiety is the condition not only of love, but of religious faith, and both arise from a manhood and womanhood now experienced as in doubt, and, like Augustine, for Auden God is the only satisfying answer to our needs for personal intimacy with a person we can trust.

Auden's voice as a poet arose, in collaboration with his then lover Isherwood, from resistance to the demands of patriarchal manhood. In contrast, however, to both Britten and Isherwood, his resistance was not later supported by loving relationships that challenged the gender binary and hierarchy and thus homophobia itself. His love for Kallman was willfully patriarchal, and, in the trauma of a broken heart, he turned, like Augustine, to an interpretation of religion that was also patriarchal. In this regard, Auden is a much more conventional gay man of his time and place than were Britten, Pears, and Isherwood. Although Britten lived in a Britain from which Auden fled and Isherwood turned to a non-Western Indian religion, Vedanta, that Auden disdained, what set them apart was that through loving relationships they experienced a more humane world more real and more authoritative than the patriarchal "loud angry crowd/ Very angry and very loud" that Auden, in his sense of loss and abandonment, came to accept as inevitable and inexorable. What Britten and Pears and Isherwood found through loving relationships was a deepening of their ethical and artistic voices in resisting injustice, challenging patriarchy in general and homophobia in particular. In contrast, the resisting ethical voice of the earlier Auden – a voice that had defended liberal values, including personal love, in *September* 1, 1939 – was stilled and muted. And because of his religion, his suffering over the loss of love became, like Aeneas, a stoical badge of honor, a mark of the hold patriarchal manhood continued to exert over Auden's sense of his duties. At bottom, Auden's anxiety arose from his growing sense of the deep loneliness to which *The Age of Anxiety* gave voice, a loneliness that ended in a life of carelessness and disorder that shocked Hannah Arendt, and a poetry whose subject increasingly was human suffering as our ultimate lot, a poetry that shocked George Orwell. However, while for this reason he never carried his resisting voice as far or as deep as Britten and Isherwood, he always spoke honestly from the sense of the human ethical plight as he had come to understand and live it, stoically accepting, like Aeneas and Augustine before him, a desolate patriarchal loneliness that brought him so much anxiety and so much suffering. Britten and Isherwood, once close friends, show us there was always another path. It is Auden's personal tragedy, both as a man and as an artist, that – when he saw this in the love and art of Britten and Pears – he not only refused disassociatively to see what was before his eyes, but contemptuously devalued such love because, as he put it with an astonishing obtuseness and stupidity that would wound and permanently alienate his close friend and collaborator, an artist needs "to suffer, and make others suffer."

5

Bayard Rustin on Nonviolence

The previous three chapters explored the struggle for the resisting voice of four British gay artists (Britten, Pears, Isherwood, and Auden), once close friends and indeed artistic collaborators, joined in resistance to British patriarchal manhood and the imperialism it supported as well as, implicitly, to British homophobia. My analysis connected their resistance on all these fronts to the role resistance to patriarchy played both in their early relationships to their families of origin and in later friendships and loves. Sometimes that resistance was supported by their mothers, and sometimes it contested their mothers' complicity with patriarchy (for Isherwood, throughout his life; for Auden, until his religious conversion). My focus was on the role such resistance played as the crucial variable in explaining when breaking the Love Laws freed creative ethical voice to resist injustice and when it did not. This chapter and the next turn to the similar resistance of Americans – the resistance of two black gay men to American racism and homophobia; in Chapter 7, the resistance of two remarkable white American women, whose lesbian love unleashed a voice resisting American sexism and racism and, implicitly, homophobia. If my analysis works for these Americans, as it did for the Britons, it shows how this resistance illuminates very different contexts and backgrounds. Resistance to patriarchy, suitably nuanced and contextual, is the heart of the matter. That the point has not been seen illustrates, I believe, how deeply an uncritical patriarchy continues to dominate our thinking even though it contradicts our experience, certainly, our experience of resisting injustice as a continuing force in our private and public lives.

The resistance to British imperialism of the Britons I studied resisted, implicitly, the racism that sustained it. All these men were, however, white, and they were from fairly privileged backgrounds in the structure of British life and the imperialism that sustained it. It is all the more remarkable that they come to resist British imperialism, but they do so very much from within, yet also from outside; their struggles as gay men to find love is one of their shared motives to form the kind of "Society of Outsiders" – both within and outside British patriarchy – that Virginia Woolf had called for.

This chapter and the next also explore the deeply American problem of racism, rooted in American slavery, which only a bloody civil war ended, and yet persisted long thereafter. It is an issue that affects all Americans, including those Americans from ethnic groups who, although white, were coded by racist America as black – including Irish Americans, Jews, and Italian Americans, among others. It is an issue close to my own struggles as an Italian American and as a gay man and those of my partner, who is Jewish, and I have always regarded the resistance of African Americans as deeply connected to my own struggles. The difference, of course, is that Italian Americans and Jews, like gay men and lesbians, can cover their differences,[1] thus avoiding prejudice in a way people of color usually cannot. However, the pressure to assimilate into American culture tempts such unjustly stigmatized groups to cover in ways that endorse the evil of racism and homophobia they should, as among its victims, resist.[2] The consequence is what D. W. Winnicott calls "the compliant false self appears, with the hiding of the true self that has the potential for the creative use of objects."[3] How does one resist this deadly temptation?

For this reason, I turn in this chapter and the next to two remarkable American black, gay men, whose example always inspired me because it spoke to my experience, as a gay man from an Italian culture, itself quite patriarchal and, in the United States, racialized. The resistance of Bayard Rustin and James Baldwin absorbed me because it arose directly from the sense of themselves as among the victims of both American racism and homophobia and thus tempted to assimilate to and accept such demands as in the nature of things (as Baldwin's stepfather had), an experience I shared, at least in part. But, they resisted. What role might breaking the Love Laws play in understanding their or my resistance, perhaps freeing me and others from the false self of covering through a personal and ethical voice that contests the interlinked racist, sexist, and homophobic stereotypes that repress moral individuality and voice? Put another way, how does one come to a sense, after covering for so long, of the difference in oneself between acting and living? In my experience, breaking the Love Laws is one such way, an experience like waking up from a deep sleep and seeing and exploring the world with open eyes. Both Rustin and Baldwin tread this path through love both to self-knowledge and to a life centered in an authentic and creative personal ethical voice.

Bayard Rustin and James Baldwin were both black gay men, whose lovers were sometimes white men. They thus both break the Love Laws as gay men, men loving men, and as black men, loving persons not of their race. Rustin was essentially always

[1] On covering, see Kenji Yoshino, *Covering: The Hidden Assault on Our Civil Rights* (New York: Random House, 2006).
[2] See David A. J. Richards, *Italian American: The Racializing of an Ethnic Identity* (New York: New York University Press, 1999); David A. J. Richards, *Tragic Manhood and Democracy: Verdi's Voice and the Powers of Musical Art* (Brighton: Sussex Academic Press, 2004).
[3] See D. W. Winnicott, *Playing and Reality* (London and New York: Routledge, 2005) (first published, 1971), p. 137.

a political activist and an important figure in the American civil rights movement, particularly with regard to the role of nonviolence in the movement for civil rights. Baldwin was essentially an artist, but his artistic voice arose in such articulate resistance to American racism that he became an important figure in the growing American understanding of its own racism, and thus an important figure in the civil rights movement. By the end of their lives, each of them was also an articulate black voice for gay rights among both blacks and non-blacks. What makes each of them so important to our study is the ways in which their breaking the Love Laws both as gay men and as black men took the form of resisting patriarchy, enabling them both to forge new ethical voices effectively to both reveal and resist American racism through nonviolence (Rustin) and, in Baldwin's novels and essays, to reveal and resist the role the violence of patriarchy played in both American racism and homophobia.

At the heart of Bayard Rustin's life and work was a pacifism that brought attention to nonviolence as giving ethical voice to resistance to injustice. I have already explored pacifism in three other gay men – Benjamin Britten, Peter Pears, and Christopher Isherwood – all of whose pacifism, like Rustin's, included refusal to fighting in World War II (Britten and Pears are, on their return to Britain in 1942, given exemptions, Isherwood in the United States does alternative service, Rustin – the black pacifist – goes to prison). We see in Rustin a distinctively American approach to nonviolence, one with long roots in one of the most important resistance movements in American history, namely, antebellum radical abolitionism.[4] Placing him within the American tradition of nonviolence, and particularly in relationship to the seminal figure of William Lloyd Garrison, casts a flood of light on Rustin's distinctive resisting voice, in particular, its connections to nonviolence.

I have written at some length elsewhere about Garrison and his important connections to the international movement of nonviolent civil disobedience of Leo Tolstoy, Mohandas Gandhi, and Martin Luther King, Jr.[5] I draw here rather briefly on that account to show that Rustin works within this American tradition (which he both assumes and elaborates) because the point underscores the impor-tance in resisting injustice of ongoing forms of friendship and love, including traditions, that defy the gender binary and hierarchy to form such networks across the patriarchal boundaries that forbid such associations. Garrison during the antebellum period developed and supported such traditions. Although he was white and did not himself love sexually across the boundaries, he formed and promoted loves and friends across such boundaries. Garrison was a crucial figure in giving resonance to the resisting voices not only of abolitionist feminists, as we

---

[4] See David A. J. Richards, *Women, Gays, and the Constitution: The Grounds for Feminism and Gay Rights in Culture and Law* (Chicago: University of Chicago Press, 1998).

[5] See David A. J. Richards, *Disarming Manhood: Roots of Ethical Resistance* (Athens, OH: Swallow Press/Ohio University Press, 2005).

shall see, but of the resistance of blacks, including the former slave Frederick Douglass, the most important leader of black resistance to injustice in the nineteenth century, for whom Garrison supplies a stage and an audience of both whites and blacks who would hear his astonishing ethical voice.[6] No person who resists injustice effectively is alone, and nothing shows this better than the ways in which Rustin's voice arises within a supportive tradition that already challenged the gender binary and hierarchy. It is, I believe, a mark of the continuing power of patriarchy that we balkanize our discussions of the evils of religious intolerance, racism, sexism, and homophobia, when, in fact, all such serious movements resisting injustice arise from common grounds, resisting patriarchy. Garrison, resisting patriarchy, exemplifies this point, more than any other man in the antebellum period, as he resisted not only religious intolerance but also American racism and sexism, calling for and developing networks of friendship and love across the boundaries that led to such resistance.

I connect Rustin to Garrison for two reasons. First, both men come to nonviolence through a developmental psychology, which, unlike the psychology of more patriarchal men, stayed in close relationship to the ethical voices of those mothers or maternal figures, who found in Jesus of Nazareth's "Sermon on the Mount" a religious and ethical justification for resisting traditional forms of patriarchal violence and the evils it supported through nonviolence. Second, because of this background, both men found an ethical voice freed from the gender binary and hierarchy that patriarchy requires and found and developed that ethical voice through relationships of friendship and love that defied patriarchal boundaries. Through such relationships, a man like Garrison empowered and supported the free and equal ethical voices of women and black men (some of whom challenged the patriarchal Love Laws). Rustin followed and elaborated this tradition – in his case, as a gay man. What Rustin's struggle adds to this tradition is the two distinctive ways he himself broke the Love Laws: as a black man loving white men, breaking the Love Laws both of gender and of race/ethnicity.

A.   GARRISON ON RESISTING PATRIARCHAL VIOLENCE

Garrison, a journalist, was the leading figure in the antebellum period among a small group of radical abolitionists, who opposed not only slavery but the cultural racism that they believed had come unjustly to support not only slavery in the South but unjust forms of racial discrimination in the North.[7] If this were not radical

---

[6]   See, on this point, Henry Mayer, *All on Fire: William Lloyd Garrison and the Abolition of Slavery* (New York: St. Martin's Griffin, 1998), pp. 248, 323, 366–71.

[7]   See, for an excellent recent study on which I draw throughout my argument, Henry Mayer, *All on Fire.* See, for fuller discussion of the abolitionists in general and the radical abolitionists in particular, David A. J. Richards, *Conscience and the Constitution* (Princeton, NJ: Princeton University Press, 1993). I draw here upon arguments in my earlier book, David A. J. Richards, *Disarming Manhood: Roots of Ethical Resistance* (Athens, OH: Swallow Press/Ohio University Press, 2005), pp. 8–42.

enough, Garrison supported and encouraged the work of radical women like Lydia Maria Child who offered not only the most probing analysis of American racism in the antebellum period, but who also carried the argument further into the unchartered territory of women's rights. Indeed, it was Garrison who encouraged and published the work of the Grimké sisters, Angelina and Sarah, that gave rise to abolitionist feminism, an ethical analysis of both racism and sexism reflecting a common form of unjust moral slavery that was later to be elaborated by Lucretia Mott and Elizabeth Stanton and others (a form of which underlies even the contemporary understanding of rights-based feminism).[8] Garrison supported a number of other radical causes, including nonresistance, the pacifist view that violence was never justified in resisting injustice.[9] Garrison's advocacy of such unconventional views before the Civil War placed him well outside the dominant consensus, even of antislavery thought. Of course, after the Civil War, Garrison's views opposing slavery and racism quickly became mainstream, as Lincoln (who regularly had read Garrison's newspaper, *The Liberator*) included Garrison among the dignitaries attending the raising of the American flag over Ford Sumter to celebrate the end of the Civil War.[10]

What is compelling about Garrison was his voice of resistance to forms of injustice sustained by violence on the basis of a liberal political theory that includes both a robust principle of free conscience and speech and a principle that condemns the political force of irrational prejudice (like extreme religious intolerance and racism). The two principles are related in the following way.

The principle of free conscience and speech rests on the argument for universal toleration that had been stated earlier, in variant forms, by Pierre Bayle and John Locke.[11] That principle forbade a dominant religion or group from unreasonably depriving other groups of their rights of conscience and speech. A prominent feature of the argument for toleration was its claim that religious persecution corrupted conscience itself. Such corruption, a kind of self-induced blindness to the evils one inflicts, is a consequence of the political enforcement of a conception of religious truth that immunizes itself from independent criticism in terms of reasonable standards of thought and deliberation. Paradoxically, the more the tradition becomes seriously vulnerable to independent reasonable criticism (indeed, increasingly in rational need of such criticism), the more it is likely to generate forms of political irrationalism (including scapegoating of outcast dissenters) in order to secure allegiance. The worst ravages of anti-Semitism illustrate this paradox of

---

[8] See, for a fuller discussion of this development, David A. J. Richards, *Women, Gays, and the Constitution: The Grounds for Feminism and Gay Rights in Culture and Law* (Chicago: University of Chicago Press, 1998).

[9] See Henry Mayer, *All on Fire*, at pp. 222–28.

[10] See Henry Mayer, *All on Fire*, at pp. 577–80.

[11] For fuller examination of the argument in Locke and Bayle and its American elaboration notably by Jefferson and Madison, see David A. J. Richards, *Toleration and the Constitution* (New York: Oxford University Press, 1986), at pp. 89–128.

intolerance. Precisely when the dominant religious tradition gave rise to the most reasonable internal doubt (for example, about transubstantiation), these doubts were displaced from reasonable discussion and debate into blatant political irrationalism against one of the more conspicuous, vulnerable, and innocent groups of dissenters (the irrationalism centered on fantasies of ritual drinking of human blood that expressed the underlying worries about transubstantiation).[12]

The second liberal principle condemns the unjust force in politics of extreme religious intolerance like anti-Semitism and any form of irrationalist prejudice that arises from abridging the basic human rights of whole groups of persons, including the right of free speech to resist such injustice. Earlier I called this pattern of structural injustice moral slavery, an analysis of how and why constitutional principles have progressively condemned not only a politics actuated by anti-Semitism, but also by ethnic prejudice (including racism), sexism, and homophobia.[13] The claim of an analogy among such prejudices (for example, racism and sexism) is in the similar method of structural injustice inflicted in both cases, namely, "that others have controlled the power to define one's existence."[14] I call this injustice moral slavery because a category of persons, subject to this injustice, has been culturally dehumanized (as nonbearers of human rights) to rationalize their servile status and roles. For example, the long history of Christian Europe's restrictions on Jews were rationalized by Augustine, among others, in the quite explicit terms of slavery: "The Jew is the slave of the Christian."[15]

It is an important feature of the struggle against any one form of moral slavery (for example, racism) that it tends, on grounds of principle, to link its protest to related forms of such slavery (for example, sexism), a point central to Garrison's politics of resistance. For example, the American struggle against racism culminates not only in the constitutional condemnation of segregated education,[16] but antimiscegenation laws as well.[17] Antimiscegenation laws had come to bear this interpretation as a consequence of the Supreme Court's endorsement of the view of the unjust cultural construction of racism first suggested by Garrison's follower, Lydia Maria Child in 1833[18] and importantly elaborated by Ida Wells-Barnett in 1892.[19] Wells-Barnett analyzed Southern racism after emancipation in these terms, sustained by antimiscegenation laws and related practices, including lynching.[20] The point of such laws and practices was not only

[12] See Gavin I. Langmuir, *Toward a Definition of Anti-Semitism* (Berkeley: University of California Press, 1990) and *History, Religion, and Anti-Semitism* (Berkeley: University of California Press, 1990).
[13] See David A. J. Richards, *Women, Gays, and the Constitution.*
[14] See William H. Chafe, *Women and Equality: Changing Patterns in American Culture* (New York: Oxford University Press, 1977), p. 77; on the similar methods of repression, see *ibid.*, pp. 58–59, 75–76.
[15] Cited in David I. Langmuir, *History, Religion, and Anti-Semitism*, p. 294.
[16] See *Brown v. Board of Education*, 347 U.S. 483 (1954).
[17] See *Loving v. Virginia*, 388 U.S. 1 (1967); cf. *McLaughlin v. Florida*, 379 U.S. 184 (1964).
[18] For citations and commentary, see Richards, *Conscience and the Constitution*, pp. 80–89.
[19] For citations and commentary, see Richards, *Women, Gays, and the Constitution*, pp. 182–90.
[20] For citations and commentary, see Richards, *Women, Gays, and the Constitution*, pp. 182–90.

to condemn all interracial marriages (the focus of Child's analysis), but the legitimacy of all sexual relations (marital and otherwise) between white women and black men; illicit relations between white men and black women were, in contrast, if not legal, certainly socially acceptable, even normative. The asymmetry was rationalized in terms of gender stereotypes: a sectarian sexual and romantic idealized mythology of asexual white women and a corresponding devaluation (indeed, dehumanization) of black women and men as sexually animalistic. Illicit sexual relations of white men with black women were consistent with this political epistemology, and thus were tolerable. Both licit and illicit consensual relations of black men with white women were not, and thus were ideologically transformed into violent rapes requiring lynching. The thought that could not be spoken, for it flouted the idealizing pedestal on which white women were placed, was that white women had sexual desires at all, let alone sexual desires for black men.

Both Harriet Jacobs (supported by Child as her editor) and Ida Wells-Barnett had analyzed this injustice from the perspective of black women who had experienced its indignities first hand. For example, the slave narrative of Harriet Jacobs, *Incidents in the Life of a Slave Girl*,[21] told the story, under the pseudonym Linda Brent, of the indignities she suffered under slavery, her moral revolt against them (leading to her hiding for seven years in a small garret), and her eventual escape North to freedom. Jacobs importantly examined the role of slave-owning women from the perspective of the slave. Her portrait of her slave-owner's wife (Mrs. Flint) explored "her constant suspicion and malevolence."[22] Pridefully virtuous, standing tall on her idealized pedestal of Southern womanhood, Mrs. Flint denied any virtue to a woman slave; indeed, "[i]t is deemed a crime in her to wish to be virtuous."[23] The basis of marriage in a slaveholding family was hypocrisy and denial, treating white women contemptuously as pets on a very tight leash: "[t]he secrets of slavery are concealed like those of the Inquisition."[24] To Brent's certain knowledge, Dr. Flint was "the father of eleven slaves,"[25] but the reality was known and not known; as Mrs. Chesnut confided to her diary: "every lady tells you who is the father of all the Mulatto children in every body's household, but those in her own, she seems to think drop from the clouds or pretends so to think."[26] White slaveholding women themselves sustained this mythology by falsely idealizing their virtue and denigrating that of slaves, whose

---

[21] See Harriet A. Jacobs, *Incidents in the Life of a Slave Girl*, edited by Jean Fagan Yellin (Cambridge, MA: Harvard University Press, 1987) (originally published, 1861). For important commentaries, see Deborah M. Garfield and Rafia Zafar, eds., *Harriet Jacobs and Incidents in the Life of a Slave Girl* (Cambridge: Cambridge University Press, 1996).

[22] See *id.*, at p. 31.

[23] See *id.*, at p. 31.

[24] See *id.*, p. 35.

[25] See *id.*, at p. 35.

[26] See C. Vann Woodward and Elisabeth Muhlenfeld, *The Private Mary Chesnut: The Unpublished Civil War Diaries* (New York: Oxford University Press, 1984), at p. 42.

unjust situation, on Jacobs's view, made such virtue unreasonably difficult. Thus, Jacobs laid the foundation for later antiracist and antisexist analysis of the role that unjust gender stereotypes, based on abridgment of basic human rights, played in the dehumanization not only of black but of white women as well. It is resistance to such gender stereotypes that often makes possible resistance to forms of structural injustice.

How could Garrison's radical resisting voice have arisen and flourished in a man of his period and place? In fact, Garrison's remarkable voice, resisting dominant conceptions of patriarchal manhood that violently targeted such a voice, only makes sense when seen as motivated by Garrison's drive to stay in relationship to the anti-patriarchal voice of his mother, Frances Lloyd Garrison, and women who also spoke in that voice. Frances had broken with her Anglican parents to embrace the more personal Christian religion of dissenters, and herself spoke extemporaneously at prayer meetings[27]; after her marriage to Abijah Garrison, they had moved from Nova Scotia to Newburyport, Massachusetts, where Frances had joined "a populist insurgency that elevated the individual conscience and disdained the ordained clergy, cherished the words of the Bible, and spurned formal theology."[28] In the absence of her mariner husband at sea, Frances, the mother of four children (including William Lloyd), formed a close friendship with another married woman, Martha Farnham, who led prayer meetings that Frances attended. After Abijah abandoned his family, Frances

> seemed indomitable to her son, but her churchfolk knew the heaviness of her heart. Her sorrows and her faith made her eloquent in prayer, and she became a familiar voice in the community. "God's people is a praying people," she believed, and the weekly female prayer meetings stood as "the very gate of Heaven to our souls."[29]

Later when Frances had moved with her son to Baltimore, "she established a women's prayer meeting – the first among evangelicals in Baltimore – and presided over it with passion and eloquence."[30] The son always remembered his mother's "powerful voice in its torrents of pious exhortation."[31] His mother had also given him a powerful counterexample to the dominant racism of his culture in writing of the kindly care she had received from a black woman named Henny: "'Although a slave to man, [she is] yet a free-born soul by the grace of God,' Sister Garrison declared, and she admonished her son to 'remember her for your poor mother's sake.'"[32] When Garrison came to the recognition of the wrongness of cultural racism expressed in

[27] Henry Mayer, *All on Fire*, at pp. 5–7.
[28] *Id.*, p. 11.
[29] *Id.*, p. 14.
[30] *Id.*, p. 21.
[31] *Id.* p. 13.
[32] *Id.*, p. 69.

his book attacking colonization (the only book he published),[33] it was not only through abstract argument, but through his experience in Boston with the black religious community.[34] Later, on hearing the black woman preacher, Maria Stewart, he heard a voice he "knew so well from his mother."[35]

Garrison's developmental psychology led him to place value on his mother's prophetic ethical voice and thus to identify himself as, like her, a preacher inspired by the life and teaching of Jesus of Nazareth.[36] Such Christian-speaking witness included enduring violence. In 1835, Garrison himself was famously dragged by a rope and beaten, his life at threat, by a lynch mob through the streets of Boston for his radical abolitionist views.[37] Garrison's patient endurance of such violence was very much inspired by the abolitionist women who had accompanied him; as he put it, "Such a mob – 30 ladies routed and . . . demolished by 4,000 men."[38] Garrison had earlier addressed the mob, who were disrupting an abolitionist meeting, in terms that bring out how much the issue of protesting voice had become, for him, a criticism of the conventional understanding of manhood:

> his lame joke, "If any of you gentlemen are ladies in disguise . . . give me your names . . . and you can take your seats in the meeting," further dramatized the issue as one that pitted Christian meekness against established power, feminine sentiment against masculine patriotism, with Garrison identified with the women.[39]

Garrison had clearly come to develop and express a sense of his own free ethical voice in protest of slavery and racism by challenging a conventional sense of manhood that unleashed violence on any threat to its sense of honor, an American expression of codes of patriarchal honor.[40] Garrison's growing commitment to nonviolence tracks closely his sense that the enormity of the evil of American slavery and racism required not only men but women to resist the violent repression of voice required by a patriarchal manhood threatened by criticism of American slavery, racism, and sexism. Garrison nurtured and supported such a free ethical voice not only in himself, but in a woman of the North (Lydia Maria Child) and two women of the South (the Grimké sisters, Angelina and Sarah), authors of pathbreaking works of

---

[33] See William Lloyd Garrison, *Thoughts on African Colonization* (1832; reprint, New York: Arno Press and *The New York Times*, 1968).

[34] Henry Mayer, *All on Fire*, p. 69.

[35] *Id.*, p. 134.

[36] For Garrison's identification with Jesus, see *id.*, at pp. 125, 204–5, 210, 224, 449.

[37] See Henry Mayer, *All on Fire*, pp. 203–5.

[38] See *id.*, p. 207.

[39] See *id.*, p. 202.

[40] See, for example, Kenneth S. Greenberg, *Honor and Slavery* (Princeton, NJ: Princeton University Press, 1996); Joanne B. Freeman, *Affairs of Honor: National Politics in the New Republic* (New Haven, CT: Yale University Press, 2001); Bertram Wyatt-Brown, *Southern Honor: Ethics and Behavior in the Old South* (New York: Oxford University Press, 1982).

ethical criticism of the linkages between unjust racial and gender stereotypes,[41] as well as through his crucial support for the resisting voice of Frederick Douglass[42] (Garrison and Douglass would later disagree on many issues[43]).

There is certainly a criticism of conventionally accepted political violence implicit in these struggles, but it is not obvious that the criticism reflected an ethically grounded form of pacifism.[44] There is, rather, a more specific focus to the criticism, namely, on the forms of political violence, intimidation, and social sanctions imposed on any voice that contested the patriarchal demands of gender stereotypes. These forms of violence, broadly understood, included not only killing (Lovejoy), beatings (Garrison), public abuse, insult, and throwing objects (the Grimké sisters), but also a range of social sanctions, including withdrawal of support (Child), shaming and bullying, contempt and opprobrium, and the like. Nonviolence was rooted in a criticism of the role such patriarchally rooted violence pervasively played in both personal and political psychology in ante-bellum America, directed against any voice in a woman or man that would reasonably test the unjust terms of dominant patriarchal conceptions of political authority, including extreme religious intolerance, racism, sexism, and the like. The repudiation of violence in this domain made possible speaking and hearing a new kind of free ethical voice. Garrison's nonresistance speaks to women, in particular, because it dignifies their ethical voice and intelligence as equals. It makes possible new forms of democratic political action in which women emerge as equal moral and political agents in collaboration with men.[45]

Such disarming of patriarchal manhood may also have opened to Garrison a psychology of manhood more responsive to the humanity of women not only politically but personally. Garrison was not only a companionate husband, but a tender and supportive father:

> He took upon himself "burdens which most husbands and fathers shun," ...
> "His shining quality was that of nurse," Fanny [his daughter] emphasized, feeding
> and tending the children with such "unbounded love" and skill that the little ones
> were "drawn to him as if by a magnet."[46]

People who had only read Garrison's provocative and uncompromising rhetoric as an abolitionist journalist expected to encounter an intransigent, difficult man; they were shocked on meeting the person. One such notable example was Harriet Beecher Stowe, who "confided that while she had once considered Garrison a

---

[41] See Henry Mayer, *All on Fire*, at pp. 264–69.

[42] See, on this point, Henry Mayer, *All on Fire*, pp. 248, 323, 366–71.

[43] See Henry Mayer, *All on Fire*, pp. 371–74, 429, 431–33, 472, 536.

[44] As it was for Adin Ballou; see Adin Ballou, *Christian Non-Resistance, in All Its Important Bearings, Illustrated and Defended* (Philadelphia: J. Miller McKim, 1848) (reprinted, Philadelphia: Jerome S. Ozer, 1972).

[45] See Henry Mayer, *All on Fire*, at pp. 266, 557–58.

[46] Henry Mayer, *All on Fire*, at p. 356.

wolf in sheep's clothing, she now knew that he was really a lamb in a wolf's disguise."[47] Another such example was Frederick Douglass, who was struck by Garrison's lack of any of the conventional marks of the gender binary and hierarchy in his relationships to both men and women, black and white: "'The place the people struck me as the most democratic I had ever met,' said Douglass, visiting in the midst of a lecture tour. 'There was no high, no low, no masters, no servants, no white, no black. I felt myself in very high society.'"[48]

The great interest of Garrison (including the radical abolitionists he led and inspired) is the role accorded nonviolence not only in the understanding of the proper scope of free speech, but in new forms of democratic resistance to injustice that were later to inspire, for example, Tolstoy[49] and Gandhi.[50] Garrison was no philosopher and had no formal education, but his journalistic skills and his personality empowered new forms of resistance, notably, nonresistance societies in which women participated equally with men, black and white.[51] These "nonresistance societies" were, in fact, new forms of resistance to injustice that empowered the moral and political agency of women on equal terms with men. In founding such a nonresistance society in 1838, Garrison told his wife Helen that it "took its mandate from the Sermon on the Mount . . . (Matt. 5:38–39)."[52] Its inspiration is the life and teaching of Jesus on the repudiation of patriarchal violence, which Garrison and the radical abolitionist women allied with him saw so conspicuously all about them – not only in Southern slavery and violence, but in the Northern mobs of Boston, even, eventually, on the floor of Congress when a leading abolitionist senator, Sumner of Massachusetts, was beaten nearly to death by a Southerner.[53]

Such activities of nonresistance expressed themselves in the antebellum period in a range of forms of resistance, including the refusal of Frederick Douglass to sit in a Jim Crow car on a railroad in the North[54] and refusals to comply with the requirements of the Fugitive Slave Act in the name of what the New England Anti-Slavery Convention called its "theory of civil disobedience."[55] In 1848 the Concord writer Henry David Thoreau lectured in the town's lyceum on the topic "The Rights and Duties of the Individual in Relation to Government," in which he expressed his views that if a law "requires you to be the agent of injustice to another, then, I say, break the law. Let your life be a counter friction to stop the machine,"[56] a lecture

---

[47] See *id.*, p. 465.
[48] See Henry Mayer, *All on Fire*, p. 323.
[49] See *id.*, at pp. 249–51
[50] See *id.*, at p. 264.
[51] See *id.*, pp. 249–51.
[52] See *id.*, at p. 250.
[53] See, in general, David Potter, *The Impending Crisis*, 1848–1861, edited by Don E. Fehrenbacher (New York: Harper & Row, 1976).
[54] See Henry Mayer, *All on Fire*, at pp. 306–7.
[55] See *id.*, p. 413.
[56] Elizabeth Hall Witherell, ed., *Henry David Thoreau: Collected Essays and Poems* (New York: The Library of America, 2001), "Civil Disobedience," pp. 203–24, at p. 211.

published as an essay the next year. Born of his opposition to slavery and the Mexican War (leading to a refusal to pay taxes and imprisonment) and formed by the Garrisonian spirit of his household, Thoreau's lecture was a passionate protest against the loss of moral voice that allowed such injustices to continue.

Thoreau would never have joined nonresistance societies of the sort Garrison sponsored. His later enthusiastic support of John Brown shows a position on legitimate political violence much closer to that of Theodore Parker than Garrison,[57] and his defense of resistance is grounded in an individual's refusal of complicity, not a more political empowerment of associational practices of resistance. In his masterpiece, *Walden*, Thoreau writes of higher laws, but they are laws, for Thoreau, discovered not through association but through an austere autarky.[58]

In contrast, Garrison's ethical genius was not only journalistic, but relational and associational like that of Gandhi and King. My suggestion is that this genius was rooted in a developmental psychology in which, unlike more conventionally patriarchal men of his time, Garrison stayed in close relationship to his mother's prophetic ethical voice as well as the comparable voices of the abolitionist women he supported and inspired and who inspired him. Garrison's interest in securing a forum for these women's voices was more than an issue of the principle of free speech (although it was certainly that). It was also a conviction that something fundamental about the evil of American slavery and racism could *only* be learned by bringing such women's ethical voices, including black women's, into the public discussion. Garrison's concern is not just with removing the forms of censorship that encumbered women's basic human and constitutional rights of free exercise and free speech, but also with forging a cultural sense of resonance that strengthens women's otherwise traditionally silenced ethical voices, emboldening a creativity and brilliance of voice by being an audience that hears and values such brilliance. All these women carried the argument into places Garrison could not himself have gone, seeing connections and drawing inferences that express and advance humane intelligence about issues the culture could barely acknowledge, let alone discuss. His passion for truthful voice against lies took, then, the form of encouraging the different voices of such women as crucially necessary for the truth to be spoken and heard, acknowledging their roles as ethical prophets, very like Hawthorne's view of Hester Prynne in *The Scarlet*

---

[57] For Thoreau's speeches in praise of Brown, see "A Plea for Captain John Brown," pp. 111–38, in Henry D. Thoreau, *Reform Papers*, edited by Wendell Glick (Princeton, NJ: Princeton University Press, 1973); "Martyrdom of John Brown," *id.*, at pp. 139–43; "The Last Days of John Brown," *id.*, at pp. 145–53. For commentary on Thoreau's support of Brown and his abolitionist stance in general, see Daniel Walker Howe, "Henry David Thoreau on the Duty of Civil Disobedience," An Inaugural Lecture delivered before the University of Oxford on May 21, 1990 (Oxford: Clarendon Press, 1990).

[58] See Robert F. Sayre, ed., *Henry David Thoreau* (New York: The Library of America, 1985), *Walden*, pp. 321–588, at pp. 490–500. For illuminating commentary, see Stanley Cavell, *The Senses of Walden* (Chicago: University of Chicago Press, 1992), pp. 83–87.

Letter (see Chapter 1).[59] Bayard Rustin, as a gender nonconforming gay man, can and should be regarded in the same way.

B.   RUSTIN ON NONVIOLENCE

Bayard Rustin, born in rural Pennsylvania in 1912, "was well into boyhood before he learned that his oldest sister, Florence, was actually his mother."[60] "In every way that mattered, Julia and Janifer Rustin [his grandparents], not Florence and Archie [his father], were his Mamma and Pappa, Julia, a nurse by training, attended the birth ..., and a few days later made the decision with Janifer to raise the newborn as their youngest." They kept his origins from the child until, teased by a classmate about it, he asked Julia about it, and she answered: "Well now I think it's been too long ... Florence is your mother, but we're one big family and we are all mothers for everybody."[61] West Chester, Pennsylvania, was Quaker country, with strong anti-slavery traditions (many houses once served as locations for the Underground Railroad) and a small community of African Americans who lived there since before the Civil War. Julia had been educated in the local Friends School and was one of the first blacks in the town to receive a high school education. While a member of the African Methodist Church, "she absorbed Quakerism at home and in school, and its influence, including its historical role in respecting women's voices, on her remained powerful."[62] Of her influence on Bayard, his brilliant biographer John D'Emilio observes:

> Without question, Julia was the dominant presence in Bayard's early life, exerting an influence that stayed with him forever.... The messages he received from her, both by observation and through long hours of sitting with her in the kitchen and listening to her talk as she cooked, were many: to treat everyone with respect, to hear every side of a controversy, to put oneself at the service of others. Most of all, she impressed on him the need to present a calm demeanor to the outside world. "One just doesn't lose one's temper," Bayard heard often, and it became a lesson he later took to heart as he crafted a public role for himself. "She was a remarkable, remarkable woman," he told an interviewer near the end of his life.[63]

Rustin shared with Garrison a similar developmental psychology of a close and continuing relationship to a maternal caretaker, whose voice, like Garrison's mother, expressed Quaker values not only of pacifism resting on an interpretation

---

[59]   Carol Gilligan makes the same point in her *In a Different Voice: Psychological Theory and Women's Development* (Cambridge, MA: Harvard University Press, 1982).

[60]   John D'Emilio, *Lost Prophet: The Life and Times of Bayard Rustin* (Chicago: University of Chicago Press, 2003), p. 7.

[61]   John D'Emilio, *Lost Prophet*, p. 8.

[62]   See *id.*, p. 9.

[63]   See *id.*, p. 11.

of the Sermon on the Mount, but also of a democratic respect for the free voices of all, women and men, black and white. Rustin thus found his resisting voice and his nonviolent activism within the radical abolitionist tradition of Garrison, who had already shown how challenges to the gender binary and hierarchy could and would lead to transformative constitutional and political activism against the evil of American slavery and its attendant evils, American racism and sexism.

Rustin was both a good student and a popular athlete (on the football team) at his integrated public high school, and his love for music (including a quite good singing voice) was a central interest then and throughout his life; his closest friendship was with a white boy, although the boy's family did not allow Bayard into their home.[64] The pattern of breaking boundaries surfaces early on. Unlike his white friend, when they graduated from high school in 1932, "Bayard had no prospects commensurate with his talents. No scholarship offers arrived from colleges, and the Rustin family did not have the means to support him at a school away from home."[65] At the last moment, however, Julia approached a wealthy leader of her church, who had just become president of Wilberforce University, "an African American institution in western Ohio with a famed music school and choir."[66] The leader had heard Rustin sing, and secured him a music scholarship at Wilberforce, where he studied music. Rustin left before graduation because of his objection to the requirement to participate in ROTC activities,[67] and then goes in 1934 to a school nearer home, Cheyney State Teacher's College, a Quaker-founded school for black students. Dr. Leslie Pinckney Hill, "its Harvard-educated president, was the most eminent African American in the country, respected for his learning and the uncompromising standard he held out to his students." Rustin again received a music scholarship, and found in Dr. Hill "someone to guide and stretch him intellectually," leading to Rustin's first close reading of a philosopher, George Santayana, as well as William James.[68]

There was at this time growing concern in the country about the emergence of fascist violence by Germany, Italy, and Japan, and "[i]n the years before Pearl Harbor, a vigorous peace movement in the United States resisted the rush toward militarism."[69] President Hill made sure Cheyney State would be a voice in such resistance by having his campus play host in 1937 to the Institute of International Relations, sponsored by the American Friends Committee (AFSC) and the Emergency Peace Campaign. Bayard was the only Cheyney student to participate,

[64] See *id.*, p. 18.
[65] See *id.*, p. 21.
[66] See *id.*, p. 21.
[67] See *id.*, p. 23.
[68] See *id.*, p. 24.
[69] See *id.*, p. 25.

and the Institute's antiwar message resonated with him, as he had become a Quaker the year before. Soon after, he met "Norman Whitney, a Quaker activist from the area.... Two decades Bayard's senior, the balding, bespectacled, and somewhat portly Whitney was single and ... lived in a household with an unmarried sister.... A professor of English at Syracuse University, ...[f]or Bayard, he became something of a spiritual mentor and confessor."[70] It was to Whitney that Rustin revealed his homosexual feelings and life, either then or later, and he always supported Rustin without any condemnation, a trust and support from a respected mentor that few gay men of that time and place would have enjoyed. Rustin would need it when, later on, other Quaker mentors would traumatically break with him over publicity about his criminal prosecution in California for gay sex.

Probably because of his sense of his homosexuality, Rustin leaves Cheyney before graduation. He moves to Harlem, presumably hoping to lead a more urban life style away from his family.[71] His family had seemed accepting of his bond with his male friends, "although sex was never the subject of conversation. Once, he remembered, Julia broached the subject obliquely, 'I want to recommend something to you,' she told him. 'In selecting your male friends, you should be careful that you associate with people who have as much to lose as you have.' When Bayard pushed her to explain, she said, 'You have good reputations.... People who do not have as much to lose as you have can be very careless.' Bayard sensed that Julia was telling him something very important."[72] Julia's concern appears to be not with homosexuality as such, but with concerns about the choice of sex partners, a worry about her grandson that suggests unusual understanding of his trust in partners not worthy of such trust with possibly calamitous consequences (prefiguring events in California that later almost ruined Rustin's public life). Julia's willingness even to discuss such issues even indirectly, in a period of such homophobic unspeakability, suggests an unusual loving support and understanding, like that of Norman Whitney as well. Moreover, Julia was clearly sympathetic to Quakerism, and Whitney was a Quaker activist. Quakerism, famously, was unique among forms of Christianity in the respect accorded women's voices, sometimes, as themselves ministers, which was why so many of the abolitionist feminists in the antebellum period were Quakers, often quite explicitly indicting the role patriarchy had been allowed to play in the interpretation of Christian texts and tradition.[73] Quakerism's indictment of slavery, racism, and sexism (all deeply patriarchal practices) and the role it accorded women's free and equal democratic voices show clearly its deeply anti-patriarchal, democratic, and rights-respecting character. Julia's willingness to engage her grandson even about the unspeakable and Norman Whitney's active later support, when Rustin

---

[70] See *id.*, pp. 26–27.

[71] For further on this point, see *id.*, pp. 27–29.

[72] *Id.*, pp. 28–29.

[73] See, on this point, David A. J. Richards, *Women, Gays, and the Constitution.*

desperately needed it, show a love for him that was not patriarchally confined, but a love outside the boundaries, humanely responsive to the person he was.

Moreover, Rustin's political resistance begins, after a short period with the Communist Party, through his association with other Quakers or Quaker sympathizers. In 1941 he joins the staff of A. J. Muste's Fellowship of Reconciliation (FOR), a Christian pacifist organization.[74] This job would forge his early aspirations, as political activism for American pacifism became the center of his life. Muste was a towering figure not only in pacifist resistance to World War II, but in labor activism and in opposition to imperialism and to the racism that motivated it, both abroad and at home. Inspired by the success of Gandhi's Satyagraha in South Africa and India, Muste saw early that such techniques might work in America as well. Having two blacks on his staff, Bayard Rustin and James Farmer, was an important way of linking resistance to the war to the growing sense that, in light of the fanatical racism of Hitler overseas, FOR and other such organizations must develop new ways of resisting racism at home. Rustin was almost from the start one of his most effective, courageous, and eloquent field operatives, his singing voice playing an important role.[75] When Rustin traveled for FOR in the American South, he refused to obey the requirements of racial segregation on buses, and was beaten by police officers when he refused to move to the back. According to D'Emilio, "Rustin maintained a Gandhian posture of refusing to fight back physically, attempting to communicate with his assailants, and holding out the religious grounding of his disobedience.... A few of the white passengers were moved enough to urge the police to desist from beating him, and one took the trouble of coming to the police station to speak up on his behalf."[76] All this was long before Montgomery.

Rustin could, as a Quaker, have legally sought exemption from military service as a conscientious objector, and performed alternative service in Quaker work camps, as Isherwood did. As a matter of conviction, however, he chose not to apply for the exemption, since he believed that the forms of alternative service would not express the resistance to war he believed was needed. He was convicted of violating the Selective Service Act of 1940 and imprisoned in 1943 in the federal prison at Ashland in Kentucky. Later, Rustin would describe his three years in federal prison as "the most profound and important experience I've ever had."[77] Some of this was, as John D'Emilio observes, that "[f]or Rustin, the crime of incarceration lays in its attempt to obliterate moral autonomy."[78] However, protest of the prison conditions themselves, including its racial segregation, became itself the object of Rustin's activism in collaboration with the many others, like himself, imprisoned there who had also

---

[74] See John D'Emilio, *Lost Prophet*, pp. 37–38.
[75] See *id.*, pp. 39–71.
[76] See *id.*, pp. 36–37.
[77] See *id.*, p. 85.
[78] Quoted at *id.*, p. 85.

refused to claim conscientious objector status.[79] Rustin apparently had consensual gay sex with other inmates, which led to further problems with the authorities and, as it turns out, with A. J. Muste, who made clear in a letter to Rustin that he had to choose between promiscuous gay sex or celibacy.[80] Much of the world, even well-intentioned people like Muste, imagined gay life as a simplistic binary, either promiscuous or celibate. Rustin, like so many other men of his era, struggling to be honest with himself within a culture that attacked such honesty, sought a way out of this binary.

After release from prison in 1946, Muste urged Rustin to focus on strategies of resistance to the racist caste system of the American South. Rustin was one of the key figures, in consultation with other civil rights leaders, who planned and executed the Journey of Reconciliation in which activists rode on interstate buses (that the Supreme Court had ordered desegregated just a few months prior, and challenged any attempt to enforce the racial segregation that was now illegal).[81] He also worked closely with A. Philip Randolph, who in 1942 had formed the March on Washington Movement that had successfully pressured President Roosevelt to establish the Fair Employment Practices Committee and to prohibit racial discrimination not only in the federal government but also in the defense industries.[82] Rustin now worked with Randolph to put pressure on the Truman administration to desegregate the American military; the effort succeeded.[83] There was also an increasingly international dimension to Rustin's work for FOR, including travel to India to talk with those who had worked with Gandhi and to Africa to talk with leaders there about anti-imperialism and decolonization.[84]

Rustin had a loving relationship for several years with David Platt,[85] later a similar relationship with Tom Kahn,[86] and the deeply loving relationship at the end of his life with Walter Naegle.[87] All these men were white. Rustin's first significant relationship came when a mutual friend introduced him to David Platt in 1943, and Platt visited and corresponded with him while Rustin was in prison; when in 1945 Rustin was allowed out of prison, at Julia's request, to visit his seriously ill grandfather, the couple had an unexpected opportunity to meet and make love. Rustin also had a long conversation with a woman who was in love with him, who offered him love and understanding. In a letter to Platt in 1945, Rustin writes of what the woman offered, namely, what she called "real love, real understanding, and confidence . . . to be with you thru light and darkness, to give all that I possess that the

---

[79] See *id.*, pp. 72–92.
[80] See *id.*, pp. 113–14.
[81] See *id.*, pp. 121–40.
[82] See *id.*, pp. 56–58.
[83] See *id.*, pp. 141–60.
[84] See *id.*, pp. 161–83.
[85] See, for example, *id.*, pp. 29, 68–71, 171–72.
[86] See *id.*, pp. 277–78, 320, 327, 340, 372–73, 466.
[87] See *id.*, pp. 483–86, 488–90.

goodness within you shall live and flower."[88] However, Rustin could not accept her offer "because I came to see after the most complete searching that the best for me lies elsewhere," and, without such an effort of choice, "I am less than a man."[89] Rustin thus defines manhood not patriarchally, as Muste did, but in terms of a free ethical voice and conviction, revealing that the gender binary and hierarchy had little hold on him. The letter ends with a reference to "Marie," which is code for Platt: "my promise to Marie (the details of which you have) stands not only as a barrier to any promiscuity but as a bond of real and spiritual love that can cut off any tendencies to feel lost or cut off from someone who cares."[90] What the letter reveals is that, against all the pressures Muste was then putting on him and the real alternative choices placed before him, Rustin as a matter of reflective conviction turns to a gay loving relationship with Platt. What the letter also reveals is Rustin's worries about temptations to "promiscuity" that would soon prove all too disastrously real.

The great crisis in Rustin's sense of vocation came with his highly publicized arrest and conviction for consensual gay sex in 1953 in Pasadena, California. Rustin was walking back to his hotel after giving a lecture in Pasadena:

> Just before 3:00 A.M., a car with two young white men cruised by slowly, and Rustin waved. After the driver pulled over, Rustin approached the car. "He asked us if we wanted a good time," one of them said later. "We asked him what he meant, he replied that he couldn't offer much, but he could blow us." The two still had with them the box of unused condoms . . . from their unsuccessful search for female companionship, and they accepted Rustin's offer. Rustin was in the back seat performing oral sex when two county police officers approached the car. The police promptly arrested the three of them on charges of lewd vagrancy. . . . In court that afternoon, the judge rejected an appeal to free Rustin on the condition that he leave the state immediately. Instead, he sentenced all three defendants to sixty days.[91]

Rustin's conviction was made public by local California papers. Muste felt betrayed after having warned Rustin against having gay sex. With no dissent within FOR, Muste fired Rustin.[92] "The FOR distributed the statement [of dismissal] widely among pacifists. In doing so, it ensured that a story buried deep within the local southern California press became common knowledge among the circles of people who mattered most to Rustin. Thus ended his dozen years of service to a Christian organization dedicated to peace and justice."[93]

---

[88] Bayard Rustin, *I Must Resist: Bayard Rustin's Life in Letters*, edited by Michael G. Long (San Francisco: City Lights Books, 2012), p. 65.

[89] *Id.*, p. 66.

[90] *Id.*, p. 67.

[91] See *id.*, p. 191.

[92] See *id.*, pp. 184–205.

[93] *Id.*, p. 193.

It was, of course, the homophobic McCarthy years, and Muste had warned Rustin nearly a decade earlier that he had to make a choice between his work and his gay sex life. The panic that motivated Muste's action was not very different, I believe, from the same motives of panic that led later black leaders, even Martin Luther King, Jr., not to acknowledge the role Rustin was crucially later to play in helping him understand and effect successful strategies of nonviolent resistance, when help was desperately needed by the quite inexperienced King. However, Muste's break with Rustin was more savagely homophobic, not only abruptly cutting off employment at a time when little other employment was available to a black man like Rustin, but breaking a relationship in which Rustin had, as a Quaker, invested his ethical heart and mind. A social worker at the time suggested cleaning jobs or a job as a domestic like a butler. D'Emilio acidly comments: "[s]uch was the plight of the man whom, a few months earlier, many were calling an American Gandhi."[94]

When Rustin returns to New York from California, he is understandably distraught, but receives the unconditional support of his closest friend Norman Whitney. Rustin later recalled Whitney's support with deep feeling: "When I got out of prison, he invited me to come and spend the week. And I think that saved me from myself because I was so despairing. . . . If it had not been for [his] support at that period, I would never have had the courage to pick myself up and go on."[95] Rustin also received help from a New York therapist, Dr. Robert Ascher, who came, like Rustin, from a pacifist background and thus "brought an understanding ear to the values and outlook of his patient whose principles, he thought, 'were absolutely right.'"[96] Ascher's aim was not, unlike much conventional psychiatry in that period, to change Rustin's sexual desires, but to put them in a perspective that might remove self-destructive forms of pursuing his desires (for example, the sex in Pasadena that had had such destructive consequences on his career). Why, in such a homophobia era, had Rustin been so self-destructively reckless? What emerged in therapy was Rustin's anger:

> He was angry at his mother for the circumstances of his birth, angry at his grandmother for approving everything he did, angry at whites for the constraints they placed on his life from an early age. "It's interesting that this boy with all this rage later becomes a pacifist," Ascher noted at the time.[97]

Ascher helped Rustin see that his childhood rage was quite justified, and urged him to see his pacifism as trying to master something, rage, he knew in himself and thus recognized in others. Ascher was concerned to help Rustin pursue his vocation without the public scandal, like his arrest and conviction, that could

[94] John D'Emilio, *Lost Prophet*, p. 205.
[95] Quoted in D'Emilio, *Lost Prophet*, p. 202.
[96] *Id.*, p. 202.
[97] *Id.*, p. 203.

destroy his work. He focuses, therefore, on getting Rustin to see his sexual adventures as an expression of anger, a way of getting back. The aim of Ascher's therapy was to channel Rustin's sexual desires in a less self-destructive way; believing that all sex combined erotic and aggressive features, Ascher's aim was to help Rustin change the balance in his sexual desires, whatever their object. Although it was not Ascher's purpose, he might equally well have made the same point about Rustin's pacifism: In light of Rustin's anger, which emerged in his psychoanalysis, was his pacifism or the way he practiced it as a counter-phobic defense against his own anger (as it may also have been for Isherwood)? Asher's point, however, was to help Rustin see that all sexual love combined loving and aggressive features, and the balance might well be altered in less self-destructive ways. What the therapy reveals, I believe, is that there can be an ethically creative role for anger and indignation like Rustin's insofar as it made him a shrewd student of violence in others, in particular, violent patriar-chal men. In helping Rustin give voice to his own anger, therapy may have deepened Rustin's sense of freeing ethical voice from the inner and outer forms of violence that repress voice. Thus, his therapy helps us understand how and why nonviolence played so important a role in his life and work and why, after his analysis, he became, if anything, a more effective and intelligent advocate and practitioner of nonviolence. Better understanding his own unconscious propensities to violence enabled him better to understand and deal with such propensities in others.

We saw earlier, in Isherwood's pacifism, that it was only in a relatively late novel, *A Single Man*, that Isherwood is able to give expression to the anger and indignation of gay men at the indignities homophobia inflicts on them. However, another ingredient of Rustin's anger must have been anger at homo-phobia, in particular, at Muste for his panic and cowardice in breaking with a man he loved and who loved him. What this sorry episode shows is how, even in men as committed to nonviolence as Muste was, patriarchal homophobia violently divides men from one another. Quakers were remarkable among Christians for the ways in which they had ethically resisted slavery as well as racism, sexism, and anti-Semitism. Yet here, when it comes to homophobia, there is not only no ethical voice to resist it, but there is complicity with its savage enforcement against a man who had surely earned Muste's love and respect. We see here yet again the consequences of the long homophobic tradition of the unspeakability of homosexuality so that even the most tolerant of men could react to a gay man and friend with fear and loathing and violence on the basis of some intimate sense of their manhood that homosexuality put at threat.

It is against all these odds that Bayard Rustin refuses to surrender either his vocation or his gay sexual relationships to men who understood and shared his interests. His relationships with Tom Kahn and, later, Walter Naegle are illustrative:

Though Kahn was quarter-century younger than Rustin [they met in 1956 when Kahn was a teenager], he was intellectually precocious, well read, a good writer, and, already as a teenager, thoroughly engrossed by progressive politics and social movements. He could more than hold his own in conversations. Even while Rustin was mentoring Kahn politically, the relationship had a quality of peerness that had been missing in Rustin's romantic life before. The fact that Kahn was also, in the memory of Dave McReynolds, "very good looking . . . a very attractive guy," made the budding relationship all the more appealing. It was all "love and romance." . . . Before long, Kahn was spending many of his evenings at Rustin's apartment and, in the observation of friends, had practically moved in. As the decade drew to a close, Rustin seemed to have found not only thrilling political engagement but also an intimacy with someone who shared his public commitments.[98]

Rustin met Walter Naegle in April 1977 in Times Square when Naegle was twenty-seven and Rustin was sixty-five. They would live together as lovers until the end of Rustin's life at age seventy-five in 1987. In an interview in the last year of his life, Rustin reflected on what Naegle meant to him:

The most important thing is that after many years of seeking, I've finally found a solid, ongoing relationship with one individual with whom I have everything in common, everything. . . . I spent years looking for exciting sex instead of looking for a person who was compatible. I really did. I overemphasized sex and underemphasized relationships. I'm not talking for anyone but myself. That was the basis of my problem. I had three other early experiences. One lasted for four years and one for three, but they were never really real. I was trying to make something of them, but they were not real. It seems unbelievable at my age, particularly. Let me tell you what my final answer is in this regard. . . . It's a matter of being lucky enough to run into someone with whom one is just completely *simpatico*. I don't think that we do it. I think it is, somehow, done unto us. It's like being born. We haven't anything to do with it.[99]

Rustin here expresses the sense of awe that many of us feel in the arms of our beloved. However, his impression of love as luck belies the fundamental parts of his personality, a lifetime in the making, that made such love with Neagle possible.

The key to Rustin's resisting voice is, I believe, that Rustin, like Garrison, was released from the patriarchal gender binary and hierarchy by loving relationships with maternal caretakers, good friends like Norman Whitney and the understanding of Dr. Ascher whose voices he had come to value and respect. He carried this ethical freedom further and more creatively by the way in which challenging patriarchy was at the heart of how he broke the Love Laws. Breaking the Love Laws, as we saw in earlier chapters, does not in itself release creative resisting voice; it may, as in the case of Rustin's Pasadena encounter, disastrously ruin lives as targets of patriarchal violence. It is part of what is remarkable about Rustin that, after such a disaster, he

---

[98] *Id.*, p. 278.
[99] Quoted at *id.*, p. 485.

found a way through loving gay relationships to expose and resist through nonviolence the violence that patriarchy enforces. Rustin carries that ethical voice within
him, and for this reason breaks the Love Laws by resisting patriarchy. Loving men
and white men is an expression of that ethical voice's resistance to the lies and
violence of racism and homophobia, both of which he experienced first hand in his
life, as a black gay man. What makes this possible is coming into loving relationship
with another person as the individual he or she is without imposing on oneself or
them a gender binary and hierarchy that rests on disassociation and idealizing or
denigrating stereotypes. Rustin was able to carry this ethical voice so far because, in
loving across the boundaries of both gender and race, he released his ethical
intelligence from the role patriarchy plays in dividing us from one another, both
in terms of gender and in terms of race. His own experience of loving relationship
made possible a moral authority in himself stronger than the powerful homophobic
forces arrayed against him.

It is because Rustin broke the Love Laws in both these ways that he came through
love to the creative ethical intelligence that could see something more that patriarchal black men could not see, namely, that racism, which had certainly harmed
blacks, had harmed whites as well. Rustin did not bring to his love for men, and
white men in particular, the patriarchal gender binary and hierarchy and thus came
to see both in himself and in them a common humanity – both the full range of
thoughts and emotions all persons share, and the empowering sense of equal voice in
real relationships of love and respect. Very early on, as I earlier observed, Rustin saw
that nonviolence as a response to injustice had a resonance in whites: "Rustin
maintained a Gandhian posture of refusing to fight back physically, attempting to
communicate with his assailants, and holding out the religious grounding of his
disobedience.... A few of the white passengers were moved enough to urge the
police to desist from beating him, and one took the trouble of coming to the police
station to speak up on his behalf."[100] American racism, like other forms of irrational
prejudice, rested on what I earlier called moral slavery, the violent suppression of
any voice that might reasonably contest its stereotypes. Nonviolent resistance to
such injustice, precisely because it expressed such an ethically resisting voice,
elicited racist violence, and thus exposed the ugly truth of racism, namely, that it
rested on violence and lies. What Rustin knew from his love for white men (like
Tom Kahn and Walter Naegle) is that, under the armor of patriarchal manhood
that had been instilled in them, there was a human ethical voice that was still alive
and could respond to a loving relationship of free and equal persons. Rustin had
experienced this in his own love life, so he knew there was a basis in experience for
love across the boundaries of gender and race. It was this basis in experience
(breaking the Love Laws in the way he did) that led Rustin to play the creative role
he did in practicing nonviolence as mode of resistance to injustice. It was a way of

[100] See *id.*, pp. 36–37.

giving voice to ethical resistance as an expression of love that could and would find resonance in the ethical voice of whites, joining in a new form of relationship based on justice, not violence.

Tested in the crucible both of his experience in his gay love life and his experience as an activist, Rustin played a crucial and creative role in introducing nonviolence as a strategy of resistance long before other black leaders saw its importance. After the crisis of 1953, when he was fired from FOR, he worked for the War Resisters League (WRL) for the next twelve years, his work for them focusing largely on pacifism.[101] His experience and background in nonviolence would lead to his important contributions to the civil rights movement that began to transform American political culture in the late 1950s.

Crucially, there was Rustin's involvement with Martin Luther King, Jr., and the Montgomery bus boycott. "In King, Rustin found the person who might take his own deepest aspirations and broadcast them to the nation and the world."[102] In response to his leadership, King's home had been bombed, as had the home of another leader; pacifists worried "that the black community might respond in kind and unleash a race war that the oppressed were sure to lose."[103] Leaders of the WRL decided that someone with experience with nonviolence had to be sent to Montgomery to advise King, and in February 1956, Rustin was chosen. Rustin and King initiated "a long and complex relationship that would last until King's assassination. Rustin became teacher to a pupil whose fame would soon outstrip his mentor's."[104] Rustin had long experience with Gandhian techniques of nonviolence, and he advised King to make it central to his leadership and to undertake the kind of disciplined training of his followers that the correct execution of nonviolence required. King modeled his leadership on Rustin's advice. After worries about the Pasadena scandal of 1953 surfaced, Rustin left Montgomery but continued to be a crucial adviser to King, putting him in contact with supporters in New York and raising money. Rustin returned to Montgomery to advise King on the need for a more permanent organization when the boycott ended, conversations that led to the Southern Christian Leadership Conference,[105] and Rustin continued to work with King and build Northern support for the struggle in the South,[106] including placing a full-page appeal in The *New York Times*, signed by various luminaries, calling for support of King's nonviolent movement.[107] Once again, however, homophobia intervened, only of a sort without any basis in fact whatsoever. Representative Adam Clayton Powell was jealous of King's growing support and the role Rustin was playing in advancing his aims and program, so Powell threatened to go public about a sexual

---

[101] See John D'Emilio, *Lost Prophet*, pp. 206–22.
[102] *Id.*, p. 226.
[103] *Id.*, p. 226.
[104] *Id.*, p. 230.
[105] See *id.*, pp. 223–38.
[106] See *id.*,, pp. 262–78.
[107] See *id.*, pp. 292–93.

affair of King and Rustin (no such affair had occurred) unless King broke his relationship with Rustin, which King did, once again removing Rustin from a role he loved and played so brilliantly. What shocked Rustin was that, in contrast to Muste's breaking with him, there was no truth in Powell's allegation, but King experienced such panic that he acquiesced.[108] King's panic marks the psychological hold of American homophobia even on him.

Despite his break with King, Rustin was drawn back into civil rights activism through his relationship to A. Philip Randolph, who "began to reminisce about the march that never happened on the eve of World War II, when he threatened to bring the black masses to Washington to demand jobs. Perhaps Rustin raised the idea of a march himself, aware of what it meant to the older man. In either case, Rustin knew in a flash that he would devote himself to the project."[109] In fact, Rustin would play the central organizational role in planning and executing the 1963 March on Washington, which, in the wake of the events in Birmingham, would play a pivotal role in giving the voice of Martin Luther King, Jr., the resonance with and the connection to the American people that would lead to the Civil Rights Act of 1964 and the Voting Rights Act of 1965.[110] Rustin's public role in the March on Washington made him a target for attacks in the Senate by Senator Strom Thurmond, including an explicit statement in the Congressional Record about the Pasadena conviction and that Rustin was a sexual pervert. Thurmond had, however, gone too far for civil rights leaders, who, led by Randolph, publicly defended Rustin's integrity.[111] For Rustin, it was an extraordinary moment of validation by black civil rights leaders, some of whom (King) had once broken with him. Black leaders may have felt a public need to protect one of their own from a conspicuously racist white leader (in contrast, King's earlier breaking with Rustin arose from the rather hysterical homophobic threat of a black leader, Adam Clayton Powell, and was never made public until much later). The long-term, unbroken affection for Rustin of A. Phillip Randolph, conspicuously not a Baptist minister, may also have been crucial.

Both Rustin's life and work centered on the innovation and increasingly effective implementation of nonviolent civil disobedience as a way of exposing the crucial role irrational repressive violence played in enforcing the structural injustices I have called moral slavery, including extreme religious intolerance (anti-Semitism), racism, sexism, and homophobia. Enforcing the gender binary and hierarchy enlists gender stereotypes to stigmatize a group – Jews, people of color, women, homosexuals – as essentially feminized inferiors, and requiring hierarchical controls by their superiors. What makes Rustin so remarkable among those who resist the injustices arising from moral slavery is the way he found, well before other leaders of the civil

---

[108] See *id.*, pp. 297–301.
[109] See *id.*, p. 327.
[110] See *id.*, pp. 326–57.
[111] See *id.*, pp. 346–50.

rights movement in the United States, the key to effective resistance in nonviolence based on challenging the gender binary and hierarchy. If a black gay man like Rustin – stigmatized as a feminized man, being black and gay – could find and speak in a nonviolent free and equal resisting voice, cooperating in a movement of resistance, the very terms of his resistance – freedom and equality – freed both himself and others, black and white, gay and straight, from the patriarchal controls on voice that had long held them unjustly in subjection.

No one better understood than Rustin the irrational violence directed against blacks and gays, and he himself, as his psychoanalysis by Dr. Ascher shows, carried in his psyche rage and indignation against such injustice, including the constraints on resisting voice that such injustice imposed. I include in Rustin's wholly just rage and indignation what he experienced in the homophobic abandonment endured at the hands of Muste and others, men he loved and who he thought loved him. Rustin could at this point have abandoned pacifism and his gay lifestyle, but he did not. Having come to better understand his own rage and the intrapsychic role pacifism played in his defense against such anger, Rustin – through the understanding and support of Ascher and Norman Whitney, both white men – held on both to his pacifism and his gay loves, only now with a more real, complex understanding of the ambivalent balance between rage and voice in his own psyche. His own commitment to nonviolence may now have made more critical personal sense to him than ever before, as the voice he expressed in his analysis revealed to him his own anger, and, if anything, showed how voice may liberate us from unconscious impulses to anger we can understand in both ourselves and others, and can acknowledge and integrate. This self-understanding may have deepened the intelligence and self-mastery he brought both to nonviolence, as he played the crucial role he did in the civil rights movement (despite homophobic rebuffs), and to his love life. It was because Rustin's psyche so well understood the role violence played in the psyches of all men, black and white, distorted by patriarchy, that he understood as well how such violence might be understood and exposed and even resisted by holding onto a sense of personal connection even with those who despised and rejected him. Rustin here drew upon the long tradition of nonviolent resistance of Garrison and the radical abolitionists – women and men, black and white – as an example of what might be done in the United States. What he brought to this remarkable transformative enterprise was what he knew about the role violence played in American patriarchal manhood, black and white. No one understood this injustice better than Bayard Rustin, both as a black man and a gay man, who experienced violence when he challenged the inferiority of both black men and gay men. The power of nonviolent civil disobedience – if one was disciplined enough to bear its demands – was that its very nonviolence (just saying that a practice was unjust) was greeted with violence, thus exposing the fascist basis of structural injustice. If the evils of structural injustice rested on legitimating violence against voice, its injustice could be revealed, at least in a nation with increasingly strong traditions of free speech, precisely by nonviolence. What made this psychologically possible for Rustin and thus made him a leader in understanding and implementing nonviolence in the civil rights movement was a sense of the loving moral community that could exist between white and black people. Martin Luther King, Jr., expressed the same thought when he gave an ethically compelling sense to Jesus's injunction, "Love your enemies," Matthew 5:44, to which he appealed as early as 1957 as the proof text for the demands of his movement. As he put the point:

> So this morning, as I look into your eyes, and into the eyes of all my brothers in Alabama and all over American and over the world, I say to you, "I love you. I would rather die than hate you." And I'm foolish enough to believe that through the power of this love somewhere, men of the most recalcitrant bent will be transformed. And then we will be in God's kingdom.[112]

For Bayard Rustin, the though "I love you. I would rather die than hate you," was not only the interpretation of a Biblical text; it arose from his experience of the loves across the boundaries that had made him whole, including his passionate sexual loves of white men.

It was Walter Naegle, the love of Rustin's life, to whom Rustin disclosed more of himself than he ever had, who persuaded Rustin, as the culmination of his life's work, to take a public stance in defending gay rights. It was the experience of this loving relationship, like the comparable relationship of Isherwood and Bachardy and its consequences in Isherwood's advocacy of gay rights, that enabled Rustin to find and speak the ethical voice of gay rights, publicly lobbying the New York City Council to add sexual orientation to the list of protected categories in the human rights code. He observed: in the 1960s, "The barometer of people's thinking was the black community. Today, the barometer of where one is on human rights questions is no longer the black, it's the gay community."[113] It was such love that clearly made possible, near the end of his life, the ethical voice for gay rights that was the capstone of his life of brilliant resistance to injustice.

---

[112] See Martin Luther King, Jr., "Loving Your Enemies," in Clayborne Carson and Peter Holloran, eds., *A Knock at Midnight: Inspiration from the Great Speeches of Reverent Martin Luther King, Jr.* (New York: Warner Books, 2000), pp. 41–64, at p. 59.

[113] *Id.*, p. 490.

6

James Baldwin on Love and Voice

If vocation and love are the two questions that must be faced in a well-lived life, Bayard Rustin and James Baldwin shared both a vocation, finding a voice of ethical resistance to the racism that afflicted them as black men, and struggling to find a voice as well for loving gay relationships, including relationships with white men. Both found it easier to voice their resistance to racism, even though their gay loving relationships gave rise to the remarkably creative voices of each man as leaders in resisting American racism, as I have already shown in the case of Rustin and will now show for Baldwin. Only at the end of their lives do both men give voice to gay rights. Both men were raised in loving relationship to maternal caretakers, and religion was an important force in their lives. However, whereas Rustin drew inspiration from anti-patriarchal Quakerism, Baldwin's voice, as an artist resisting racism, developed in resistance to the Baptist patriarchal religion of his tyrannical and violent stepfather. Baldwin's artistic voice arose in trying to understand the violence of his father's religion that regarded all whites as evil and all blacks as good, which Baldwin saw as connected to the role patriarchy played in shaping the sexuality and sense of manhood of black men. In coming to terms with these issues both as a black and gay man, Baldwin's novels and essays explored the intrapsychic structure of the propensities to violence, in both white and black men, arising from patriarchy. It is the central subject of both his essays and novels. Because Baldwin had experienced so much violence from his stepfather, his struggle for resisting voice was, I believe, much more difficult and fraught than that of Bayard Rustin. Baldwin always had the love of his mother, but she had eight additional children with Baldwin's stepfather, who clearly preferred his natural children. The stepfather's violence not only took the form of abuse of his wife and beatings of all his children, but the humiliation of Baldwin in particular: "I was not only considered by my father to be ugly, I was considered by everyone to be 'strange,'"[1] a euphemism, I believe, for Baldwin's gender-bending style as a black boy and man (including his interests in and

---

[1] James Baldwin, *The Devil Finds Work*, in *Collected Essays*, edited by Tony Morrison (New York: The Library of America, 1998), pp. 479–572, at p. 483.

voracious reading of literature) all of which would have been interpreted not only by his stepfather, in this homophobic period, as effeminacy. The intrapsychic effects of such judgments on the self-conception of a sensitive, highly intelligent boy, who early on recognized his homosexuality, must have been crippling, including on his early gay sex life in New York City – a gay world that uncritically valorized both conventional good looks and masculinity. What apparently sustained him during this dark period was not only the love of his mother and the love of his siblings, for whom Baldwin, the eldest, was a central caretaker (assisting his besieged mother), but also, as we shall see, his education in the public schools of the New York City of this period and, for a brief period, holding off his stepfather, as Baptist minister, by competitively becoming himself an admired youthful religious speaker (the subject of his first novel, Go Tell It on the Mountain). Bayard Rustin never endured, at least as a boy, these kinds of conflicts. The question must be, and it is the real question we must ask ourselves about Baldwin, is how he not only survived, but found his astonishing, revelatory, honest voice in his novels, plays, and essays. This process crucially included leaving New York City and his family and living in Paris and falling in love with a white man. All his novels were written in Europe, and yet they are, like those of Henry James (whom Baldwin admired), deeply American. It was, I argue, Baldwin's way of breaking the Love Laws (loving a man, and a white man) that empowered his remarkable artistic and critical voice. Love across the boundaries is, I believe, the key – a love so central to Baldwin's finding his voice that breaking the Love Laws becomes the central subject of both his art and his essays.

Baldwin was born to Berdis Jones in New York City's Harlem Hospital on August 2, 1924, an illegitimate child who never knew who his real father was.[2] Baldwin's stepfather, David Baldwin, was a preacher and laborer who came to the North from New Orleans in the early 1920s and married Berdis; they would have eight children together in addition to James, the eldest child of the family. Reverend David Baldwin became, for Baldwin, in the words of his brilliant biographer and close personal friend, David Leeming, "the archetypal black father, one generation removed from slavery, prevented by the ever-present shadow and the frequently present effects of racial discrimination from providing his family with what they needed most – their birthright, their identity as individuals rather than as members of a class or a race."[3] In the pulpit, following the tradition of the Pentecostal black church, David Baldwin "called down the wrath of God on the sinners of the white Sodom and Gomorrah"; at home, "the father's prophecy took the form of an arbitrary and puritanical discipline and a depressing air of bitter frustration which did nothing to alleviate the pain of poverty and oppression."[4] The stepfather humiliated his stepson, "making fun of his eyes and calling him the ugliest child

[2]   David Leeming, *James Baldwin: A Biography* (New York: Knopf, 1994), p. 4.
[3]   *Id.*, p. 5.
[4]   *Id.*, p. 5.

he had ever seen."[5] And, "[t]here were times in Baldwin's adolescence when he nearly came to blows with his stepfather. They fought because he read books, because he liked movies, because he had white friends. For Reverend Baldwin all these interests were a threat to the salvation which could only come from God."[6] His bitterness and hardness alienated even members of his church, and he was less sought after as a minister. In his late years, he became suspicious even of his family, accusing them of wanting to poison him. Eventually, Reverend Baldwin lost his job and went mad; in 1943, he was committed to a mental hospital, where he died of tuberculosis. James Baldwin came to see that "this man, who frightened him so much that 'I could never again be frightened of anything else,' was a victim of a morally bankrupt religion, a morally bankrupt society, that he was a black parody of that bankruptcy."[7]

That Baldwin was able at least to stand his ground against a father he and all his siblings came to hate was due to countervailing influences on his early life. The greatest such influence was his mother, to whom he remained close throughout his life. If his stepfather saw the world in terms of racist stereotypes, "Berdis Baldwin constantly reminded her children that people must not be put on pedestals or scaffolds, that people have to loved for their faults as well as their virtues, their ugliness as well as their beauty."[8] There was also a white schoolteacher, Orilla Miller, and her sister, Henrietta, and later Evan Winfield, who "included him in their family, not only sharing cultural activities [taking him to the theatre] but as a participant in their political discussions."[9] These friends could not, however, help him with his blackness. Two African American teachers at Frederick Douglass Junior High School, which Baldwin – then called Jimmy – entered in the fall of 1935, afforded models of how to fill the gap: Countee Cullen (already an important poet of the Harlem Renaissance) and Herman W. Porter. Cullen, in particular, "brought him into the school's literary club, which he had founded, and spent a great deal of time working with him on both poetry and fiction."[10] Baldwin graduated from junior high school in the summer of 1938, "a summer during which he was to be nearly overwhelmed by sexuality and, almost at the same moment, by religion," becoming a rather successful preacher for a few years, which enhanced his self-confidence. On Countee Cullen's advice, he had applied to and been accepted in 1938 into the well-known De Witt Clinton High School in the Bronx, where he was exposed to excellent largely white teachers, some with Ph.D.s, formed close friendships with other boys, all white and Jewish, and read and wrote. Baldwin shared with one of these friends, Emile Capouya, that he had

[5] *Id.*, p. 6.
[6] *Id.*, p. 7.
[7] *Id.*, p. 8.
[8] *Id.*, p. 9.
[9] *Id.*, p. 16
[10] *Id.*, p. 22.

recently learned of his illegitimacy, and, bursting into tears, had decided his stepfather's church could not be his, and left the pulpit. Capouya suggested to Baldwin that he should meet the black painter, Beauford Delaney, who lived in Greenwich Village. "Jimmy was not yet fully aware of his own homosexuality or of the demands of his vocation, and Beauford, himself a homosexual, a minister's son, and an artist, was there, as a father in art, to help his younger version of himself though a crucial passage."[11] Delaney would remain a good friend to Baldwin both in New York City and later in Paris, when they had each moved there.

At the end of his high school and preaching careers, Baldwin felt increasingly trapped as the eldest male child of a family with a jobless father in ill health, a working mother, and eight hungry brothers and sisters; however, at the same time, he felt pulled away from them by the sense of himself as an artist and as a gay man. For a while, he joined Capouya working at a defense-related job in New Jersey, but his heart was not in his work, and, when a waitress refused to serve him because of his race, he exploded. In a rage, he threw a mug at her; it missed, but shattered the window behind her. He got away, "[b]ut, what worried him more than the fact that he 'had been ready to commit murder,' the fact 'that my *real* life was in danger, and not from anything other people might do but from the hatred I carried in my heart.'"[12] After the death of his stepfather in 1943, Baldwin moved back with his family in their Harlem apartment, but soon after decided he had to move again, living first with Beauford in Greenwich Village and then with others.

He had some affairs with women, including a white Jewish woman, but more numerous one-night relationships with men, now telling Capouya that he was homosexual. Prejudice interfered with his sex life, as his manner was effeminate and he was often verbally abused "as a 'queer' by men who acted very differently when they were alone with him. Baldwin was well aware then of the agony that plagued the lives of these ostensibly 'straight' males, who roamed the streets and men's rooms of the Village … searching for 'faggots.' Not being attracted to men whom he considered to be pretentiously effeminate – men who 'pretended to be women'" and thus "inevitably found himself in bed with the more ambiguous sort, and he suffered the abuse that derived from their shame."[13]

The great love of these Village years was Eugene Worth, an African American man who was not gay and with whom Baldwin did not have sex, and who, like Rufus in *Another Country*, committed suicide in 1946 by jumping off the George Washington Bridge. Vivaldo, an Italian American, straight man who is Baldwin's voice in *Another Country*, comes to regard with guilt his failure of physical intimacy with Rufus as a failure of love when such love was desperately needed; and Baldwin himself, although as a gay man, expressed a similar remorse over the death of Worth,

[11] *Id.*, p. 33.
[12] *Id.*, p. 40.
[13] *Id.*, pp. 45–46.

who had once wondered to Baldwin whether he, Worth, was in love with him; Baldwin confesses in one of his late essays, "I was to hurt a great many people by being unable to imagine that anyone could possibly be in love with an ugly boy like me. . . . However, when he was dead, I realized that I would have done anything whatever to have been able to hold him in this world."[14] Baldwin had been breaking the Love Laws for some time, but had not yet been in love and acted on such love. It is only when Baldwin goes to France that he confesses: "I fell in love. Or, more accurately, I realized, and accepted for the first time that love was not merely a general, human possibility, not merely the disaster it had so often, been for me . . .; it was among *my* possibilities, for here it was, breathing and belching beside me, and it was the key to life."[15]

Baldwin was haunted by the death of Worth both as an artist (Rufus in *Another Country*) and as a man, expressing his own fears about the loss of love or the inability to love and a rage – the uncontrollable rage that frightened him in his response to the New Jersey waitress – that he might turn on himself. "Suicide was a subject that obsessed him throughout his life. He lost several close friends by that route and attempted it himself at least four times."[16]

Through friends, Baldwin was now introduced to writers, including Richard Wright, who read some of his work and liked it. Baldwin wrote essays, but wanted to work on novels; he "had gone about as far as he could without facing his 'demons' head-on."[17] By 1948, a good friend advised him: "Get out – you'll die if you stay here."[18]

Baldwin moved from New York to Paris for the same kind of personal and artistic reasons that Isherwood and Auden had earlier moved from Britain to America. First, there was the sense that their lives as gay men could not flourish without some separation from their families and the larger values their families embodied. Second, the artistic voices of all these men arose as an expression of their resisting voices to British patriarchal manhood (Isherwood and Auden) or to American patriarchal racism (Baldwin), and all these men came to believe they would be freer to develop as artists outside the country whose homophobia so afflicted them. Isherwood's whole artistic voice arose in resistance to his mother's Myth of the Dead War Hero, just as Baldwin would find his artistic voice through resistance to his patriarchally violent stepfather and the racism that destroyed him.

The move from his home country to a foreign country was profoundly transformative for Baldwin. Falling in love for the first time in his life and with a white

---

[14] See James Baldwin, *The Price of the Ticket*, in James Baldwin, *Collected Essays*, edited by Toni Morrison (New York: The Library of America, 1998), pp. 830–42, at p. 833.

[15] James Baldwin, *No Name in the Street*, *op. cit.*, pp. 365–66.

[16] David Leeming, *op. cit.*, p. 12.

[17] *Id.*, p. 53.

[18] Quoted at *id.*, p. 54.

European man in Europe released both the astonishing ethical voice of his pathbreaking investigation of the psychology of American racism in his influential essay, *Notes of a Native Son* (1955), and the artistic voice that revealed this psychology in his first three pathbreaking novels, *Go Tell It on the Mountain* (1952), *Giovanni's Room* (1956), and *Another Country* (1962). Both the essay and the novels – probably Baldwin's most enduring achievements – arose from his loving gay relationship to a white man:

> Lucien Happersberger was a Swiss who had left home in search of excitement and success in Paris. In Lucien, Jimmy found the "love of my life." He was a street boy, motivated at first more by the drive to survive in a hostile environment than by any homosexual cravings, but he came to love Jimmy with genuine depth. Apparently, oblivious to what people thought of their relationship, he did not mind being called Jimmy's lover even though, during the greater part of their friendship over the next thirty-nine years, he technically was not.[19]

During their several years together, "Jimmy and Lucien developed an emotional closeness that Baldwin had never experienced before,"[20] an experience Baldwin himself called the "love of my life." The love affair did not last: "Lucien was easygoing and relaxed about the relationship. Jimmy was not. He wanted a mate, Lucien wanted a copain who would understand his need for women as well. During the years that they knew each other, Lucien was to marry three times and to produce two children. The first marriage would occur within two years of their initial meeting."[21] Baldwin would go on to have many other sexual relationships to white and increasingly young black men, always seeking what he had discovered in his love affair with Lucien in what he imagined and hoped would be a long-term creative relationship of equals. His last novel, *Just Above My Head* (1978), gives expression to what he sought in the relationship of two black men, Arthur, a singer, and Jimmy, a pianist, who both loved and inspired one another and performed together – not unlike, I believe, the reality of the Britten–Pears relationship. Baldwin never found any such long-term relationship, in part "because he was drawn not to other homosexuals but to men who were sometimes willing to act homosexually, importantly, in response to the need for money and shelter or to what can only be called his personal magnetism and persuasiveness"[22]; the resentment of these men "sometimes led to beatings, and in later years to his becoming the victim of outrageous acts of embezzlement and theft"[23]; and he sometimes despaired (thus, the suicide attempts). Nevertheless, he held onto the sense of its possibility and, of course, its value, something he could not conceive before Lucien: "Every lover he had after Lucien had to compete with the memory of him, the possibility of his return, or his

[19] *Id.*, pp. 74–75.
[20] *Id.*, p. 75.
[21] *Id.*, pp. 75–76.
[22] *Id.*, p. 76.
[23] *Id.*, p. 76.

presence down the street, next door, or in the next room."[24] Something in his relationship to Lucien opened Baldwin's heart and mind not only to the possibility and value of gay love, but to its reality, which was, he discovered, close at hand if he could but grasp and hold onto it. It was the sense of this reality, so close at hand, that led to Baldwin's astonishing investigation of what held him and others back, namely, the violence directed at any love that challenged the irrational boundaries imposed by patriarchy – in particular, anti-Semitism, racism, sexism, and homophobia. Strikingly, "the love of his life," Lucien, was with him as death approached. Songs of Bessie Smith were on the television. "These were songs he had listened to on the Swiss mountain with Lucien as he wrote his first novel. Now Lucien was there and Bessie Smith was singing again."[25] It was when he lived intimately with Lucien in an isolated Swiss village that he found the creative voice of his essay, *Notes of a Native Son*, and his astonishing first novel, *Go Tell It on the Mountain*,[26] and Baldwin would continue to draw on what he had learned from the relationship even after it ended, in his remarkable next two novels, *Giovanni's Room* and *Another Country*.

Baldwin broke the Love Laws with a man and a man who was white and from a different culture, but in a way that Baldwin had never experienced before because he had never fallen in love and been loved in this way. It was this experience of real relationship, free and improvisatory, full of "laughter, food, sex, and, above all, drink,"[27] that released Baldwin from the hold of the internalized racial stereotypes that afflicted his violently racist stepfather. Through this loving experience Baldwin came to see in himself and Lucien the same range of human thoughts and feelings and free voice in relationship (thus, free of both the gender binary and hierarchy), and the centrality for both of them of the human need for loving and being loved, the north star of Baldwin's life and work. The question this raised for Baldwin is how and why such love had previously been for him so unthinkable, indeed the object of fear and anger and violence by others and himself. The question became real for Baldwin through the experience of gay love, and in several of his novels he answers the question in terms of what divides gay men from such love, or what brings a straight man to such love with a gay man. In *Giovanni's Room*, David, a white American, had come to acknowledge and explore his homosexuality in a love affair in Paris with an Italian, Giovanni; when he abruptly rejects Giovanni in a rather savagely unfeeling way, ostensibly to marry a white woman, Giovanni confronts David with his coldness and terror and his resulting self-deceived failure of relationship, which would poison his life: "Giovanni has no one to talk to, and no one to be with, and where he has found a lover who is neither man nor woman, nothing that

---

[24] *Id.*, p. 76.

[25] *Id.*, p. 385.

[26] See James Baldwin, *Go Tell It on the Mountain*, in James Baldwin, *Early Novels and Stories*, edited by Toni Morrison (New York: The Library of America, 1998), pp. 1–215.

[27] David Leeming, *James Baldwin*, p. 75.

I can know or touch."[28] What David cannot and will not see is what Giovanni had seen revealed in him in their passionate love, that he "is neither man nor woman." Similarly, in *Another Country*, when Vivaldo, a straight man, unburdens his heart to and eventually makes love to a gay man, Eric, he sees that Eric lives in the truth of human love and relationship: "It was a quality to which great numbers of people would respond without knowing to what it was that they were responding. There was great force in the face, and great gentleness. But, as most women are not gentle, nor most men strong, it was a face which suggested, resonantly, in the depths, the truth about our natures."[29] The truth about our natures is that the gender binary and hierarchy – the heart of patriarchy – are false, and destructively false because they cut us off from loving relationships based on freedom and equality. Baldwin saw this destructive force as quite general, cutting off straight women and men as well from real relationship, as when, in *Another Country*, Vivaldo and his married woman friend, Cass, approach having a relationship in which Vivaldo can speak of his deepest worries, Vivaldo draws back: "feeling his hope and his hope of safety threatened by invincible, unnamed forces within himself."[30] Baldwin now could see from experience that his stepfather's demonization of whites was as false as his idealization of blacks, resting on the violence and lies by which patriarchy enforces the gender binary and hierarchy, violence and lies that Baldwin had himself endured, as an effeminate and "strange" boy at the hands of his stepfather and so many others. Everything we know about trauma, and the violence Baldwin endured at the hands of his stepfather and others was traumatic, and clarifies how Baldwin, a child, would have identified with his aggressor, absorbing his gender stereotypes into his own psyche, clarifying why he would, before Lucien, have acted on his homosexual feelings in self-punishing ways. Perhaps Baldwin never entirely freed his personal life from the burdens of such trauma, but his love affair with Lucien showed him there was a way out, and he was to spend the rest of his life showing others what he had discovered even though, tragically, he never fully realized his hope for enduring love with another man. It is a mark of the continuing power of patriarchy that it sometimes remains intractably at work in our intimate lives, long after we have resisted it elsewhere. Nonetheless, effectively freed, for the first time in his life, from the gender binary and hierarchy that enforces patriarchy by repressing resisting voice, Baldwin found the voice to write his first great essay and most brilliant novel, a novel in which he shows what he had learned through the experience of love about how patriarchy destroys love, as it had destroyed his stepfather. Lucien was at this time his lover and companion.

---

[28] See James Baldwin, *Giovanni's Room*, in James Baldwin, *Early Novels and Stories*, pp. 221–360, at pp. 334–35.
[29] James Baldwin, *Another Country* (New York: Vintage International, 1990) (first published, 1960), p. 330.
[30] *Id.*, p. 237.

What Baldwin had discovered that would become the subject of his essays, novels, and plays was both an astonishing insight into the personal and political psychology of patriarchy, and a corresponding insight into how culture, in particular, American culture had both constructed its sense of identity in terms of this repressive psychology and yet made possible and imperative a resisting voice that might and would and should challenge its injustice. Baldwin was himself to exemplify such liberal voice for Americans, white and black, gay and straight, of his remarkable generation of both transformative political change and reaction, in which he came to play an increasingly important role as a public figure in America's vibrant civil society.

Baldwin explains how he came to a sense of the American dimension of the problem in *Stranger in the Village*,[31] the last essay in *Notes of a Native Son*.[32] He reflects on his experience of living with Lucien in an isolated Swiss village, where no blacks had ever been seen. Baldwin was struck by the response to his strangeness of the Swiss: "All of the physical characteristics of the Negro which had caused me, in America, a very different and almost forgotten pain were nothing less than miraculous – or infernal – in the eyes of the village people. . . . In all of this, in which it must be conceded there was the charm of genuine wonder and in which there was certainly no element of intentional unkindness, there was yet no suggestion that I was human: I was simply a living wonder."[33] The very different response to him of the Swiss prompted reflection on the distinctive history of America, in which blacks were coercively brought to America as slaves stripped of their history and yet, in contrast to the relationship of European imperialists to the blacks and other ethnicities they ruled over in distant colonies, American blacks were intimately part of American culture, including, paradoxically, its ideals of democracy and human rights. It was this very intimacy and the contradiction of slavery and racism to their democratic ideals that led Americans to "the idea of white supremacy," an idea central to "the heritage of the West," but "Americans made themselves notorious by the shrillness and the brutality with which they have insisted on this idea." Americans did not invent the idea, but "it has escaped the world's notice that these very excesses of which Americans have been guilty imply a certain, unprecedented uneasiness over the idea's life and power, if not, indeed the idea's validity." What it called for was to deny the "human reality" of black people, with whom they lived so closely: their "human weight and complexity, and the strain of denying the overwhelmingly undeniable forced Americans into rationalizations so fantastic that they approach the pathological."[34] It was only when Baldwin came to Europe (fleeing a country he thought he despised) and fell in love with a white European that he realized how American he was, how much his own psyche, as an American

[31] See James Baldwin, *Stranger in the House*, in James Baldwin, *Collected Essays*, pp. 117–29.
[32] See James Baldwin, *Notes of a Native Son*, id., pp. 5–116.
[33] *Id.*, p. 119.
[34] *Id.*, pp. 126–27.

black, was framed by its distinctive history: both its democratic ideals and its savage racism. What Baldwin came to realize on his Swiss mountaintop with Lucien is that, in light of this history, American blacks "could turn his peculiar status in the Western world to his own advantage and, it may be, to the great advantage of the world. It remains for him to fashion out of his experience that which will give him sustenance and a voice."[35]

What this voice could show us, Baldwin now writing in his own resisting voice as a black American, is that, because of both their democratic ideals and their racism, "Americans are as unlike any other white people in the world as it is possible to be." For example, "the American vision of the world – which allows so little reality, generally speaking, for any of the darker forces in human life, which tends until today to paint moral issues in glaring black and white – owes a great deal to the battle waged by Americans to maintain between themselves and black men a human separation which could not be bridged. It is only now beginning to be borne in on us . . . that this vision of the world is dangerously inaccurate, and perfectly useless. For it protects our moral high-mindedness at the terrible expense of weakening our grasp of reality."[36]

Stranger in the Village leads to the question: How had such a dangerously unreal and unjust separation become part of the fabric of American life? Once Baldwin realized how deeply American he, a black and gay American, was, he saw that exploring racism within the American black community, something he knew at first hand from his stepfather, was a way of understanding the personal and political psychology of American racism generally. If blacks, so clearly the victims of American racism, could themselves reactively embrace a form of it, that would reveal the power of the psychology that sustains racism, something American blacks and whites, as Americans, tragically shared. Falling in love with a European white man in Europe – showing him that he could love and be loved – released Baldwin from the fear and anger he had experienced in his sexual life in America, an uncontrollable rage that he had come to fear in himself (the incident with the New Jersey waitress). It is often a feature of thus falling in love that each of the lovers, in falling in love with and coming into real relationship with the individual they come to love, come to know and understand the web of relationships stretching from early childhood forward that made the beloved the person he or she is, including the traumas and losses, the loves and hates, the hopes and fears that are always part of the complex fabric of a human life. Baldwin experienced such a love for and with Lucien, and thus, through the experience of being loved for the complex person he was, could see himself and give honest voice to the web of persons and relationships that shaped his psyche, including the rage and anger he absorbed from his violently racist stepfather.

[35] *Id.*, p. 128.
[36] *Id.*, pp. 128–29.

Baldwin thus writes, while living with Lucien, his intimately autobiographical first novel, *Go Tell It on the Mountain*,[37] about a young black man, John Grimes, modeled on Baldwin and his early relationships, at the time Baldwin first found his voice as a magnetic religious preacher, a vocation that he soon abandoned, but a vocation that prefigures the compelling and truthful ethical voice of his novels and essays (at times, Baldwin seems like the thundering and piercing Jonathan Edwards of his time). John is portrayed as in love with an older black straight boy, Elisha, his teacher, and, although their relationship is not sexual at all, it is John's love for Elisha that brings him to a sense of his own voice as a preacher (just as, later on, it would be Baldwin's sexual love for Lucien that would lead to his voice as an essayist and artist). What the novel is essentially about is John's struggle for voice and for love, coming to understand his struggle in light of the impact on him of the three main influences on his early life – his mother, his violent stepfather, and his stepfather's sister, all of whom moved from the South to Harlem and were important persons in his early life. The question explored in *Go Tell It on the Mountain* is why his preacher stepfather not only did not love as his mother did, but was indeed consumed and ultimately destroyed by hatred.

What makes the novel so riveting is that Baldwin focuses on the damage to love in intimate life as the key to understanding how blacks and whites, living, unlike Europeans, so closely together, could accept a racism that requires their separation. The damage Baldwin identifies is the moral injury inflicted on the human psyche by the patriarchal Love Laws, an injury that he analyzes as the source of his stepfather's violently self-destructive racism, which arises, reactively, as a response to the racism of Southern whites.

The racism of Southern whites rested on the racialized pedestal that ascribed an idealized purity to all white women, and unjustly ascribed to all blacks a degraded, indeed rapacious sexuality, and thus rationalized extraordinary forms of violence (lynchings) directed at any suggestion or suspicion of sex between black men and white women, much of which was, in fact, consensual. Sex between white men and black women, often exploitative, was, in contrast, conventional, although officially condemned, because it was supported by the stereotype of degraded black sexuality. What kept American whites and blacks in the American South, who were otherwise so intimately connected, apart was the internalization of the patriarchal Love Laws, which held Southern white women, in particular, on a tight leash of patriarchal control of their sexual desires and love lives. Antimiscegenation laws were thus very much at the American heart of darkness expressing itself in a wanton violence and irrationalist dehumanization. As Baldwin put the point, what American racism called for was to deny the "human reality" of black people, with whom they lived

---

[37] See James Baldwin, *Go Tell It on the Mountain*, in James Baldwin, *Early Novels and Stories*, edited by Toni Morrison (New York: The Library of America, 1998), pp. 1–215.

so closely: their "human weight and complexity, and the strain of denying the overwhelmingly undeniable forced Americans into rationalizations so fantastic that they approach the pathological."[38] It was precisely because intimate affections and loves, including sexual loves, were so humanly natural among people so intimately connected, as blacks and whites in the American South clearly were, that the moral injury inflicted by the violently irrational repression of such love made thinkable what should have been unthinkable, the massive cultural dehumanization of people of color.

What Baldwin comes to see in his stepfather is that, brought up in the racist South as he was, his own racism against whites mirrored the basis of the racism of whites, since both accepted the unjust terms patriarchy imposed on intimate life. Patriarchy draws its power and appeal from the way it rationalizes the abridgment of basic human rights of whole classes of persons by dehumanizing them through enforcing stereotypes that, in a vicious circularity, arise from the repression of the resisting voice of those who might and would challenge such stereotypes. It is these stereotypes that idealize those who conform to patriarchal demands on a pedestal, and that denigrates those who do not conform. The only difference between white and black racism is whom they idealize or denigrate. Both seek to control sex and love to the ends of patriarchy, as they understand it. For blacks like Baldwin's stepfather, since the racialized pedestal unjustly ascribed to all blacks a degraded sexuality, resistance to such unjust images in the black churches led to insistence on a form of idealization of good black women's sexuality that rested on repression of sexual voice, and a corresponding devaluation of any women who had a free sexual voice and lived accordingly. There was to be no friendship or love across the boundaries patriarchy required.

What Baldwin shows us in his first novel is the effects of the patriarchal pedestal (good asexual vs. bad sexual women) on the psychology and ethics of black men and women of the South. Baldwin is mainly concerned with the impact of this form of the pedestal on men like his stepfather, which was first urged on Gabriel (based on Baldwin's stepfather) by Gabriel's devout mother and, after a history of sexual dalliance, adopted by him at her death when he becomes a minister. In the novel, Gabriel's devotion to her ideals takes the form of marrying Deborah, a woman scorned by other black men as tainted because she had been raped by white men. In dreams he has before deciding to marry her, Gabriel first dreams of having armored himself in chastity, about to be stoned, and then battling (he wakes with a nocturnal emission) and then dreams of being on a cold mountaintop and asked by a voice to go higher, finally coming to the sun and to peace.[39] As his dream shows, he married Deborah not from love, but from a sense of better meeting his religious ideals, which disfavor any sexual feeling for the woman he marries; in fact, she is

---

[38] *Id.*, pp. 126–27.
[39] See James Baldwin, *Go Tell It on the Mountain, op. cit.*, pp. 105–7.

childless. Gabriel is then attracted to and has an affair with a young woman, Esther, who gets pregnant by him. He refuses to consider her proposal – to leave his wife and run off with her – because he regards her as a fallen woman.[40] Esther is repelled by his dishonesty, his fear, and his shame, which in turn shames her "before my God – to make me cheap, like you done . . . I guess it takes a holy man to make a girl a real whore."[41] Gabriel steals money from Deborah to help Esther leave for Chicago; she dies in childbirth, leaving a son, Royal, whom Gabriel never acknowledges as his own and is killed as a young man. After the boy's death and before her own, Deborah confronts Gabriel with the truth, questioning his judgment about not going with the woman he evidently sexually loved but regarded as a "harlot" ("Esther weren't no harlot,"[42] Deborah opines); he has, Deborah says, done the wrong thing both ethically and before God.[43] Both Esther and Deborah identify Gabriel's sense of the pedestal as the root of what cuts him off from any real relationship to them or to any person or God. The heart of Gabriel's problem is that his enforcement of the patriarchal Love Laws rests on an irrationalist propensity to violence at any challenge to his patriarchal authority, including his violence against and thus moral injury to his own capacity for love, and his violence against others, including his gender-bending stepson.

There can be little doubt that Baldwin, whom his stepfather found ugly, effeminate, and "strange," came to see his own plight, as a black gay man, as at one with the pedestal's denigration of black sexual women. In his first play, *The Amen Corner* (1968), Baldwin studied the same issue from the perspective of a black woman minister, Sister Margaret, who, like his stepfather, reacts to the racism she endured by placing herself on an idealized pedestal, breaking any real loving relationship to her husband and son; as Baldwin put the point of the play, "Her sense of reality is dictated by the society's assumption, which also becomes her own, of her inferiority. Her need for human affirmation, and also vengeance, expresses itself in her merciless piety, and her love, which is real but is also at the mercy of her genuine and absolutely justifiable terror, turns her into a tyrannical matriarch."[44] Baldwin had come through the experience of love to see his own internalized fear and anger as arising from his own internalization of his stepfather's violence against any form of sexual love that defied patriarchal controls, a violence that black women under patriarchy could and did enact as well. In contrast, John's love for Elisha leads to his resonant voice as a minister, which clearly anticipates the voice Baldwin would find through his love for Lucien. Baldwin would not and did not make his stepfather's disastrous mistake.

[40] *Id.*, p. 126.
[41] *Id.*, p. 128.
[42] *Id.*, p. 143.
[43] *Id.*, pp. 142–44.
[44] James Baldwin, *The Amen Corner* (New York: Vintage International, 1996), at p. xvi.

Baldwin elsewhere describes the boundaries that the racialized pedestal, when absorbed into the minds and lives of blacks, imposes on any possibility of real relationships among them, a traumatic break in relationship "like one of those floods that devastate counties, tearing everything down, tearing children from their parents and lovers from each other, and making everything an unrecognizable waste."[45] The consequence is damning:

> You very soon, without knowing it, give up all hope of communion. Black people, mainly, look down or look up but do not look at each other, not at you, and white people, mainly, look away. And the universe is simply a sounding drum; there is no way, no way whatever, so it seemed then and has sometimes seemed since, to get through a life, to love your wife and children, or your friends, or your mother and father, or to be loved.[46]

The pedestal kills real sensual relationships of mutual voice, and thus kills relationships:

> To be sensual, I think, is to respect and rejoice in the force of life, of life itself, and to be *present* in all that one does, from the effort of loving to the breaking of bread. . . . The person who distrusts himself has no touchstone for reality – for this touchstone can be only oneself. Such a person interposes between himself and reality nothing less than a labyrinth of attitudes.[47]

The pedestal is one component of this "labyrinth of attitudes," a stereotypical assumption that cuts one off not only from the voice of others, but from one's own personal emotional voice. It thus stultifies emotional intelligence, without which love is narcissism. Baldwin had seen this in his stepfather and other preachers and had come, for this reason, to be skeptical about the Christianity of the black churches in particular and of established religion in general. He would be skeptical to the end of his life, although his own voice, as an essayist and artist, was an ethically transformative voice that he first found early in his life as a black minister.

The importance of his homosexuality to Baldwin's life and work, only dealt with peripherally in *Go Tell It on the Mountain*, is stage central in his second novel, *Giovanni's Room*, dedicated to Lucien. *Giovanni's Room* contrasts with his other five novels in both style and content. Whereas all the other novels deal with complex webs of interpersonal relationships, *Giovanni's Room* has the starkness of Greek tragedy, and has no black characters. It is about the relatively short sexual relationship of a white American, David, living in Paris and an Italian bartender, Giovanni; there are two other gay characters, Jacques and Guillaume, Giovanni's boss whom he murders; and Hella, an American woman, whom David will ask to marry him at

---

[45] James Baldwin, *The Fire Next Time*, in James Baldwin, *Collected Essays*, pp. 291–347, at p. 304.
[46] *Id.*, p. 304.
[47] *Id.*, pp. 311–12.

the end of the novel. The novel's narrative voice is David's, the white American, who had had a gay relationship with another boy when young and then abruptly ended it, and thought of himself and acted thereafter as straight. Giovanni, in his village in Italy, had had a child with a woman, the child and woman dying in childbirth, and he comes to Paris to escape, and, quite handsome, becomes a bartender in a gay bar, where he meets and falls in love with David. Both David and Giovanni are white, quite good looking, and neither effeminate, so Baldwin is editing out of the narrative issues that were, in fact, central to his own struggles as a black gay man. Their passionate sexual affair lasts a few months in Giovanni's one-room apartment, which becomes for them both a kind of new world of thought and feeling but one confined, claustrophobically, to Giovanni's room. Abruptly, David abandons Giovanni, who is distraught in losing the person he thought was the love of his life, loses his job when Guillaume sexually exploits and then falsely accuses him of theft, and murders Guillaume and, at the end of the novel, is punished by the guillotine. Hella, when she discovers the nature of David's relationship to Giovanni, rejects him, and David clearly will settle into a life quite like the ostensibly straight men Baldwin knew in New York City who haunted gay bars to pick up gay men like Baldwin, with whom they have sex and for whom they have contempt.

Baldwin's voice in the novel is the novel's victim, Giovanni [since Italians were racialized in both France and the United States, Baldwin sometimes uses Italian ethnics to capture his experience as a black men, as he does in *Giovanni's Room* and would again do with Vivaldo in his next novel, *Another Country*, and with Jerry and his Sicilian friends in his fourth novel, *Tell Me How Long the Train's Been Gone* (1968)[48]]. Giovanni's voice is, as one would expect, wonderfully intelligent, funny, loving, and compelling (like Baldwin's), and his indictment of David in the gripping scene of David's rejection of him has the force of an ethical sermon on the problematic and crippling homophobia of American manhood in a man like David who cannot love the one man who loved him and whom he loved, settling instead for a life of self-deception and furtive homosexual liaisons. David would remain haunted to his death by a sense of moral guilt and responsibility for Giovanni's death, killing the man he loved, as the violence of homophobia requires.

Baldwin's motives in writing *Go Tell It on the Mountain* arose from his experience of and desire to understand and make sense of his stepfather's violence and its intrapsychic impact on him, as a gay man. It was because his stepfather's violence against Baldwin was so clearly directed at his stepson's effeminacy and "strangeness" that Baldwin saw so early the roots of such violence in patriarchy, albeit a black reactive interpretation of patriarchy, which he saw had poisoned not only the intimate lives of white men and women, but blacks as well. It is this insight, arising

---

[48] See, for example, James Baldwin, *Tell Me How Long the Train's Been Gone* (New York: Dell, 1968), at pp. 118–19.

from his close observation of his stepfather and of himself and others, that led him in *Giovanni's Room* to offer one of the first and most piercing indictments of American homophobia, whose cold cruelty rests, as it did with David, on an irrational panic at any threat to a self-conception of American manhood that men like David could not question, even though its costs to them and others were, for Baldwin, catastrophic. Baldwin strips race from the novel because he wants to identify the American pathology as rooted in a powerful conception of American manhood and womanhood, which extended to both whites and blacks, both of whom Baldwin came to see, through his love in Europe for a European white man, as deeply American.

Baldwin's most ambitious attempt to bring together his insights into American racism, sexism, and homophobia is his third novel, *Another Country*. In one of his most remarkable later essays, *No Name in the Street* (1972), Baldwin wrote of these insights in terms of an American disassociation that could not connect the evils of public life to those of private life:

> I have always been struck, in America, by an emotional poverty so bottomless, and a terror of human life, of human touch, so deep, that virtually no American appears able to achieve any viable, organic connection between his public stance and private life. This is what makes them so baffling, so moving, so exasperating, and so untrustworthy.[49]

Another Country examines the moral injury inflicted on American private life by the patriarchal Love Laws, in particular, the interlinked evils of American racism, sexism, and homophobia. What Baldwin wanted to expose for discussion was the "connection between public stance and private life," and *Another Country* thus examines a broad range of cases in which conforming to or breaking the Love Laws are the center of discussion, sometimes leading to disaster, sometimes liberation through love, resisting patriarchy. These include a black straight man's (Rufus's) disastrously violent sexual affair with a white Southern woman; Vivaldo, a white writer and the closest friend of Rufus, who fails to give Rufus the support he needs when his depression will lead to committing suicide, leading Vivaldo to wonder if he should have made love to Rufus; Eric, a gay American actor, who had had a unhappy love affair with Rufus, and would find love in France with a younger man, Yves, and, on his return to America, has a sexual affair with Vivaldo, which helps Vivaldo resolve his guilt about Rufus and better understand the problems in his sexual affair with Rufus's black singer sister, Ida; Eric also has an adulterous affair with Cass, the unhappily married white wife, with two children, of a successful American novelist, Richard, leading to the end of the marriage, and the possibility for Cass of a life in which she might realize more fully both her need for real relationships and a vocation that might fulfill her.

---

[49] James Baldwin, *No Name in the Street*, in James Baldwin, *Collected Essays*, pp. 353–475, at p. 385.

The heart of the novel is Vivaldo's interracial love for Rufus's black sister, Ida; Baldwin later wrote of "my heroine, Ida, who in effect dictated a great deal of the book to me."[50] While it is clear Ida loves Vivaldo, and Vivaldo her, the relationship is fraught with misunderstanding, and Ida, an ambitious and talented singer, has an affair with a rather repellent agent to advance her career, as Vivaldo has an affair with Eric. Nonetheless, Ida's internal life only emerges into the open late in the novel, as she and Vivaldo acknowledge to one another what they have each done, making love to others, and what they have been struggling with in their relationship (namely, the spectre of Rufus, whom they both loved, and failed). What is striking about the Ida–Vivaldo relationship is that they are lovers and also ambitious artists, and that they come to a sense of the value of their love, as now free and equal, through honest voice, finally opening up to one another about the legitimacy of their ambitions and their common love of Rufus.

Baldwin shows us in *Another Country* what he had come to understand about being American when he found love in Europe with a European man, namely, that breaking the Love Laws could release an ethical voice that resisted the injustices of patriarchy. For this to be possible, we need to find in our intimate relationships "another country," a love based in freedom and equality on the basis of which a good and just life would be possible. Breaking the Love Laws may, if patriarchal domination of women by men remains unquestioned, be disastrous (Rufus and his Southern mistress). However, failure to break the Love Laws (Vivaldo not having a love affair with Rufus) may also be disastrous, if it reflects a homophobic panic leading to a disastrous failure of love. And, breaking the Love Laws may be the key to new relationships if, like the adultery of Cass and Eric, or the love of Eric and Yves, or the love of Eric and Vivaldo, or the love of Eric and Cass, or, finally, the love of Vivaldo and Ida, it frees people from the patriarchal disassociation that has blighted their lives and makes possible a life lived in the truth and value of free and equal love – another country.

Baldwin may have tried to do too much in *Another Country*, but its ambition is to show us quite concretely what our lives might be like if we took seriously what he had come to believe was the heart of the greatest evils in American cultural and political life – its racism, sexism, and homophobia. Its narrative is undoubtedly sometimes forced, more working out the abstract logic of Baldwin's insight into the importance of breaking the Love Laws, than plausibly showing us how lives embody these insights. A gay man may certainly love and help straight friends, as Eric does transforming the lives of Vivaldo and Cass, but, in the context of the novel, his erotic availability and goodness, as a kind of gay savior, strain credulity, exemplifying the kind of idealization of sexuality of which Baldwin was usually so skeptical. Nonetheless, the novel has moments of shattering tragic force (the suicide of Rufus), and of transcendent erotic power (as Baldwin relives his love affair, now

---

[50] James Baldwin, *Words of a Native Son*, in James Baldwin, *Collected Essays*, pp. 707–13, at p. 708.

ended, with Lucien, narrating the only relationship in the novel that seems deeply loving, the love of Eric and Yves in France, a love that Eric believes will end as Yves matures).

Baldwin continued to write novels: *Tell Me How Long the Trains Been Gone* (1968), *If Beale Street Could Talk* (1973), and *Just Above My Head* (1979). These novels draw upon Baldwin's experience as now a public celebrity and an influential activist in the civil rights movement; it was a telegram from Baldwin, over the violence in Birmingham calling for action by the federal government, to then attorney general Robert Kennedy, which led to an angry meeting with Baldwin and other black leaders in New York City, a meeting that may have prompted a speech by President Kennedy that he would propose pathbreaking civil rights legislation.[51] Baldwin also now increasingly depended on the love of his family and their children, including their active involvement in helping manage his demanding life of writing and public appearances (he was particularly close with his brother, David, who was a manager of his affairs). Baldwin had, of course, been the eldest child in a large family, and thus had been a caretaker of his younger brothers and sisters, and the sensitivity of his treatment of young children in his works arose from this experience (for example, *Go Tell It on the Mountain* and his short children's novel, *Little Man Little Man*, written from the point of view of black boys in Harlem[52]); Baldwin never forgot the traumatized boy in the sometimes violent and unhappy man. While he fled America to find his voice in Europe and continued largely to live in Europe (including Turkey, both in Europe and Asia), he had deeply missed his family, and no doubt experienced guilt for abandoning them, and his now frequent visits to America allowed him to reconnect and deepen relationships that were to prove among the most supportive in his later life. Baldwin continued to have love affairs with younger men, and, after the murders of Medgar Evers, Martin Luther King, Jr., and Malcolm X, all of whom he knew personally and admired, he was drawn to younger militant black men, and was involved with and supported, as did his close friend, the actor Marlon Brando, the Black Panthers, and others.[53] These experiences, including a sense for him of the emotional hollowing of his celebrity, are drawn upon in his three later novels.

Two of these novels – *Tell Me How Long the Trains Been Gone* and *Just Above My Head* – are long and dense with a web of interpersonal relationships. The first of them is written in the voice of a highly successful black actor, Leo Proudhammer, reflecting, after a serious heart attack, on his life and its direction forward. Leo is bisexual, having had a long affair with his closest friend, the actress and Southern white woman, Barbara, and the novel ends with an affair with a black militant, Black

[51] See David Leeming, *James Baldwin*, p. 222.
[52] See James Baldwin, *Little Man Little Man: A Story of Childhood*, written by James Baldwin and illustrated by Yoran Cazac (New York: The Dial Press, 1976).
[53] See *id.*, pp. 290–95.

Christopher (interestingly, at the novel's end, after Black Christopher expresses an intention to buy arms, the affair apparently abruptly ends: Proudhammer appears again to be alone with his art). Much of the novel deals with the racist violence inflicted on him and Barbara for their rather conspicuous interracial affair, and Baldwin draws quite directly on his own experience in the theatre with leading teachers and directors (including a thinly disguised portrait of Elia Kazan) and with actors, indeed mentioning the name of Marlon Brando. By centering the narrative in a black actor, Baldwin gives a sense of the price he had paid for being a celebrity, the sense of himself as an actor on a stage (more acting than living), increasingly out of touch with the creative voice of his three earlier novels.

Just Above My Head is mainly about two black artists and lovers – a singer and pianist, Arthur and Jimmy, and their respective families, who were close friends. The novel is Baldwin's longest, written in the voice and from the perspective of Arthur's brother and manager, Hall Montana, and thus lacks the authority of Baldwin's earlier novels, clearly rooted in his own voice and experience. The parents of Hall and Arthur are loving and supportive; the parents of Jimmy and his sister, Julia, disastrously allow Julia, as a young woman to tyrannically dominate the family as a preacher, refusing to allow her mother to seek health care, leading to her death. Julia is crushed, losing her vocation, and her father becomes quite monstrous, repeatedly raping his daughter. Julia goes to Africa to get away, and returns to New York to become a leading model. Arthur and Jimmy fall passionately in love, and work closely and creatively with one another as singer and pianist, and are brilliantly successful. Arthur, at the novel's end, dies suddenly, but previously had had a short affair in Paris (while Jimmy was in London) with a Frenchman, Guy Lazar. Arthur, as a character in the novel, only comes alive in his affair with Lazar, in which there is much intelligent discussion about the differences between American and European racism, including French imperialist racism in Algeria and Indochina, reopening and deepening the discussion of Baldwin's early essay, *Stranger in the Village*.[54] Arthur embraces Lazar's invitation to discuss these issues in depth, "the Puritan in him having announced that the horizontal position will soon be joyless if the vertical position is a lie."[55] What makes this interlude so remarkable, revelatory, and lively is that, finally, Baldwin writes in his own (Arthur's) voice about a love affair very similar to his love for Lucien, only now imagined as a love of equals in which feeling and thought, opposites under the gender binary, are one.

In *Just Above My Head*, Baldwin is clearly paying tribute to his own brother David, who was, like Hall Montana, his manager and a straight black man, and who came, like his other siblings, to support and care for Baldwin as a gay man and artist. The novel is very much about the impact of their love and acceptance of a gay brother; in the character of Julia, in the other family in the novel, Baldwin shows how even the

---

[54] See James Baldwin, *Just Above My Head* (Laurel: New York, 1979), at pp. 455–93.
[55] *Id.*, p. 474.

traumatic sexual abuse and rape of Julia by her own father can nonetheless be healed through love, including Julia's affair with Hall, and her supportive love of her brother Jimmy, who becomes the lover of Hall's brother, Arthur. In *Just Above My Head*, Baldwin investigates, building on his experience of his own family, how some black families, even after the traumatic abuse of a father like Baldwin's stepfather, survive such abuse and, through their caring love for one another, come to resist injustice.

The contrast between two quite different black families is also the subject of Baldwin's short novel, *If Beale Street Could Talk*, the only one of his novels written in the voice of a young black woman. *If Beale Street Could Talk* is also concerned to show very different black families, one of whom supports their daughter, Fonny, in resisting the injustice of her lover, Alonzo, his unjust imprisonment for a rape he never committed, and the other, the family of Alonzo, whose mother and sisters – very much on the morally corrupt idealized pedestal that Baldwin exposed in his play, *The Amen Corner* – condemn and do not help their brother, who is, in fact, innocent and the victim of a racist policeman. The policeman, stung by Alonzo's contempt when the officer earlier tried unjustly to arrest him (for a crime that an Italian American grocery store owned publicly and floridly attests that Alonzo did not commit), unjustly later fabricates the arrest of Alonzo for a rape he did not commit. What makes this novel of some interest is that it is the only one of Baldwin's six novels that focuses not on personal life, but on the connections of personal life to resistance to injustice. This narrative of love, giving rise to resistance, is told in the voice and dialect of a young black woman, Fonny, in love with and now pregnant by Alonzo, whose mother goes to Puerto Rico to find the woman allegedly raped by Alonzo, and whose older, well-educated sister connects Fonny to a white liberal lawyer, who, despite objections from fellow whites, effectively represents Alonzo. Alonzo, an artist, is eventually released.

Baldwin shows us in this novel the political consequences of a social movement of resistance to injustice in which breaking the Love Laws played an increasingly important role. It made a difference in terms of black families, some of whom increasingly challenged the gender binary and hierarchy and became agents of resistance to injustice, and some of whom, staying on the racialized pedestal, did not. It also made a difference in the increasing importance of whites joining the resistance of blacks, exemplified by the liberal white lawyer in *If Beale Street Could Talk*. Why does Baldwin tell his narrative of resistance in the voice of a young black woman very much in love with a man unjustly persecuted on racist grounds, and why the role in resistance of the white lawyer?

Baldwin had increasingly returned to the United States both to observe and participate in the civil rights movement, the most important challenge to American racism in our history. His essays, for example, are often a personal narrative of both what he observed and experienced during his increasingly frequent returns, riveting, indignant, and incisive. And, many of my generation of liberal whites, who often despaired, as Baldwin did, in response to the murder a number of both white and black leaders of resistance, some of whom (like Medgar Evers and King practiced nonviolent resistance) found in Baldwin's essays and in his increasingly frequent appearances on American television, the honest, uncompromising ethical voice we then desperately needed to hear to keep alive our own resisting voices and hopes during a dark, increasingly reactionary time – the presidencies of Richard Nixon and Ronald Reagan.

Baldwin had been born and brought up in Harlem, but had experienced the effects of Southern racism in the psyches of his stepfather, mother, and aunt, all of whom have moved from the South to Harlem. Now, for the first time in his life, Baldwin went South as a celebrity, and told us truths we have never heard before about the character of racism in the South, which arose, as he showed us, from the terror racist Southerners brought to the enforcement of the Love Laws, including – as Baldwin, a gay black man, insists on showing in harrowing personal terms – its homophobia. His words from *No Name in the Street* (1972) bear repeating:

> I have written elsewhere about those early days in the South, but from a distance more or less impersonal. I have never, for example, written about my unbelieving shock when I realized that I was being groped by one of the most powerful men in one of the states I visited. He got himself sweating drunk in order to arrive at this despairing titillation. With his wet eyes staring up at my face, and his wet hands groping for my cock, we were both, abruptly, in history's ass-pocket. It was very frightening – not the gesture itself, but the abjectness of it, and the assumption of a swift and grim complicity: as my identity was defined by his power, so was my humanity to be placed at the service of his fantasies. . . . This man, with a phone call, could prevent or provoke a lynching . . . Therefore, one had to be friendly, but the price for this was your cock.
>
> This will sound an exaggerated statement to Americans, who will suppose it to refer, merely, to sexual (or sectional) abnormality. This supposition misses the point: which is double-edged. The slave knows, however his master may be deluded in this point, that he is called slave because his manhood has been, or can be, or will be taken from him. . . . In the case of American slavery, the black's right to his women, as well as to his children, was simply taken from him, and whatever bastards the white man begat on the bodies of black women took their condition from the condition of their mother: blacks were not the only stallions of the slave-breeding farms! And one of the many results of this loveless, money-making conspiracy was that, in giving the master every conceivable sexual and commercial license, it also emasculated them of any human responsibility – to their women, to their children, or to themselves. The results of this blasphemy resound in this country, on every private and public level, until this hour. When the man grabbed my cock, I didn't think of him as a faggot, which, indeed, if having a wife and children, house, cars, and a respectable and powerful standing in the community, mean anything, he wasn't: I watched his eyes, thinking, with great sorrow, *The unexamined life is not worth living.*[56]

---

[56] James Baldwin, *No Name in the Street*, in James Baldwin, *Collected Essays*, pp. 353–475, at pp. 390–91.

What is poignant about this observation is that it centers not only on the moral injury the Love Laws inflict on blacks, but on whites. Baldwin's second and most important play, *Blues for Mister Charlie* (1964), further explores this observation. The play arose from the racist murder of Emmett Till and the resulting trial and acquittal, dramatizing the very different ways the black and white communities interpret the evidence given to the court. The play takes seriously the burdens nonviolence imposed on a black community subjected to racist violence, but its main attention is on the burden Southern racism imposed on the two white men, Lyle Britten (the store owner, who murders a black boy for disrespectfully speaking to his wife) and Parnell James (a wealthy liberal newspaper editor). Parnell is a close friend both of the black family of the boy who was killed and of Lyle, and is thus caught between the opposing parties at the trial. Both Parnell and Lyle have slept with black women in the town; but, Lyle, seeking respectability, married a white, well-educated librarian, Jo, whereas Parnell has continued to sleep with blacks, expressing both his desire and ambivalence: "Out with it, Parnell! The nigger lover! Black boys and girls! I've wanted my hands full of them, wanted to drown them, laughing and dancing and making love – making love – wow! – and be transformed, formed, liberated out of this grey-white envelope."[57] Both Lyle and Parnell broke the Love Laws, sleeping with black women, but Lyle did so in the clandestine way white men of the South did, acting on the racialized pedestal that idealized white women as asexual and degraded black women as sexual; thus, Lyle marries a good white woman to preserve his respectability, and indeed the motive for the murder of the black boy is a perceived insult to his white wife. Parnell is in a very different place, himself regarding his breaking of the Love Laws as the explanation for his ethical feeling for blacks and his objection to Southern racism. Of all the people who testify at the trial, only Parnell speaks truthfully (resisting injustice), and he later challenges Lyle for making his wife, Jo, lie at the trial that the black boy sexually assaulted her, when in fact he only spoke disrespectfully. The pathos of the play – blues for Mister Charlie – is the pathos of Parnell, now regarded as a renegade to the white race, and, at the end of play, allowed by blacks to "walk in the same direction."[58] Parnell exemplifies Baldwin's lifelong view that American racism inflicted devastating moral injury on whites, in particular, on their intimate sexual lives.

Baldwin returned to exploring this theme in his powerful short story, "Going to Meet the Man," one of the two stories expressly written (the others had been written earlier) for his collection of short stories published under that title in 1965,[59] the year after *Blues for Mr. Charlie*. The story connects racism to white sexuality, written from the point of view and in the voice of a Southern racist

[57] See James Baldwin, *Blues for Mister Charlie* (New York: Vintage International, 1992), at p. 106.
[58] *Id.*, p. 121.
[59] See James Baldwin, "Going to Meet the Man," in *Going to Meet the Man*, in James Baldwin, *Early Novels and Stories*, pp. 757–950, pp. 933–50.

sheriff, who as a boy experienced the lynching and castration of a black man, and at the end of the story is only able to be sexually potent with his wife by thinking of himself as not white but as black: "Come on, sugar, I'm going to do you like a nigger, just like a nigger, come on, sugar, and love me just like you'd love a nigger."[60] David Leeming, who was with Baldwin when he wrote the story, comments perceptively: "The black man who is lynched during the sheriff's childhood is . . . a scapegoat for the facing of the race problem. Hanging on the tree, deprived of his masculinity in a violent ritual of castration rooted in the white man's myth of black sexuality, he provides the white man – represented by the sheriff – with the actual power he otherwise lacks. Only by remembering the lynching and pretending that the woman under him is a black woman can the sheriff 'perform' with his wife."[61]

If Beale Street Could Talk and *Blues for Mister Charlie* explore the ways in which, through resisting the Love Laws, whites were joining blacks in a common resistance to racist violence and injustice, they also underscore the role of black women in such resistance (thus, Flory is the voice of the novel). Baldwin brought his remarkable psychological and ethical insights critically to bear not only on whites, but on the black male leaders of the civil rights movement, whom he supported and deeply admired, but whose leadership rested on a form of the racialized pedestal, as Baldwin insists on showing us – a truthful voice speaking of injustice not only by whites, but by blacks, all rooted in the same problem, patriarchy.

When Baldwin met Martin Luther King, Jr., he commented, "Reverend King is not like any preacher I have ever met before. For one thing, to state it baldly, I liked him."[62] He was thinking, of course, of his stepfather and the other such ministers he had known. King was clearly a counterexample to Baldwin's negative view of black preachers; "[w]hat he says to Negroes he will say to whites; and what he says to whites he will say to Negroes. He is the first Negro leader in my experience, or the first in many generations, of whom this can be said."[63] However, Baldwin, for all his admiration of and active support for King and his movement, did take critical note of a problem in black leadership, including King: "[o]ne of the greatest vices of the white bourgeoisie on which they have modeled themselves is its reluctance to think, its distrust of the independent mind."[64] Even King had uncritically absorbed a conventionality that mirrored white conventionality, acquiescing, for example, in pressure brought "to force the resignation of his (King's) extremely able organizer

---

[60] See *id.*, p. 950. For illuminating commentary on the short story and its background, see David Leeming, *James Baldwin*, pp. 248–49.

[61] See David Leeming, *James Baldwin*, p. 249.

[62] James Baldwin, "The Dangerous Road Before Martin Luther King," in James Baldwin, *Collected Essays*, pp. 638–58, at p. 638.

[63] *Id.*, p. 639.

[64] *Id.*, p. 655.

and lieutenant, Bayard Rustin."[65] The resignation had been forced by Rustin's homosexuality. For Baldwin (a gay man), yielding to such pressures reflects the hypocritical public face of sexual conventionality, compromising the central aim of the civil rights leadership, recognition of the human rights of all on equal terms, which "necessarily carries with it the idea of sexual freedom: the freedom to meet, sleep with, and marry whom one chooses."[66] Baldwin is making reference to the racist obsession with miscegenation; the response of such conventionality is: "I am afraid we must postpone it [the right to sexual freedom] for the moment, to consider just why so many people appear to be convinced that Negroes would then immediately meet, sleep with, and marry white women; who, remarkably enough, are only protected from such undesirable alliances by the majesty and vigilance of the law."[67] The issue of sexual freedom is not, Baldwin argues, peripheral to the civil rights movement, but central, as the Supreme Court itself recognized in 1967 when it struck down antimiscegenation laws in *Loving v. Virginia*.[68]

Baldwin found in Martin Luther King, Jr., a preacher in many respects quite different from his stepfather, but sensed in some areas the same kind of dishonest sexual voice, required by patriarchal conventionality, that he found in his stepfather. The problem, of course, arose from the ways in which the black churches, in resisting the racialized pedestal, adopted a form of the pedestal to accentuate their own sexual virtue and, correlatively, condemning any blacks who deviated from it (for example, Bayard Rustin). The problem was, if anything, aggravated when some black churches under King's leadership became active in the civil rights movement. In order to be credible critics of dominant racist opinion (with its racialized pedestal), protesters had to be, if anything, hyper-respectable in the terms of Southern white respectability, including the pedestal.[69] King had been prepared for this role by the ways in which, as a black man, he had accommodated himself to its public requirements of respectable manhood once he decided that his vocation was that of his father and maternal grandfather, a Baptist minister.

There was, of course, a problem of black manhood under racism correlative to the problem of black womanhood, the consequences of which Orlando Patterson has

---

[65] *Id.*, p. 656. The purging of Rustin from the Southern Christian Leadership Conference, where King had wanted Rustin appointed as coordinator and publicist, was King's response to a grotesque threat by Adam Clayton Powell that, otherwise, he would publicly state that King and Rustin had had a homosexual affair; see Taylor Branch, *Parting the Waters: Martin Luther King and the Civil Rights Movement* 1954–63 (London: Papermac, 1988), pp. 328–29.

[66] James Baldwin, "The Dangerous Road Before Martin Luther King," in James Baldwin, *Collected Essays*, pp. 638–58, at p. 653.

[67] *Id.*, pp. 653–54.

[68] See *Loving v. Virginia*, 388 U.S. 1 (1967).

[69] See, on this point, Marisa Chappell, Jenny Hutchinson, and Brian Ward, "'Dress modestly, neatly . . . as if you were going to church': Respectability, Class and Gender in the Montgomery Bus boycott and the Early Civil Rights Movement," in Peter J. Ling and Sharon Monteith, *Gender in the Civil Rights Movement* (New York: Garland Publishing, 1999), at pp. 69–100.

argued are still very much with us.[70] The racialized pedestal defines the problem, a pedestal that allowed white Southern men to indulge their sexuality on black women while rigidly controlling the sexuality of white women; the sexual desire of white women for anyone, let alone for black men, was such a threat to this ideology (rationalizing lynching) because it threatened the idealized pedestal itself (a point powerfully made by Ida Wells-Barnett).[71] Black men were correlatively trapped in a kind of sexual cage. Any sexual interest in white woman called for lynching, and their ability to protect their own black women was compromised by the terms of white racism, which rationalized its sexual exploitation of black women on the basis of dehumanizing stereotypes of black sexuality as of animals not of humans. The more promiscuous the sexuality of blacks, the more they accommodated themselves to the racist stereotype. Black men like King had as strong sexual interests as white men, but their manhood as Baptist preachers required that they keep their sexual interests undercover, so to speak, conforming in their public roles to idealized roles of husband and father and hold their wives under comparable idealizing controls, all to make the appropriate public statement in rebuttal of the racialized pedestal. It was as much a role at which black men like King played as it was for Tolstoy when he decided that, as a man, he must play to the hilt the roles of husband and father.[72] James Baldwin, a gay man and an outsider to this conception of manhood, shows us the price in real relationships black men and women paid when they took this line, and he apparently sensed with the sensitivity and psychological insight of the great artist he was that King had paid and was paying such a price.[73]

We have already seen the price Bayard Rustin paid, not so much as a black man but as a gay man, as both white (Muste) and black (King) leaders, who received indispensable advice and support from Rustin, broke with him, in the case of King, on no real ground whatsoever other than baseless accusations by Adam Clayton Powell, Jr. And, Eldridge Cleaver turned on Baldwin "for his homosexuality and for his supposed rejection of his blackness."[74]

Such hurtful expressions of homophobia arise from a larger problem in the black male leadership of the civil rights movement, namely, patriarchy. The problem is further illustrated by their sexist failure to acknowledge the absolutely crucial role black women played in starting, leading, and executing the nonviolent forms of civil disobedience central to the successes of the civil rights movement. It was pivotally important, in this connection, that the Montgomery bus boycott not only began in

[70] See Orlando Patterson, *The Rituals of Blood: Consequences of Slavery in Two American Centuries* (Washington, DC: Civitas, 1998).
[71] See, for her brilliant analysis, David A. J. Richards, *Women, Gays, and the Constitution*, pp. 182–90.
[72] For fuller exploration of this point, see David A. J. Richards, *Disarming Manhood*, pp. 43–91.
[73] For fuller exploration of this point, see David A. J. Richards, *Disarming Manhood*, pp. 172–80.
[74] David Leeming, *James Baldwin*, p. 292.

the 1955 refusal of a woman, Rosa Parks,[75] to obey the laws governing segregation on buses, but that its initial groundswell of support came spontaneously from women and that women were disproportionately involved in the boycott itself.[76] This ethical leadership of women had become so conspicuous that when black male leaders of Montgomery first met to discuss tactics and some urged keeping their names secret, E. D. Nixon, a railroad porter and admirer of A. Philip Randolph, exploded in rage at their timorousness in comparison to the courage of women:

> Let me tell you gentlemen one thing. You ministers have lived off their wash-women for the last hundred years and ain't never doing anything for them.... We've worn aprons all our lives.... It's time to take the aprons off.... If we're gonna be mens, now's the time to be mens.[77]

Nixon's trenchant, salty observations question a black manhood that was apparently less ready, willing, and able effectively to resist injustice than womanhood. Constance Baker Mottley, an NAACP lawyer during this period, notes in this connection that, as regards nonviolence:

> [King] sometimes had problems with young men who believed that violence was the answer, but ... [w]hen he preached nonviolence to the largely elderly females in those Birmingham churches at night, King was preaching to the converted.... They were always there, night after night. Strong black women had always set the tone in Southern black communities.[78]

We are only now, in light of the feminist project to recover women's roles in history, coming to some understanding of the role women played not only in mass demonstrations throughout the South, but important leadership roles.[79] These women

---

[75] See Taylor Branch, *Parting the Waters*, pp. 128–34, 139, 655.; see also Taylor Branch, *Pillar of Fire: America in the King Years 1963–65* (New York: Simon & Schuster, 1998).

[76] See, on these points, Mary Fair Burks, "Trailblazers: Women in the Montgomery Bus Boycott," in Vicki L. Crawford, Jacqueline Anne Rouse, and Barbara Woods, eds., *Women in the Civil Rights Movement* (Bloomington: Indiana University Press, 1993), pp. 71–84; Belinda Robnett, *How Long? How Long?: African-American Women in the Struggle for Civil Rights* (New York: Oxford University Press, 1997), pp. 53–70; Lynne Olson, *Freedom's Daughters: The Unsung Heroines of the Civil Rights Movement from 1830 to 1970* (New York: Scribner, 2001), pp. 87–131; Taylor Branch, *Parting the Waters*, p. 149.

[77] Taylor Branch, *Parting the Waters*, p. 136.

[78] Constance Baker Mottley, *Equal Justice Under Law* (New York: Farrar, Straus and Giroux, 1998), p. 157.

[79] See, for important studies, Peter J. Ling and Sharon Monteith, *Gender in the Civil Rights Movement*; Lynne Olson, *Freedom's Daughters*; Belinda Robnett, *How Long? How Long?*; Vicki Crawford, Jacqueline Anne Rouse, and Barbara Woods, *Women in the Civil Rights*; Bettye Collier-Thomas and V. P. Franklin, eds., *Sisters in the Struggle: African American Women in the Civil Rights-Black Power Movement* (New York: New York University Press, 2001); Paula Giddings, *When and Where I Enter. The Impact of Black Woman on Race and Sex in America* (New York: William Morrow and Company, 1984).

included, among many others, Ella Baker,[80] Septima Clark,[81] Diane Nash,[82] and Fannie Lou Hamer.[83] King was enough of a patriarchal man to maintain the Baptist tradition that top leadership was rightly kept in the hands of men; some of these women, notably Ella Baker, resisted him on this and other points. However, these and other women were drawn into such active participation, including leadership roles (for example, the role of Diane Nash in proposing the Birmingham campaign), by something that moved them, as women, in King's prophetic ethical voice and in his actions. The patriarchal problem was not just King's, of course; it was endemic in the civil rights movement. One of the important motives to feminism was the ethical empowerment of some women by participation in the civil rights movement that led them to question its sexism and sexism generally, both as an aspect of racism and as an independent evil.[84]

The problem illustrated by both the homophobia and sexism of the civil rights movement is patriarchy, a problem, as we have seen, also very much at work in white leaders of human rights movements (Muste). It was a particular problem in the civil rights movements because of the leadership role played by the black churches and their uncritically patriarchal conceptions of religious authority, and no one was more critical of this fact than, as we have seen, James Baldwin, whose stepfather was a preacher in one of the black Christian churches.

Baldwin did not regard the problem as unique to black Christianity. Baldwin also knew and admired Malcolm X as a leader of black resistance to racism and was horrified by his murder. In writing his screenplay on the life of Malcolm, *One Day When I Was Lost* (1972), a revised form of which was made into a movie on Malcolm directed by Spike Lee after Baldwin's death,[85] Baldwin naturally sees in Malcolm's turn to the racism of the Black Muslim faith as akin to the racism of his stepfather's Christianity; but, it is when Malcolm rejects the racism of this version of Islam for the more traditional Islam that embraces all races and ethnicities that Baldwin perceives his true moral stature as a black leader. If the racism of whites motivated the murder of Martin Luther King, Jr., Baldwin sees the patriarchal racism of the Black Muslim faith, now challenged by Malcolm, as what leads to his murder.

---

[80] See Taylor Branch, *Parting the Waters*, at pp. 231–33, 258, 264, 273–76, 292–93, 317, 392, 466–67, 487, 518; Taylor Branch, *Pillar of Fire*, pp. 192–93, 439, 457.

[81] See Taylor Branch, *Parting the Waters*, pp. 263–64, 290, 381–82, 573, 576–77, 899; Taylor Branch, *Pillar of Fire*, pp. 124, 191.

[82] See Taylor Branch, *Parting the Waters*, pp. 279–80, 295, 392, 424, 428–29, 437, 439, 449, 455, 466–67, 487, 559, 588, 712, 754, 892–93; Taylor Branch, *Pillar of Fire*, pp. 54–55, 68, 139–41, 165, 285, 524, 553, 559, 579, 587, 599.

[83] See Taylor Branch, *Parting the Waters*, pp. 636, 819; Taylor Branch, *Pillar of Fire*, pp. 57, 71, 74, 109, 179, 219, 240, 329, 458–59, 461, 465, 474, 481, 547–48.

[84] See, on this development, Sara Evans, *Personal Politics: The Roots of Women's Liberation in the Civil Rights Movement and the New Left* (New York: Vintage Books, 1980).

[85] See, for discussion, David Leeman, *James Baldwin*, pp. 284–302.

The great importance of both Bayard Rustin and James Baldwin to the civil rights movement is that because they broke the Love Laws as gay black men loving the white men they had, as black men repudiating the gender binary and hierarchy in their love lives, come to see something other black men could not or would not see until much later, namely, the uncritical role patriarchy continued to play in their conceptions of authority. In this, they compromised their own ethical authority, rooted in a struggle for human rights, by not recognizing the crucially important role women and gay men played in that struggle at every level.

Baldwin lived until 1987, and thus saw the emergence from the civil rights movement of second-wave feminism and gay rights. Baldwin framed the resistance narrative of *If Beale Street Could Talk* in the voice of a young black woman because he had observed and criticized both the sexist and homophobic strands in the civil rights movement, and wanted truthfully to acknowledge the crucial role of freeing women's, as well as gay people's, voices and lives from patriarchal constraints in the resistance he observed in the United States.

There had always been a feminist edge to Baldwin's art and essays, because, as we have seen, it was through releasing himself from the gender binary and hierarchy in his love for Lucien that breaking the Love Laws gave rise to the remarkable resisting voice of all his work. This feminist edge appears in his earliest essays on homosexuality, and is starkly clear in his later essays.

His early essay, *The Male Prison* (1954), discusses Andre Gide's homosexuality.[86] What rivets Baldwin's attention is the way Gide dealt with his homosexuality in his remarkable *Madeleine*,[87] in which he discusses his sexless marriage to his cousin, Madeleine. Baldwin does not discuss his own homosexuality in the essay, but he expresses dismay at the shocking way Gide, confessedly a gay man, dealt with this marriage, namely, his arid idealization of her as "an utterly disincarnate love,"[88] "the least carnal perturbation to whom would have been an insult."[89] Gide had himself been shocked when his fellow gay artist, Marcel Proust, told him that in creating gay characters in his great novel he had always attributed the good features of gay men he had observed to his female characters, and their abject, bad features to the gay men he portrayed in his novel.[90] For Gide, this was dishonest to Proust's own experience as a gay man, and thus unconscionable in terms of his demanding Protestant conscience.[91] Gide thought of himself, as a gay man and artist, as always honest to

---

[86] See James Baldwin, "The Male Prison," in James Baldwin, *Collected Essays*, pp. 231–35 (first published, 1954).

[87] See Andre Gide, *Madeleine*, translated by Justin O'Brien (Chicago: Elephant Paperbacks, 1952).

[88] See *id.*, p. 16.

[89] *Id.*, p. 17.

[90] See, on this point, Didier Eribon, *Insult and the Making of the Gay Self*, translated by Michael Lucey (Durham: Duke University Press, 2004), at p. 86.

[91] For a plausible defense of Proust as breaking through the unspeakability of homosexuality and thus preparing the way for its honest discussion and ethical evaluation, see Didier Eribon, *Insult and the Making of the Gay Self*, pp. 23–140.

his experience. What he tells us about his marriage to his cousin is unflattering to both him and her, but honest; and, in his one explicit apologetic work about homosexuality, *Corydon*,[92] the only form of homosexuality he defends is the one he preferred, namely, pederastic sexual relations to quite young boys. What understandably shocks Baldwin is the narrowness of Gide's experience, in particular, the role that idealization played in what he called love for his cousin. Baldwin had come to see the idealized pedestal as what marks the lack of any real loving relationship between persons as individuals. It is not the lack of sex in Gide's marriage to his cousin that shocks Baldwin, but that the relationship is so idealized that he is never in real relationship to her, or she to him, and Baldwin would clearly see this as a failure of love in all relationships, heterosexual and homosexual, the consequence of what he calls "the male prison," which is patriarchal masculinity.

Another early essay, *Preservation of Innocence* (1949),[93] questions the conventional condemnation of homosexuality as unnatural, and offers an explanation for the "hysteria" leading to the "present untouchability" of male homosexuals:

> Let me suggest that his present debasement and our obsession with him corresponds to the debasement of the relationship between the sexes, and that his ambiguous and terrible position in our society reflects the ambiguities and terrors which time has deposited on that relationship as the sea piles seaweed and wreckage along that shore.[94]

The problem, as Baldwin sees it, is the falseness to experience of the gender binary itself, that men and women correspond to its terms:

> It is observable that the more we imagine we have discovered the less we know and that, moreover, the necessity to discover and the effort and self-consciousness involved in this necessity make this relationship more and more complex. Men and women seem to function as imperfect and sometimes unwilling mirrors for one another, a falsification or distortion of the nature of the one is immediately reflected in the nature of the other. A division between them can only betray a division within the soul of each. Matters are not helped if we thereupon decide that men must recapture their status as men and that women must embrace their function as women; not only does the rigidity of attitude put to death any possible communion, but, having once listed the bald physical facts, no one is prepared to go further and decide, of our multiple human attributes, which are masculine and which are feminine.... The recognition of this complexity is the signal of maturity; it marks the death of the child and the birth of the man.[95]

---

[92] See Andre Gide, *Corydon*, translated by Richard Howard (New York: Farrar, Straus & Giroux, 1983) (original French edition, 1983).

[93] See James Baldwin, "Preservation of Innocence," in James Baldwin, *Collected Essays*, pp. 594–600 (first published, 1949).

[94] See *id.*, p. 595.

[95] See *id.*, pp. 596–97.

Freaks and the American Ideal of Manhood (1985)[96] and *The Price of the Ticket* (1985),[97] published late in this life, deal with his own personal experience as a gay man, the first with the kind of abuse he endured as a black gay man, the second with the importance in his life as a gay artist of his relationships to various artists, and in particular, Beauford Delaney.

In the most striking of these essays, *Freaks and the American Ideal of Manhood*, Baldwin frankly discusses his early life as a young gay black man in New York City, in which there was much gay sex but no love: in a world in which "humiliation is the central danger of one's life," "since one cannot risk love without risking humiliation, love becomes impossible."[98] Baldwin's experience was one of continual violence directed at his being gay:

> The condition that is now called gay was then called queer. The operative word was *faggot*, and later pussy, but these epithets really have nothing to do with the question of sexual preference: You were told simply that you had no balls.
>
> I certainly had no desire to harm anyone, nor did I understand how anyone could look at me and suppose me physically capable of *causing* any harm. But boys and men chased me, saying I was a danger to their sisters. I was thrown out of cafeterias and rooming houses because I was "bad" for the neighborhood.
>
> The cops watched all this with a smile, never making the faintest motion to protect me or to disperse my attackers; in fact, I was even more afraid of the copies than I was of the populace.[99]

Such violence, including being beaten by mobs of boys and men, were elicited by Baldwin's sense of his effeminacy:

> It wasn't only that I didn't wish to seem or sound like a woman, for it was this detail that most harshly first struck my eye and ear. I am sure that I was afraid that I already seemed and sounded too much like a woman. In my childhood, at least until my adolescence, my playmates had called me a sissy. It seemed to me that many of the people I met were making fun of women, and I didn't see why. I certainly needed all the friends I could get, male or female, and women had nothing to do with whatever may trouble might prove to be.[100]

It is this kind of experience that led Baldwin, though deeply unhappy, not to be "even remotely tempted by the possibilities of psychiatry or psychoanalysis," because "anyone who thought seriously that I had any desire to be 'adjusted' to this society

---

[96] See James Baldwin, "Freaks and the American Ideal of Manhood," in James Baldwin, *Collected Essays*, pp. 814–29 (first published, 1985).

[97] See James Baldwin, "The Price of the Ticket," in James Baldwin, *Collected Essays*, pp. 830–42 (first published, 1985).

[98] See James Baldwin, "Freaks and the American Ideal of Manhood," in James Baldwin, *Collected Essays*, pp. 814–29 (first published, 1985), p. 817.

[99] *Id.*, p. 819.

[100] *Id.*, p. 823.

had to be ill; too ill, certainly, as time was to prove, to be trusted."[101] His problem was a matter of American culture,

> the American ideal of masculinity, This ideal has created cowboys and Indians, good buys and bad guys, punks and studs, tough guys and softies, butch and faggot, black and white. It is an ideal so paralytically infantile that it is virtually forbidden – as an unpatriotic act – that the American boy evolve into the complexity of manhood.[102]

He now saw developments within feminism as the key to taking seriously and resisting the pernicious role gender continued to play in our culture: "The present androgynous 'craze' … strikes me as an attempt to be honest concerning one's nature."[103] He concludes:

> But we are all androgynous, not only because we are all born of a woman impregnated by the seed of a man but because each of us, helplessly and forever, contains the other – male in female, female in male, white in black and black in white. We are a part of one another. Many of my countrymen appear to have found this fact exceedingly inconvenient and even unfair, and so, and, very often, do I. But none of us can do anything about it.[104]

We are, Baldwin argues, androgynous, by which he means that the gender binary and hierarchy do not correspond to human experience – men have characteristics ascribed to women, and women those ascribed to men, so that the gender binary is false and falsifying, and does not correspond to what we experience in real relationships between equal persons with free voices. It was the experience of such a relationship with Lucien – the first loving gay relationship in his life – that led him to see the cultural role that America's rigid enforcement of the gender binary and hierarchy had played not only in crippling his own capacity to love, but the lovelessness that he came to see motivated racism, sexism, and homophobia as well. Long before American feminists like Carol Gilligan gave a name to this phenomenon, Baldwin found his vocation and voice in exploring the role the Love Laws played in sustaining both black and white racism, as well as sexism and homophobia, as I believe my argument has now shown. It is an astonishing achievement of both psychological and ethical insight, confirming yet again the power of art to deepen our understanding of our common humanity in ways that other disciplines are not yet able to do. Near the end of his life, Baldwin was working on his last play, *The Welcome Table*, that he did not live to finish,[105] in which the main characters were women, and its main character Edith, living in the South of France, is modeled on the black singer-dancer, Josephine Baker. Baldwin was coming to believe that the

[101] *Id.*, p. 816.
[102] *Id.*, p. 815.
[103] *Id.*, p. 827.
[104] *Id.*, pp. 828–29.
[105] For discussion, see David Leeming, *James Baldwin*, pp. 372–78.

best way to express his own complexities was through the prism of a woman artist and the way her loves and her art challenged conventional barriers, in the same way that Tennessee Williams, another gay American artist, would find in Blanche DuBois in *Streetcar Named Desire* the fullest expression of his life as a gay man seeking a voice and resonance for his struggles for love and vocation and the tragic forces in American masculinity that not only refused to see such love for what it was, but destroyed and maimed it. Baldwin was, of course, acutely sensitive, as a gay man, to how patriarchy killed loving relationships between men, and he knew, from the experience of his loving relationship to Lucien, that it was that experience that gave rise to his voice resisting patriarchy. Like D. H. Lawrence in *Women in Love*, Baldwin believed that we will not have taken seriously the deepest injustices that afflict us until we resist patriarchy in our intimate lives, and thus make possible not only love between women and men, but between men and men.

What a late essay like *Freaks and the American Ideal of Manhood* shows us, in terms starker and more personal than Baldwin had ever used before, is the violence he endured, which he saw from the beginning to be rooted in his gender-bending gay life style, or, even before he had a sex life, in his gender-bending "strangeness." It is his great achievement to give voice to the roots of this violence in a conception of American manhood and womanhood that, in demanding compliance with the Love Laws that held people in their racist or sexist or homophobic place, destroyed the possibility of love and real relationship, indeed gave rise to violence to any love that challenged the rigid gender binary and hierarchy. What makes Baldwin's achievement so remarkable is that he saw the central issue, patriarchy, in such complex and nuanced ways, interconnecting evils (racism, sexism, and homophobia), not usually seen whole but in compartments. Is it perhaps because, as a black man who was gay and loved white men and black and gender-bending, he saw and experienced all these evils as one and found nonetheless a love that resisted all of them, giving him both life and voice to tell his terrible and terrifying story with such emotional force and yet intellectual precision? If there is any example of how challenging the gender binary and hierarchy makes life and love and ethical voice possible, it is James Baldwin.

7

Eleanor Roosevelt, Margaret Mead, and Ruth Benedict on Resisting Patriarchy

Gay men stand in a different relationship to patriarchy than women in general, and lesbian women in particular. The demands of the gender binary and hierarchy require that, at a young age, boys must be indoctrinated into these demands – taking on the activities and interests of men (sharply separated from those of women – thus, the gender binary), and observing the hierarchies among men as well as hierarchies of men over boys and women. Gay love challenges these demands, and has thus historically been subject to extraordinary levels of punishment (burning at the stake). When a boy like James Baldwin fails to observe these demands, he is subject to humiliation and violence, marking his psyche, requiring, if he is to live and love as a gay man, resistance challenging the gender binary. We have now explored such resistance – both successful and unsuccessful – in various gay men, and how and why a certain experience of love across the boundaries expresses itself in such resistance.

In contrast, patriarchy tends to take less interest in women until they approach sexual maturity and marriage, demanding then that they conform to patriarchal controls as obedient wives and mothers, including controls of voice. Until that time, girls live in a world of women, and often have relationally complex relationships with one another, and, within the confines of women's space, girls are free and have a voice until they are sexually mature. It is for this reason that women often have stronger voices in resisting patriarchy than men, who experience trauma and patriarchal identification when developmentally quite immature, leading to both loss of memory and voice, the marks of trauma. The comparable demands on women come later when they are developmentally more mature, and still have voices, and can sometimes resist the demands placed on them, whether from their mothers or fathers or others. The consequence is that men, like Garrison, who come to resist patriarchy through relationships to women who resist patriarchy, often sponsor and support women's resistance voices because such voices carry the argument into areas he cannot (see Chapter 5).[1]

---

[1] On all these points, see Carol Gilligan, "The Centrality of Relationship in Human Development: A Puzzle, Some Evidence, and a Theory," in K. Fischer and G. Hoam, eds., *Development and Vulnerability in Close Relationships* (New York: Erlbaum, 1996); Carol Gilligan, *The Birth of Pleasure*; and Carol Gilligan, *Joining the Resistance* (Cambridge, UK: Polity, 2011).

The very fact that women are of less interest to patriarchy until they are developmentally mature can give them more freedom to explore lesbian relationships to one another, sometimes masking such relationships as yet another form of those intense friendships among women that flourish under the radar of patriarchy.[2] Under certain forms of patriarchy, like that of ancient Rome, many such relationships, even when sexual, were often not perceived as such. As Bernadette Brooten put the point, contrasting Roman views of male homosexuality and lesbianism:

> the permanent passivity expected of women contrasted with the understanding that free men might penetrate either females or males or even be penetrated themselves. The focus on penetration as the principal sexual image led to a simplistic view of female erotic behavior and a complex view of the erotic choices of men.[3]

Brooten convincingly argues in her important book that Christian patriarchy was more homophobic than Roman patriarchy: Christianity, unlike pagan law, not only brutally condemned male homosexual relationships as such (death by burning) but lesbian relationships as well, and went beyond Jewish law in condemning lesbian relationships as well as male sexual relationships.[4] An "American colonial statute from New Haven (and the many others that have placed the death penalty on male-male sexual relationships throughout history) illustrates this legacy" when it explicitly extends the death penalty to lesbian sex as well.[5] The target of such extraordinary Christian criminal and moral condemnations of lesbianism were those relationships conspicuously challenging conventional feminine gender roles, women dressing as men and engaging in sex acts involving penetration (dildos).[6] Transvestite lesbianism, in particular, merited the death penalty in America, Britain, and Europe:[7] "What was most threatening to both Europe and America from the sixteenth to the eighteenth centuries was not lesbian sex by itself, but male impersonation and all that was implied in rejection of the feminine status."[8]

In contrast, "[i]t is doubtful that [lesbian] women who did not change their female appearance suffered such penalties"[9] as death; and sometimes lesbian sexual relationships were not criminally condemned at all: The British law, which criminalized male gay sex until 1967, did not criminalize lesbianism as such.[10]

---

[2] For an illuminating study of the spectrum of such relationships, see Martha Vicinus, *Intimate Friends: Women Who Loved Women, 1778–1928* (Chicago: University of Chicago Press, 2004).

[3] Bernadette J. Brooten, *Love Between Women: Early Christian Responses to Female Homoeroticism* (Chicago: University of Chicago Press, 1996), at p. 49.

[4] See *id.*

[5] Brooten, *Love Between Women*, p. 195.

[6] On the Roman form of this view, see Brooten, *Love Between Women*, p. 54.

[7] See, on this point, Lillian Faderman, *Surpassing the Love of Men: Romantic Friendship and Love Between Women from the Renaissance to the Present* (New York: Perennial, 1998), pp. 47–61.

[8] *Id.*, p. 54.

[9] *Id.*, p. 49.

[10] See en.wikipedia.org/LGBT rights in the United Kingdom.

Such relationships could, however, be the subject of criminal law in other ways, for example, homophobic enforcement of prostitution laws and laws against public indecency,[11] and remain even today the targets of homophobic public and private violence[12] and discriminatory treatment.[13] And, there was, of course, denial. In an 1811 case in Scotland, the sexual relationship of two women, observed by a young school girl, was successfully argued by their lawyer as not possible (ostensibly because there was no penetrating object).[14] Women under patriarchy have close relationships to one another, which can easily mask lesbian feeling as they themselves have children or care for them and live lives under the radar of patriarchy. Lesbians may thus break the Love Laws (loving persons of the same gender) without needing to conspicuously challenge patriarchy.

When, however, do these relationships express themselves in resistance to patriarchy in all its forms? What appears to be the key to such resisting voice is when lesbian love leads to freeing the voice and lives of women from the traditional patriarchal constraints imposed on women's choices, including not only to love in a way that breaks the Love Laws, but to speak and write and live in ways that resist and often question patriarchal constraints on women's voices and lives. Many lesbian artists, inspired by their lovers, illustrate how lesbian relationships inspire new forms of artistic and ethically creative voice. Gertrude Stein and her lover, Alice B. Toklas, immediately come to mind.[15] Stein's art is not as hermetic as many suppose; one of her most moving explorations of lesbian love and the homophobic violence inflicted on such love, "Melanctha" in *Three Lives*,[16] is portrayed from within black American culture and its enforcement of the Love Laws. Other such relationships include, among others, the poet Elizabeth Bishop and Lota de Macedo Soares,[17] and the plays of Mercedes de Acosta inspired by her lesbian relationships to

---

[11]   See, in general, Joey L. Mogul, Andrea J. Ritchie, and Kay Whitlock, *Queer (In)justice: The Criminalization of LGBT People in the United States* (Boston: Beacon Press, 2011).

[12]   See, in general, Gregory M. Herek and Kevin T. Berrill, eds., *Hate Crimes: Confronting Violence Against Lesbians and Gay Men* (Newbury Park, CA: Sage, 1992); Less E. Ross, ed., *The War Against Domestic Violence* (Boca Raton, FL: CRC Press, 2010), pp. 129–38.

[13]   See, for example. Ruthann Robson, *Lesbian (Out)Law: Survival under the Rule of Law* (Ithaca, NY: Firebrand, 1992); Ruthann Robson, "Convictions: Theorizing Lesbians and Criminal Justice," in Martin Duberman, ed., *A Queer World: The Center for Lesbian and Gay Studies Reader* (New York: New York University Press, 1997), at pp. 418–30.

[14]   Bernadette J. Brooten, *Love Between Women*, pp. 189–90.

[15]   For an illuminating selection of Stein's art, see Carl Van Vechten, *Selected Writings of Gertrude Stein* (New York: Vintage, 1990). For a complete edition, see Catharine R. Stimpson and Harriet Chessman, eds., *Gertrude Stein: Writings 1903–1932* (New York: The Library of America, 1998); Catharine R. Stimpson and Harriet Chessman, eds., *Gertrude Stein: Writings 1932–1946* (New York: The Library of America, 1998).

[16]   See Stimpson and Chessman, *Gertrude Stein: Writings 1903–1932*, pp. 124–239.

[17]   See Carmen L. Oliveira, *Rare and Commonplace Flowers: The Story of Elizabeth Bishop and Lota de Macedo Soares*, translated by Neil K. Besner (New Brunswick, NJ: Rutgers University Press, 2003). For Bishop's works, see Robert Giroux and Lloyd Schwartz, eds., *Elizabeth Bishop: Poems, Prose, and Letters* (New York: The Library of America, 2008).

leading actresses of her period, including Greta Garbo.[18] Like Benjamin Britten and Peter Pears, the lesbian relationships of de Acosta paired a creative and performing artist, and her plays, not unlike the operas of Britten, prominently challenged not only women's traditional roles, but, in her most successful play, *Jacob Slovak*,[19] the Love Laws, destroying the love of a woman for a Jewish man. Even Willa Cather, so reticent about her lesbian loves, writes early in her creative life the astonishing 1905 short story, "Paul's Case," one of the most sensitive, intelligent, and harrowing explorations of the psyche of a deeply alone, young gay man, imprisoned by the homophobia of his father and teachers and fellows in unreal and crippling fantasies of freedom, that end in theft, acting out his dreams of extravagance (including taking rooms at the Waldorf in New York City), despair, and suicide under a train.[20] Cather deals with the issues the short story raises circumspectly (the homosexuality is not explicit, but nonetheless clearly recognizable), but yet with remarkable honesty, integrity, and humane feeling for Paul's unspeakable plight – an imaginative freedom that could, with a courage and intelligence and discipline like that of Cather herself, have been the basis of revelatory art, rather than suicidal fantasies. The short story shows that gay people under American homophobia – isolated and unspeakable and thus without voice – live unjustly at a knife's edge of despair and suicidality.

Perhaps, the most underappreciated of these lesbian artists – as the remarkable student of homophobia she clearly was – is the novelist, Patricia Highsmith. We now know, from the astonishing biography of Highsmith by Joan Schenkar,[21] that all of Highsmith's many novels, some of them made into important movies (for example, Hitchcock's *Strangers on a Train*), were inspired by her succession of lesbian lovers. All of her novels, with one exception, involve murders, usually motivated by rage and anger. Highsmith saw her plight as a gender-bending lesbian in gay men, imprisoned by a violent internalized homophobia to which they reacted by homicide. Although one would not know it from the several movies based on her novel, *The Talented Mr. Ripley*,[22] Ripley's murderous violence – killing both Dickie

[18] See Robert A. Schanke, *"That Furious Lesbian": The Story of Mercedes de Acosta* (Carbondale: Southern Illinois University Press, 2003); for Acosta's plays, see Robert A. Schanke, *Women in Turmoil: Six Plays by Mercedes de Acosta* (Carbondale: Southern Illinois University Press, 2003).

[19] See Robert A. Schanke, *Women in Turmoil*, pp. 45–94.

[20] See Willa Cather, "Paul's Case," in Willa Cather, *Collected Stories* (New York: Vintage, 1992), pp. 170–89. For an excellent interpretive study of Cather's life and works, see Hermione Lee, *Willa Cather: Double Lives* (New York: Vintage, 1989). For Cather's ambivalence about her sexuality, see Joan Acocella, *Willa Cather and the Politics of Criticism* (New York: Vintage Books, 2000), pp. 45–65. I am indebted for these references to Phillip Blumberg.

[21] Joan Schenkar, *The Talented Miss Highsmith: The Secret Life and Serious Art of Patricia Highsmith* (London: St. Martin's Press, 2009).

[22] See *Purple Noon*, directed by René Clément (1960); *The Talented Mr. Ripley*, directed by Anthony Minghella (1999).

and Freddie – is triggered, in both cases, by homophobic insults.[23] Highsmith's portrait of Ripley as wearing two masks, which he exchanges as circumstances require, anatomizes gay men under homophobia as actors, split and divided from themselves, indeed having no selves – mimicking a geniality that covers murderous rage. Only in her important novel of lesbian love, *The Price of Salt*,[24] does Highsmith show us the inner world of lesbian lovers, as the artistic Therese's love for Carol, an older married woman with a young son in a miserable patriarchal marriage, opens each of them to an imaginative world of new possibilities resisting patriarchal demands. It is her only novel, and her best written, without homicide at its center. It is also the most hopeful.

We can, I believe, see the same transformative power of lesbian love in lesbian pairs who were not artists, but whose love freed a new kind of ethical public voice that challenged patriarchal demands. Perhaps, the now most well-known lesbian relationship is that of Eleanor Roosevelt and Lorena Hickok, and I begin with a discussion of their relationship and its impact on freeing ethical voice. I then turn to a more extended discussion of a less well-known lesbian relationship, that of Margaret Mead and Ruth Benedict, two brilliant academic anthropologists, who challenged then-dominant gender stereotypes by breaking the gender barrier on women in higher education as teachers and pathbreaking scholars, critics of American sexism and racism, but of patriarchy generally. None of these women had, as some of the artists had, lived openly as lesbians. This is, I believe, more understandable in their circumstances than it may be in ours (feminist criticism of Susan Sontag for closeting her passionate loves of women comes to mind[25]). However, there can be no doubt that lesbian love in both cases I study here freed ethical voice, in a period when patriarchal constraints on women's voices were powerful.

The Roosevelt–Hickok relationship has now been well studied.[26] Eleanor Roosevelt had led a much more conventional life as wife and mother than Hickok, who had, at the time they met, already broken with dominant gender stereotypes of the woman's role by becoming the leading American woman political journalist of the Associated Press, assigned to interview the wife of the governor of

---

[23] See, on this point, Patricia Highsmith, *The Talented Mr. Ripley*, in Patricia Highsmith, *The Talented Mr. Ripley, Ripley Under Ground, Ripley's Game* (New York: Everyman's Library, 1999), pp. 1–290, at pp. 98–99, 142, 146–47.

[24] See Patricia Highsmith, *The Price of Salt* (Mineola, NY: Dover, 2015).

[25] See, for an illuminating recent discussion, Kate Webb, "From Desert Girl to Dark Lady" (reviewing two recent biographies of Sontag), *The Times Literary Supplement*, January 23, 2015, no. 5834, at pp. 8–9.

[26] For the most illuminating study of the relationship, see Blanche Wiesen Cook, *Eleanor Roosevelt, Volume 1: 1884–1933* (New York: Penguin, 1992); Blanche Wiesen Cook, *Eleanor Roosevelt, Volume 2: The Defining Years 1933–1938* (New York: Penguin, 1999). For insight into their loving intimacy, see Rodger Streitmatter, *Empty Without You: The Intimate Letters of Eleanor Roosevelt and Lorena Hickok* (New York: Da Capo, 1998).

New York and later the president of the United States.[27] Eleanor was very much a woman of her rather American aristocratic class (the niece of Theodore Roosevelt). If women of her class did not go to college, Eleanor didn't,[28] although she did have a superb liberal education at an all-women's school in Britain, where her remarkable intelligence and independence were acknowledged and recognized.[29] Like other women of her class, her apparently privileged family life concealed a cold, rejecting mother and an alcoholic, self-destructive father (adored by his daughter), both of whom died when Eleanor was young (Eleanor was eight when her mother died, and her father died two years later).[30] Eleanor fell in love with and married a man of her class and indeed a relative (conspicuously, not breaking the Love Laws), a man of great good humor and open-hearted (not unlike her alcoholic father), the "gay cavalier,"[31] who always valued his wife's remarkable intelligence, independence, and ethical integrity, even when he disagreed with her views or, as a politician, could and would not act on them. It was, however, very much a power marriage always on stage, and Eleanor early in the marriage settled into a life as dutiful patriarchal wife of an upcoming politician, mother of five children (another died in infancy), and subject to her demanding and controlling mother-in-law.[32] Her husband's affair with Lucy Mercer (discovered by Eleanor in 1918) ended the sexual aspect of their marriage, and broke Eleanor's heart (Eleanor was willing to divorce, but Franklin's mother threatened to disown him if he did so).[33]

Eleanor Roosevelt continued to support her husband's ambitions, crucially not allowing his crippling polio to end his political career (opposing, in this, her mother-in-law, who wanted her son to retire from politics).[34] Eleanor played her role as political wife brilliantly, but she spent her personal life at her own home, Val-Kill, and her closest friends were two lesbian couples[35] (FDR and Louis Howe "called many of ER's new friends 'she-men,'"[36] conscious, as they certainly were, that Eleanor's new intimates challenged the gender binary). For her part, in 1925, Eleanor would write in her private journal: "No form of love is to be despised."[37]

Hickock becomes a crucial intimate figure in Eleanor's life in 1932, indeed they become lovers, as Eleanor experiences depression when it becomes clear she will be

[27] See, on this point, Blanche Wiesen Cook, *Eleanor Roosevelt, Volume 1*, pp. 448–76.
[28] See, on this point, *id.*, p. 156.
[29] See, on this point, *id.*, pp. 102–24.
[30] See on these points, *id.*, pp. 56–78.
[31] See *id.*, p. 218.
[32] See *id.*, pp. 125–86.
[33] See *id.*, pp. 228–32.
[34] See *id.*, pp. 307–37.
[35] Esther Everett Lape and Elizabeth Fisher Read; see *id.*, pp. 296–97; Nancy Cook and Marion Dickerman, with whom she built and lived at Val-Kill; see *id.*, pp. 318–19.
[36] *Id.*, p. 302.
[37] See *id.*, p. 318.

first lady of the United States.[38] A poignant expression of Eleanor's sense of the dark side for women of patriarchal marriage (including marriage to a president of the United States) were her visits to the monument, Grief, in Washington, DC, dedicated to Clover Adams, the wife of Henry Adams; Clover had committed suicide on learning of her husband's affair with another woman.[39] Eleanor had certainly known such despair and perhaps even suicidality. The day before Franklin's inauguration as president Eleanor goes to the monument with Lorena Hickok.[40] Their love at this point and for the next few years may have crucially shown Eleanor a way to go creatively on. It was the lesbian relationship to Hickok that made possible and indeed directly inspired the development of Eleanor Roosevelt's pathbreaking ethical voice, including, as first lady, both not only speaking and writing in a more public way (Hickok urges her to start writing a column, and speaking in public), but also about new topics like the state of poor Americans during the New Deal (Hickok's reports directly inspire – through its impact on Eleanor, Harry Hopkins, and FDR himself – a new federal program for a community for the poor, Arthurdale[41]), the changing roles of women and women's work,[42] and the ethical claims of people of color against American racism, including Eleanor's unsuccessful campaign for a federal law against lynchings.[43] Many of these issues were brought to the attention of Eleanor and FDR through Hickok's work as chief investigator for Harry Hopkin's Federal Emergency Relief Association (she gives up her career in journalism in part to remain closer to Eleanor – with her own bedroom in the White House).[44] Eleanor experienced in her relationship to Hickok something she may never have experienced in her life before, what she called in her letters to Hickok "a world of love."[45] The power of such mutual understanding, tenderness, and support is revealed by the way Eleanor wrote of Hickok's absence: "empty without you even though I'm busy every minute."[46] Eleanor had, through her relationship to Hickok, experienced an alternative to the demanding patriarchal sense of duty that had dominated her life into false compliance and silenced her inner voice. Love of an equal, who understood and valued her as a person and understood her wounded, despairing sense – from her childhood (a cold mother, and an alcoholic, self-destructive father) and her marriage – of being unloved and unlovable, opened her heart and mind to how love across the boundaries frees an ethical voice that resists and challenges those boundaries, including the boundaries

---

[38] See, on this point, Blanche Wiesen Cook, *Eleanor Roosevelt, Volume 1*, pp. 477–500.

[39] On this point, see *id.*, p. 235.

[40] See *id.*, pp. 492–93.

[41] See, on this point, Blanche Wiesen Cook, *Eleanor Roosevelt, Volume 2*, pp. 130–52.

[42] On Hickok's indignation at the treatment of women's work, see *id.*, pp. 294–95, 302; on her influence on this point on Eleanor, see *id.*, pp. 118–19.

[43] See, on this point, *id.*, pp. 153–89.

[44] See *id.*, pp. 48, 116–17.

[45] See Rodgers Streitmatter, ed., *Empty Without You: The Intimate Letters of Eleanor Roosevelt and Lorena Hickok* (New York: Da Capo Press, 1998), p. 64.

[46] *Id.*, p. 16.

not only of gender but of race and religion (Eleanor was a lifelong critic of political anti-Semitism). Eleanor's relationship to Hickok parallels, at this point, the adulterous and emancipatory loves of George Eliot and Henry Lewes, and Harriet Taylor and John Stuart Mill. Eleanor, in one of her love letters to Hickok, comments on how incendiary adultery, when heterosexual, remains, and clearly regards her relationship to Hickok as adultery, although not incendiary because lesbian love was so easily covered and denied: "How lucky you are not a man!"[47]

The relationship between Eleanor and Hickok did not last on the intense terms of exclusive intimacy that Hickok craved, even though they remained close friends to the end of Eleanor's life and Eleanor supported her financially. Eleanor wore until her death a ring given to her by Hickok in 1932 that had been given to Hickok by her great friend, the legendary diva, Ernestine Schumann-Heink.[48] Hickok's enduring impact on freeing Eleanor's patriarchally silenced voice can no longer be doubted, ending in the role Eleanor Roosevelt would crucially play in the drafting of the Universal Declaration of Human Rights,[49] the culmination of the freeing of ethical voice made possible by her loving relationship to Lorena Hickok.

There is yet another example of the transformative powers of such lesbian love – in particular, how they can make possible new ethical voices resisting both racism and sexism, indeed patriarchy itself – which I want now to examine in some depth, namely, the lesbian relationship of two very great American anthropologists, Margaret Mead and Ruth Benedict. If the general form of my argument can, suitably nuanced to their experience as women, make illuminating sense of their creative voices, it confirms, I believe, the power of the approach. Garrison certainly believed that women could carry the arguments against patriarchy further and deeper than men. My argument here builds on Garrison's insight, showing how lesbian love enabled these two women to carry the argument further than others in their period could and did: raising questions about the gender binary and hierarchy itself (Mead) and extending that argument into one of the most profound analyses of the evils of racism, sexism, and homophobia, and the connections of such evils to the imperialist violence of fascism in Germany and Japan (Benedict).

Margaret Mead and Ruth Benedict were close friends throughout their professional lives; Mead becomes an anthropologist because Benedict inspired her to do so, and Benedict finds in Mead's love and friendship the support she needed to come to the remarkable insights she did into racism and homophobia, insights ahead of their time but laying the foundation for future work and resistance. Mead and Benedict were lesbian lovers for some part of their lives. Both also had sexual relationships to men: Mead married three different men over the course of her

[47] Streitmatter, *Empty Without You*, p. 40.
[48] See Blanche Wiesen Cook, *Eleanor Roosevelt, Volume 2*, p. 394.
[49] See Mary Ann Glendon, *A World Made New: Eleanor Roosevelt and the Universal Declaration of Human Rights* (New York: Random House, 2001).

life, and had a daughter with one of them, and Benedict had been married, quite unhappily, prior to meeting Mead. Both had other lesbian relationships, and Benedict had two other long-term lesbian lovers after Mead.[50] My interest here is how a loving lesbian relationship between Margaret Mead and Ruth Benedict enabled each of them to carry the argument further than others. It empowered critical insights into then-dominant gender stereotypes, including the gender binary and hierarchy, that were central features of the work of both anthropologists, and led both of them to question not only American sexism, but also racism. Ruth Benedict extended the analysis to homophobia as well, and developed a pathbreaking distinction between shame and guilt cultures that she used brilliantly to help Americans understand the culture of imperial Japan with which the United States fought in World War II.

The lives and work of Mead and Benedict became closely intertwined in the same way the creative lives of Britten and Pears were closely intertwined. To do justice to each of them, we must, like the examination of Britten and Pears, study each of them in relationship to one another, a relationship of supportive mutual friendship that continued long after their sexual relationship ceased. It is for this reason that I tell their love story in the same way I told the love story of Britten and Pears, in one narrative in one chapter about two remarkable people who found themselves and their resisting voices in loving relationship to the other.

Margaret Mead was born in 1901 in Philadelphia. Emily Fogg Mead, Margaret's mother, was a highly educated intellectual with a passion for social reform. "She had enjoyed studying the all-female environment of Wellesley College until a reversal in the family fortunes necessitated her return home to the Mid-west, where she taught school and then, supported by a scholarship and the money she had saved, completed her degree at the University of Chicago and embarked on graduate study."[51] In Chicago, she met and married Edward Mead, an economist who was to have a lifelong position at the Wharton School of Commerce at the University of Pennsylvania. The household included her widowed mother-in-law, Martha, who was a college graduate and resumed her teaching career after her husband died. Her presence in the household allowed Emily to continue to pursue her doctoral research on Italian immigrants and her social causes. Mead observed of them: "the two women I knew best were mothers and had professional training. So I had no reason to doubt that brains were suitable for a woman. And as I had my father's kind of mind – which was also his mother's – I learned that the mind is not sex-typed"[52] (the gender binary thus never made sense to Mead). Emily had a postpartum breakdown after the birth of Margaret's younger sister, Katherine, and

---

[50] For important studies of their relationship, see Hilary Lapsley, *Margaret Mead and Ruth Benedict: The Kinship of Women* (Amherst: University of Massachusetts Press, 1999); Lois W. Banner, *Intertwined Lives: Margaret Mead, Ruth Benedict, and Their Circle* (New York: Vintage Books, 2003).

[51] Hilary Lapsley, *Margaret Mead and Ruth Benedict*, p. 136.

[52] Quoted at *id.*, p. 13.

soon after the father had taken a mistress, who urged him to divorce. Martha, who had a strong influence on her son, stopped that possibility, and was a steadying influence on Margaret during the period of her mother's breakdown. Margaret eagerly anticipated following her mother at Wellesley, but because of financial reverses, her father could not afford to send her there, so she attended Edward's alma mater, DePauw University in Indiana; she later persuaded her father to allow her to transfer to Barnard College in New York City, where she would study anthropology with Franz Boas and would meet Ruth Benedict.

Ruth Benedict was born in 1887 in New York City, but grew up on her grand-father's farm in New York State. Benedict's mother, Bertrice, went to Vassar and graduated Phi Beta Kappa in 1885. At graduation, she was already engaged to a homeopathic physician, Frederick Fulton. When Ruth was two, Frederick died, and as an adult, according to Hilary Lapsley, "Ruth believed that her father's death was the formative event in her life."[53] What apparently impacted the child was the way her mother "made a cult of grief out of my father's death, and every March [the anniversary of her loss] she wept in church and in bed at night."[54] For Benedict, the trauma of her father's death and her mother's response marked her continuing sense of a divided self, divided between two worlds: "the world of my father, which was the world of death and which was beautiful, and the world of confusion and explosive weeping which I repudiated. I did not love my mother. I resented her cult of grief, and her worry and concern about little things. But I could always retire to my other world, and to this world my father belonged. I identified him with everything calm and beautiful that came my way."[55] The practical world of women's conventional duties as wife and mother was divided from her imaginative world of the intimate voice of her loving father. Lapsley describes the psychological consequences of such a division:

> Within the two worlds of her childhood she had long practiced the dissociation between public and private self often forced on women by the requirement that they put others' needs before their own. Yet if her self was silenced, at least it was not negated, for it existed in her rich, imaginative life. Her depression arose from the collision and conflict between the inner life and the outer world which seemed to offer no room for what she really valued. . . . It was not until years later, after having experienced unhappiness and battles against thoughts of suicide, that Ruth was to find the conditions that would lead to a resolution of these dualities and a sense of wholeness.[56]

Benedict thus faced a dilemma strikingly similar to that of Isherwood: what for Isherwood was his mother's Myth of the Dead War Hero was for Benedict her mother's rigid conception of the womanly duties central to her cult of grief for her

[53] *Id.,* p. 35.
[54] Quoted at *id.,* p. 35.
[55] Quoted at *id.,* pp. 35–36.
[56] *Id.,* pp. 40–41.

dead husband. The struggle in both cases was to find an authentic voice within that might resist such patriarchal duties of manhood or womanhood. The sense of a divided self corresponds to the terms of a gender binary, only her father being imaginative experience, and her mother patriarchal duty.

A generous benefactor gave Benedict and her sister (both of whose grades were top-of-the class) four-year scholarships to Vassar, where Benedict studied literature. Upon graduation, a Vassar patron offered her an all-expenses-paid one-year tour of Europe. She became fascinated by a portrait of Mary Wollstonecraft in the National Portrait Gallery in London, confessing later that she was "haunted by the terror of youth before experience. I wanted so desperately to know how other women had saved their souls alive. And the woman in the little frame arrested me."[57] Upon return to the United States, Benedict considered her options, and tried social work and then teaching. A young scientist, Stanley Benedict, pursued her, and in the year of their engagement became a full professor at the Cornell University medical school. A rising source of tension in the marriage was Ruth's desire to have children. She learned that she had blocked fallopian tubes that could be remedied only by complicated surgery, "but Stanley, exercising his male prerogative, would not give his consent to the operation."[58] Meanwhile, Benedict struggled with a manuscript on Wollstonecraft and women, but could not make progress. The marriage deteriorated, and Benedict went to New York City to study at Columbia University and the New School for Social Research. A teacher at the latter institution, Alexander Goldenweiser, "first recognized Ruth's potential as a scholar and persuaded her to pursue her studies seriously. He suggested that she enroll for graduate studies with Franz Boas at Columbia. In 1921, at the mature age of 33, Ruth entered Columbia as a doctoral student."[59]

Franz Boas was a Jewish immigrant from Germany, a pacifist and socialist, who played a central role in the development of a cultural anthropology that was to debunk the racism common in both Germany and the United States in the late nineteenth century.[60] Consider, for example, the Supreme Court's decision in 1896,[61] which held that state-imposed racial segregation was consistent with the Equal Protection Clause of the Fourteenth Amendment (a decision unanimously reversed in 1954).[62] What rendered such segregation acceptable in 1896 was certainly in part, as Charles Lofgren has shown,[63] the dominant racist social science of the late nineteenth century. This "science" of American ethnology used alleged physical

---

[57] Quoted at *id.*, p. 43.

[58] *Id.*, p. 51.

[59] *Id.*, p. 53.

[60] See Hilary Lapsley, *Margaret Mead and Ruth Benedict*, pp. 55–61.

[61] See *Plessy v. Ferguson*, 163 U.S. 537 (1896).

[62] *Brown v. Board of Education*, 347 U.S. 483 (1954) (state-imposed racial segregation violation of equal protection).

[63] Charles A. Lofgren, *The Plessy Case: A Legal Historical Interpretation* (New York: Oxford University Press, 1987).

differences (physically measured by brain capacity or cephalic indices) to argue that there were inherent differences in moral capacity between the races.[64] These measurements afforded a putatively scientific basis for making the allegedly reasonable judgment that the separation of the races was justified. Segregation in transportation (the issue in *Plessy*) might thus discourage forms of social intercourse that would result in degenerate forms of miscegenation; and segregation in education would reflect race-linked differences in capacity best dealt with in separate schools, as well as discourage social intercourse.

The antebellum abolitionists, however, had offered plausible objections to the scientific status of American ethnology, and similarly forceful objections were available at the time *Plessy* was decided in 1896. For example, Franz Boas had two years prior published a paper debunking the weight to be accorded race in the social sciences.[65]

What Boas had shown was that the weight accorded race in the racism of German anti-Semitism or American racism did not rest on a physical fact that marked the subhuman abilities of certain groups of people, but rather a cultural tradition of dehumanizing whole groups of persons by, first, depriving them of the basic rights accorded other persons, and second, the rationalizing such treatment in terms of cultural stereotypes whose appeal, in a vicious circularity, rests on the abridgment of the basic rights of the group, in particular, the repression of any voice that might reasonably challenge this injustice. From this perspective, racism does not rest on a reliable science of race differences: There are none that could justify unequal treatment. Rather, it reflects an entrenched structural injustice, rooted in culture and tradition – what I have earlier called moral slavery. In making this argument, Boas urged a paradigm shift from the crude physical anthropology on which racism rested to a cultural anthropology that took account of the weight of unjust cultural traditions in human societies, traditions that were subject to ethical criticism and change.

Ruth Benedict found her intellectual home at Columbia. "Boas's mentoring was crucially important in her decision to advance in anthropology. This was a critical juncture in her life and one where she could not have tolerated discouragement. She had failed as a social worker, as a teacher, and as a writer, her marriage was failing, and she had been denied the opportunity of motherhood. Goldenweiser and Boas

---

[64] See, for good general treatments, Stephen Jay Gould, *The Mismeasure of Man* (New York: W.W. Norton, 1981); Thomas F. Gossett, *Race: The History of an Idea in America* (New York: Schocken Books, 1965); George M. Fredrickson, *The Black Image in the White Mind: The Debate on Afro-American Character and Destiny, 1817–1914* (Middletown, CT: Wesleyan University Press, 1981); John S. Haller, Jr., *Outcasts from Evolution: Scientific Attitudes of Racial Inferiority, 1859–1900* (New York: McGraw-Hill, 1971); Reginald Horsman, *Race and Manifest Destiny: The Origins of American Racial Anglo-Saxonism* (Cambridge: Harvard University Press, 1981).

[65] See Franz Boas, "Human Faculty as Determined by Race" (1894), in George W. Stocking, Jr., *A Franz Boas Reader: The Shaping of American Anthropology, 1833–1911* (Chicago: University of Chicago Press, 1974), pp. 221–42.

represented an anthropology that could prove an outlet for her literary imagination. It offered a route to different worlds and provided a relief from her own."[66] After her first year of graduate study, Ruth Benedict became the teaching assistant for the Barnard course in which Margaret Mead was a student. Benedict had just returned from a summer of fieldwork with the Serrano people in the American Southwest, and was just finishing her doctorate. She very much wanted to be financially independent of her husband, and had hoped to lead the first anthropology department ever established at a women's college (Barnard); Boas thought another of his earlier woman graduate students, who was unmarried, would be preferable. As an alternative, Boas secured her employment with a private group, the Southwest Foundation, where she continued to do fieldwork and study the mythology of Southwest peoples.[67] Benedict would be appointed assistant professor at Columbia in 1931.[68]

Ruth Benedict and Margaret Mead became close friends soon after they stepped into the same classroom. Mead found her vocation through Benedict. "Ruth noted in her diary in March 1923: 'Lunch with M. Mead – discussed her going into anthropology. I hope she does. I need a companion in harness. . . .' What tipped the balance, apparently, was Ruth's saying, 'Professor Boas and I have nothing to offer but an opportunity to do work that matters.'"[69] After Mead graduated from college, sometime in 1923 or 1924, she and Benedict became lovers.[70] While they actually lived together for only a short period, the sexual relationship continued until 1928 in the midst of frequent separations because of Mead's fieldwork in the Pacific.

The sexual relationship was intensely important for Benedict, who would later write that what made her marriage to Stanley so disastrous was that his harshness and disapproval "made her lose faith in the transformative power of love."[71] The relationship with Mead allowed Benedict to give expression to her long suppressed sexuality and need for sexual love in terms that remind one of Baldwin on what his love for Lucien meant to him. "Now she found that she could love a woman completely, with sensual abandonment and the investment of all her emotions. She wrote of the physical satisfactions of love. 'Here bliss/Is for the taking,' and she asked how anything could 'compete/ With sleep begotten of a woman's kiss.' In an unpublished poem, 'For Faithfulness,' she wrote, 'I lie so in quiet at your breast. . . . I am so safe with you, so blindly blest.'"[72] The sense of the power of passionate sexual love and the comfort and clarity about oneself and the beloved could have been written by Baldwin, albeit about a man not a woman. There was, however, an aspect of Benedict's love for Mead that was not at work in Baldwin's relationship to Lucien.

[66] Hilary Lapsley, *Margaret Mead and Ruth Benedict*, p. 60.
[67] See *id.*, pp. 61–62.
[68] See *id.*, p. 200.
[69] *Id.*, p. 69.
[70] *Id.*, p. 75.
[71] *Id.*, p. 90.
[72] *Id.*, p. 95.

Benedict had come out of an unhappy marriage to an educated but patriarchal man who exercised his authority to stop her from having the child she wanted, and she had through Boas found a vocation that expressed, and allowed her to feel confidence in, her brilliant intelligence and imagination. No relationship to a man had enabled her to overcome the division of her psyche, modeled on the gender binary, that was the legacy of her father and mother. Now, she found in her relationship to Mead, very much her equal in intelligence and imaginative insight into other peoples and voice, a sensual release of her passions and a fuller exercise of her intelligence engaging with the honest voice of another – the first sexual loving experience in her life that flourished on terms of a greater equality and freedom than any she had known, allowing her to experience in herself and in Mead the full range of human thoughts and feelings. There was no gender binary or hierarchy separating her from the person she loved: Mead was, like her, a woman and, under patriarchy, her equal. However, more importantly, both came to the relationship as women already much more outside of or in tension with patriarchy than other women of their generation, very much a Society of Outsiders, in Woolf's sense.

Mead had already come, through her relationship to her highly educated and ambitious mother (including her study of Italian immigrants) and grandmother and even her father, to see that the mind was not, as she put it, "sex-typed," that she could and would exercise the full range of her intelligence, as a person, not defined by the gender binary. While she clearly sexually liked men, her relationships to men were sometimes fraught, and, in the case of one of her husbands, patriarchally violent on his part. She had also had the experience of her father's infidelity and her mother's depression, so she always knew women did not always flourish in conventional marriages.

Benedict also had the experience of a highly educated mother, but a mother whose patriarchal demands, after the early death of her father, caused her daughter a sense of conflicted internal division itself defined by the gender binary, and led her into a marriage that stifled both her sexuality as a woman (including her desire to have a child) and her intelligence. Benedict had begun her journey into resisting patriarchal demands when she effectively left her husband and found a vocation through Boas in higher education that had been traditionally defined patriarchally as men's domain. Entering into this field was itself a challenge to the patriarchally defined limitation of rights of free speech and conscience and work to men, which made Benedict already a rebel against conventional ideals of patriarchal femininity.

It is against this background that their meeting, as teacher and student, at Barnard was for both of them an inspiration to yet further challenge patriarchal constraints on women, enabling each of them to carry their resistance to patriarchal demands on women much further than they could otherwise have done. What Garrison had found in women (namely, that they could carry the resistance to patriarchy further than anti-patriarchal men like himself), Benedict and Mead discovered in their passionate lesbian sexual love an attachment, a communion freed in unexpected and liberating ways from the patriarchal constraints on women's sexuality and voice (in particular, Virginia Woolf's Angel in the House). In 1927, Margaret wrote quite explicitly in these terms about the effects on her of her relationship to Benedict (trusting the authority of one's own experience, resisting patriarchal authority, finding one's own voice) in a poem, "The Gift," in which

> she thanks Ruth for helping her sharpen her intellect and understand her sexuality . . . the implication is that she learned about a range of sexual expression from Ruth. Through Ruth, Margaret has also overcome her fear of her academic elders. . . . Moreover, because of Ruth, she no longer fears her desire for both sexes. . . . Yet Ruth has also freed her to follow "untraveled ways" as well as "traveled" ones. . . . She writes poetically that she will press "all encountered beauty" upon Ruth's "lips of loveliness."

> > For you have given me speech!
> > No more I'll sit, an anxious child
> > Awed by articulate elders,
> > Dumb in envy of the melodies
> > The fall from human lips, while mine
> > Can only give straight, formal kisses. . . . [73]

Their lesbian sexual relationship, although never public while they lived, led them to challenge patriarchal limits on the right of intimate life not only for women, but for lesbian women in new, remarkably creative ways. Each of them, already living outside patriarchy, embraced more fully than they previously had been able to do so the basic human rights of speech, conscience, work, and intimate life, and, for this reason, saw the deepest problem for women hungering for justice was patriarchy itself. The best evidence for this is their work itself. Their loving sexual relationship – both highly sexual and also full of intelligent, indeed creative voice – could only have taken place if both women found in their love what Britten and Pears found in theirs, a world of freedom and equality in intimate life that resisted the patriarchal constraints on love, in particular, the Love Laws. It is out of their mutually shared experience of sexual love on terms of freedom and equality that they came together to the brilliant insight that enabled Benedict and Mead to work to make creative advances, through identifying and questioning the gender binary and discuss publicly its sometimes quite pernicious significance in human cultures. What Boas had discovered about the unjust cultural construction of anti-Semitism and race, they discovered about gender, including, in Benedict's pathbreaking works, the role the patriarchal gender binary played in all these evils. If intelligence is seeing true connections previously not seen, sexual love here was the key to their astonishing intelligence as scholars and activists advancing justice in America. Could anything

[73] See *id.*, pp. 261–62.

better challenge the gender binary than this union of the unleashed sexual passion of women and intelligence?

The sexual aspect of their relationship did not last, even though both acknowledged, as we have just seen, its pivotal importance in their lives and their work. The problem was Mead's other relationships, including other lesbian relationships and her marriages to men. In 1923, Mead would marry Luther Cressman,[74] who was training for the ministry, and later would marry two anthropologists with whom she would do fieldwork, Reo Fortune[75] and Gregory Bateson.[76] She would divorce all of them, and, at the end of her life, live with Rhoda Metraux, who was her lover.[77] For her part, Benedict pressed Mead, in 1924, the year after her marriage to Cressman, for a stronger commitment from her, reproaching Margaret for idolizing her as a "favorite teacher" and not regarding her as an equal, clearly pressing her lover for a more real, more equal relationship, unburdened by idealizing pedestals.[78] It was the sense of equality and freedom in relationship that was, I believe, so liberating for both these remarkable women, and Benedict clearly sensed the importance of equality in any real relationship when she urged her lover not to hold onto her sense of Benedict as her idealized teacher, and, to this extent, not her equal. Mead's marriage to Reo Fortune was tempestuous and violent; at its worst, he hit her, causing a miscarriage.[79] Her marriage to Bateson, involving collaborative fieldwork, was much happier,[80] but ended when he fell in love with a dancer. When Ruth saw that Margaret Mead's sexual passion for Reo Fortune was consuming, she decided in 1928 that the sexual dimension of her relationship to Mead should end, and she should seek more committed lesbian lovers.[81] By the mid-1930s, Benedict had become a committed lesbian, and she had had two long-term lesbian lovers, Natalie Raymond[82] and Ruth Valentine.[83] "Margaret didn't like it; she wanted Ruth to remain both homosexual and heterosexual, a 'mixed type.'"[84]

The intensely collaborative friendship between the two women flourished to the end of Benedict's life: reading and commenting on one another's work, indispensable support and conversation. From the beginning to the end, their relationship was what Benedict wanted it to be: "I need a companion in harness." Mead remained this companion.

Both Benedict and Mead came from families in which they had seen either how a grieving mother could become an unloving and insensitive enforcer of patriarchal

[74] See *id.*, p. 21.

[75] See *id.*, p. 154.

[76] *Id.*, pp. 245–49.

[77] See *id.*, pp. 309.

[78] *Id.*, p. 223.

[79] See Lois W. Banner, *Intertwined Lives*, pp. 335–36.

[80] See Hilary Lapsley, *Margaret Mead and Ruth Benedict*, pp. 247–49.

[81] See Lois W. Banner, *Intertwined Lives*, pp. 272–74.

[82] See Hilary Lapsley, *Margaret Mead and Ruth Benedict*, pp. 203–5, 210–13, 245–53, 262–63.

[83] See *id.*, pp. 278–86, 299.

[84] Lois W. Banner, *Intertwined Lives*, p. 254.

demands on her children (Benedict) or how a patriarchal father could seek other women when his wife has a breakdown (Mead). Benedict would marry a patriarchal man who had contempt for her intelligence and ambition, and stopped her from having an operation she wanted that might allow her to have children. And, at least one of Mead's husbands was violently patriarchal. Patriarchy rests, as we have seen, on the enforcement of the gender binary and hierarchy, and Benedict and Mead both knew what such enforcement meant. Indeed, one of them, Benedict, had been psychologically traumatized by her mother's enforcement. It is against this background that we can understand how and why a loving sexual relationship between these two free and equal persons, based on equal respect for their intelligence and equal voice, enabled them more clearly to see that the gender binary and hierarchy rested on lies and violence. What they experienced in themselves and in one another was the full range of human thoughts and emotions, not, as the gender binary requires, only one side of the spectrum. And, their sense of equal loving voice in relationship made possible a resisting voice to both the gender binary and hierarchy. It is through the experience of this kind of loving relationship that, as Mead put it, "you have given me speech," no longer "[a]wed by articulate elders." As we have seen earlier, a loving relationship between equals affords an experience of ethical authority that breaks patriarchal disassociation and expresses an ethical voice resisting patriarchy. It is this experience that explains, I believe, why Mead's work so focuses on debunking the gender stereotypes that support the gender binary and hierarchy. The whole drive of her work is to show us that these gender stereotypes are not based in reality, and thus may and should be questioned. The consequence is obvious: If we lead lives in abject thrall to these stereotypes, we are living lives, as Baldwin would put it, based on a demonstrably false and perniciously false American mythology of manhood and womanhood. Baldwin and Mead would, as we shall shortly see, find common ground on this point – the black gay man, the bisexual woman – arising from a journey resisting patriarchy that they shared.

Following Boas's method of cultural relativism, Mead's *Coming of Age in Samoa*,[85] *Sex and Temperament in Three Primitive Societies*,[86] and *Male and Female*[87] are variations on one theme: the remarkably different ways non-Western cultures understand gender and sexuality, and yet flourish in their own contexts and circumstances. Cultural relativism is a means to gain insight into cultures very different from one's own, trying to see them as a participant observer, suspending, to the extent one reasonably can, one's own cultural prejudices, in order to better understand the unfamiliar culture. It is a method intended to make anthropology

[85] Margaret Mead, *Coming of Age in Samoa: A Psychological Study of Primitive Youth for Western Civilisation* (New York: Harper Perennial, 2001) (first published, 1928).

[86] Margaret Mead, *Sex and Temperament in Three Primitive Societies* (New York: Perennial, 2001) (first published, 1935).

[87] Margaret Mead, *Male and Female* (New York: Perennial, 2001) (first published, 1949).

more scientifically reliable in taking seriously the range, variety, and plasticity of human cultural arrangements, and then trying to look, holistically, and to explain how they arose in light of the circumstances and history of the people under examination. The consequence of the method is that unexpected light can be cast on the sometimes unquestioned and unquestionable prejudices that motivate the interpretation of foreign, and supposed inferior, cultures. There was thus an intrapsychic dimension to the method of participant observation: The more truthful interpretation of foreign cultures that the method made possible sometimes revealed the most intractable prejudices of one's own culture. Boas's use of the method thus revealed the ugly irrationalism of German anti-Semitism and American racism, evils he was shocked to find that both his native Germany and his adopted country, the United States, shared. Mead's and Benedict's use of the method revealed the irrationalism of American sexism, as well of its racism and homophobia.

Mead's work is so influential because, like Boas's similar work on race, it showed that gender is not an innate biological construction in the nature of things. Rather, gender, like race, is a cultural construction arising in certain times and places, and that is nearly always used to justify unjust treatment of women. The circumstances that enable such construction may include long-standing cultural patterns of unjust treatment, which rest on false natural facts, which serve to rationalize and perpetuate injustice. Whatever true natural facts there are about gender differences support, if anything, the more just treatment of women both in public and in private life.[88] What Boas's cultural anthropology meant to the ethical criticism of racism, Mead's anthropology meant to the ethical criticism of sexism. Despite ongoing controversies over Mead's work,[89] her voice as a cultural anthropologist is, on balance, an ethical voice resisting patriarchy.

Some sense of Mead's ethical largeness of spirit, no doubt connected to her work in debunking gender binaries, appears in her 1970 conversation with James Baldwin, *A Rap on Race*.[90] Baldwin's anger and indignation are conspicuously voiced, as he defends, in the wake of the assassination of Martin Luther King, Jr., in 1968, the black power argument for the separation of the races. Mead, an integrationist, ably resists this view. What is of interest in the conversation is Baldwin's emphasis on the need for an honest intimate loving voice[91] and the problem of love as the central American problem,[92] and Mead's insistence that any conversation between them take seriously their different backgrounds, including Baldwin's traumatic experience

---

[88] See, on this point, Melvin Konner, *Women After All: Sex, Evolution, and the End of Male Supremacy* (New York: W.W. Norton & Company, 2015); for an earlier treatment to similar effect, see Ashley Montagu, *The Natural Superiority of Women*, 5th ed. (Lanham, MD: Altamira Press, 1999).

[89] For a balanced recent defense of Mead's contribution, against her critics, see Peter Mandler, *Return from the Natives: How Margaret Mead Won the Second World War and Lost the Cold War* (New Haven, CT: Yale University Press, 2013).

[90] See Margaret Mead and James Baldwin, *A Rap on Race* (New York: Dell, 1971).

[91] See Margaret Mead and James Baldwin, *A Rap on Race*, pp. 20–21, 188.

[92] See *id.*, p. 156.

of his stepfather and his sense of being an exile from America and Mead's sense of the happiness of her childhood in a comparatively liberal and open-minded household on issues of both race and gender.[93] In the midst of so much that separates them, Mead tells a story about images, a story Baldwin finds "beautiful":

> Sometimes there are images. . . . They made a cover for a magazine once in Hawaii, where you have people from everywhere in the world. Around the edges they put faces that were unmistakably Asian, African, Polynesian, Caucasian. Then as you moved toward the center the faces became less and less definite, until you reached the center, where you had a face that you couldn't place. It was beautiful. And of course you see this all the time in Hawaii.[94]

Mead's thought about race comes from her thought about the falseness of sharp gender binaries, "in which masculine and feminine stood at the edges of her point of view, to support a more unified person at the center."[95] Baldwin and Mead come to common ground on this point.

Ruth Benedict came from a darker psychological place than Margaret Mead, her sense of self divided by her mother's sense of the patriarchal duties of womanhood and a private imaginative world whose voice was silenced. Just as Isherwood's resistance was to his mother's Myth of the Dead War Hero, Benedict's resistance was to what she called her mother's "cult of grief" made out of her father's death, fierce and rigid dedication to what her mother regarded as the duties of patriarchal womanhood. Benedict observed what Proust observed, namely, that sons and daughters observe that their mothers are more rigidly bound to patriarchal demands than their husbands, the patriarchs themselves, who can dispense with the law, as they will. Sensitive and perceptive children in this position – Proust, Isherwood, Benedict – often develop acute insights, expressed in their distinctive resisting voices as artists or writers, into patriarchy and the psychology of disassociation that supports it. What made Benedict such a creative cultural anthropologist was that she came to break through the disassociation of imaginative voice that had afflicted her since childhood, and she found that voice through the loving relationship to Mead and, after Mead, to her other lesbian lovers. It was through this struggle that Benedict came finally into a sense of completeness or integration as a person, and her voice expressed itself in three notable achievements: her use of cultural anthropology to examine homophobia as an unjust cultural construction like racism and sexism, her brilliant criticism of American and European racism, and her articulation of the distinction between shame and guilt cultures in her remarkable study of Japan, a country she never visited.

Benedict's *Patterns of Culture*, published in 1934, sets out her defense of cultural anthropology as an intellectual discipline, focusing on three peoples, the Zuni, the

---

[93] See *id.*, pp. 221–22.

[94] *Id.*, p. 125.

[95] Lois W. Banner, *Intertwined Lives*, p. 400.

Dobu, and the Kwakiutl.[96] What made her argument of such importance was not only her emphasis on cultural variation, but on the broad cultural themes, Apollonian in the case of the Zuni,[97] Dionysian in the case of the Kwakiutl,[98] that organized each culture's sense of itself and the psychology each culture supported to realize its sense of itself[99] (prefiguring the distinction between the shame and guilt cultures she was later to articulate). What is from today's perspective remarkable is that Benedict in 1934 uses the argument she would use to show racism as an unjust cultural construction to suggest that what we today call homophobia has a similar character, taking cultural anthropology into an area Mead did not take it. Benedict knew personally the gay psychiatrist, Harry Stack Sullivan, who had tried to develop within psychiatry a more humane understanding of homosexuality than the then-dominant view of it as a mental illness.[100] As we become "increasingly culture-conscious,"[101] Benedict suggests we may want to reformulate our conception of what counts as neurotic, for what we count as disordered may simply reflect a culture where "he is trapped in a repugnant situation which is reinforced by every contact he makes and which will extend past his mother to his school and his business and his wife."[102] In her concluding chapter, she calls, as Sullivan might have called, for "a valid comparative psychiatry"[103] that takes seriously that what we call abnormals have a legitimate and sometimes valued place in other cultures, whereas, in our culture, "abnormals are those who not supported by the institutions of their civilization."[104] Citing the men–women of the Amerindian institution of the berdache (homosexual men living as women, with whom other men sometimes lived),[105] who have an esteemed place in Amerindian cultures, Benedict explicitly argues, on grounds of justice, that our homophobia cannot be justified. We blame homosexuals, in a vicious circularity, for what our injustice has made of them:

> the invert is exposed to all the conflicts to which aberrants are always exposed. His guilt, his sense of inadequacy, his failures, are consequences of the disrepute which social tradition visits upon him, and few people can achieve a satisfactory life

---

[96] Ruth Benedict, *Patterns of Culture* (Boston: A Mariner Book, 2005) (first published, 1934).

[97] See, *id.*, pp. 238, 242.

[98] See *id.*, pp. 175, 181.

[99] See, on this point, Ruth Benedict, *Patterns of Culture*, pp. 232–33.

[100] See, for illuminating studies of Sullivan, A. H. Chapman, *Harry Stack Sullivan: The Man and His Work* (New York: G.P. Putnam's Sons, 1976); Helen Swick Perry, *Psychiatrist of America: The Life of Harry Stack Sullivan* (Cambridge, MA: The Belknap Press of Harvard University Press, 1982); Naoko Wake, *Private Practices: Harry Stack Sullivan, the Science of Homosexuality, and American Liberalism* (New Brunswick, NJ: Rutgers University Press, 2011); Mark J. Blechner, *Sex Changes: Transformations in Society and Psychoanalysis* (New York: Routledge, 2009).

[101] See Ruth Benedict, *Patterns of Culture*, p. 245.

[102] *Id.*, p. 245.

[103] *Id.*, p. 258.

[104] *Id.*, p. 258.

[105] *Id.*, p. 263.

unsupported by the standards of their own society. The adjustment that society demands of them would strain any man's vitality, and the consequences of this conflict we identity with their homosexuality.[106]

Benedict published *Race and Racism* in 1942 in the midst of World War II.[107] It is a work of a responsible liberal public intellectual of the highest quality and, given its context, of the greatest and most prophetic political importance. Benedict's argument draws together all of Franz Boas's lifelong work on the unjust cultural construction of anti-Semitism and racism, and gives it a powerfully argued form to bring the British and Americans, allies in World War II, to a sense of understanding what World War II was about and what victory in that war would and should mean to postwar reconstruction in Britain, the United States, Europe, and Asia. What Benedict shows is that racism has no rational basis, corresponding to no natural fact that justifies unequal treatment. Rather, at some length, Benedict shows how the irrational prejudices of anti-Semitism and racism rose historically through the abridgment of the basic human rights of whole groups of persons, and then rationalizing such treatment on the basis of stereotypes whose appeal rests, in a vicious circularity, on the abridgment of basic human rights, including the suppression of any voice that might reasonably challenge such injustice. "[R]acist persecutions replaced religious persecutions in Europe,"[108] only now based on an alleged science of race that was just as irrational because it was supported by the same vicious circularity of dehumanization and violent repression of the voice of reasonable doubt. "It is ironic," she observes, "that it is those very European nations in which anthropometric investigation shows no pure race which base their claims to superiority on allegation of their 'pure' blood."[109]

It is a brilliant, powerful, and convincing argument. What made it of such importance is that it clarifies what was at stake in the aggressively violent fascism of Germany, Italy, and Japan, namely, aggressive violence rooted in racism, creating scapegoats (the Jews) to rationalize its violence, and hostile to any conception of liberal democracy or basic human rights. The defeat of the fascist powers would be justified in terms of the defeat of their aggressive and mindless racism. The argument is prophetic because its reasonable consequence is that, if Britain and the United States were victorious, they have responsibility to take their own racism seriously – whether the American racism of racial segregation or antimiscegenation laws, or British imperialism rationalized on racist grounds. Correspondingly, if Europe is to be sensibly reconstructed, it must be on foundations of liberal democracy, at the national and even the European levels. These latter points are not explicitly raised in a book written in 1942, but the implications

---

[106] *Id.*, p. 265.
[107] Ruth Benedict, *Race and Racism* (London: Routledge & Kegan Paul, 1942).
[108] *Id.*, p. 153.
[109] *Id.*, p. 60.

are clear, and are prophetic of postwar developments, with which we are still struggling.

Finally, in her *The Chrysanthemum and the Sword*,[110] published in 1946, Benedict applies her cultural anthropology to the interpretation of Japan. Benedict had been commissioned by the U.S. government to write a cultural analysis of Japan in June 1944 to help us understand our war-time enemy and how we should deal with them after the war. She never went to Japan, but consulted written sources, movies, and Japanese Americans. Benedict had long been interested in the role violence plays in shame cultures,[111] and her study of Japan is her fullest and deepest exploration of this question.

In *Patterns of Culture*, Benedict had interpreted the Kwakiutl as a Dionysian culture, in which "the Kwakiutl reaction to the death of a noble adult was to carry out some plan for getting even, to strike back against a fate that had shamed them."[112] Kwakiutl culture thus encouraged a highly competitive will to power among its people, and any insult, including death of a leader, was experienced as shaming manhood, thus eliciting violence. In her study of Japan, Benedict further developed and elaborated this insight into the idea of shame versus guilt culture, and studied Japanese culture as a shame culture. Shame is, of course, one of the moral emotions central to our sense of ourselves as competent, arising from failures of competence, and expressing itself in the attempt to better exercise our sense of competence and mastery in the future. Guilt, another similarly important moral emotion, arises from failures of moral reciprocity in relationships to other persons, expressing itself in forms of apology and atonement to acknowledge personal culpability and, if feasible, reparation to the victim.[113] All human cultures display both emotions, but, in Benedict's view, every culture emphasizes one more than the other. Some cultures rely on shame, while others rely on guilt:

> In anthropological studies of different cultures the distinction between those which rely heavily on shame and those that rely heavily on guilt is an important one. A society that inculcates absolute standards of morality and relies on men's developing a conscience is a guilt culture by definition. . . . Where shame is the major sanction, a man does not experience relief when he makes his fault public even to a confessor. So long as his bad behavior does not "get into the world" he need not be troubled and confession appears to him merely as a way of courting trouble. . . .
>
> True shame cultures rely on external sanctions for good behavior, not, as true guilt cultures so, on an internalized conviction of sin. Shame is a reaction to other

---

[110] Ruth Benedict, *The Chrysanthemum and the Sword: Patterns of Japanese Culture* (Boston: A Mariner Book, 2005) (first published, 1946).

[111] See, on this point, Lois W. Banner, *Intertwined Lives*, pp. 204–5.

[112] See Ruth Benedict, *Patterns of Culture*, p. 239.

[113] On shame and guilt, see Gerhart Piers and Milton B. Singer, *Shame and Guilt: A Psychoanalytic and Cultural Study* (Springfield, IL: Charles C Thomas, Publisher, 1953).

people's criticism. A man is shamed either by being openly ridiculed and rejected or by fantasying to himself that he has been made ridiculous. In either case it is a potent sanction. But it requires an audience or at least a man's fantasy of an audience. Guilt does not.[114]

From this perspective, the difficulties Americans had in understanding the Japanese, one of their enemies in World War II, arose from America being a guilt culture and Japan a shame culture.

To understand the kind of shame culture Japan was, Benedict puts great emphasis on the role hierarchy played not only in the individual Japanese family, and in social and political life, but in shaping the nation's imperial ambitions: "it was necessary for her to fight to establish a hierarchy – under Japan, of course, since she alone represented a nation truly hierarchical from top to bottom and hence understood the necessity of taking 'one's proper place.'"[115] The Japanese imperial system was a crucial feature of this hierarchy, which explained something otherwise puzzling to democratic Americans, namely, the role of a divinized God-Emperor at the top of the hierarchy, "an ecstatic contemplation of a fantasied Good Father untainted by contacts with the world,"[116] an imperial system, or so the Japanese came to believe, whose succession "had been unbroken 'from ages eternal.' Japan was no China with thirty-six different dynasties in recorded history."[117] Rigid hierarchy extended to the family, the emphasis being not "to achieve loving-kindness in the family,"[118] but to observe one's duties and obligations. The Japanese said of young children they knew no shame, because the system of patriarchal controls had not yet had their effect.[119] Such controls were enforced at school and later in military service by brutal hazing and ridicule.[120] Such breaking of personal relationships gave rise, Benedict argues, to anger at any threat to one's self-esteem, which could take the form of suicide or aggression against others. What saved the Japanese from self-destruction was an ethnic nationalism:

> they embraced nationalistic goals and turned the attack outward again, away from their own breasts. In totalitarian aggression against outside nations they could "find themselves again" again. They saved themselves from a bad mood and felt a great new strength within them. They could not do it in personal relationships but they believed they could as a conquering nation.[121]

[114] Ruth Benedict, *The Chrysanthemum and the Sword*, pp. 222–23.
[115] *Id.*, p. 21.
[116] *Id.*, pp. 125.
[117] *Id.*, p. 127.
[118] *Id.*, p. 124.
[119] See, on this point, *id.*, pp. 270, 275.
[120] See *id.*, pp. 276–79.
[121] *Id.*, p. 169.

Even the Japanese interpretation of Buddhism, Zen Buddhism, transformed a universalistic religion of loving kindness[122] into a discipline for warriors.[123] Japan's militaristic discipline puzzled Americans by the degree of self-sacrifice required (for example, suicide when defeated), but the Japanese thought of the matter as meeting the hierarchical duties of manhood, which made the question of self-sacrifice irrelevant.[124]

What Benedict's analysis brilliantly illuminates is the larger question of the violence of patriarchal manhood, what the psychiatrist James Gilligan has recently exposed as the psychological root of violence, namely a shaming of manhood.[125] The experience of shame that leads to violence has, of course, a very different character from the shame involved in achieving competence: The violence is often irrational, corresponding to a perceived threat – loss of faith, dishonor, an insult to manhood. Men are particularly vulnerable to such shame when, often through a history of traumatically violent abuse of them earlier in their lives, they have identified with the patriarchal conception of manhood of their abuser, identifying with the aggressor. Identification in such cases covers lack of caring relationships or the trauma arising from broken relationships. Such men invest their sense of personal competence in a self-image of patriarchal manhood marked by a strictly observed gender binary and hierarchy (men over women) in which their often fragile sense of manhood requires them strictly to confine themselves to what they take to be their male gender role to be, and the violence is triggered by any insult to this patriarchally defined sense of manhood.

What makes their sense of manhood psychologically fragile is that the gender binary is in fact false to experience (men have many of the features the gender binary deems feminine, and women the features the gender binary deems masculine), and the idea of gender hierarchy is not only not in the nature of things, but condemned by the moral powers of rationality and reasonableness that men and women, as human and as democratic equals, share. The cultural power and appeal of patriarchal manhood and womanhood can be reasonably understood as yet another example of culturally entrenched forms that illustrate the two features of moral slavery, dehumanization from basic rights, and stereotypes that rest, in a vicious circularity, on the abridgment of such rights. The irrationalist vulnerability to shame of James Gilligan's violent men arises from the psychology of traumatic breaks in real relationships that leads these men to identify with the patriarchally imposed gender stereotypes of their oppressors.[126] What holds such cultural patterns in place

---

[122] See, on this point, Richard Gombrich, *What the Buddha Thought* (London: Equinox, 2009).
[123] See *id.*, pp. 241–43.
[124] See *id.*, pp. 230–3.
[125] See James Gilligan, *Violence: Reflections on a National Epidemic* (New York: Vintage Books, 1996).
[126] I am indebted for the importance of the distinction between shame and guilt cultures, as well as for the irrational shame underlying patriarchal violence, to conversations with James Gilligan.

is precisely the propensity to violence elicited by any challenge to these gender stereotypes.

What Gilligan's study of men illuminates is the larger political psychology of fascist violence that underlies and indeed supports all the forms of prejudice so far discussed: extreme religious intolerance (anti-Semitism), racism, sexism, and homophobia against any reasonable challenge or doubt. The key to all of them is some form of the patriarchally imposed gender binary and hierarchy that gives rise to a political psychology based on identification with stereotypes that arises from traumatic breaks in relationship.

What makes Ruth Benedict's interpretation of Japan so remarkable is that she was able to so intelligently grapple with these issues so early and so profoundly. The key, I believe, to such brilliant work is that she brought to the interpretation her own struggles with American patriarchy, and the fact that her mother, in a ritual of mourning for her dead husband, had rigidly imposed on her daughter a conception of the duties of womanhood that silenced Benedict's personal voice. As Benedict came, through her loving relationships to Mead and others, to see the lies and violence on which patriarchy rested, her resistance to patriarchy released the astonishing voice of *The Chrysanthemum and the Sword*, which so truthfully investigates the repressive violence at the heart of patriarchy. The prophetic challenge Benedict leaves us is whether, having defeated the aggressive fascisms of Germany, Italy, and Japan, we can responsibly address our own patriarchal traditions, which are inconsistent with our democratic values of equality, liberty, and human rights.

The works of Margaret Mead and Ruth Benedict are complementary: Mead focusing on the falseness of the gender binary, Benedict on the pernicious consequences of the hierarchy associated with the gender binary. From my point of view, Benedict's pathbreaking insights into the common evils of anti-Semitism and racism as well as homophobia, and her astonishing analysis of the roots of fascism's irrationalist violence in patriarchal hierarchy, are, I believe, more remarkable and enduring than Mead's more conventional life and work. Benedict may have been able to carry the analysis further than Mead because she was more personally courageous about her lesbianism than Mead, who, coming from a much happier family background (although not without its problems, as we have seen), may have craved a more conventional, certainly a publicly conventional life (three marriages perhaps made this point) than Benedict. Benedict's early life was much more like that of Isherwood and Baldwin, in which, like Isherwood on his mother's Myth of the Dead War Hero or Baldwin for his stepfather's mythology of racist supremacy, she was more injured by patriarchal demands. Only gay love freed each of them from the harm patriarchy had done each of them, or, at least, enabled them to understand and struggle to resist the continuing effects of the harm as artists and writers, freeing the remark-able resisting voice in their works that we have now studied in some depth. It was a feature of each of their lives that, only through questioning patriarchy, could they experience and live in love.

Benedict's achievement seems to me comparable to Baldwin's: both carrying the analysis of patriarchy and its evils further and deeper that anyone else of their respective generations. What is, I think, the heart of the matter is the personal burden of patriarchal violence each carried in their psyches. There were in each of their psyches feelings of anger and rage, arising from traumatic violence, and gay love in each case took on the liberating significance it did because it enabled them, through a love that resisted patriarchy, to experience the healing and the creative voice that could, finally, speak of the injustice they and others suffered. We can see this in all of Baldwin's work, I believe, and in Benedict's late work on fascist violence. Benedict could understand the roots of this violence against America from Japan in the same way Woolf had earlier argued in *Three Guineas* that the British should understand the violence of Germany against Britain, namely, as violence rooted in patriarchal hierarchy. The British certainly had difficulty in even hearing that Germany's violence might be connected to the forms of patriarchy still in place in Britain's family and intimate life. Even Benedict does not explicitly make this point, although it is because (like Virginia Woolf) she came to recognize the evils of patriarchal hierarchy in her own experience as a child and wife that she is, I believe, able so intelligently to analyze and reveal the roots of Japanese fascist violence. It should not surprise us, in light of the argument of this book, that it should be two women, Virginia Woolf and Ruth Benedict, both who passionately sexually loved other women, who give us this insight, whose deep truth we are only now beginning to understand and take seriously in our lives and politics.

By exploring the connections between American cultural racism and sexism, both Mead and Benedict set the stage for the growing American recognition, in the wake of World War II, of our own racism, leading to the overruling of *Plessy v. Ferguson* (which legitimated racial segregation as consistent with equal protection)[127] by *Brown v. Board of Education* in 1954,[128] and, later on, for the interpretation of the principle of equal protection to condemn sexism as well.[129] Perhaps no work was more important in calling for this American recognition than Gunnar Myrdal's *An American Dilemma*,[130] first published in 1944, and cited as authority by the Supreme Court of the United States in its unanimous opinion

---

[127] See *Plessy v. Ferguson*, 163 U.S. 537 (1896).

[128] See *Brown v. Board of Education*, 347 U.S. 483 (1954).

[129] See, for example, *Frontiero v. Richardson*, 411 U.S. 677 (1973); *Craig v. Boren*, 429 U.S. 190 (1976); *United States v. Virginia*, 518 U.S. 515 (1996).

[130] See Gunnar Myrdal, *An American Dilemma: The Negro Problem and Modern Democracy*, Volume I (New Brunswick, NJ: Transaction, 2009); Gunnar Myrdal, *An American Dilemma: The Negro Problem and Modern Democracy*, Volume II (New Brunswick, NJ: Transaction, 2009).

in *Brown v. Board Education.*[131] Myrdal's work shows how Boasian cultural anthropology and other work and developments reveal that American racism is based not on science, but on an unjust cultural construction of race, supported by lies and violence. It is striking that, in making this argument, Myrdal argues that the same argument can and should be made about American sexism.[132] Both Margaret Mead and Ruth Benedict had made this argument credible and reasonable, and thus set the stage for the constitutional developments that were to follow in post–World War II in the areas of both racism and sexism and, more recently, in homophobia.[133] Love across the boundaries, once again, leads to justice.

---

[131] See, on this point, *Brown v. Board of Education*, reprinted in Kathleen M. Sullivan and Noah Feldman, *Constitutional Law*, 18th ed. (St. Paul, MN: Foundation Press, 2013), pp. 620–23, footnote 1, at pp. 622–23.

[132] See Gunnar Myrdal, *An American Dilemma, Volume II*, Appendix 5, pp. 1073–78.

[133] See, on this point, *Romer v. Evans*, 517 U.S. 620 (1996); *Lawrence v. Texas*, 539 U.S. 558 (2003).

Conclusion

Moral Injury and Love: Why Love Leads to Justice

The question – why love matters to justice? – has very concrete applications: as a means to understand the psychology of empathy; as a means by which public institutions might foster and encourage empathy as an important value in democratic cultures.[1] My way of understanding the question starts in a different place, namely, intimate loving relationships, and asks, more dynamically, why such relationships can and do lead to justice, and how. I here review my overall argument, and then reflect on the two issues that are, I believe, implicit in the relationships I have studied: The moral injury inflicted by patriarchy, and the role love across the boundaries can and does sometimes play in healing the injury and giving voice to the injustice of patriarchy.

As we have seen, again and again, what holds in place some of the worst structural injustices of our world (anti-Semitism, racism, sexism, and homophobia) are the Love Laws – the series of written and unwritten rules that enforce patriarchy, and as a result, tell each of us who we may love, and how, and how much, all in order to maintain control over the choices central to intimate life. Because the Love Laws play this role, resistance to them can play a pivotal role in resistance to injustice, as I hopefully have shown.

The argument began (Chapter 1) with setting out the framework of my analysis, and showing its explanatory value in understanding when breaking the adultery laws, the high crime and misdemeanor of patriarchy, has led to resistance, as Nathaniel Hawthorne suggested it might in his classic novel, *The Scarlet Letter*. I then turned to two adulterous couples – Henry Lewes and George Eliot, and Harriet Taylor and John Stuart Mill – and showed why and how falling in love led both Eliot and Mill not only to break but to question the Victorian Love Laws, empowering George Eliot's remarkable resisting voice showing how patriarchy destroys love, and the collaborative works resisting patriarchy of Harriet Taylor and John Stuart Mill on both the subjection of women and the liberal values of free speech and personal autonomy in intimate life, both of which patriarchy represses.

---

[1] See, for such an approach, Martha C. Nussbaum, *Political Emotions: Why Love Matters to Justice* (Cambridge, MA: Belknap Press of Harvard University Press, 2013).

The remaining focus of this book was on gays and lesbians: Benjamin Britten and Peter Pears (Chapter 2), Christopher Isherwood (Chapter 3), Wystan Auden (Chapter 4), Bayard Rustin (Chapter 5), James Baldwin (Chapter 6), and Eleanor Roosevelt, Margaret Mead, and Ruth Benedict (Chapter 7). Western homophobia is one of the most extreme forms of structural injustice in that the unspeakability of homosexuality is at its heart and has been allowed hegemonically to dominate Western cultures for millennia. In contrast, there have been, certainly since the Enlightenment, voices protesting religious intolerance, racism, and sexism. Moreover, homophobia has come down with particular force on gay male loving relationships because such relationships threaten the hierarchy and hostility among men that patriarchy requires and encourages. It is for this reason that my argument has centered on the struggles to resistance through loving relationships of gay men: Britten and Pears, Isherwood, Auden, Rustin, and Baldwin. If breaking the Love Laws plays an important role in resisting injustice, the close study of these men's struggles for loving relationship, against such homophobic odds, would cast a flood of light on why and how love matters to resisting injustice.

Four of these men (Britten, Pears, Isherwood, Auden) were British and gay, and were, at least for certain periods of their lives, good friends. What they shared was their common resistance to British patriarchal manhood both because of its imperialism (which they all opposed) and its homophobia. All of them at one point left Britain for America, and two of them (Isherwood and Auden) remained in part because, once Berlin was no longer available as an experiment in sexual freedom, America seemed the only alternative available as Europe descended into world war.

The loving relationship between Benjamin Britten and Peter Pears is perhaps the most revelatory and powerful confirmation of why and how love matters to resisting injustice. It was after Britten, the composer, and Pears, the singer, fell passionately in love in America that they decided both to return to a Britain still at war and to work collaboratively on a series of music dramas, some of them masterpieces, that would expose both the destructiveness of homophobia and how it depended on hierarchy and violence. It helps one understand what their pacifism meant to them, as men and as artists, to connect their return to a Britain now embattled in World War II to their collaborative work during the war on one of their masterpieces, *Peter Grimes*. *Grimes* gives voice to threats to moral individuality – as Virginia Woolf earlier saw – not only from the aggressive violence of the fascist enemies Britain was fighting, but, as the opera shows us, from the violence – external and internal – of British homophobia, ending in Grimes's suicide. What pacifism may have meant to them was the freeing of ethical voice from such repressive and aggressive violence, and it is a tribute to how English they were that they regarded Britain as the forum they must challenge, that must hear and respond to that voice. It was their love, centering on the equal freedom of voice in relationship, that released them from the gender binary and hierarchy, and thus to see and resist the violence and lies on which homophobia rests. With Pears literally as his collaborative voice, Britten found and gave expression to his artistic resisting voice; and with Britten as the music dramatist who wrote for Pears's voice, Pears found his own voice as a performing artist. Their voices were not only complementary, but mutually supportive and empowering, breaking the silence of homophobic unspeakability by the powers of art to touch emotions and voices still alive under the armor of patriarchal manhood and woman-hood. Their love created, as love in such circumstances sometimes does, a kind of new world more real than the hostile world around them, yet they did not withdraw but rather found an understanding and support in one another that enabled them to give public artistic voice both to the loving world of freedom and equality in relationship they had found with one another, and to their indignation at the injustice of homophobia, which I believe they always associated with patriarchal violence – thus, their version of pacifism. Two of their greatest operas resisting homophobia – *Peter Grimes* and *Billy Budd* – were written and performed in one of the most homophobic periods in modern British history, finding a resonance suggestive of democratic and liberalizing changes to come. Their love gave rise to courage, not the courage of war heroes, but the courage of artists who discovered through love an authoritative ethical voice to resist the patriarchal forces that imperiled their love and, as I believe they thought, all love.

Christopher Isherwood's resistance to homophobia is a much more complex, drawn-out process, one in which leaving Britain and traveling abroad plays an important role. The link of Isherwood's creative artistic voice to exile is quite similar to that of James Baldwin, only whereas Isherwood's journey is from Britain to Berlin and ultimately to America, Baldwin's is from America to Europe. Isherwood's sense of homelessness arises from his resistance to his mother's Myth of the Dead War Hero, a resistance joined by his friend and sex partner, Wystan Auden, leading to collaborative works, including three plays, which deal with the violence and emotional fragility and lovelessness of British imperial manhood. However, what was always at the heart of Isherwood's resistance was his sense of homelessness in Britain. As a gay man, he hungered for a loving sexual relationship not burdened by the stifling hierarchy and exploitation of the secretive and unspeakable world of homosexual sex that gay boys of his generation had learned in the British public schools, and brought to their experience of gay sex as adults. For all the pleasure and even inspiration he obviously took in his sexual relationship with Auden, Isherwood wrote of it in terms of a continuation of school boy gay sex, which suggests why, for him, the relationship never went further than it did. What made living in Berlin for several years so important in Isherwood's life both as a gay man and artist was both the culture of scientific and ethical resistance to homophobia he found in Magnus Hirschfeld's institute and the ambient world of gay sex freely available to him. It is in Berlin that Isherwood falls in love with a German youth, Heinz, and much of his life for the next several years centers in traveling with him around Europe. Isherwood desperately tried to protect the relationship from the hostile forces around it, including what he regarded as the British homophobia in not allowing Heinz into Britain and the aggressive German fascism that ultimately separates them, when Heinz is compelled to serve in the German military (even though he had no sympathy with fascism). It was while he was in loving relationship with Heinz that Isherwood writes the novel for which he is now largely remembered, *The Berlin Stories*, in which he stays close to what the experience of Berlin meant for him. In these stories, he shows us both its monsters and its victims in unforgettably vivid and humane terms, both the sexual freedom for both men and women and the civilized world of German Jews now at murderous threat from fascist violence. When the Berlin experiment abruptly ends with Hitler's election, and when later Isherwood and his lover are abruptly separated, Isherwood turns to pacifism, which was, I believe, his way of resisting the homophobic violence – both German and British – that he had experienced. Whenever he defended his pacifism, Isherwood did not appeal to Vedanta, but spoke of his former German lover as a German soldier in World War II and how ethically unimaginable it was for him to kill a man he loved. This echoes the ending of Britten's great *War Requiem* in which a British soldier (played by Peter Pears) and a German soldier (Dietrich Fiescher-Dieskau) sing of their common plight and death at each other's hands. The pacifism of Isherwood, Britten, and Pears may have had common emotional roots in the gay experience of breaking the Love Laws not only with men in general but with German men in particular (before Pears, Britten had been in love with a German boy[2]).

What Isherwood experienced in his loving relationship with a German was a way of breaking the Love Laws that made possible a creative artistic and ethical freedom. By freeing himself from the disassociation of homophobia, he was able to write so truthfully about people, Germans, for whom the British had contempt, and about others, sexually free women and gay men, who were not even acknowledged as human. While Isherwood's novels before and after *The Berlin Stories* all have distinction, the only two that, in my judgment, achieve the revelatory artistic power of the Berlin works are the two that arise from loving relationship, the first, *Prater Violet*, from his experience of an asexual, but loving relationship with a heterosexual Austrian film director with whom he worked closely in London, and the second, *A Single Man*, that arises from his experience of a threat to his loving sexual relationship with Don Bachardy, the man with whom Isherwood spent the later part of his life. *Prater Violet* shows us the inner terrors of an Austrian Jewish director working in Britain whose wife is at threat from fascism in Austria and connects these terrors to Isherwood's own struggles for a gay loving relationship. Isherwood writes *A Single Man* during a period when his loving relationship with Bachardy had become fraught, giving expression not only to his anger at Bachardy but also to his rage and indignation at the a homophobic culture that renders gay

---

[2]   See, on this point, John Bridcut, *Britten's Children*, pp. 89–125.

relationships unspeakable. The artistic voice that gives expression to both anger and love marks the maturity of Isherwood's relationship with Bachardy, which remained intact. This relationship empowered the voice of Isherwood's autobiography, *Christopher and His Kind*, in which he sees his whole life as part of the universal struggle for gay rights, which is as much German as British or as American.

Wystan Auden's life, as a gay man, took a very different turn when he and Isherwood both came to the United States in 1939. They had shared in Britain a common resistance to British imperial manhood, a resistance not only expressed in their collaborative works but in Auden's poetry. In his debunking of British manhood in *The Orators* and in his powerful, moving poems about disappointment in love and men's emotional frailties as well as his more public, historical poems, Auden expressed his anxieties over how imperial masculinity in Germany and Britain was leading to yet another, perhaps more catastrophic war. Auden always remained a sexually active gay man, but he had not had Isherwood's experience with loving gay relationships, for which he longed, before they came to New York City, nor would he have Isherwood's good fortune in loving relationships in Los Angeles.

We can never know what direction Auden's life as a gay man and artist would have taken had he met and fallen in love with someone who loved him on terms of equality and reciprocity. Chester Kallman was not such a man. Once Auden's heart was broken by Kallman's sexual infidelities and carelessness, Auden continues the relationship but now experienced his love for Kallman as a Christ-like sacrifice of his own happiness, an embrace of suffering required by the homophobic reading of gay sexuality Auden internalized from his mother's interpretation of Christianity. Auden had defended his moving to America as a way of getting away from a family that had limited his life and art. However, because of his psychological crisis over Kallman, he becomes closer to his mother, although now dead, than he had ever been while she was alive. Both the traumatic loss of Kallman and his mother, the two people Auden most loved, were covered by an idealization of suffering and denigration of sexual life, although Auden continued to live as a sexually active gay man until his death.

Auden's poetry continued to express the anxieties of manhood and his poetry had a resonance for the postwar generation. His collaborative work with Kallman on opera libretti brought them both the greatest happiness in their relationship they would ever know, and produced at least one libretto (to Stravinsky's *The Rake's Progress*) that is now a universally recognized masterpiece of twentieth-century musical art. Strikingly, it is the work – centering on the conflict between the rake and the faithful lover – closest to the experience of their own fraught relationship. Auden, with one of the most intelligent minds of his generation, never saw or understood the degree to which he, who had challenged and continued to challenge patriarchal manhood in so many ways, blindly accepted patriarchy in his love life (idealizing his own suffering, as what gay love must be, covering desolating loss). Patriarchy darkens intelligence, but it also kills love, as we see, I believe, in Kallman's response to the domineering, willful, increasingly miserable man who continued to support him financially, namely, not only lack of feeling for Auden's loneliness at their separations, but a callous, exploitative carelessness about Auden's well-being. Patriarchy also may have led to the diminution in the quality of Auden's poetry, after coming to America, that many have noted. It certainly clarifies what so horrified Hannah Arendt in her good friend, Auden, in the last years of his life, namely, his inexplicably willful loneliness and misery, a punishment, he may have thought, for what his embrace of patriarchal religion led him to see as sins.

Bayard Rustin and James Baldwin broke the Love Laws. By loving men and white men, they crossed the boundaries of gender and race. In both cases, breaking the Love Laws released them from the gender and racial binary and hierarchy. Through their loving relationships to white men, they came to see the falsity of these binaries of both gender and race, experiencing themselves and the men they loved as human, who shared the full range of human thoughts and emotions and who were capable of living together, indeed intimately, as equals, with free and equal voices in relationship.

Such loving relationships, including Rustin's relationship with his grandmother, gave rise to the pathbreaking role he played in understanding the potential non-violence could and would have in resisting injustice in the United States. Long before other black leaders, who were more burdened by conceptions of patriarchal manhood, Rustin, the gay man, saw nonviolent resistance as a voice that would not only empower men and women, blacks and whites, to join in resisting the injustice that afflicted all of them, but was also a voice that might have a resonance across the boundaries of both race and gender. The black man who loved white men knew that, under the armor of patriarchal manhood, there was a loving human voice that, once manhood was disarmed by nonviolence, could and would hear and respond to claims it knew were just. Rustin was afflicted throughout his life as an activist for human rights by both white and black homophobia, and he is still not appreciated for his contributions to the most important and transformative social movement in recent constitutional history, the civil rights movement. Despite all our progress, including constitutional recognition of gay marriage as a human right, Americans remain, as a people, still so uncritically in thrall to homophobic denial that we cannot and do not do justice to the astonishing courage, born of gay love, of Bayard Rustin. Perhaps, appreciating the creative role of breaking the Love Laws may help us better understand the roots of resistance to injustice in love, which Rustin and others exemplify so powerfully.

James Baldwin's struggle for a resisting voice required an exile from America very similar to Isherwood's exile from Britain. Just as Isherwood's resistance was always to his mother's patriarchal voice, Baldwin's was to his stepfather's patriarchally violent and racist religious voice as a black minister. Baldwin's teachers, both white and black, in the quite good public education in New York City nourished his sense of artistic voice; and his friends at school were largely white. His friendship with the black gay artist, Beauford Delaney, living in Greenwich Village and later in Paris, gave him a supportive model for how he might live. Moving to Paris was what living in Berlin was to Isherwood: not only a culture of supportive bohemian artists, some black and some gay and some both, but the place where he fell in love with a white Swiss youth, Lucien, whom he regarded as the love of his life. It was while living with Lucien, a European, in Switzerland, writing his essay, *Stranger in the Village*, that Baldwin came to a sense of how American he was, and how racism had afflicted both blacks and whites, the subject of his first and most revelatory novel, *Go Tell It to the Mountain*. The novel places at the heart of racism how patriarchy breaks real loving sexual relationships between equals, and expresses itself in stereotypes that idealize those who conform and denigrates those who do not. Conformity with such stereotypes, which place on an idealized pedestal those who conform, kills real relationship and honest intimate voice, and expresses itself in violence against those who fail to conform. Humiliated by his stepfather as ugly and shamed as effeminate, Baldwin had experienced such violence at first hand, and it was only in loving relationship with Lucien that he found a resisting voice that could expose the lovelessness and violence of patriarchy that, as he clearly saw, motivated both racism and homophobia. It was this insight that he would explore further in his second novel, *Giovanni's Room* (dealing with American homophobia), and his third novel, *Another Country*, his most ambitious (dealing with racism, sexism, and homophobia, as aspects of the same underlying American problem, patriarchy). In Baldwin's later three novels, as well as his plays and essays, Baldwin draws on his own experience of patriarchal violence, as both a black and a gay man, to offer one of the most profound studies of the common evils of racism, sexism, and homophobia, all rooted, as he shows and argues, in killing any love that might challenge patriarchal demands. What is implicit in all Baldwin's works and explicit in his final essays on homosexuality is the root of the problem in the patriarchal gender binary and hierarchy, false to experience and enforced by lies and violence. Of all the artists studied in this book, Baldwin sees and explores and exposes this problem in all its complexities, uniting the common evils of racism, sexism, and homophobia, all of which divide us from our common humanity.

Women stand in a different relationship with patriarchy than men. Patriarchy bears heavily on young boys, initiating them into patriarchal manhood through sometimes traumatic breaks in relationship with their mothers (for example, the British public school). In contrast, girls are only of interest to patriarchy later when, as young women, their role as patriarchal wives and mothers make them of interest. By this time, they are more mature, and often resist patriarchal demands in a way young boys cannot and do not.[3] This difference may explain why homophobia sometimes bears more heavily on men and boys than women and girls, although, as we have seen, both have historically been severely condemned to the death penalty by Christian teaching. What apparently brought such severe punishment on lesbian relationships was when a lesbian impersonated a man; it was not lesbian relationships as such that were condemned, but those that conspicuously challenged the patriarchal definition of women's proper role. The lesbian relationships I have studied here do not just break the Love Laws, but do so in ways that challenged patriarchal definitions of women's role – for example, a woman as a creative artist (Virginia Woolf, or Gertrude Stein, or Patricia Highsmith), or as politically independent ethical voice as first lady (Eleanor Roosevelt), or as a university professor of anthropology (Margaret Mean and Ruth Benedict). When lesbian resistance arises in such a loving sexual relationship that challenges patriarchal demands, it takes astonishingly creative forms (Virginia Woolf) and finds a resonance during periods when gay men's voices remain silenced and have no or little resonance (as in the period when Ruth Benedict lived and wrote).

The loving relationship of Margaret Mead and Ruth Benedict illustrates this point. Mead and Benedict come into relationship through their common conviction of the importance of Franz Boas's cultural anthropology, carrying forward his insights into the unjust cultural construction of anti-Semitism and racism into their investigations into the unjust construction of sexism and, in the case of Benedict, homophobia. Their loving sexual relationship freed both of their voices from the patriarchal gender binary and hierarchy, as they saw in each of themselves and the other in relationship the full spectrum of human thoughts and emotions, including high intelligence and moral passion, and experienced as well the liberating effects of equal voice in relationship. What they experienced was not only a sexual release and fulfillment unfettered by patriarchal demands, but a new way of working as cooperative equals in relationship. Throughout their lives thereafter, long after their relationship ceased to be sexual, they remained in constant conversation about their work and thought, supporting and energizing each other.

Margaret Mead's great contribution, through her studies of comparative cultures, was to show the range and variety of ways cultures interpret both gender and sexuality, thus questioning the naturalness of the traditional Western understanding of the gender binary and hierarchy. Cultures were best understood not in terms of a binary, but a spectrum of variations in the interpretation of gender. Thus, the weight our culture places on gender (the gender binary and hierarchy) is no more rooted in natural facts than race, as Boas had shown. Both are largely cultural constructions, and if unjustly constructed, are subject to ethical and political criticism as sexist or racist and to reform.

---

[3]   See, on all these points, Carol Gilligan, *The Birth of Pleasure*.

Ruth Benedict's journey to resisting voice was certainly not supported by her mother and grandmother, as was Mead's. Benedict's mother, after her father's death when Ruth was two, developed a ritual of mourning, as Isherwood's mother had after his father's death in World War I. This took the form of imposing on her daughter a rigid conception of the duties of patriarchal womanhood that silenced her daughter's imaginative voice, and divided her between two worlds, the public world of a woman's duties, the private world of inner imagination and voice. It is against this conception of patriarchal womanhood, just as Isherwood resists his Myth of the Dead War Hero and Baldwin resisted his stepfather's conception of patriarchal manhood, that Benedict finds her path of resistance. Her patriarchal husband's lack of respect for her interests, including her desires to be a mother, increasingly alienates her. It is only when she begins her study of cultural anthropology that Benedict comes to a sense of the power of her own voice. And it is through her loving relationship with Mead and her two later long-term lesbian relationships that she finally integrates her divided self, leading to the remarkable voice of her studies of racism, homophobia, and the violence of Japanese patriarchal manhood. At the heart of these creative shifts in voice lie loving relationships that belied the gender binary and hierarchy, unleashing the incisive ethical intelligence of Benedict's later works.

Why and how does love matter to justice?

It matters because some of the most intractable injustices (anti-Semitism, racism, sexism, and homophobia) take hold on our psyches and thus our personal and public lives. An illuminating way of addressing the harm such injustices inflict on the human psyche and the role love plays in resisting them is a proposal recently made by Carol Gilligan that we understand the psychological harm of patriarchy in terms of an extrapolation of what the psychiatrist Jonathan Shay has called "moral injury."[4]

Shay's conception of moral injury was developed to understand the effects of trauma on the moral character of veterans of the Vietnam War. Shay ministered, as a psychiatrist and therapist, to these veterans, identifying in their experience three features that injured their moral character: (1) the betrayal of what is right, (2) in a high-stakes situation, where (3) the betrayal is sanctioned by someone in a position of legitimate authority. The consequence of such betrayal is a shattering of trust. The moral injury thus inflicted (as with Achilles after he is betrayed by Agamemnon's refusal to give him the woman to whom he had a right), can lead, as it did with Achilles's grief over the death of his lover (Patroclus), to going berserk, wantonly killing others with no sense of limits, a kind of terrorism. Shay found, as a therapist, that healing from such trauma turns on "communalization of the trauma – being able to tell the story of someone who is listening and who can be trusted to retell it

---

[4] See Jonathan Shay, *Achilles in Vietnam: Combat Trauma and the Undoing of Character* (New York: Scribner, 1994), p. 20.

truthfully to others in the community."[5] When soldiers shared with their therapist and one another their stories, they came to recognize and speak about an experience that was not idiosyncratic, but shared by others. Such communalization enabled them to recover from the twin marks of trauma, loss of voice and memory.

Carol Gilligan has recently argued, in an important paper,[6] about "the resonances I found in Shay's description of moral injury. In the very different context of studying development, my colleagues and I had also observed a shattering of trust following an experience of betrayal in a situation where the stakes were high and the betrayal was culturally sanctioned. Shay's work led me to identify the betrayal as a betrayal of 'what's right' and to see the ethical implications in which I had recognized as trauma, although not of the extremity that Shay encountered."[7] Gilligan goes on to interpret her well-known work on the development of girls in terms of how their initiation into patriarchy as good girls traumatically breaks real relationships and silences resisting voice and memory. And, she discusses as well the recent work of her student Judy Chu that shows the comparable effects of the earlier initiation of boys into patriarchy,[8] as well as the work of another of her students, Niobe Way, showing how later on such initiation traumatically breaks the real relationships to other boys for which adolescent boys hunger.[9]

In her foreword to Judy Chu's book on the initiation of boys into patriarchy by other boys, Gilligan beautifully illustrates the intrapsychic effect on boys of such initiation in the epilogue to the psychoanalyst Donald Moss's *Thirteen Ways of Looking at a Man*.[10] Gilligan observes:

> Moss tells the following story. When he was in first grade, they learned a new song every week and were told that at the end of the year, they would each have a chance to lead the class in singing their favorite, which they were to keep a secret. For Moss, the choice was clear: "The only song I loved was the lullaby 'When at night I go to sleep, thirteen angels watch do keep . . .' from *Hansel and Gretel*." . . . *Every night he* would sing it to himself, and as the song said, the angels came, saving him from his night terror *and* and enabling him to fall asleep. It "was, and would be the most beautiful song I have ever heard."
>
> The first graders had learned the song in early autumn and in late spring when Moss's turn came, he stood at the front of the class. The teacher asked what song he had chosen. Moss remembers:

---

[5] *Id.*, p. 4.

[6] Carol Gilligan, "Moral Injury and the Ethic of Care," *Journal of Social Philosophy*, 45, no. 1 (Spring 2014): 89–106.

[7] *Id.*, p. 92.

[8] See Judy Chu, *When Boys Become Boys: Development, Relationships and Masculinity* (New York: New York University Press, 2014).

[9] Niobe Way, *Deep Secrets: Boys' Friendships and the Crisis of Connection* (Cambridge, MA: Harvard University Press, 2011).

[10] See Donald Moss, *Thirteen Ways of Looking at a Man: Psychoanalysis and Masculinity* (New York: Routledge, 2012).

I began to tell her: "it's the lullaby. . . . " But, immediately out of the corner of my eye, I saw the reaction of the boys in the front row. Their faces were lighting up in shock. . . . What the boys were teaching me was that I was to know now, and to always have known, that "When at night I go to sleep" could not be my favorite song, that a lullaby had no place here, that something else was called for. In a flash, in an act of gratitude, not to my agents, but to my boys, I changed my selection. I smiled at the teacher, told her I was just kidding, told her I would now lead the class in singing the "Marines' Hymn": "From the Halls of Montezuma to the shores of Tripoli. . . . "[11]

For Gilligan, Moss "reminds us when looking at a man to think of the boy and to ask whether around the time of the first grade, he may have learned not to reveal what he originally had loved unconditionally,"[12] an experience of moral injury arising from a traumatic initiation into patriarchy, here enforced by other boys. There is a shattering of trust by the socially sanctioned demands of patriarchal authority as it requires doing the wrong thing in a high-stakes situation, thus blunting relational capacities and inner personal voice and leaving injuries that are carried into later life as requisites of manhood and womanhood.

All of the men and women I have studied in this book – straight and gay – suffered from the moral injury to their characters, in Gilligan's sense.[13] Patriarchy has had the power it has had over people's lives and supported injustices like anti-Semitism, racism, sexism, and homophobia because it satisfies the three features of Gilligan's analysis: Its demands require us to do what we know to be morally wrong; it shatters trust in relationships, and it legitimates violence at any challenge to patriarchal demands. This is a life and death matter, because the violence of patriarchy, in killing love, unleashes violence not only against others but against our selves, as James Baldwin (the most profound analyst of the violence of patriarchy studied in this book) saw early in the suicide of his friend Eugene Worth, which haunted Baldwin all his life, and saw again in his own despairing suicide attempts. However, despite all this struggles, Baldwin's gospel was always love, a love he saw and wrote about, with astonishing insight in his novels and essays, that defied the gender binary and hierarchy, a love that resists moral injury nourishes and holds us to life. Once having tasted its power in his love for Lucien, Baldwin turned to life and saw lovelessness as the motor of the irrational and unjust prejudices that, in warring on love, maimed and killed our psyches. It had certainly maimed Baldwin, but he

---

[11] Carol Gilligan, "Foreword," Judy Y. Chu, *When Boys Become Boys*, pp. ix–xv, at ix, quoting Donald Moss, *Thirteen Ways of Looking at a Man*, p. 140 (I have redacted both Gilligan's commentary and quote from Moss).

[12] Carol Gilligan, "Foreword," Judy Y. Chu, *When Boys Become Boys*, pp. ix–xv, at x.

[13] I am indebted for this analogy to extensive conversations with Carol Gilligan after discussing with her Shay's book, which we taught in our collaborative seminar, Resisting Injustice, and after we attended a lecture at New York University School of Law by Jonathan Shay. I am indebted also to the psychiatrist James Gilligan, with whom I have co-taught another seminar, Retributivism in Criminal Law Theory and Practice.

found a way, through the experience of love and his unleashed artistic powers, to tell Americans we were all maimed, but there was healing and there was hope.

The underlying premise of seeing patriarchy as inflicting moral injury is that our sense of ethics, a distinctive feature of our humanity, rests on our ability to see ourselves as persons, not only from our own point of view but in the shoes and from the perspective of other persons, what the philosopher Stephen Darwall, building on the Kantian ethical theories of John Rawls and T. M. Scanlon, has called the second-person standpoint.[14] Darwall argues that this capacity "requires empathy in the sense of simulation or imaginative projection into the other's point of view (while, it should be noted, retaining a sense of one's own independent perspective)."[15] There is now considerable evidence, based on research on human babies and evolutionary psychology,[16] that this distinctive human capacity of mutual understanding, reading the human world, arises from early interpersonal relationships of babies to caretakers, which, in the human case, includes not only mothers and fathers but a web of caretakers (distinctive of humans) that Sarah Blaffer Hrdy calls "alloparents."[17] Human babies first experience themselves as persons in interpersonal relationship with such caretakers, learning to read themselves as persons and to see others as persons through the caring love of others. Such care includes assuring the child of continuing love as she or he, after an early period when the baby sees itself as at one with caretakers, experiences frustration as it realizes it is a separate person from caretakers and others. Such loving relationships, enduring even through periods of stress, are thus crucial to human ethical development, fostering the development of the human capacity of empathy, the imaginative projection, as Darwall calls it, into the minds and feelings and lives of other persons. It is these capacities of feeling and thought that give rise to the sense of ethical relationships to other persons, requiring them and us to regulate our lives on terms that respect the dignity of all persons, as free and equal persons with basic human rights. The Kantian idea of ethics, as principles all persons – understood as free and equal – could reasonably accept as binding them and others – is a way of making philosophical sense of these features of our humanity.

Patriarchy inflicts moral injury because its gender binary and hierarchy rationalize the abridgment of the basic human rights of whole classes of persons (in particular, its repression of the ethical voice through which we come to understand and give effect to what ethics requires of us and all persons). Such an immoral practice would not have had the hold on our psyches it has had unless, among other

---

[14] See Stephen Darwall, *The Second-Person Standpoint: Morality, Respect, and Accountability* (Cambridge, MA: Harvard University Press, 2006).

[15] See *id.*, p. 45.

[16] For two recent important studies to this effect, see Sarah Blaffer Hrdy, *Mothers and Others: The Evolutionary Origins of Mutual Understanding* (Cambridge, MA: Belknap Press of Harvard University Press, 2009); Paul Bloom, *Just Babies: The Origins of Good and Evil* (New York: Crown Publishers, 2013).

[17] See Sarah Blaffer Hrdy, *Mothers and Others*, pp. 22, 177.

things, it had not enforced on us its Love Laws. The sense of ethical relationships arises developmentally from love, and what makes patriarchy so pernicious, both personally and politically, is that it attacks so violently, both through external sanctions and internal self-punishment, the love that the Love Laws condemn. However, love is the basis for empathy and ethical intelligence, and patriarchy, in regulating love, kills empathy and ethical intelligence, and thus the sense of ethical relationships to classes of persons whose basic human rights patriarchy has abridged. Patriarchy thus injures our very sense of what ethics is.

There is also the connection between the enforcement of patriarchy and violence, which is explained by the break in relationship in young boys that patriarchy requires, as identification with patriarchal stereotypes of manhood take the place of real relationships. It is this identification that leads to the idealization of those who conform to the stereotypes and the denigration of those who do not, and explains the sometimes uncontrollable violence (going berserk) visited, in particular, on those who challenge or violate these stereotypes (thus, the role scapegoats play anti-Semitism, racism, sexism, and homophobia – as innocent people are transformed into aggressors – the Jew, the black, the sexually free woman, the faggot – and murder is rationalized as self-defense). Moral injury in this sense does not just make us less sensitive to the claims of others; it monstrously rationalizes and motors aggressive inflictions of evil without any sense of compunction, but in service of some imagined pernicious ideal of purity or devotion, some idealization resting on denigration and disgust. Such moral injury rationalizes moral evil.

Perhaps, the starkest example of such patriarchally inflicted moral injury in the men and women I have studied in this book is James Baldwin, as he tells us in his autobiographical essay, *Freaks and the American Ideal of Manhood*, as well as in his novels, essays, and plays. Baldwin always knew, even as a young boy, that there was something wrong in his stepfather's racist and homophobic violence, which enforced patriarchal demands as the word of God. He admits as well that he knew the extraordinary levels of homophobic violence he endured as a boy and young man in New York City were triggered reactively by his gender-bending gay style, a violence he barely understood yet knew to be wrong (why was being a sexual woman, or like such a woman, so objectionable?). However, like the psychoanalyst Moss reflecting on how the objections of other boys had led to betray his inner sense of beauty and pleasure, Baldwin explains as well that he had internalized a sense of humiliation about his sexual desires and actions, and had accepted exploitative gay sex but not love as in the nature of things. And, he wondered as well about his own propensities to uncontrollable violence or enduring such violence not only in his sex life, but in his reaction to the New Jersey waitress who refused to serve him because he was black. Baldwin's life and work show why moral injury inflicted by patriarchy is, like the trauma Shay studied, a life and death matter.

However, Baldwin's life and work show something else as well, namely, the difference between breaking and resisting the Love Laws. All through his life before going to Europe, Baldwin had broken the Love Laws, but their lies and violence led him to accept them, indeed to internalize a self-hating and self-punishing image of himself as a sexually active gay man, thus accepting a false image of himself. Throughout this period, however, Baldwin is not even tempted to adopt the false self of covering that more discrete gay men of his period adopted. It is the experience of loving and being loved by Lucien that not only leads Baldwin to see the lies and violence that enforce homophobia, but also to see that covering as well was not the course for him, precisely, because love had freed both his artistic and ethical voice. Coming into a real relationship led him to embrace the truth and value of free and equal love, requiring not only an ability to love openly, but to accept the risks and losses of love.[18] Love always remained for Baldwin his north star, freeing his astonishing ethical and artistic voice.

In his study of the war trauma of Vietnam veterans, Shay speaks not only to moral injury, but to how such injury can be and is healed. There is, of course, the process of therapy, which, in its most humane and gifted practitioners, is itself "a cure through love," as Freud himself observed.[19] This therapy for Shay includes what he calls the "communalization of the trauma,"[20] in which traumatized veterans, isolated and alone with their loss and their grief and their uncontrollable violence, come to see themselves and other veterans as sharing something very human, which they can share with others. Such communalization enables them to break through the two marks of trauma, loss of voice and memory, and both to find their voice through remembering what they endured and speaking of it as a shared human experience. As victims who care for and understand and console one another, they experience a reparative love very similar to the love stories studied in this book.

This book is itself, I believe, such an effort at communalization, trying to show what men and women, straight and gay, have unjustly endured at the hands of a patriarchy that remains, I believe, still little understood and still marginalized as a serious subject for study. If we take seriously some of the deepest injustices that continue to afflict us and all other human societies, then we must address how and why patriarchy remains a dominant force in culture and religion, in private and public, and we must resist. My study has been mainly of gays and lesbians whose moral injury has been so little understood and whose resistance even less understood, but the argument clearly has much more general force (Harriet Taylor and John Stuart Mill, Henry Lewes and George Eliot).

---

[18] I am indebted for this way of putting the point to Naomi Snider.

[19] Cited in Jonathan Lear, *Love and Its Place in Nature: A Philosophical Interpretation of Freudian Psychoanalysis* (New Haven, CT: Yale University Press, 1998), at p. 27.

[20] Jonathan Shay, *Achilles in Vietnam*, p. 194.

The focus of my analysis, in all the cases I examined closely, has been the moral injury inflicted by the Love Laws, and also the role that love across the patriarchal boundaries has played both in healing the injury and in enabling persons to speak and write in resistance to injustice. It should now be quite clear that my argument does not turn merely on breaking the Love Laws as such, but to breaking them in a way that allows lovers, afflicted by moral injury, to experience one another as free and equal in relationship, communally sharing memory about what they have each endured and finding a voice to see and resist such treatment as the injustice it is. The relationship itself thus becomes perhaps the first concrete experience in their lives of what freedom and equality among persons means and can mean, "another country," in Baldwin's sense, from which they may speak and seek to enlarge the democratic community they have found in their intimate lives and now demand in their public lives as well.

What I believe my argument has shown – through the close study of a range of diverse examples – is that a key to understanding transformative ethical resistance – moral progress, if you will – is the connection between the experience of love across the boundaries patriarchy imposes and the freeing of ethical voice. It is precisely because patriarchy quashes, indeed silences, such voice that the freeing of voice plays the role it does in ethical transformation. An important feature of this process is the way such love itself defies the gender binary and hierarchy, the marks of patriarchy, uniting both thought and feeling, enlarging empathy as it extends and deepens ethical intelligence. The experience of such love breaks the psychological disassociation of thought and feeling that patriarchal stereotypes require as the psychological supports for the unethical divisions (of religion, race, class, gender, and sexual orientation) that make these divisions seem so much in the nature of things, indeed a kind of pseudo-ethical bedrock (as in the nationalisms based on religion or ethnicity or gender or sexual orientation that have rationalized and rationalize even today not only unjust wars but atrocity, including genocidal slaughter). If we are serious about the study of our human susceptibilities to forms of ethical and political evil, some of which have now proven to be catastrophic to our survival as a species, the study of the ways in which patriarchy inflicts moral injury on our humanity and how it may be healed must take a more prominent role among the human sciences.

As I conclude the argument of this book, it is important to take seriously what it has shown, namely, the role patriarchy plays and continues to play in the crippling of both ethical feeling and intelligence not only in private life but public life as well. The evidence for this is the case studies of this book, all of which show how when love leads to ethical resistance, it frees a voice patriarchy has crushed and releases and marries feeling and thought not only to resist the Love Laws, but the larger structures that patriarchy imposes both on private and public life. We can see and resist – on the basis of democratic values of free and equal voice – the false values of the gender binary and hierarchy that have imprisoned and poisoned our lives and relationships. Ethics – based on free and equal voice – may now more fully express its reasonable demands, and indeed has done so, as my argument shows. It is for this reason that the three British gay men I study, building on the gay and lesbian experiences of the Bloomsbury Group, are among the most intelligent and trenchant critics of imperialism and the unjust wars to which it led. It is for the same reason that Bayard Rustin and James Baldwin not only through love resist American homophobia, but are among the most effective and profound critics of their generation of American racism, including, in the case of Rustin, the brilliant use of nonviolence to expose the basic of American racism in violence and lies. And, it is for the same reason that Eleanor Roosevelt, Margaret Mead, and Ruth Benedict not only love across the boundaries, but through love free an ethical voice that not only more profoundly criticizes and resists American sexism, but, in the case of Roosevelt and Benedict, anti-Semitism, racism, and the roots of fascist violence, calling for and, in the case of Roosevelt, playing the central role she did in the design and announcement of the Universal Declaration of Human Rights. What is extraordinary about all these resisters is both the empathy and ethical intelligence of their resistance, which has transformed our world much for the better. The feeling and intelligence arises, so I have hopefully shown, from the roots of their resistance in a love that freed their ethical voices from patriarchy.

It is important for this reason to underscore yet again how important resistance to patriarchy is to understanding ethical transformation and progress. The marginalization of this issue both in our universities and our public life itself marks, I believe, how much such resistance is yet required of each and every one of us and the degree to which reactionary forces remain still powerfully alive in American politics, culture, and even higher education. Indeed, for this reason, the perspective taken in this book may clarify why some injustices remain so entrenched in American law and politics and are so difficult to acknowledge, let alone resist.

Take prisons. There is a powerfully reasonable case to be made and indeed that has been made that the role of prisons in American criminal justice is indefensible, indeed that these institutions not only do more harm than good, but violate human rights; and, there are humane alternatives that are both more effective and less expensive.[21] I find these arguments plausible, indeed compelling. Why has the issue (why prisons at all) been so little seen, let alone acknowledged? The most penetrating analysis of this problem comes from much the best book of the French social theorist and historian, Michel Foucault, namely, *Discipline and Punish: The Birth*

---

[21] See, for defense of this position and a proposal for humane alternatives, James Gilligan and Bandy Lee, "Beyond the Prison Paradigm: From Provoking Violence to Preventing It by Creating 'Anti-Prisons'" (Residential Colleges and Therapeutic Communities), *Ann. N.Y. Acad. Sci.* 1036: 300–324 (2004).

of the Prison.[22] At the end of this book, Foucault trenchantly observes that both the early studies of the prison and the more recent studies, separated by centuries, make quite clear that the prison not only did not achieve its claimed humane purposes (in contrast to earlier in-kind punishments of mutilation, and the like) of deterrence, reform, reintegration, and the like, but frustrated such purposes (imprisonment often leads to recidivism).[23] Foucault then addresses the question no one else raises: why do we keep them when we could more effectively pursue these ends in other, less costly ways? His answer is that, in contradiction to the values of democratic liberalism (which he associates with contractualism in political theory[24]), there are interests, which remain largely invisible though nonetheless powerful, to create and maintain a docile underclass,[25] "attenuating the effects of revolt that...[such treatment] may...arouse."[26] But, as Foucault puts it with characteristic understatement, "this choice is somewhat 'unjust'."[27] But, why are these forces so hegemonically powerful, yet invisible? What has Foucault – unlike everyone else – seen, and why has he seen it?

Foucault was certainly no feminist, but it is, I believe, quite clear that much of the argument of this remarkable book – with its emphasis on the objectification of criminals through the panoptical "disciplinary gaze"[28] (enforcing loss of voice) and the maintenance of hierarchy and yet the invisibility of the contradiction he reveals – is best understood as arising from feminist insights resisting patriarchy, whose political power depends on a disassociated political psychology that renders patriarchy invisible, a psychology arising from the repression of voice, in this case, the voice of criminals. The invisible interests Foucault identifies are those of patriarchy, which he traces to the impact of Roman patriarchy[29] on religious orders and Napoleonic militarist imperialism, framing prisons in the image of a militaristic patriarchal hierarchy completely inappropriate to a reasonable policy of humane reform, education, and reintegration.[30] It is precisely because patriarchy is so rarely seen, let alone resisted, that it has the force it has and continues to have. The consequences are catastrophic. The brilliance of Foucault's analysis is that it sheds light on the dimensions of the problem. Criminal justice, and certainly American criminal justice, is thus

---

[22]   See Michel Foucault, *Discipline and Punish: The Birth of the Prison* translated by Alan Sheridan (New York: Vintage Books. 1977).

[23]   See *id.*, pp. 257–71.

[24]   See, on the role of "the theory of contract," id., p. 303.

[25]   See *id.*, pp. 272–92.

[26]   *Id.*, p. 303. My interest in Foucault was illuminated by conversations with Dr. James Gilligan, who first brought to my attention Foucault's trenchant analysis of the history of prisons and how the problem persists today. For an exploration of the role such resistance plays in prison revolts, see Tom Wicker, *A Time to Die: The Attica Prison Revolt* (Chicago: Haymarket Books, 2011 (first published, 1975).

[27]   Michel Foucault, *Discipline and Punish*, p. 296.

[28]   Michel Foucault, *Discipline and Punish*, p. 174.

[29]   See Michel Foucault, *Discipline and* Punish, p. 146.

[30]   See *id.*, pp. 141, 217.

revealed as what much of it is, a mindless war against evils and evildoers (the war on drugs) that often cannot be justified on liberal principles,[31] reflecting and enforcing a populist racism that should morally disgust us (mass incarceration),[32] a war unjust both in its ends and its means.

Why does Foucault see so deeply into this problem? What one finds, on closer examination of Foucault's life as a gay man, is the psychological roots of such resistance in love, in this case, his love for his lifelong partner, Daniel Defert. Foucault's struggles as a gay man in significant ways were very like those of James Baldwin: a tyrannical patriarchal father whom Foucault hated, closeness to his mother (who outlived him), shame and conflict over his homosexuality (resulting in suicide attempts as a young man), a sense of being ugly and thus unattractive to a gay world in which conventional good looks were prized, a compensatory craving for celebrity (with its benefits and burdens), and continual travelling and living outside France throughout his life (searching perhaps, like Baldwin, for "another country"), including, at the end of his life, the gay S/M world of Berkeley/San Francisco, California and New York City, where he probably contracted the AIDS from which he died in 1984.[33] Both lives have tragic dimensions of self-destruction (residual marks of the trauma both, as gay men in a homophobic culture, endured), but also of unrelenting resistance in the light of ethical values of free and equal voice they shared. What is astonishing to me is how far each of them came in their resistance to injustice against such homophobic odds. There were, of course, many differences between the lives of Foucault and Baldwin, most notably, the esteem in which Foucault's father (a surgeon) was held in France, which may clarify why Foucault's early resistance focused on the abuses of medicine and psychiatry, not, in contrast to Baldwin (Baldwin's homophobic stepfather was a minister), on the abuse of religion. But, it should strike us that the struggles for resistance to homophobic self-hatred arose in both cases from the moral injuries homophobia inflicted on both Foucault and Baldwin, and that passionate reciprocal love (loving and being loved) played a crucial role in their resilience – healing their respective moral injuries, leading to the freeing of creative ethical voice.

---

[31] See David A.J. Richards, *Sex, Drugs, Death and the Law: An Essay on Human Rights and Overcriminalization* (Totowa, NJ: Rowman and Littlefield, 1982), pp. 157–212. On the reactionary politics of the war on drugs, see David A.J. Richards, *Resisting Injustice and the Feminist Ethics of Care in the Age of Obama: "Suddenly,... All the Truth was Coming Out," pp. 91–117.*

[32] See, on this point, Michelle Alexander, *The New Jim Crow: Mass Incarceration in the Age of Colorblindness* (New York: The New Press, 2010).

[33] See, on all these points, David Macey, *The Lives of Michel Foucault* (New York: Vintage Books, 1995); James Miller, *The Passion of Michel Foucault* (New York: Anchor Books, 1993); Didier Eribon, *Michel Foucault* translated by Betsy Wing (Cambridge, MA: Harvard University Press, 1992). See also David M. Halperin, *Saint Foucault: Towards a Gay Hagiography* (New York: Oxford University Press, 1995) (commenting on all these biographies).

Foucault and Daniel Defert had lovers outside the relationship, but it was the central relationship for both of them;[34] Foucault, a usually reticent man, acknowledged as much in a 1981 interview:

> I am living in a state of passion with someone. Perhaps, at some given moment, this passion took a turn for love. Truly, this is a state of passion between the two of us, a permanent state with no reason to come to an end and other than itself, one in which I am entirely invested, one running through me. I think there is nothing in the world, nothing, no matter what, that could stop me from going to see him again, or speaking to him.[35]

Defert was much more politically active and radical (for a period, a Maoist) than Foucault. But, there was one period in their lives together when they joined forces for three years (1970–73) publicly to protest French prisons[36]: "The goal of Foucault's political activity was the empowering of others by giving, for instance, prisoners the voice they were denied."[37] Although Foucault never shared Defert's Maoism, there was during this period a deeply collaborative enterprise between them, leading to the most politically active period of Foucault's life (Foucault, "the professor militant"[38]). Foucault's entire corpus may plausibly be understood as a struggle to resist patriarchy, in particular, his sense as a gay man as living within a patriarchal prison, which extended not only to prisons, but to the organization of the military, schools, asylums, hospitals, religious orders, and much else in modern life. But, it is striking that the most intelligent and profound expression of such resistance arises from his common enterprise of resistance with his lover (like that of Britten and Pears), as they come to see in prisons the clearest example of the ways in which patriarchy had undermined French liberalism in service of fighting yet "another war,"[39] as unjust as most wars are both in their ends and means, indeed, more unjust, mindlessly rationalized as self-defense against putative aggressors who are, in fact, victims of injustice.[40] The use of prisons was so personal for him because it supported what he calls illegitimate state "normalization"[41] of personal life, including marginalizing and silencing not only homosexuality[42] but, as he observes, both commercial sex and drug

---

[34] See, on this point, David Macey, *op. cit.*, pp. 92–93, 145; James Miller, *op. cit.*, pp. 185–87.

[35] Quoted by Didier Erisbon, *Michel Foucault*, pp. 141–42.

[36] Foucault had also early in his career done psychiatric clinical work in hospitals and prisons. See, on this point, David Macey, *op. cit.*, pp. 56–59.

[37] David Macey, *op. cit.*, p. 237.

[38] See David Macey, *Id.*, p. 290, and fuller description of these events at pp. 257–322.

[39] Michel Foucault, *Discipline and Punish*, p. 116.

[40] See, on this point, James Gilligan, *Why Some Politicians Are More Dangerous than Others* (Cambridge, UK: Polity Press, 2011).

[41] Michel Foucault, *Discipline and Punish*, p. 308.

[42] On disciplining homosexuality and sexual morality in general, see, for example, Michel Foucault, *Discipline and Punish*, pp. 172, 211, 212.

use and much else,[43] and was often used most aggressively against the most vulnerable– the poor, political dissenters, and people of color.[44] The result is Foucault's most brilliant and well argued book, *Discipline and Punish*.

It is for me a real question why Foucault himself failed to see the connections of his argument to feminist resistance to patriarchy. It is only at the end of his life that he writes several books on the history of sexuality and openly discusses his homosexuality,[45] and these discussions are remarkable for their lack of sensitivity to the feminist issues these topics raise.[46] What may lie at the root of the problem is the assumption that feminism is only for and about women, when in fact, as the argument of this book shows, the feminist critique of patriarchy touches men and women, straight and gay, indeed, is the key to a resistance arising from love across the boundaries that advances justice. Foucault's resistance illustrates, and certainly does not contradict, this thesis. The argument Foucault makes in *Discipline and Punish* may best be understood, indeed clarified, as a resistance by two gay men arising from their love and the freeing of a voice that resists the ways patriarchy harms men, who largely inhabit prisons (and largely fight unjust wars) and are all too easily objectified and demonized in democratic politics, rationalizing an indefensible retributivism based on an endless cycle of patriarchal violence (including not only prisons, but the death penalty):

> the criminal designated as the enemy of all, whom it is in the interest of all to track down, falls outside the pact, disqualified himself as a citizen and emerges, bearing within him as it were, a wild fragment of nature; he appears as a villain, a monster, a madman, perhaps a sick and, before long, "abnormal" individual. It is such that, one day, he will belong to a scientific objectification and to the "treatment" that is correlative with it.[47]

Once again, it is love across the boundaries and its freeing of ethical voice that makes possible the ethical empathy and intelligence of Foucault's study of prisons. And resistance to patriarchy is the heart of the matter. It is a resistance for men as well as women, straight and gay. It remains, I believe, a research project for the future closely to study men, like Foucault and others, who find in loves that resist patriarchy

---

[43] Michael Foucault, *Discipline and Punish*, pp. 279–80.

[44] See, on these points, Michel Foucault, *Discipline and Punish*, pp. 272–92 The political activism underlying *Discipline and* Punish included protests of police abuse against resisting journalists as well as Africans, including Algerians. See, on this point, David Macey, *The Lives of Michel Foucault*, pp. 290–322. For the American experience of racism and mass incarceration, see Michelle Alexander, *The New Jim Crow: Mass Incarceration in the Age of Colorblindness* (New York: The New Press, 2010).

[45] For a charitable reading of Foucault on sexuality and homosexuality, see Didier Eribon, *Insult and the Making of the Gay Self* translated by Michael Lucey (Durham: Duke University Press, 2004), pp. 247–338.

[46] On this point, see Carol Gilligan and David A.J. Richards, *The Deepening Darkness*, p. 16. For illuminating commentary on Foucault, see Sara Mills, *Michel Foucault* (London: Routledge, 2003).

[47] Michael Foucault, *Discipline and Punish*, p. 101.

the empathy and ethical intelligence to investigate other injustices that remain largely invisible, for example, how and why young men in particular are so easily drawn into gang violence and initiating and fighting unjust wars, and not to resist, though some do.[48] We need more such work so that men – straight and gay – come to see how much patriarchy injures and maims them. The power of patriarchy rests, as the Romans – perhaps the most brilliantly successful and influential patriarchs in human history[49] – well understood, on divide and conquer, dividing enemies from one another. We will not reasonably seize the opportunities for progress now available to us and understand our ethical responsibilities accordingly, until men refuse complicity with such Roman balkanization, and join with other men and women, straight and gay, in a common feminist resistance to injustice. Love across the boundaries – both passionate erotic love and deep friendship – is not to be feared, but to be embraced.

Feminism and gay rights have certainly come a long way from the period of the lives of Benjamin Britten and Peter Pears, Christopher Isherwood, Wystan Auden, Bayard Rustin, James Baldwin, Eleanor Roosevelt, Margaret Mead, and Ruth Benedict, and many millennials may wonder why study them at all. Let me answer in my own personal voice as a gay man and racialized Italian American, who has lived in love with my Jewish partner, Donald Levy, for now some forty years. I know the struggle of the gay men and women studied in this book from, as it were, the inside. I was one among many resisting voices of people of my generation to speak and write about both feminism and gay rights as human rights and as rights worthy of constitutional protection under the United States Constitution. Some of the people studied in this book were much closer to my experience (Britten and Pears) than others (Isherwood, Auden, Baldwin), and I doubt I would have undertaken the research and writing of this book if some of them were not so different from my own experience and, for this reason, all the more fascinating to me – so attractive because they were so different. Much of what I have found came to me with a sense of both discovery and surprise as a landscape of struggle and terrible suffering that I, like others, share only in part and did not see in its complex human reality (including those, like Auden, one of the most intelligent men of his time, who, questioning everything but the patriarchy that held his psyche in thrall, suffered stoically from an injury he never recognized and a maimed love that gave little solace or understanding). Why didn't I and perhaps you see this? Why? Is it perhaps the residual hold on us of patriarchy – its idealization and denigration – that yet hold me and perhaps you back from seeing what is before our eyes? What some of the people here studied did, against much greater odds than I and perhaps you faced, is quite remarkable and worthy of greater understanding and respect. We should cherish them for how far they came, and what they showed us

---

[48] See, on gang violence and resistance, Gary T. Barker, *Dying to be Men: Youth, Masculinity and Social Exclusion* (London: Routledge, 2005).

[49] See, for fuller defense of this view, Carol Gilligan and David A.J. Richards, *The Deepening Darkness*.

about our humanity – both about the difficulties they faced and how many of them found or never gave up the search for a love that fulfilled them and made possible ethical voices that resisted injustice, voices of dignity. What they overcame was an injustice enforced through trauma, and they found through the love forbidden by the patriarchal Love Laws the memory of what they suffered and an ethical voice to resist. The moral injury such trauma inflicts will, if not communalized in works of memory and ethical voice, endlessly repeat itself. The injury of patriarchy continues from generation to generation, leading to the horrors of twentieth-century totalitarianism and of terrorism today, a cycle of violence apparently without end. We can, however, break it. We can break the chain of injustice if we never forget how such injustices have been and are resisted, and thus keep alive in ourselves our ethical voice and our sense of ethical responsibility. If I am right, my argument offers a map of the continuing struggle of gays and lesbians for love and its freeing of voice, which resonates not only for Americans but all peoples, including for those, in Zimbabwe and elsewhere,[50] afflicted by shameful forms of political homophobia (mobilized by the violence against scapegoats so familiar in fascism) in the name of ethnic nationalism (African, or Asian, or Russian values).[51] There is, however, an alternative, grounded in universal human rights, that arose as humanity's response to the catastrophic aggressive violence of European and Asian political fascism. It should strike us that it was a lesbian love – breaking and resisting the Love Laws – that may have opened Eleanor Roosevelt's heart and mind to forge with others such an alternative, playing the central role she did in the design and announcement of the Universal Declaration of Human Rights that called, in the wake of World War II, for a new dedication of all peoples to the protection of universal human rights, the measure of a humane politics everywhere.

Five of the persons I study here in depth were artists (Britten, Pears, Isherwood, Auden, Baldwin), two of them pathbreaking scholars working at the creative edge of their professions (Mead and Benedict); Eleanor Roosevelt, however, was a path-breaking first lady speaking in an ethically grounded political voice that challenged some of America's and Europe's worst injustices. And Rustin was a political activist understanding and implementing the crucial role of nonviolence in the civil rights movement, and Baldwin, an artist, played an increasingly important role in activism for the rights of blacks. What all of them share is the struggle for honest, ethical voice. It was such voices that broke the silence of unspeakability that had held gay men and lesbians in abject subordination for so long. Innovations in artistic voice often express or prefigure innovations in ethical and political voice (Britten and Pears, Isherwood, and Baldwin exemplify these close connections), and the artists

---

[50] See, on this point, David A. J. Richards, *The Rise of Gay Rights and the Fall of the British Empire*, pp. 218–22.

[51] I am indebted for these points to Tsion Gurmu and Donald Cooley.

I study played a crucial role in this process, making possible the ethical voice of gay rights that is increasingly resonant in America and elsewhere.

Why does art play this role, as it does in many of the people I have studied in this work? First, there is the power of art, often by the very freedom of its associations, to extend and deepen human imagination, an imperative need for the artists studied in this book to imagine an alternative world in which homophobia did not violently war on gay love.[52] Second, the tools of art themselves challenge the gender binary, showing in literature – whether novels or poetry – the full range of human experience in both men and women, straight and gay.[53] Music transcends the gender binary in the same way, as my argument makes quite clear. The role of music in the operas of Britten sung by Pears – appealing to both our emotions and our intelligence – appeals to our psyches under the armor of patriarchy that otherwise imprisons our hearts and minds; it reveals injustices, as Britten's remarkable operas do from *Peter Grimes* to *Death in Venice*, we cannot otherwise acknowledge, and moves us to convictions and feelings we would not otherwise have or acknowledge.[54] That art is borne in the love of Britten and Pears, which may say something about our often false conceptions of the romantic artist, alone and defiant.[55] Art, in defying the gender binary, subverts its unjust hold on our psyches. And third, because art is interpretively ambiguous, it may subversively explore injustices that cannot otherwise be acknowledged because they are historically unspeakable.[56] The role artists play in my argument illustrates all these points, and confirms the subversive powers of artistic voice in resisting injustice. It is no accident that totalitarian and authoritarian regimes always attack and censor the arts.

Many gay men and lesbians of my generation wonder how America could have come so far in a relatively short period of time, as gay marriage – which George W. Bush would have constitutionally forbidden – is now, just a few years later, an issue embraced even by some Republicans and may be accepted as a basic constitutional right, perhaps even in my own lifetime (I finished this book in early April 2015). Gay men and lesbians remain a quite small political group in the United States, but the emancipation of their ethical voice – the study of this book – has, if

---

[52] I am indebted for this point to Luke Fredericks.

[53] I am indebted for this point to Naomi Snider.

[54] I am indebted for this point to David Billingsley.

[55] Consider, for example, Vincent Van Gogh, often invoked as an example of such a lonely, isolated artist. However, as recent biographies and Van Gogh's letters to his brother Theo clearly show, the love between Van Gogh and his brother went well beyond his brother's financial support, as Theo was the resonance for his brother's artistic voice. Indeed, Van Gogh's mental breakdown may plausibly be traced, at least in part, to his terrors about the loss of his brother and his support when Theo decides to marry. Why has this love not been better seen and appreciated? See, on all these points, Julian Bell, *Van Gogh: A Power Seething* (Boston: New Harvest, 2015); Steven Naifeh and Gregory White Smith, *Van Gogh: The Life* (New York: Random House, 2012); Mark Roskill, ed., *The Letters of Vincent Van Gogh* (New York: Touchstone, 2008). These reflections were stimulated by comments of Callie Lefevre.

[56] I am indebted for this point to Michael Stachiw.

I am right, always been closely linked to resistance to the patriarchal Love Laws. Through writers like Baldwin and feminists like Roosevelt, Mead, and Benedict and many others, the broader American society has increasingly come to see and resist the moral injury these laws have inflicted on their own lives in the form of anti-Semitism, racism, and sexism, all of which were enforced through Love Laws. Recognizing homophobia as another such evil comes relatively late, but, if am right, rests on precisely the same injustice. As matter of principle, the right to love, including marriage, should be extended to all persons on equal terms. My argument thus explains why gay marriage should have had and increasingly does have such a resonance for Americans, as many have come to see, even though a range of resistance movements (opposing anti-Semitism, racism, sexism, and, now homophobia) that an attack on love perpetuates and enforces some of the worst injustices that have afflicted human societies and led to unimaginable savagery. Love that crosses the boundaries leads us to question and reject the divisions of race, class, gender, and sexuality from an ethical stance of our common humanity, the basis of human rights.

What I have found in this book about the emancipatory potential of love across the boundaries may extend further than the loves I have studied in depth. Dalma Heyn[57] and Esther Perel[58] have explored the unhappiness of heterosexual women and men in many American marriages, and the psychoanalyst Stephen Mitchell[59] has investigated the same territory of how and why once loving marriages deteriorate. All of them trenchantly observe how the secure boundaries of marriage, rooted in still powerful patriarchal assumptions that idealize and denigrate sexual relationships, hold captive our erotic intelligence and deaden the erotic play that makes sexual love so absorbing and creative. If heterosexual couples still carry patriarchal assumptions with them into marriage, they are, in the terms of Perel's book, mating in captivity, losing the free voice of an erotic love – improvisatory and experimental and inexhaustible – that gives life relish and delight, and links erotic and ethical intelligence in the ways that distinguish the creative voice of our species. If so, what I have found in the adulterous straight couples and the gay/lesbian couples I have studied touches on the central issues of a good and ethical life. The depth of the problem may be seen in how difficult it is to see the problem, how much patriarchy still rules our psyches in our intimate lives. What I have shown here comes from the margins of the conventional love stories that absorb us all, but, if true, what we learn from the margins – from the domain of the conventionally unspeakable – is a submerged but resisting voice in all our love stories, a voice freed from patriarchy through love and the creative play that loving trust makes possible, a

---

[57] See, Dalma Heyn, *The Erotic Silence of the American Wife* (New York: Turtle Bay Books, 1992); Dalma Heyn, *Marriage Shock: The Transformation of Women into Wives* (New York: Delta, 1997).

[58] Esther Perel, *Mating in Captivity: Unlocking Erotic Intelligence* (New York: Harper, 2007).

[59] See Stephen A. Mitchell, *Can Love Last? The Fate of Romance Over Time* (New York: W.W. Norton, 2002).

voice that calls for recognition and acknowledgment and that we ignore at peril to our ethics and our happiness.

Why and how does love matter to justice? It matters, so I have now argued and hopefully shown, because love crosses the boundaries that patriarchy sets up and enforces – thus it overflows or overrides patriarchy. Loving relationships of a certain kind (those that challenge the gender binary and hierarchy) empower a voice that resists injustice. And, it matters because, through relationships based on freedom and equality, we – you and I and each of us – find and hold onto the intimately personal ethical voice that is the true north guiding us to a life lived in justice. Love leads to justice.

Bibliography

Acocella, Joan. *Willa Cather and the Politics of Criticism* (New York: Vintage Books, 2000).

Alexander, Michelle. *The New Jim Crow: Mass Incarceration in the Age of Colorblindness* (New York: The New Press, 2010).

Annan, Noel. *Leslie Stephen: The Godless Victorian* (Chicago: University of Chicago Press, 1984).

Anselm of Canterbury. *The Major Works* (Oxford: Oxford University Press, 2008).

Ansen, Alan. *The Table Talk of W.H. Auden* (Princeton, NJ: Ontario Review Press, 1990).

Auden W.H., and Chester Kallman. *Libretti and Other Dramatic Writings 1939–1973* (Princeton, NJ: Princeton University Press, 1993).

Auden, W.H. *The Complete Works of W.H. Auden: Prose*, Volume 1, 1926–1938, edited by Edward Mendelson (Princeton, NJ: Princeton University Press, 1996).

Auden, W.H. *The Complete Works of W.H. Auden: Prose*, Volume II, 1939–1948, edited by Edward Mendelson (Princeton, NJ: Princeton University Press, 2002).

Auden, W.H. *The Complete Works of W.H. Auden: Prose*, Volume III, 1949–1955, edited by Edward Mendelson (Princeton, NJ: Princeton University Press, 2008).

Auden, W.H. *The Complete Works of W.H. Auden: Prose*, Volume IV, 1956–1962, edited by Edward Mendelson (Princeton, NJ: Princeton University Press, 2010).

Auden, W.H., and Christopher Isherwood. *Journey to a War* (London: Faber and Faber, 1986) (first published, 1939).

Auden, W.H., and Christopher Isherwood. *Plays*, edited by Edward Mendelson (Princeton, NJ: Princeton University Press, 1988).

Auden, W.H. *The Living Thoughts of Kierkegaard* (New York: New York Review Book, 1999) (first published, 1952).

Auden, W.H. *Collected Poems*, edited by Edward Mendelson (New York: Vintage International, 1991).

Auden, W.H. *Lectures on Shakespeare*, edited by Arthur Kirsch (Princeton, NJ: Princeton University Press, 2000).

Auden, W.H. *Selected Poems*, selected and edited by Edward Mendelson (New York: Vintage International, 1989).

Auden, W.H. *The Orators: An English Study* (London: Faber and Faber, 1966) (first published, 1932, revised edition, 1934).

Augustine, *The City of God*, Henry Bettenson translation (Harmondsworth, Middlesex, England: Penguin, 1972).

Augustine, *The Confessions*, Henry Chadwick translation (Oxford: Oxford University Press, 1991).

Bach, Sheldon. *The Language of Perversion and the Language of Love* (Northvale, NJ: Jason Aronson, 1994).

Baldwin, James. *Another Country* (New York: Vintage International, 1990) (originally published, 1960).

Baldwin, James. *Blues for Mister Charlie* (New York: Vintage International, 1992).

Baldwin, James. *Collected Essays*, edited by Tony Morrison (New York: The Library of America, 1998).

Baldwin, James. *Early Novels and Stories*, edited by Toni Morrison (New York: The Library of America, 1998).

Baldwin, James. *Just Above My Head* (Laurel: New York, 1979).

Baldwin, James. *Little Man Little Man: A Story of Childhood*, written by James Baldwin and illustrated by Yoran Cazac (New York: The Dial Press, 1976).

Baldwin, James. *Tell Me How Long the Train's Been Gone* (New York: Dell, 1968).

Baldwin, James. *The Amen Corner* (New York: Vintage International, 1996).

Ballou, Adin. *Christian Non-Resistance, in All Its Important Bearings, Illustrated and Defended* (Philadelphia: J. Miller McKim, 1848) (reprinted, Philadelphia: Jerome S. Ozer, 1972).

Bamforth, Nicholas, Maleiha Malik, and Colm O'Cinneide. *Discrimination Law: Theory and Context* (London: Sweet & Maxwell, 2008).

Banner, Lois W. *Intertwined Lives: Margaret Mead, Ruth Benedict, and Their Circle* (New York: Vintage Books, 2003).

Banville, John. "Learning a Lot About Isaiah Berlin," *The New York Review of Books*, December 19, 2013, Vol. LX, no. 20.

Barker, Gary T. *Dying to Be Men: Youth, Masculinity and Social Exclusion* (London: Routledge, 2005).

Barker, Pat. *Regeneration* (New York: Plume, 1993).

Bedford, Sybille. *Aldous Huxley: A Biography* (Chicago: Ivan R. Dee, 1974).

Bell, Julian. *Van Gogh: A Power Seething* (Boston: New Harvest, 2015).

Benedict, Ruth. *Patterns of Culture* (Boston: A Mariner Book, 2005) (first published, 1934).

Benedict, Ruth. *Race and Racism* (London: Routledge & Kegan Paul, 1942).

Benedict, Ruth. *The Chrysanthemum and the Sword: Patterns of Japanese Culture* (Boston: A Mariner Book, 2005) (first published, 1946).

Berg, James J., and Christopher Freeman. *Conversations with Christopher Isherwood* (Jackson: University Press of Mississippi, 2001).

Bethencourt, Francisco. *Racisms: From the Crusades to the Twentieth Century* (Princeton, NJ: Princeton University Press, 2013).

Blackstone, William. *Commentaries on the Laws of England* (1765–69) (Chicago: University of Chicago Press, 1979).

Blaffer Hrdy, Sarah. *Mothers and Others: The Evolutionary Origins of Mutual Understanding* (Cambridge, MA: Belknap Press of Harvard University Press, 2009).

Blechner, Mark J. *Sex Changes: Transformations in Society and Psychoanalysis* (New York: Routledge, 2009).

Bloom, Paul. *Just Babies: The Origins of Good and Evil* (New York: Crown Publishers, 2013).

Brabins, Martin, conductor. Birmingham Contemporary Music Group, *Benjamin Britten on Film* (London: NMC Recordings, 2007).

Branch, Taylor. *Parting the Waters: Martin Luther King and the Civil Rights Movement 1954–63* (London: Papermac, 1988).

Branch, Taylor. *Pillar of Fire: America in the King Years 1963–65* (New York: Simon & Schuster, 1998).

Brecht, Bertolt. *Three Plays*, edited by Eric Bentley (New York: Grove Press, 1964).

Brett, Philip. *Music and Sexuality n Britten: Selected Essays*, edited by George E. Haggerty (Berkeley: University of California Press, 2003).

Bridcut, John. *Britten's Children* (London: Faber and Faber, 2006).

Britten, Benjamin. Libretto, *Billy Budd*, conducted by Benjamin Britten. London label, available on CD, 1989.

Britten, Benjamin. *Settings of Poems by W.H. Auden* (London: Collins Classics, 1998).

Britten, Benjamin. Libretto, *War Requiem*, Benjamin Britten conducting, on the London label, and available on CD, recorded in Kingsway Hall, London, January 1963.

Brooten, Bernadette J. *Love Between Women: Early Christian Responses to Female Homoeroticism* (Chicago: University of Chicago Press, 1996).

Brown, Lyn Mikel, and Carol Gilligan. *Meeting at the Crossroads: Women's Psychology and Girls' Development* (Cambridge, MA: Harvard University Press, 1992).

Brown, Peter. *Augustine of Hippo* (London: Faber & Faber, 1967).

Brown, Peter. *The Body and Society: Men, Women, and Sexual Renunciation in Early Christianity* (New York: Columbia University Press, 1988).

Burton, Humphrey. *Leonard Bernstein* (New York: Doubleday, 1959).

Carpenter, Humphrey. *Benjamin Britten: A Biography* (New York: Charles Scribner's Sons, 1992).

Carpenter, Humphrey. *W.H. Auden: A Biography* (Boston: Houghton Mifflin Company, 1981).

Carson, Clayborne, and Peter Holloran, eds. *A Knock at Midnight: Inspiration from the Great Speeches of Reverent Martin Luther King, Jr.* (New York: Warner Books, 2000).

Cather, Willa. *Collected Stories* (New York: Vintage, 1992).

Cavell, Stanley. *The Senses of Walden* (Chicago: University of Chicago Press, 1992).

Chafe, William H. *Women and Equality: Changing Patterns in American Culture* (New York: Oxford University Press, 1977).

Chapman, Sullivan, A.H. *Harry Stack Sullivan: The Man and His Work* (New York: G.P. Putnam's Sons, 1976).

Chu, Judy Y. *When Boys Become "Boys": Development, Relationships, and Masculinity* (New York: New York University Press, 2014).

Clark, Thekla. *Wystan and Chester: A Personal Memoir of W.H. Auden and Chester Kallman* (New York: Columbia University Press, 1995).

Clément, René, director of movie. *Purple Noon* (1960).

Collier-Thomas, Bettye, and V.P. Franklin, eds. *Sisters in the Struggle: African American Women in the Civil Rights-Black Power Movement* (New York: New York University Press, 2001).

Cooke, Mervyn, ed. *The Cambridge Companion to Benjamin Britten* (Cambridge: Cambridge University Press, 1999).

Crawford, Vicki L., Jacqueline Anne Rouse, and Barbara Woods, eds. *Women in the Civil Rights Movement* (Bloomington: Indiana University Press, 1993).

Crick, Bernard. *George Orwell: A Life*, new edition (London: Penguin 1992).

Darwall, Stephen. *The Second-Person Standpoint: Morality, Respect, and Accountability* (Cambridge, MA: Harvard University Press, 2006).

Davenport-Hines, Richard. *Auden* (New York: Pantheon Books, 1995).

D'Emilio, John. *Lost Prophet: The Life and Times of Bayard Rustin* (Chicago: University of Chicago Press, 2003).

Dover, Kenneth J. *Greek Homosexuality* (London: Duckworth, 1978).

Duberman, Martin ed. *A Queer World: The Center for Lesbian and Gay Studies Reader* (New York: New York University Press, 1997).

Duberman, Martin. *The Worlds of Lincoln Kirstein* (Evanston, IL: Northwestern University Press, 2007).

Egremont, Max. *Siegfried Sassoon: A Life* (New York: Farrar, Straus and Giroux, 2005).

Eliot, George. *Daniel Deronda* (Oxford: Oxford University Press, 2009).

Eliot, George. *Middlemarch* (Oxford: Oxford University Press, 2008).

Eribon, Didier. *Insult and the Making of the Gay Self*, translated by Michael Lucey (Durham: Duke University Press, 2004).

Eribon, Didier. *Michel Foucault*, translated by Betsy Wing (Cambridge, MA: Harvard University Press, 1992).

Evans, Sara. *Personal Politics: The Roots of Women's Liberation in the Civil Rights Movement and the New Left* (New York: Vintage Books, 1980).

Faderman, Lillian. *Surpassing the Love of Men: Romantic Friendship and Love Between Women from the Renaissance to the Present* (New York: Perennial, 1998).

Falby, Alison. *Between the Pigeonholes: Gerald Heard 1889–1971* (Angerton Gardens: Cambridge Scholars Publishing, 2008).

Farnan, Dorothy J. *Auden in Love: The Intimate Story of a Lifelong Love Affair* (New York: New American Library, 1984).

Feldstein, Ruth. *How It Feels to Be Free: Black Women Entertainers and the Civil Rights Movement* (New York: Oxford University Press, 2014).

Fischer, K., and G. Noam, eds. *Development and Vulnerability in Close Relationships* (New York: Erlbaum, 1996).

Fontanella-Khan, Amana. "India's Feudal Rapists," *The New York Times*, Thursday, June 5, 2014.

Forster, E.M. *Howards End* (New York: Vintage International Edition, 1989).

Forster, E.M. *Two Cheers for Democracy* (New York: A Harvest Book, 1938).

Foucault, Michel. *Discipline and Punish: The Birth of the Prison*, translated by Alan Sheridan (New York: Vintage Books. 1977).

France, David. *How to Survive a Plague* (DVD, MPI Media Group, 2012).

Fredrickson, George M. *The Black Image in the White Mind: The Debate on Afro-American Character and Destiny, 1817–1914* (Middletown, CT: Wesleyan University Press, 1981).

Freeman, Joanne B. *Affairs of Honor: National Politics in the New Republic* (New Haven, CT: Yale University Press, 2001).

Fussell, Paul. *The Great War and Modern Memory* (New York: Oxford University Press, 2013) (originally published, 1975).

Garfield, Deborah M., and Rafia Zafar, eds. *Harriet Jacobs and Incidents in the Life of a Slave Girl* (Cambridge: Cambridge University Press, 1996).

Garrison, William Lloyd. *Thoughts on African Colonization* (1832; reprint, New York: Arno Press and *The New York Times*, 1968).

Giddings, Paula. *When and Where I Enter. The Impact of Black Woman on Race and Sex in America* (New York: William Morrow and Company, 1984).

Gide, Andre. *Corydon*, translated by Richard Howard (New York: Farrar, Straus & Giroux, 1983) (original French edition, 1983).

Gide, Andre. *Madeleine*, translated by Justin O'Brien (Chicago: Elephant Paperbacks, 1952).

Gilligan, Carol. *The Birth of Pleasure: A New Map of Love* (New York: Vintage, 2003).

Gilligan, Carol. *In a Different Voice: Psychological Theory and Women's Development* (Cambridge, MA: Harvard University Press, 1982).

Gilligan, Carol. *Joining the Resistance* (Cambridge, UK: Polity, 2011).

Gilligan, Carol. "Joining the Resistance: Psychology, Politics, Girls and Women," *Michigan Quarterly Review* 24, no. 4 (1990).

Gilligan, Carol. "Moral Injury and the Ethic of Care: Reframing the Conversation about Differences," *Journal of Social Philosophy* 45, no. 1 (Spring 2014): 89–106.

Gilligan, Carol. "Strong Democracy: A Different Voice, What Stands in the Way," unpublished essay, 2014.

Gilligan, Carol, Nona P. Lyons, and Trudy Hanmer, eds. *Making Connections: The Relational Worlds of Adolescent Girls at Emma Willard School* (Cambridge, MA: Harvard University Press, 1990).

Gilligan, Carol, and David A.J. Richards. *The Deepening Darkness: Patriarchy, Resistance, and Democracy's Future* (Cambridge: Cambridge University Press, 2009).

Gilligan, Carol, Annie G. Rogers, and Deborah Tolman, eds. *Women, Girls, and Psychotherapy: Reframing Resistance* (New York: Hayworth Press, 1991).

Gilligan, James, and Bandy Lee. "Beyond the Prison Paradigm: From Provoking Violence to Preventing It by Creating 'Anti-Prisons' (Residential Colleges and Therapeutic Communities)," *Ann. N.Y. Acad. Sci.* 1036 (2004): 300–24.

Gilligan, James. *Violence: Reflections on a National Epidemic* (New York: Vintage Books, 1997).

Gilligan, James. *Why Some Politicians Are More Dangerous than Others* (Cambridge, UK: Polity Press, 2011).

Gilmour, David. *The Ruling Caste: Imperial Lives in the Victorian Raj* (New York: Farrar, Straus & Giroux, 2005).

Giroux, Robert, and Lloyd Schwartz, eds. *Elizabeth Bishop: Poems, Prose, and Letters* (New York: The Library of America, 2008).

Glendon, Mary Ann. *A World Made New: Eleanor Roosevelt and the Universal Declaration of Human Rights* (New York: Random House, 2001).

Goldhill, Simon. *Victorian Culture and Classical Antiquity: Art, Opera, Fiction, and the Proclamation of Modernity* (Princeton, NJ: Princeton University Press, 2011).

Gombrich, Richard. *What the Buddha Thought* (London: Equinox, 2009).

Gossett, Thomas F. *Race: The History of an Idea in America* (New York: Schocken Books, 1965).

Gould, Stephen Jay. *The Mismeasure of Man* (New York: W.W. Norton, 1981).

Graves, Robert. *Good-Bye to All That* (New York: Anchor, 1998) (originally published, 1929).

Greenberg, Kenneth S. *Honor and Slavery* (Princeton, NJ: Princeton University Press, 1996).

Gregg, Richard B. *The Power of Non-Violence* (Ahmedabad, India: Navajivan Publishing House, 1938).

Hall Witherell, Elizabeth ed. *Henry David Thoreau: Collected Essays and Poems* (New York: The Library of America, 2001).

Haller, Jr., John S. *Outcasts from Evolution: Scientific Attitudes of Racial Inferiority, 1859–1900* (New York: McGraw-Hill, 1971).

Halperin, David M. *Saint Foucault: Towards a Gay Hagiography* (New York: Oxford University Press, 1995).

Hartocollis, Anemona. "Credibility Among Gay Men Gives Leverage to City's New Chief of H.I.V. Prevention," *The New York Times*, Tuesday, July 22, 2014.

Hawthorne, Nathaniel. *The Scarlet Letter* (New York: Penguin, 1983).

Headington, Christopher. *Peter Pears: A Biography* (London: Faber and Faber, 1992).

Heard, Gerald. *Pain, Sex, and Time: A New Outlook on Evolution and the Future of Man* (Rhineback, NY: Monkfish Book Publishing Company, 1967) (first published, 1939).

Heard, Gerald. *The Five Ages of Man: The Psychology of Human History* (New York: The Julian Press, 1963).

Herek, Gregory M., and Kevin T. Berrill, eds. *Hate Crimes: Confronting Violence Against Lesbians and Gay Men* (Newbury Park, CA: Sage,1992).

Herman, Judith. *Trauma and Recovery* (New York: Basic Books, 1997).

Heyn, Dalma. *Marriage Shock: The Transformation of Women into Wives* (New York: Delta, 1997).

Heyn, Dalma. *The Erotic Silence of the American Wife* (New York: Turtle Bay Books, 1992).

Highsmith, Patricia. *The Price of Salt* (Mineola, NY: Dover, 2015).

Highsmith, Patricia. *The Talented Mr. Ripley, Ripley Under Ground, Ripley's Game* (New York: Everyman's Library, 1999).

Himmelfarb, Gertrude. *The Jewish Odyssey of George Eliot* (New York: Encounter Books 2009).

Hitchens, Christopher. *Why Orwell Matters* (New York: Basic Books, 2002).

Horsman, Reginald. *Race and Manifest Destiny: The Origins of American Racial Anglo-Saxonism* (Cambridge: Harvard University Press, 1981).

Huxley, Aldous. *Ends and Means: An Inquiry into the Nature of Ideals* (New Brunswick, NJ: Transaction, 2012) (first published, 1937).

Huxley, Aldous. *Eyeless in Gaza* (New York: Harper Perennial, 1995) (originally published, 1936).

Hynes, Samuel. *The Auden Generation: Literature and Politics in England in the* 1930's (New York: The Viking Press, 1976).

Isherwood, Christopher. *A Meeting by the River* (Minneapolis: University of Minnesota Press, 1999) (first published, 1967).

Isherwood, Christopher. *A Single Man* (Minneapolis: University of Minnesota Press, 2001) (first published, 1964).

Isherwood, Christopher. *All the Conspirators* (New York: A New Directions Book, 1979) (first published, 1926).

Isherwood, Christopher. *An Approach to Vedanta* (Hollywood, CA: The Vedanta Press, 1963).

Isherwood, Christopher. *Christopher and His Kind* (Minneapolis: University of Minnesota Press, 2001) (originally published, 1976).

Isherwood, Christopher. *Down There on a Visit* (Minneapolis: University of Minnesota Press, 1999) (first published, 1959).

Isherwood, Christopher. *Kathleen and Frank* (London: Vintage Books, 2013) (originally published, 1971).

Isherwood, Christopher. *Lions and Shadows* (London: Vintage Books, 2013) (originally published, 1938).

Isherwood, Christopher. *My Guru and His Disciple* (Minneapolis: University of Minnesota Press, 2001) (first published, 1980).

Isherwood, Christopher. *Prater Violet* (Minneapolis: University of Minnesota Press, 1973) (originally published, 1945).

Isherwood, Christopher. *Ramakrishna and His Disciples* (Hollywood, CA: Vedanta Press, 1965).

Isherwood, Christopher. *The Berlin Stories* (New York: A New Directions Book, 2008) (*Mr. Norris Changes Trains*, originally published, 1936; *Goodbye to Berlin*, originally published, 1939).

Isherwood, Christopher. *The Memorial: Portrait of a Family* (New York: Farrar, Straus and Giroux, 2013) (originally published, 1932).

Isherwood, Christopher. *The World in the Evening* (Minneapolis: University of Minnesota Press, 1980) (first published, 1952).

Jacobs, Alan. *What Became of Wystan: Change and Continuity in Auden's Poetry* (Fayetteville: The University of Arkansas Press, 1990).

Jacobs, Harriet A. *Incidents in the Life of a Slave Girl*, edited by Jean Fagan Yellin (Cambridge, MA: Harvard University Press, 1987) (originally published, 1861).

Kallman, Chester. *The Sense of Occasion* (New York: George Braziller, 1971).

Kant, Immanuel. *Foundations of the Metaphysics of Morals*, translated by Lewis W. Beck (New York: Liberal Arts Press, 1959) (originally published, 1784).

Kildea, Paul. *Benjamin Britten: A Life in the Twentieth Century* (London: Allen Lane, 2013).

Kirsch, Arthur. *Auden and Christianity* (New Haven, CT: Yale University Press, 2005).

Koestler, Arthur. *The Yogi and the Commissar and Other Essays* (New York: The Macmillan Company, 1945.

Konner, Melvin. *Women After All: Sex, Evolution, and the End of Male Supremacy* (New York: W.W. Norton & Company, 2015).

Kramer, Jane. *Allen Ginsberg in America* (New York: Random House, 1969).

Kripal, Jeffrey J. *Kali's Child: The Mystical and the Erotic in the Life and Teachings of Ramakrishna* (Chicago: University of Chicago Press, 1995).

Kwarteng, Kwasi. *Ghosts of Empire: Britain's Legacies in the Modern World* (New York: Public Affairs, 2011).

Lakoff, George. *Moral Politics: How Liberals and Conservatives Think* (Chicago: University of Chicago Press, 1996, 2002).

Langmuir, Gavin I. *History, Religion, and Anti-Semitism* (Berkeley: University of California Press, 1990).

Langmuir, Gavin I. *Toward a Definition of Anti-Semitism* (Berkeley: University of California Press, 1990).

Lapsley, Hilary. *Margaret Mead and Ruth Benedict: The Kinship of Women* (Amherst: University of Massachusetts Press, 1999).

Lawrence, D.H. *Women in Love* (London: Vintage, 2008) (first published, 1921).

Lear, Jonathan. *Love and Its Place in Nature: A Philosophical Interpretation of Freudian Psychoanalysis* (New Haven, CT: Yale University Press, 1998).

Lee, Hermione. *Willa Cather: Double Lives* (New York: Vintage, 1989).

Leeming, David. *James Baldwin: A Biography* (New York: Knopf, 1994).

Lerner, Gerda. *The Creation of Patriarchy* (New York: Oxford University Press, 1986).

Ling, Peter J., and Sharon Monteith. *Gender in the Civil Rights Movement* (New York: Garland Publishing, 1999).

Lofgren, Charles A. *The Plessy Case: A Legal Historical Interpretation* (New York: Oxford University Press, 1987).

Macintyre, Ben. *A Spy Among Friends: Kim Philby and the Great Betrayal* (New York: Crown Publishers, 2014).

Magnus, Philip. *Kitchener: Portrait of an Imperialist* (New York: E.P. Dutton, 1968).

Mandler, Peter. *Return from the Natives: How Margaret Mead Won the Second World War and Lost the Cold War* (New Haven, CT: Yale University Press, 2013).

Mann, Thomas. *Death in Venice*, translated by Stanley Appelbaum (New York: Dover, 1995).

Mayer, Henry. *All on Fire: William Lloyd Garrison and the Abolition of Slavery* (New York: St. Martin's Griffin, 1998).

McCall Smith, Alexander. *What W.H. Auden Can Do for You* (Princeton, NJ: Princeton University Press, 2013).

McLean Taylor, Jill, Carol Gilligan, and Amy Sullivan. *Between Voice and Silence: Women and Girls, Race and Relationship* (Cambridge, MA: Harvard University Press, 1995).

McLynn, Neil B. *Ambrose of Milan: Church and Court in a Christian Capital* (Berkeley: University of California Press, 1994).

Mead, Margaret. *Coming of Age in Samoa: A Psychological Study of Primitive Youth for Western Civilisation* (New York: Harper Perennial, 2001) (first published, 1928).

Mead, Margaret. *Male and Female* (New York: Perennial, 2001) (first published, 1949).

Mead, Margaret. *Sex and Temperament in Three Primitive Societies* (New York: Perennial, 2001) (first published, 1935).

Mead, Margaret, and James Baldwin. *A Rap on Race* (New York: Dell, 1971).

Mendelson, Edward. *Early Auden* (Cambridge, MA: Harvard University Press, 1981).

Mendelson, Edward. *Later Auden* (New York: Farrar, Straus and Giroux, 1999).

Menn, Stephen. *Descartes and Augustine* (Cambridge: Cambridge University Press, 2002).

Miles, Barry. *Allen Ginsberg: Beat Poet* (Croydon, UK: Virgin Books, 2014.

Miles, Barry. *Call Me Burroughs* (New York: Hachette Book Group, 2013).

Mill, John Stuart. *Autobiography*, edited by John M Robson (London: Penguin, 1989) (first published, 1873).

Mill, John Stuart. *On Liberty and The Subjection of Women*, edited by Alan Ryan (London: Penguin 2006) (*On Liberty*, first published, 1859; *The Subjection of Women*, first published, 1869).

Mills, Sara. *Michel Foucault* (London: Routledge, 2003).

Minghella, Anthony, director of movie. *The Talented Mr. Ripley* (1999).

Mitchell, Stephen A. *Can Love Last? The Fate of Romance Over Time* (New York: W.W. Norton, 2002).

Mogul, Joey L., Andrea J. Ritchie, and Kay Whitlock. *Queer (In)justice: The Criminalization of LGBT People in the United States* (Boston: Beacon Press, 2011).

Montagu, Ashley. *The Natural Superiority of Women*, 5th ed. (Lanham, MD: Altamira Press, 1999).

Morris, Ian. *Foragers, Farmers, and Fossil Fuels: How Human Values Evolve* (Princeton, NJ: Princeton University Press, 2015).

Morris Jr., Roy. *Declaring His Genius: Oscar Wilde in North America* (Cambridge, MA: Belknap Press of Harvard University Press, 2013).

Moss, Donald. *Thirteen Ways of Looking at a Man: Psychoanalysis and Masculinity* (New York: Routledge, 2012).

Mottley, Constance Baker. *Equal Justice Under Law* (New York: Farrar, Straus and Giroux, 1998).

Myrdal, Gunnar. *An American Dilemma: The Negro Problem and Modern Democracy, Volume I* (New Brunswick, NJ: Transaction, 2009).

Myrdal, Gunnar. *An American Dilemma: The Negro Problem and Modern Democracy, Volume II* (New Brunswick, NJ: Transaction, 2009).

Naifeh, Steven, and Gregory White Smith. *Van Gogh: The Life* (New York: Random House, 2012).

Nicolson, Nigel. *Portrait of a Marriage* (New York: Athenaeum, 1973).

Nussbaum, Martha C. *Political Emotions: Why Love Matters to Justice* (Cambridge, MA: Belknap Press of Harvard University Press, 2013).

Oliveira, Carmen L. *Rare and Commonplace Flowers: The Story of Elizabeth Bishop and Lota de Macedo Soares*, translated by Neil K. Besner (New Brunswick, NJ: Rutgers University Press, 2003).

Olson, Lynne. *Freedom's Daughters: The Unsung Heroines of the Civil Rights Movement from 1830 to 1970* (New York: Scribner, 2001).

Orwell, George. *Essays* (New York: Everyman's Library, 2002) (first published, 1961).

Owen, Wilfred. *The Collected Poems of Wilfred Owen*, edited by C.D. Lewis (New York: New Directions Book, 1963) (first published, 1920).

Pagels, Elaine. *Adam, Eve, and the Serpent* (New York: Random House, 1988).

Parker, Peter. *Isherwood: A Life Revealed* (New York: Random House, 2004).

Parker, Peter. *The Old Lie: The Great War and the Public School Ethos* (London: Hambledon Continuum, 2007) (originally published, 1987).

Patterson, Orlando. *The Rituals of Blood: Consequences of Slavery in Two American Centuries* (Washington, DC: Civitas, 1998).

Paxton, Nancy L. *George Eliot and Herbert Spencer: Feminism, Evolutionism, and the Reconstruction of Gender* (Princeton, NJ: Princeton University Press, 1991).

Paxton, Robert O. *The Anatomy of Fascism* (New York: Vintage Books, 2004).

Perel, Esther. *Mating in Captivity: Unlocking Erotic Intelligence* (New York: Harper, 2007).

Piers, Gerhart, and Milton B. Singer. *Shame and Guilt: A Psychoanalytic and Cultural Study* (Springfield, IL: Charles C Thomas, Publisher, 1953).

Plotinus. *The Enneads*, translated by Stephen MacKenna (London: Penguin, 1991).

Porphyry. *The Life of Plotinus*, translated by Stephen McKenna (Edmonds, WA: Holmes Publishing Group, 2001).

Potter, David. *The Impending Crisis*, 1848–1861, edited by Don E. Fehrenbacher (New York: Harper & Row, 1976).

Powell, Neil. *Benjamin Britten: A Life for Music* (New York: Henry Holt and Company, 2013).

Rawls, John. *A Theory of Justice* (Cambridge, MA: Harvard University Press, 1971).

Rawls, John. *Lectures on the History of Political Philosophy* (Cambridge, MA: The Belknap Press of Harvard University Press, 2007).

Reed, Philip, and Mervyn Cooke, eds. *Letters from a Life, The Selected Letters of Benjamin Britten, Volume Six: 1966–1976* (Woodbridge, Suffolk: The Boydell Press, 2012).

Richards, David A.J. *Fundamentalism in American Religion and Law: Obama's Challenge to Patriarchy's Threat to Democracy* (New York: Cambridge University Press, 2010).

Richards, David A.J. *Italian American: The Racializing of an Ethnic Identity* (New York: New York University Press, 1999).

Richards, David A.J. *Sex, Drugs, Death and the Law: An Essay on Human Rights and Overcriminalization* (Totowa, NJ: Rowman & Littlefield, 1982).

Richards, David A.J. *A Theory of Reasons for Action* (Oxford: Oxford at the Clarendon Press, 1971).

Richards, David A.J. *Conscience and the Constitution* (Princeton, NJ: Princeton University Press, 1993).

Richards, David A.J. *Disarming Manhood: Roots of Ethical Resistance in Jesus, Garrison, Tolstoy, Gandhi, King, and Churchill* (Athens, OH: Swallow Press/Ohio University Press, 2005).

Richards, David A.J. *Resisting Injustice and the Feminist Ethics of Care in the Age of Obama* (New York: Routledge, 2013).

Richards, David A.J. *Sex, Drugs, Death and the Law: An Essay on Human Rights and Overcriminalization* (Totowa, NJ: Rowman and Littlefield, 1982).

Richards, David A.J. *The Rise of Gay Rights and the Fall of the British Empire: Liberal Resistance and the Bloomsbury Group* (Cambridge: Cambridge University Press, 2013).

Richards, David A.J. *Toleration and the Constitution* (New York: Oxford University Press, 1986).

Richards, David A.J. *Tragic Manhood and Democracy: Verdi's Voice and the Powers of Musical Art* (Brighton: Sussex Academic Press, 2004).

Richards, David A.J. *Women, Gays, and the Constitution: The Grounds for Feminism and Gay Rights in Culture and Law* (Chicago: University of Chicago Press, 1998).

Ricks, Christopher. *T.S. Eliot and Prejudice* (London: Faber and Faber, 1994).

Rist, John M. *Augustine: Ancient Thought Baptized* (Cambridge: Cambridge University Press, 1997).

Roberts, Adam. "No jingo! Benjamin Britten and Pacifism," *Times Literary Supplement*, November 22, 2013, no. 5773, pp. 13–15.

Robnett, Belinda. *How Long? How Long?: African-American Women in the Struggle for Civil Rights* (New York: Oxford University Press, 1997).

Robson, Ruthann. *Lesbian (Out)Law: Survival under the Rule of Law* (Ithaca, NY: Firebrand, 1992).

Roiphe, Katie. *Uncommon Arrangements: Seven Marriages* (New York: Dial, 2007).

Rose, Jacqueline. "Mothers," *London Review of Books*, 36, no. 12 (June 19, 2014), pp. 17–22.

Rose, Phyllis. *Parallel Lives: Five Victorian Marriages* (New York: Vintage, 1983).

Rosenthal, Michael. *The Character Factory: Baden-Powell's Boy Scouts and the Imperatives of Empire* (New York: Pantheon, 1986).

Roskill, Mark, ed. *The Letters of Vincent Van Gogh* (New York: Touchstone, 2008).

Ross, Less E., ed. *The War Against Domestic Violence* (Boca Raton, FL: CRC Press, 2010).

Rotberg, Robert I. *The Founder: Cecil Rhodes and the Pursuit of Power* (New York: Oxford University Press, 1988).

Rowbotham, Sheila, and Edward Carpenter. *A Life of Liberty and Love* (London: Verso. 2008).

Roy, Arundhati. *The God of Small Things* (New York: Harper Perennial, 1997).

Rustin, Bayard. *I Must Resist: Bayard Rustin's Life in Letters*, edited by Michael G. Long (San Francisco: City Lights Books, 2012).

Sayre, Robert F., ed. *Henry David Thoreau* (New York: The Library of America, 1985).

Schanke, Robert A. *"That Furious Lesbian": The Story of Mercedes de Acosta* (Carbondale: Southern Illinois University Press, 2003).

Schanke, Robert A. *Women in Turmoil: Six Plays by Mercedes de Acosta* (Carbondale: Southern Illinois University Press, 2003).

Schenkar, Joan. *The Talented Miss Highsmith: The Secret Life and Serious Art of Patricia Highsmith* (London: St. Martin's Press, 2009).

Shay, Jonathan. *Achilles in Vietnam: Combat Trauma and the Undoing of Character* (New York: Scribner, 1994).

Shenk, Joshua Wolf. "The End of 'Genius,'" *The New York Times, Sunday Review*, Sunday, July 20, 2014.

Shenk, Joshua Wolf. *Powers of Two: Finding the Essence of Innovation in Creative Pairs* (New York: An Eamon Dolan Book/ Houghton Mifflin Harcourt, 2014).

Siedentop, Larry. *Inventing the Individual: The Origins of Western Liberalism* (London: Allen & Unwin, 2014).

Soble, Alan. *Sex, Love, and Friendship: Studies of the Society for the Philosophy of Sex and Love, 1977–1992* (Amsterdam: Rodopi, 1997).

Southern, Terry, and Christopher Isherwood screenplay. *The Loved One* (1965), directed by Tony Richardson, available in CD.

Spender, Stephen, ed. *W.H. Auden: A Tribute* (New York: Macmillan Publishing Co., 1975).

Spender, Stephen. *World Within World* (New York: The Modern Library, 2001) (originally published, 1951).

Stimpson, Catharine R., and Harriet Chessman, eds. *Gertrude Stein: Writings 1903–1932* (New York: The Library of America, 1998).

Stimpson, Catharine R., and Harriet Chessman, eds. *Gertrude Stein: Writings 1932–1946* (New York: The Library of America, 1998).

Stocking, Jr., George W. *A Franz Boas Reader: The Shaping of American Anthropology, 1833–1911* (Chicago: University of Chicago Press, 1974).

Stoppard, Tom. *Rock 'n' Roll* (New York: Grove Press, 2006).

Strachey, Lytton. *Elizabeth and Essex: A Tragic History* (San Diego, CA: A Harvest Book, 1956) (originally published, 1928).

Street, Middagh, and Sherill Tippins. *February House* (Boston: Mariner, 2005).

Streitmatter, Rodger. *Empty Without You: The Intimate Letters of Eleanor Roosevelt and Lorena Hickok* (New York: Da Capo, 1998).

Sullivan, Kathleen M. and Noah Feldman. *Constitutional Law*, 18th ed. (St. Paul, MN: Foundation Press, 2013).

Sunstein, Cass R. "John & Harriet: Still Mysterious," *The New York Review of Books*, April 2, 2015, Vol. LXII, no. 6, pp. 67–70.

Swick Perry, Helen. *Psychiatrist of America: The Life of Harry Stack Sullivan* (Cambridge, MA: The Belknap Press of Harvard University Press, 1982).

TeSelle, Eugene. *Augustine the Theologian* (Eugene, OR: Wipf and Stock, 2002).

The Buddha. *The Dhammapada: The Sayings of the Buddha*, translated by John Ross Carter and Mahinda Palihawadana (Oxford: Oxford University Press, 2008).

Thoreau, Henry D. *Reform Papers*, edited by Wendell Glick (Princeton, NJ: Princeton University Press, 1973).

Tippins, Sherill. *February House* (Boston: Mariner, 2005).

Van der Kolk, Bessel A., Alex C. McFarlane, and Lars Weisaeth, eds. *Traumatic Stress: The Effects of Overwhelming Experience on Mind, Body, and Society* (New York: The Guilford Press, 1966).

Van Vechten, Carl. *Selected Writings of Gertrude Stein* (New York: Vintage, 1990).

Vicinus, Martha. *Intimate Friends: Women Who Loved Women, 1778–1928* (Chicago: University of Chicago Press, 2004).

Vlastos, Gregory. *Platonic Studies*, 2nd ed. (Princeton, NJ: Princeton University Press, 1981).

Wake, Naoko. *Private Practices: Harry Stack Sullivan, the Science of Homosexuality, and American Liberalism* (New Brunswick, NJ: Rutgers University Press, 2011).

Walker Howe, Daniel. "Henry David Thoreau on the Duty of Civil Disobedience," An Inaugural Lecture delivered before the University of Oxford on May 21, 1990 (Oxford: Clarendon Press, 1990).

Way, Niobe. *Deep Secrets: Boys' Friendships and the Crisis of Connection* (Cambridge, MA: Harvard University Press, 2011).

Webb, Kate. "From Desert Girl to Dark Lady," *The Times Literary Supplement*, January 23, 2015, no. 5834, at pp. 8–9.

Wicker, Tom. *A Time to Die: The Attica Prison Revolt* (Chicago: Haymarket Books, 2011) (first published, 1975).

Wiebe, Heather. *Britten's Unquiet Pasts: Sound and Memory in Postwar Reconstruction* (Cambridge: Cambridge University Press, 2012).

Wiesen Cook, Blanche. *Eleanor Roosevelt, Volume 1: 1884–1933* (New York: Penguin, 1992).

Wiesen Cook, Blanche. *Eleanor Roosevelt, Volume 2: The Defining Years 1933–1938* (New York: Penguin, 1999).

Wikipedia.org/wiki/Adultery.

Wikipedia.org/LGBT rights in the United Kingdom.

Williams, Craig A. *Roman Homosexuality*, 2nd ed. (New York: Oxford University Press, 2010).

Winnicott, D.W. (1958). "The Capacity to Be Alone," *Int. J. Psycho-Anal.* 39:416–20.

Winnicott, D.W. *Playing and Reality* (London and New York: Routledge, 2005) (first published, 1971).

Winnicott, D.W. *Through Paediatrics to Psycho-Analysis: Collected Papers* (New York and London: Brunner-Routledge, 1992).

Woodward, C. Vann, and Elisabeth Muhlenfeld. *The Private Mary Chesnut: The Unpublished Civil War Diaries* (New York: Oxford University Press, 1984).

Woolf, Virginia. *A Room of One's Own* (San Diego, CA: A Harvest Book, 1981) (originally published, 1929).

Woolf, Virginia. *Mrs. Dalloway* (San Diego, CA: A Harvest Book, 1997) (first published, 1925).

Woolf, Virginia. *Three Guineas*, Jane Marcus edition (Orlando, FL: A Harvest Book, 2006) (originally published, 1938).

Woolf, Virginia. *To the Lighthouse* (San Diego, CA: A Harvest Book, 1981) (originally published, 1927).

Woolf, Virginia. *Women and Writing*, edited by Michele Barrett (Orlando, FL: A Harvest Book, 1980).

Wyatt-Brown, Bertram. *Southern Honor: Ethics and Behavior in the Old South* (New York: Oxford University Press, 1982).

Yoshino, Kenji. *Covering: The Hidden Assault on Our Civil Rights* (New York: Random House, 2006).

CASES

Brown v. Board of Education, 347 U.S. 483 (1954).

Craig v. Boren, 429 U.S. 190 (1976).

Frontiero v. Richardson, 411 U.S. 677 (1973).

Lawrence v. Texas, 539 U.S. 558 (2003).

Loving v. Virginia, 388 U.S. 1 (1967).

McLaughlin v. Florida, 379 U.S. 184 (1964).

Plessy v. Ferguson, 163 U.S. 537 (1896).

Romer v. Evans, 517 U.S. 620 (1996).

United States v. Virginia, 518 U.S. 515 (1996).

Index